Palgrave Socio-Legal Studies

The Palgrave Socio-Legal Studies series is a developing series of monographs and textbooks featuring cutting edge work which, in the best tradition of socio-legal studies, reach out to a wide international audience.

George B. Radics · Pablo Ciocchini
Editors

Criminal Legalities and Minorities in the Global South

Rights and Resistance in a Decolonial World

palgrave
macmillan

Editors
George B. Radics
Department of Sociology
National University of Singapore
Singapore, Singapore

Pablo Ciocchini
Department of Sociology, Social Policy and Criminology
University of Liverpool
Singapore, Singapore

ISSN 2947-9274 ISSN 2947-9282 (electronic)
Palgrave Socio-Legal Studies
ISBN 978-3-031-17917-4 ISBN 978-3-031-17918-1 (eBook)
https://doi.org/10.1007/978-3-031-17918-1

Cover credit: Medialys Images/Medialys Images by Massimiliano Ferraro/Alamy

This Palgrave Macmillan imprint is published by the registered company Springer Nature Switzerland AG
The registered company address is: Gewerbestrasse 11, 6330 Cham, Switzerland

Preface

Work began on this edited volume as we were wrapping up our previous edited book, *Criminal Legalities in the Global South: Cultural Dynamics, Political Tensions, and Institutional Practices* published by Routledge at the end of 2019. As we started to promote our last book, and embark upon this one, the world came to a halt with COVID-19. In our last preface, we acknowledged the difficulties for scholars from the Global South on the treacherous path of knowledge production, with all the precarity involved with academia. These past three years have only exacerbated conditions, giving even those in the Global North a glimpse into what it feels like to have borders closed off to you, adapt rapidly to dramatic change, and, especially at the beginning of the pandemic, the fear associated with not knowing what to do when yourself or family members get sick. The pandemic radically reshaped the direction of this edited book many times, and understandably so since the topic of this volume concerns minorities, and those at the margins of society are often the first to suffer when the slightest change to an environment takes place and are the most vulnerable when traumatic events unfold.

But this book is not just about challenges; it is also about triumphs and survival. The editors are deeply grateful to the authors who stuck with us to the very end, the authors who jumped in at the last moment to fill in gaps left by those who could not continue, and the authors who tried their best to complete their chapters despite the monumental challenges that eventually forced them to pull out. It was through all of our collective efforts that this second edited book was made possible. And as with the first edited book, we are continually amazed by the brilliance—and resilience—of those who participate in our books and special issues considering the challenges associated with this work. We are inspired by the efforts of authors to peer into their own conditions to identify where things can be improved and by the empathy of those who work to reveal the oppressive conditions for others. We are proud of these collective efforts and are excited to keep moving forward.

Thanks to the dedication and cooperation of all involved, this volume took only a few months longer than the last to be finalized. New methods of connecting, and different uses of technology, helped sustain the development of this book. Unlike the last edited book that benefited from in-person planning sessions, workshops, and conference presentations, most of the preparation for this book took place virtually and remotely. Authors connected through a workshop co-hosted by the National University of Singapore and the University of Liverpool in January 2021, and a two-day seminar at the Oñati Socio-Legal Institute in July 2021, both conducted online. The Law and Society Association (LSA) Annual meetings in 2020 (Denver) and 2021 (Chicago), both also conducted online, served as important venues to connect, seek feedback, and promote our work. Immense gratitude must therefore be made to the LSA for its generous support of our International Research Collaborative (IRC-5) "Criminal Legalities in the Global South" in 2020 and 2021 and for our presence at the LSA in Lisbon, Portugal, in July 2022. Additionally, three of the chapters in this book were presented at the "Stigmatization, Identities and the Law: Asian and Comparative Perspectives" workshop on 23–24 June 2020, supported by Academic Research Fund Tier II (MOE2018-T2-1-101) and hosted online by the Centre for Asian Legal Studies at the National University of Singapore. The editors are grateful to their respective departments for supporting their attendance at these conferences and workshops and for providing the space for this work to continue.

Finally, special thanks must be made to acknowledge the hidden labor that goes into these books. To the numerous editors and anonymous peer reviewers who spent the time helping us improve the framing and content of this book, a big thank you. We are also extremely grateful for the fantastic editorial assistance of Lydia Ng, who helped format and edit every word in this book, and Shray Mehta for his astute thoughts and comments on several of the chapters. Lastly, we would like to thank Josie Taylor, Senior Commissioning Editor from Palgrave, who worked with us to place this edited book with the prestigious Socio-Legal Studies series.

Singapore, Singapore

George B. Radics
Pablo Ciocchini

Contents

Notes on Contributors

José Atiles is an Assistant Professor of Sociology at the University of Illinois at Urbana-Champaign. His research and publications focus primarily on the sociolegal and criminological implications of US colonialism in Puerto Rico, and to elucidate how the uses of law and exceptionality exacerbate the unequal and undemocratic condition of Puerto Rico. He has published in peer-reviewed international journals and several book chapters in peer-reviewed edited volumes and has published four peer-review books in Spanish. Currently, he is working on his book manuscript *Law in/as Crisis: Emergency Powers, Corruption, and Resistance in Puerto Rico.*

Pablo Ciocchini is a Lecturer at the University of Liverpool in Singapore. He holds an LLM from the National University of La Plata (Argentina), an M.A. in the Sociology of Law from the Oñati International Institute for the Sociology of Law (Spain), and a Ph.D. in Sociology of Law from University of the Basque Country. His research interests include criminal courts in the Global South, state violence, state-corporate crime, sociolegal theory, and critical criminology. His articles have appeared in the *British Journal of Criminology*, the criminology. His articles have appeared in the *British Journal of Criminology*, the *International Journal of Law in Context*, *Critical Criminology*, *Crime, Law, and Social Change*, the *Asian Journal of Social Sciences*, among others. He is the co-editor of *Global Legalities in the Global South* (Routledge, 2019).

Suraj Gogoi is a sociologist interested in social, political, and ethical life in South Asia. He is currently an Assistant Professor in the School of Liberal Arts, RV University, Bangalore. His forthcoming book with Routledge,

Tribal Question and Assamese Identity: Poetics and Politics of Indigeneity (co-authored with Manoranjan Pegu) frames the social and political life in contemporary Assam by situating the figure of the tribal in conversation with caste Assamese society (and culture), official language politics, and the nature of Assamese nationalism. His current research also engages with regimes of citizenship and the figure of the minority citizen-subject in South Asia. He is a social critic and writes regularly on culture, politics, and society in contemporary India.

Joseph Greener is Lecturer in the Department of Sociology, Social Policy and Criminology at the University of Liverpool. His research interests lie in critically orientated and theoretically informed analyses of state power and political economy across a range of issues including welfare, social care, crime control, neo-imperialism, and racism.

Veronica L. Gregorio received her Ph.D. in Sociology from the Department of Sociology and Anthropology, National University of Singapore, where she currently works as a teaching assistant. Her research interests are rural transformation, gender and sexuality, and youth and family relations, with a regional focus on Southeast Asia. She has published in *Current Sociology, Review of Women's Studies, Philippine Sociological Review,* and *Simulacra Jurnal Sosiologi.* Her ongoing projects include the following: co-edited volume on Resilience and Familism: The Dynamic Nature of Families in the Philippines (*Contemporary Perspectives in Family Research*), co-edited special issue on Asian Families: Networks, practices, and inequalities (*Asian Studies: Journal of Critical Perspectives on Asia*), and book manuscript based on her dissertation, *Family Ties, Social Reproduction and Rural Transformation in Southeast Asia* (under contract with Amsterdam University Press).

Sabeen Kazmi is a Ph.D. Candidate at the Centre for Criminology and Socio-Legal Studies at University of Toronto. Her research focuses on "*Katchi-Abadis*" or "non-permanent settlements" in Karachi, Pakistan. She is interested in understanding how liberal rhetorics of "security" and "development" are utilized through popular political narratives, policies, and legislations to justify the displacement of occupants residing in *katchi abadis.* Her work extends the security-development nexus through embedding her site of research within a post-colonial/anti-colonial legal framework. Beyond her thesis, she is also broadly interested in questions of belonging, visitation, South-Asian diaspora and decolonizing the South-Asian personhood. Through her community involvement, activism, teaching, and community work, she is committed to anti-racism, anti-islamophobia, and abolishment of caste-based oppression and supports LGBTQ justice and indigenous resistance on Turtle Island and with other indigenous movements across the globe.

Jayson Lamchek (Ph.D., Australia National University) is a Research Fellow at Deakin University Law School, Melbourne, Australia, and Adjunct Associate Professor of Law, University of New England, Armidale, Australia. He was a legal practitioner in the Philippines, having worked as an associate at the Public Interest Law Center (PILC). His interdisciplinary human rights scholarship queries the advancement of human rights in the extremely challenging contexts of counterterrorism and the War on Drugs in the Philippines. His is the author of *Human Rights-Compliant Counterterrorism* (CUP, 2019) and has published articles in *Australian Journal of Human Rights, Asian Studies Review* and *International Criminal Law Review*. Most recently, he engages issues related to technology development and material inequality.

Marta Machado is Full-time Professor at the Getulio Vargas Foundation Law School in Sao Paulo since 2007 and since 2019 Associate Dean for Academic Master and Ph.D. Programs. She's Master (2004) and Ph.D. (2007) in Philosophy and Theory of Law at University of Sao Paulo. During her Ph.D., she has been Visiting Researcher at the Barcelona University (Philosophy of Law Department) and the Max Planck Institute for the Study of Crime, Security and Law. She was a Postdoctoral Fellow at the Freie Universität Berlin (founded by the Ministry of Education/Capes) and at the Centre for Latin American Studies at UC Berkeley. She has been Visiting Professor at the University of Toronto and at Columbia Law School (2017). She's currently Senior Researcher at the CEBRAP; Global Fellow at the Centre on Law & Social Transformation (University of Bergen); Fellow at the International Reproductive and Sexual Health Law Program, University of Toronto School; Associate Researcher at the Oxford Human Rights Hub and one of the principal investigators at the Maria Sibylla Merian International Centre for Latin America Conviviality in Unequal Societies (MECILA).

Lara Nascimento Meneses is from Fortaleza, Ceará, Brazil. She graduated with a degree in Law from the University of Fortaleza in July 2019. During law school, she was a Researcher at the Criminal Sciences Laboratory at the University of Fortaleza, between 2018 and 2019, where she started studying the experiences of mothers in jail in the State of Ceará, Brazil, the main object of the present chapter. After graduation, she attended a specialization in Criminal Law, also at the University of Fortaleza, ending in July 2021. She is currently a lawyer in Fortaleza, Ceará, Brazil.

Emilio Meyer is a tenured, Full-time Associate Professor of Constitutional Law at the Federal University of Minas Gerais (UFMG), Brazil, since 2013, in Graduate (Masters and Ph.D.) and Undergraduate courses. He is also the Dean for Masters and Ph.D. Graduate Courses (2021–2023). He is Visiting Researcher at UFMG's Institute of Advanced Interdisciplinary Studies (2018–2019). He is Research Fellow of the Brazilian National Council for Scientific and Technological Development (CNPq, 304139/2021-1). He is Director of the Study Centre on Transitional Justice of the Federal University of Minas Gerais (http://cjt.ufmg.br). He is Former General Secretary of the Latin America Transitional Justice Network (2016–2017). He is Visiting Researcher at the King's College London Brazil Institute (2014–2015). He is Fellow at the King's College Transnational Law Summer Institute (2016). He is founding member of the Critical Transitional Justice Network. He is member of the International Law and Politics Collaborative Research Network. He is founding member of the ICON-S Brazilian Chapter. He has Masters (2006) and Ph.D. (2012) degrees from the Federal University of Minas Gerais (UFMG). In 2013, he was awarded by the Brazilian Ministry of Education's CAPES Foundation the prize for the best Law thesis in Brazil.

M. Bashir Mobasher is a Postdoctoral Fellow at the American University's Department of Sociology. In addition, he is a member of Diversity, Equity, and Inclusion Committee (DEI) and Immigration Lab at the American University. Between 2018 and 2021, he was an Assistant Professor of Political Science at the American University of Afghanistan. He also has several years of working experience with USAID's rule of law project (2010–2013), INL's legal education reform project (2017–2020), Max Planck's administrative law reform (2021), and International IDEA's multiple research projects (2021–2022). He is an expert in constitutional design in divided societies. He has authored, reviewed, and supervised numerous research projects on constitutional law, electoral systems, and identity politics. His recent research projects are centered around decentralization prospects in plural Afghanistan and the politics of discrimination law. He obtained his B.A. (2007) from the School of Law and Political Science at Kabul University, and his LLM (2010) and Ph.D. (2017) from the University of Washington School of Law.

João Araújo Monteiro Neto is a Sociolegal Scholar working in the field of criminal law, information technology governance, and digital human rights. He received his Ph.D. from Kent Law School, United Kingdom, and also has a MPhil in Constitutional Law from the University of Fortaleza. He was a Visiting Scholar at the Annenberg School for Communication (University of Pennsylvania, US) and a Research Support Officer in the Information Policy and Governance Department at the University of Malta.

Nasiruddin Nezaami is a Fellow at Stanford University Law School and the Chair of the Law Department at the American University of Afghanistan (AUAF). He started his career as an Assistant Professor of Law at Kabul University where served as Vice-Dean for the Faculty of Law and Political Science. He holds an LLM from the University of Washington and an LLB from Kabul University. He is Country Director for Afghanistan for the Higher Education Teaching and Learning (HETL) Association and serves as peer reviewer for prestigious international journals. He was a member of the Afghan Penal Code Commentary committee where he wrote the commentary on cybercrimes and environmental crimes of the Afghan Penal Code. He has worked with a number of organizations as an independent consultant. His publications include a co-editorial book titled, "*Governance and Management in Higher Education*: Innovations in Higher Education Teaching and Learning," and many articles published in reputable journals.

Stacy Ooi graduated from the National University of Singapore (NUS) with a degree in Sociology. She runs a prose fiction platform called the Rainbow Fictioneers and works in social services.

Nigel Timothy Mpemba Patel is a Malawian researcher and writer. They hold a Bachelor of Social Science majoring in Philosophy and Law and a LLB from the University of Cape Town, South Africa. They also hold a Graduate Diploma in Law and a Masters of Science in Law, Business and Management from the University of Law, United Kingdom. Nigel is a qualified solicitor of England and Wales. Nigel trained at a magic circle law firm in London and qualified into the firm's Dispute Resolution team. During their legal training, Nigel was on secondment for six months to the Mary Ward Legal Centre working in the housing team on a range of housing law matters. Nigel is currently a Judicial Assistant at the United Kingdom Supreme Court.

George B. Radics is a Senior Lecturer in the Department of Sociology and Anthropology at the National University of Singapore. He teaches Law and Society, Selected Topics on Law and Justice, Sociology of Emotions, and Classical Sociological Theory. After receiving his Ph.D. in Sociology from the National University of Singapore (NUS), he earned a juris doctor with a concentration in Asian law from the University of Washington and worked for the Supreme Court of Guam for two years. He is a member of the New York Bar. His articles have been published in the *Columbia Human Rights Law Review*, *Journal of Human Rights*, *Asian Journal of Social Science*, and the *Philippine Sociological Review*. His work involves the judicial system, notions of justice, human rights, minorities, and comparative legal studies.

Gustavo Rojas-Páez is a Lecturer in Legal Theory and Criminology at Universidad Libre of Colombia. His work addresses the relationship between structural harm and legality from a sociolegal perspective. He has held visiting fellowships at the University of Warwick and at the University of Sussex, and at the IISL in Oñati. Among his publications on crimes of the powerful stand out: the book chapter Understanding environmental harm and justice claims in the Global South: crimes of the powerful and peoples' resistance (Palgrave, 2017) and "Coal Criminals: Crimes of the Powerful, Extractivism and Historical Harm in the Global South" co-authored with José Atiles (British Journal of Criminology, Forthcoming). Currently, he is the Director of the Sociolegal Research Centre at Universidad Libre, School of Law.

Nestor Eduardo Araruna Santiago graduated in 1995 with a degree in Law from the Federal University of Minas Gerais. After graduation, he received a specialization and a master's degree in Criminal Law, and a doctorate in Tax Lax, all from the Federal University of Minas Gerais in 2005. From 2015 to 2016, he completed a postdoctoral internship at the University of Minho. He is currently a Full Professor at the University of Fortaleza (since 2007) and Associate Professor at the Federal University of Ceará (since 2006) but has been teaching since 1999. He is also a criminal lawyer in Fortaleza, Ceará, Brazil.

Ezgi Taşcıoğlu is a Lecturer in Law at the School of Law, Keele University. Her primary research interests lie in sociolegal studies, the regulation of sex, gender and sexuality, disability law, and social and cognitive justice. She holds a B.A. in Cultural Studies from Sabancı University (Turkey), an M.A. from the Oñati International Institute for the Sociology of Law (Spain), and a Ph.D. in Law and Society from the University of Milan (Italy). Following her Ph.D., she was a Research Fellow at Birmingham Law School, University of Birmingham. Her current research project on the right to legal capacity of intellectually disabled people in Turkey is funded by an ESRC New Investigator Grant (December 2022–May 2025).

1

Introduction

George B. Radics

"When they saw me dancing at birthday parties as a kid, they already knew!" declares Kathryn, a *transpinay* (Filipina transwoman) who engages in sex work to make a living. Despite Southeast Asia's rich history of non-binary people, modern Philippine law refuses to recognize even those who undergo sexual reassignment surgery, making the day-to-day lived realities for trans people precarious and invisible. This drove Kathryn, and others like her, into the illegal practice of online sex work to earn a living, express her true identity, and find love. For others, simply speaking out makes them the target of criminalization. In Puerto Rico, as a U.S. territory, it is under great pressure to keep its economy open to U.S. investments and protect American assets. In this neoliberal space, when the local government abandons its responsibility to its citizens, natural catastrophes such as hurricanes or COVID-19 exacerbate governmental control over dissent and intensifies deep-seated economic inequality. Or for countries that suffered under decades of dictatorial rule, it takes a relentless spirit to speak out against entrenched violent practices such as the mass murder of its people, as seen in the Carandiru Prison massacre in Brazil, or the practice of incentivizing the execution of the poor and falsely identifying them as rebels in Colombia. Lastly, with the

G. B. Radics (✉)
Department of Sociology and Anthropology, National University of Singapore, Singapore, Singapore
e-mail: socrgb@nus.edu.sg
NUS College, National University of Singapore, Singapore, Singapore

G. B. Radics and P. Ciocchini (eds.), *Criminal Legalities and Minorities in the Global South*, Palgrave Socio-Legal Studies, https://doi.org/10.1007/978-3-031-17918-1_1

United States' withdrawal from ethnically diverse Afghanistan, conditions can change dramatically overnight, and geopolitical decisions in the North can aggravate the situation for minorities in the South.

The examples above represent just a few scenarios from the chapters in this book and highlight how legal conditions in the Global South are many times violent, but also, how the human will to confront such violence is even stronger. Institutions in the Global North which aim to protect and venerate individual rights are often instruments of violence in the South. Criminal law and criminal justice institutions such as the police, the public prosecutor's office, and the courts that are supposed to deliver justice, rehabilitate offenders, and prevent crime do the opposite in the Global South—they violate the rights of citizens and create criminals by defining the boundaries of what constitutes "legal" and "illegal" activities and behaviors in a manner that conflicts with everyday lived realities. Minorities are often affected even more, disproportionately suffering from the symbolic and physical violence of the state due to their marginal identities. While this situation exists in the Global North, it manifests differently in the Global South in form and magnitude. Furthermore, violence is largely the product of factors such as the legacy of colonial experiences, authoritarian governments, extreme inequality, and neoliberal economic policies of the state. While this volume will explore the disproportionate vulnerabilities of minorities in the Global South, at the same time, it will examine sites of resistance and change, and how the experience of minorities in the Global South can provide invaluable lessons to the Global North on the virtues of survival, adaptation, and revolution.

This volume is composed of chapters from junior and advanced scholars, many times based in the jurisdictions they study or have strong personal connections to it. Furthermore, many of the authors demonstrate deep relationships with the people studied. As opposed to studying issues from afar, many of the chapters highlight what research looks like when those enmeshed in the social conditions of the country or region they study have to face these same conditions themselves. Building on the success of our previous volume *Criminal Legalities in the Global South: Cultural Dynamics, Political Tensions, and Institutional Practices* (Ciocchini and Radics 2019), this volume includes an even broader range of regions and nations as discussed in our last, bringing to the table new connections and ideas. Composed of 13 chapters, this volume includes nations with the largest populations in the world such as Brazil, India, and Pakistan, to smaller nations and territories, such as Singapore and Puerto Rico. It includes a chapter on the geographically and politically strategic nation of Turkey, to the rapidly developing nations of the Philippines and Colombia. The inclusion of Afghanistan, especially in light of the U.S. withdrawal, highlights how many of the nations included in this volume experience rapid growth as they rebuild from violent pasts, like Colombia, or have to reinvent themselves in the post-colonial world, like Malawi. Most importantly, in addition to the diverse range of nations covered, the chapters highlight the vast diversity within these nations. From imprisoned mothers to the LGBTQ, this volume brings the experiences of those living in the Global South into even sharper focus by delving into the relationship between minorities and the criminal law.

1 Challenges in Studying the South

Yet several issues emerge as we attempt to understand the conditions for minorities in the Global South. First is the term "minority" itself. Over the last decade or so, numerous persuasive articles have been written to encourage us to cancel the term. Rashaad Lambert, Director for Culture and Community for Forbes magazine, writes "Words matter, especially when they're inaccurate. The use of the word minority—and the comparative mentality that's formed as a result—is often introduced to Black and Brown people at the most malleable point of life: childhood" (Lambert 2020). In his piece, he highlights how the term "minority" is often projected onto others, infantilizing and disempowering a segment of the population, namely non-White people, who are already the majority outside of the United States, and rapidly becoming the majority in the United States. Ken Wibecan commenting on the National Public Radio's usage of the term states, "Many people use [minority] when they really mean African American or Latino. That is not only inaccurate, but it is also offensive… Does NPR really think that the population of America is composed of only two elements — whites and minorities? I don't think so. And if not, isn't it time to retire that insulting word and use more specific designations instead?" (Schumacher-Matos 2011). The NPR article went on to discuss how the use of the word signals America's "pathological avoidance of straight talk about race relations," ignores non-White cultural influence on the mainstream, and encourages victimization (ibid.). Raising important points, these perspectives posit race (many times "Black" or "Brown" in the United States) as the main indicator of minority status. Furthermore, they challenge the use of the term "minority" when in fact, numerically, these groups constitute a majority in many parts of the world and are rapidly becoming a "majority."

In this volume, disempowered groups such as women, the poor, and ethnic groups in highly diverse environments sometimes already are the "majority." Historically, throughout the colonial era, a small minority have oppressed, erased, and defined larger cultures, so much so that certain individuals, such as trans people or homosexuals, went from non-issue to visible "minority." Even in the North, it was considered an achievement for women to receive "minority" status, forcing institutions to recognize their disadvantaged position and the ongoing discrimination against them (Hacker 1951, 1975). Thus, for this edited volume, the term "minority" can be seen more as a *process* of marginalization and disempowerment trapped within power relations, rather than a label. While, admittedly, languages change, and concepts become outdated, for now, because this volume deals with individuals from the Global South, it will engage the term "minority" until a more appropriate concept representing the experiences of individuals from all parts of the world becomes available.

Another issue that emerges in attempting to understand the conditions for minorities in the Global South is the categories of marginalization. Initially, we intended to organize the chapters along the lines of gender, sexuality, race, and class. But as the reader will see, none of the chapters fall cleanly into any of these categories. This is because, beyond just intersectionality, Global South identities turn Global North categories on their head. A response to the increasingly diversifying North, and the civil rights and student movements in the 1960s and 1970s, "politics of recognition" became the topic of discussion for several decades in the North, with multiculturalism, immigration, indigeneity (Kymlicka 1992, 1995; Kymlicka and Banting 2006), feminism (Young 1990; Baum 2004), and exemption, accommodation, preservation, and redress (see Kivisto 2012) serving as categories of recognition. Taylor and Guttman (1994, 27) discusses the "politics of recognition" as part of the modern condition, one in which honor, esteem, and pride are replaced with dignity, mutual respect, and egalitarianism. Universalism, brought upon by economic redistribution and the promise of rights for all citizens, demands a recognition of an authentic self, and citing Franz Fanon's *Wretched of the Earth*, harm can ensue in the case of misrecognition (Taylor and Guttman 1994, 64). Kivisto (2012), referencing Jefferey Alexander's *Civil Society* (2006), also highlights "incorporation" as a method to transcend the "tribal stigmas of race, nation, and religion" (Goffman 2014 [1963], 3–4), with assimilation being replaced with multiculturalism as a preferred means of social acceptance.

While those in the Global South also demand such recognition, undoubtedly, the conditions for "recognition" are not the same. Pervasive and persistent inequality (Francis et al. 2020), illiberalism (Chua 2005), colonial divide-and-rule policies (Brown 1996; Radics and Sinha 2018), and a history of resistance to being treated as pawns in ideological battles between larger powers (Obregón 2017; Anghie 2017), the Global South stems from a different history. As opposed to a Westphalian-type, modern nation-state where sovereignty was observed between neighbors, many Global South nations were *granted* their independence by colonial powers, borders were drawn without concern for local populations, and for decades prior to independence diverse communities were intentionally kept separate to prevent cohesion. Furthermore, post-colonial ideologies of nationalism and development often emphasized unitary and homogenous visions of nationhood, leading to violence, secessionism, and civil war (Kymlicka and He 2005). And modernist and developmentalist economic theories popular from the mid-1940s till late-1960s also led to neoliberal economic policies that were presumed to lead to democracy and eventually "law and order," but instead created massive inequality (Eslava 2015; see Lipset 1959; Rostow 1960).

In this context, being Black and Brown does not immediately make one allies, and simply having female sex characteristics does not guarantee protections under the law if you fail to perform your national duty. In the Global South, the law was not a product of mutual agreement and constitutional promises. What constitutes a "citizen" is constantly evolving, and identities are messy and tied to the shifting political, economic, and social values that many times have emerged inorganically *through* the North. In the North, identities can serve as a community that transcends the individual, and when these communities don't serve the individual, new communities can be formed. In the South, minority identities are criminalized, so the act of forming a community is an act of rebellion, subject to violence, discrimination, and erasure. Nationalism in the Global South becomes entangled with notions of civilization, modernity, and progress, with minority groups serving as shameful relics of the past, unholy or backward people to be saved, or threats to the "nation" that should be eradicated.

The role of the state leads us to our final challenge: how do laws that have been used in the past to harm, protect those at the margins? For many of the nations in this edited volume, the criminal laws enacted to establish "law and order," actually cause "chaos and order" (Radics and Ciocchini forthcoming). In the North, modern law draws on notions of legitimacy of authority, inherent rights tied to the individual, rationalism, and universalism espoused by the political philosophies of Thomas Hobbes, John Locke, Immanuel Kant, and Jean-Jacques Rosseau (Tully 1995, 60). These political theories were then further developed by Michael Walzer (1983), Taylor and Guttman (1994), and John Rawls (1999) at the end of the twentieth century to make sense of individual rights within the context of the modern condition and the increasing physical and cultural diversity of globalized societies. A robust attempt to question the universal applicability of such ideas to the South was launched by a powerful group of scholars who have presented an alternative understanding of rights in the Global South. Boaventura de Sousa Santos (1995, 574) sees the South as a "frontier," where selective and instrumental use of traditions was brought from the Global North by pioneers and emigrants to invent new forms of legal sociability. Jean and John Comaroff (2006, 2009) explored how global capitalism has exacerbated the use of the law in the South to inflict violence and protect the powerful. Auyero and Sobering (2017) also remind us that rather than protecting individual rights, states in the South reproduced the same oppressive laws that were used to colonize them—often manifesting in the form of criminal laws—abandoning citizens at the margins or over policing them (see also Bonilla Maldonado 2013; Eslava 2015; Pahuja 2012; Ciocchini and Radics 2019).

This volume hopes to build on this tradition of highlighting new modes of understanding the process of marginalization for minorities, particularly in the context of criminal legalities in the Global South. Going beyond categories and histories developed in the North, this edited volume draws from young and established scholars from or based in the Global South to explore their unique understanding of rights for minorities under criminal law regimes in their countries of study. But before we can appreciate their contributions, a short discussion on the modern struggle for rights in the North will be discussed to highlight the difference between Northern demands for rights, and the Southern conditions presented in this volume.

2 Demanding Rights: Global South in the Global North?

The inspiration behind modern debates on, and for, minorities can be traced to the rebellious 1960s Western world. From its inception, ethnic studies in the United States had always attempted to be global, even though it was largely tied to the goal of changing local conditions for Black, Indigenous, and people of color. Enabled by decades of formidable African American demands for civil rights, by November 1968, the longest student-led strike in the United States was organized by the Third World Liberation Front (TWLF) at San Francisco State University. TWLF was a coalition of six autonomous non-White student organizations: Black Student Union, Latino American Student Organization, Mexican American Student Configuration, Pilipino American Collegiate Endeavors (PACE), Intercollegiate Chinese for Social Action (ICSA), and the Asian American Political Alliance (Nance 2008; Miranda, n.d.). These student protests led to the first College of Ethnic Studies in the country. Similar protests took place across the bay at U.C. Berkeley, eventually leading to an interdisciplinary department of Ethnic Studies.

Around the same time, second-wave feminism emerged, influenced by Simone de Beauvoir's famous *The Second Sex* (1953) and Betty Friedan's *Feminine Mystique* (1963). By the 1970s, the first Women's Studies Department in the United States emerged at San Diego State University—funded and backed by big business interests, such as oil (Salper 2011). LGBT organizations in the Global North can be traced to Weimar Germany, though their real influence began to spread after World War II (see Bauer 2017). For the LGBTQ, continued repression spurred radicalization by the 1960s, with monumental events such as Stonewall in the United States serving as a catalyst for similar gay rights movements in other parts of the Global North (Radics 2019; Weiss 2007). This chain reaction in terms of LGBTQ movements, as well as feminist movements, was perhaps because many of the conditions were similar: the postwar baby boom, a growing cultural revolution, and shifting sentiments against heavy-handed efforts by the church or state to enforce outdated social mores (May 1988; Edsall 2003).

By the end of the 1970s, ethnic and gender-based groups began to focus on their communities' particular issues, moving away from exclusively pan-racial or gender-based politics. In 1977, the term "identity politics" was introduced by the Combahee River Collective, a group of African American feminists. They boldly proclaimed, "we believe that the most profound and potentially the most radical politics come directly out of our own identity, as opposed to working to end somebody else's oppression" (Guy-Sheftall 1995, 234). Highlighting racism in the White woman's movement, the "notoriously negative" reaction of Black men to feminism, the narrow focus of the socialist movement that ignores race and gender, and the rejection of the expulsion of lesbians, the Combahee River Collective "arrived at the necessity for developing an understanding of class relationships that takes into account the specific class position of Black women" (Guy-Sheftall 1995, 235).

Kimberlé Crenshaw (1989, 150), by reviewing court cases that looked at Black women as either Black or women, built upon the identity politics framework by stating that courts treat "Black women in ways that deny both the unique compoundedness of their situation and the centrality of this experiences to the larger classes of women and Blacks." She continues, "neither Black liberationist politics nor feminist theory can ignore the intersectional experiences of those whom the movements claims as their respective constituents" (Crenshaw 1989, 166). Intersectionality, thus, became indispensable from the identity politics framework, and both became part of the larger Critical Race Theory movement that can be traced to law professors Derrick Bell, Kimberlé Crenshaw, Mari Matsuda, Richard Delgado, and Charles Lawrence, to name a few. Critical Race Theory aims to highlight how racism exists, "color-blindness" hides it, race itself is socially constructed, racial experiences are intersectional, and different races have different perspectives and experiences that are unique and should be told (Delgado and Stefancic 2001, 7–9).

Despite the overlap of many different identities, and the ultimate offshoot of such communities into their own subgroups, indigeneity and settler colonialism, an influential frame to study minorities, gained currency. In studying Australia, Patrick Wolfe (2006) describes settler colonialism as a land-centered project that operates through the logic of elimination. Evelyn Nakano Glenn (2015) adds that settler colonialism embeds a hetero-masculine national identity, which in the United States, rests on a hierarchy of race, with "whiteness" as the ideal, and "blackness" as backwardness, the antithesis to freedom, and non-citizenship. J. Kēhaulani Kauanui (2021), citing Haunani-Kay Trask (2000) and Candice Fujikane and Jonathan Okamura (2000), highlights that scholars have been contemplating the impact of Asian settlers in Hawaii for years. Despite the recent popularity of settler colonialism as a framework to understand racial, gender, and sexual oppression, these ideas can be traced as far back as Jean M. O'Brien's *Dispossession by Degrees* (1997) or even Fayez Sayegh in *Zionist Colonialism in Palestine* (1965), and has been used to study similar processes in Argentina, Australia, Canada, Israel, New Zealand, and the United States.

3 Decolonizing the Literature

While all helpful, these frameworks of identity politics, intersectionality, and settler colonialism do not apply to the Global South so cleanly. Drawing from a liberal, Western conception of individual rights, they presume that the state shall be impartial and that fundamental rights applied universally. In contrast, this volume argues that rights in the South are not upheld in the same way and explores four dimensions that differ strongly from the liberal conceptions of rights found in the Global North. First, while the instability of the 1960s ushered in debates in the North, Southern nations at the time were experiencing all-out war, either supported by Northern nations, or caused by their withdrawal during the period of decolonization. Second, the increasing diversity in the North that led to the demand for ethnic studies and equal representation was largely driven by migrants who were escaping growing inequality and economic deprivation in the South. Third, entrenched cultural biases were many times imported from foreign nations, reinterpreting local traditions as backwards, or the result of old societal rifts that were enflamed and exploited by external forces. And, finally, such cultural biases, in the shadow of war and growing inequality, become entrenched in the law—criminalizing diversity. This final section will highlight how the chapters in this volume will develop these four dimensions.

3.1 Rebuilding After Violence

Göran Therborn (1979) highlights how a particular form of authoritarianism emerges when an imported version of democracy, stark inequality, and asymmetrical relations between the North and the South are part of the nation-building process. Guillermo O'Donnell (1993) highlights how in Latin America, patrimonial, populist, or bureaucratic authoritarian regimes emerged as a result. In Southeast Asia, Dan Slater (2010) argues that similar conditions produced domination-type dictatorships seen in Singapore and Malaysia, fragmented dictatorships as seen in the Philippines and Thailand, and militarized dictatorships as seen in Indonesia and Burma.

Emilio Meyer and Marta Machado in the first chapter, "The Carandiru Prison Massacre," examine how, despite Brazil's transition to democracy, the ongoing failure to prosecute the police officers in charge of a massacre that took place in 1992 at the Carandiru Prison serves as evidence that the judicial system, including the police, sees poor, Black, and those considered criminals as not deserving of rights or protection. It also demonstrates the ongoing militarization of the police in the name of "national security," and the warrior-like, masculinist ethos of the police forged in the dictatorship from 1964 to 1985. M. Bashir Mobasher and Nasiruddin Nezaami, in their chapter "Politics Before Law," discuss how in the incredibly diverse nation of Afghanistan, new laws were passed in 2017 to protect minorities from hate speech. Replacing the 1976 Penal Code, the 2017 Penal Code was meant to enhance protections for ethnic and religious minorities from the rise of hate speech in cyberspace, as well as the rise of extremist political voices. Discussing five cases from outside and within the government, their chapter shows how laws on the books do not always translate into law in practice, and how laws can sometimes be used as a political bargaining chip, as opposed to a set of impartial rules to be applied universally. Returning to Latin America, in "Between Denial and Memory," Gustavo Rojas-Páez discusses the tragic phenomenon of "false positives" in Colombia, where the government creates incentives for the military to deliver high body counts, thereby encouraging the creation of fake charges against those killed extrajudicially. His chapter examines how such killings happen to those considered dispensable—namely the poor, disabled, or the indigenous. To justify the killings, trumped up charges of "drug trafficking" or other crimes are associated with minorities to justify their execution. This chapter, along with the others in this section, highlights how prolonged periods of state-sponsored violence make it difficult to transform institutions that had for decades been used to oppress citizens, into one that suddenly protects them.

3.2 Economic Interests and the State

As the Global North began to relinquish control over their colonies in the mid-twentieth century, bilateral aid to the South became replaced with multilateral aid in the form of loans that were distributed through the World Bank and the International Monetary Fund (Bello 2006; Radics 2001). These loans came with requirements that forced nations to lower tariffs, remove controls on their currency, and promote a policy of state-sponsored, foreign-run export processing zones (Broad 1988). The purpose of these policies was to increase economic competitiveness, but instead, many times had the effect of exacerbating inequality. With the fall of the Soviet Union, these neoliberal economic policies became even more widespread, as it was presumed that economic openness could help the "developing world" catch up with the West (Silva 2009).

But as will be seen in the chapters, these economic pressures have even deeper roots, starting with the competition over resources between ethnic groups, and how colonial powers exploited this competition. In Suraj Gogoi's "Formless Punishment and Exclusion," he explores how the National Register of Citizens in India is a modern manifestation of the animosity between elite Bengalese and Assamese classes that was created when the British began to fill their administration with the former, and the Bengali language was imposed in the lands of the Assamese. As if in some perverse retribution, the laws have since been structured to punish poor and migrant Bengalis, now labeled foreigners and "infiltrants," subjecting them to the indignities of "Foreigner Tribunals," a civil institution that lacks even the basic rights guaranteed in the penal code. In my own chapter,

"(Cr)Immigration and Merit-Based Migration in the Global South," the legacy of British importation of labor to Colonial Malaya left entrenched views of certain low-level jobs as being tied to various races. As a result of the need for cheap labor in modern-day Singapore, this race-based approach to managing labor was maintained and enhanced, allowing for stereotypes of vice and illegal activities to be attached to migrant laborers, and a concomitant reduction in the protections and rights afforded them.

In Pakistan, we see a similar process of economic forces labeling individuals as criminals in order to facilitate economic extraction. Sabeen Kazmi in "Colonial Legal Continuities in Post-Colonial Pakistan" argues that maintenance of British-era land acquisition laws, in addition to emergence of *katchi abadis* (non-permanent settlements), has created a situation of precarity where urban elites need the cheap labor that these *katchi abadi* dwellers provide, but demonize and criminalize them to justify their removal when their land becomes valuable and worth developing. Finally, in José Atiles' "Disciplining colonial subjects," he argues that for the residents of Puerto Rico, a territory of the United States without the same rights and privileges of a fully-fledged state in the union, poverty, and protests are criminalized. Despite the fact that neoliberal policies have exacerbated inequality and the degradation of the environment, Puerto Ricans themselves are blamed for this state of affairs with the most vulnerable and vocal the first to be punished.

3.3 Entrenched Cultural Biases

In the case of many of the nations in the South, a long-lasting effect of colonization on these societies was that forced diversity led to societal rifts between the different races and ethnicities (Goh 2008; see also Chua 2012; Radics and Sinha 2018). Efforts to transform the intimate lives of local populations through criminal laws that challenged "backward" practices affected how gender, sexuality, religion, and hygiene were seen by local populations (Manderson 1997; Stoler 1989). Upon independence, many of these new cultural practices were seen as essential to the development of a modern nation. Thus, these entrenched laws that initially were meant to train colonized populations to be more "modern" were enhanced in the post-colonial state which now viewed "wayward" cultural values as a threat to the national identity, warranting harsh and severe punishment (Kymlicka and He 2005).

In the case of Singapore, Joseph Greener and Stacy Ooi in "'Truth' and 'Consent' in Sexual Violence Reporting" highlight how in Singapore, where deeply polarized notions of gender prevail, until the beginning of this century, any sexual act outside of procreation was criminalized, and only recently, marital rape was deemed illegal, and women who report sexual violence are treated with extreme distrust and discouraged from reporting. Women who are sexually active are seen as violating the norms of only having sex within the confines of marriage and solely for reproduction, and therefore, those who suffer from sexual assault are treated as duplicitous women whose allegations cannot be trusted without incontrovertible evidence. Lara Nascimento Meneses, João Araújo Monteiro Neto, and Nestor Eduardo Araruna Santiago in their chapter, "Between Toys and Behind Bars," demonstrate how similar notions in Brazil can be taken in a different direction. Women and children are envisioned as so vulnerable that even the "national security" doctrine does not seem to affect them. In Brazil, women prisoners are constitutionally provided with the right to raise their children outside of prison—though such bold laws have yet to be fully implemented. Exploring entrenched biases against the poor, Pablo Ciocchini and Jayson Lamchek in "The 'War on Drugs' in Philippine Criminal Courts" draw from interviews with prosecutors, public attorneys, and judges to show how legal professionals' embrace of plea bargaining continue the weaponization of morality against the poor within the criminal justice system.

3.4 Criminalizing of Diversity

The final section of this edited volume will explore how many of the entrenched cultural biases become passed down through the law. In our previous volume, we explored the criminalization of adultery (Rahman 2019), sexuality (Sheikh 2019; Radics 2019), and cultural practices such as *jogo do bicho* or "animal lottery" (Neto and Santiago 2019). While our previous volume explored the cultural practices that were criminalized, in this volume we explore the criminalization of the identity itself, starting with trans sex workers in Turkey. Ezgi Taşcıoğlu in "Circuits of Law: Everyday Criminalisation of Transgender Embodiment in Istanbul" explores how in attempting to modernize Turkey's laws, fines were implemented to punish sex work. Whereas in the past, trans sex work was subject to bribery and harassment, ironically, this "modern" legal framework of fines has created a more oppressive predicament where everyday life is now subject to criminal procedures that are imbued with bias, conservative religious values, and more tangible and physical economic punishments. Veronica L. Gregorio in her chapter, "Reaffirming Womanhood: Young transwomen and online sex work in Philippines" discusses how because the state refuses to recognize and protect transgender people in the Philippines, trans women are pushed to break the law and engage in online sex work, not just for financial reasons, but for the reaffirmation of their identities and to seek companionship and love. Finally, Nigel Timothy Mpemba Patel in "A Queer *Chinkhoswe*" ends the volume on a hopeful note. Through the criminalizing of a queer couple who performed a *chinkhoswe*, or a traditional Malawian matrimonial agreement, we see how customary laws can be used to challenge the idea that homosexuality is un-African. In the shadow of Malawi's British-enacted anti-sodomy laws, this brave act, and its criminalization, brings into focus the cultural wars, colonial legacies, and deeply entrenched biases in the Global South. The chapter brings home how the criminalization of minorities is absurd, contrary to human nature, and a human-made situation that can easily be rectified to celebrate human diversity, rather than oppressing it.

4 Conclusion

While the situation may seem dire for many of the minorities in this book, there is much to be learned from their experiences. The chapters in this book give us a glimpse into the Southern processes and methods in which a minority group emerges, is treated under the law, and reacts to change their oppressive situation. They also highlight how the laws and concepts that evolved in response to Western histories and circumstances may have great value in the Global South, but by no means can be applied in the same way. And finally, what we hope you take away from this book is not to pity the struggles of minorities in the Global South, but to be inspired by them, learn from them, and respect not just the universality of "human rights," but also, the universality of the human will to survive—and nowhere is this spirit stronger than within communities of individuals who live in worlds where their day-to-day survival is criminalized, and their existence constantly under threat.

References

Alexander, Jeffrey. 2006. *Civil Society*. New York: Oxford University Press.

Anghie, Antony. 2017. Bandung and the Origins of Third World Sovereignty. In *Bandung, Global History, and International Law: Critical Pasts and Pending Futures*, ed. L. Eslava, M. Fakhri, & V. Nesiah, 535–551. Cambridge: Cambridge University Press.

Auyero, Javier, and Katherine Sobering. 2017. Violence, the State, and the Poor: A View from the South. *Sociological Forum* 32 (S1): 1018–1031.

Bauer, Heike. 2017. *The Hirschfeld Archives: Violence, Death, and Modern Queer Culture*. Philadelphia: Temple University Press.

Baum, Bruce. 2004. Feminist Politics of Recognition. *Signs* 29 (4): 1073–1102.

Bello, Walden. 2006. *Deglobalization*. Manila: Ateneo de Manila Press.

Broad, Robin. 1988. *Unequal Alliance: The World Bank, the International Monetary Fund, and the Philippines*. Berkeley: University of California Press.

Brown, David. 1996. *The State and Ethnic Politics in South-East Asia*. London: Routledge.

Chua, Beng Huat. 2005. The Cost of Membership in Ascribed Community. In *Multiculturalism in Asia*, ed. Baogang He and Will Kymlicka, 170–196. Oxford and New York: Oxford University Press.

Chua, Lynette J. 2012. Pragmatic Resistance, Law, and Social Movements in Authoritarian States: The Case of Gay Collective Action in Singapore. *Law & Society Review* 46 (4): 713–748.

Ciocchini, Pablo, and George Radics. 2019. *Criminal Legalities in the Global South: Cultural Dynamics, Political Tensions, and Institutional Practices*. London: Routledge.

Comaroff, J., and J.L. Comaroff. 2006. *Law and Disorder in the Postcolony*. Chicago: University of Chicago Press.

Comaroff, J., and J.L. Comaroff. 2009. *Ethnicity Inc*. Chicago: University of Chicago Press.

Crenshaw, Kimberlé. 1989. Demarginalizing the Intersection of Race and Sex: A Black Feminist Critique of Antidiscrimination Doctrine, Feminist Theory and Antiracist Politics. *University of Chicago Legal Forum* 1 (8): 139–167.

de Beauvoir, Simone. 1953. *The Second Sex*. New York: Knopf.

de Sousa Santos, Boaventura. 1995. Three Metaphors for a New Conception of Law: The Frontier, the Baroque, and the South. *Law & Society Review* 29 (4): 569–584.

Delgado, Richard, and Jean Stefancic. 2001. *Critical Race Theory: An Introduction*. New York: NYU Press.

Edsall, Nicholas C. 2003. *Toward Stonewall: Homosexuality and Society in the Modern Western World*. Charlottesville: University of Virginia Press.

Eslava, Luis. 2015. Development and the Nation-State. In *Local Space, Global Life: The Everyday Operation of International Law and Development*, ed. Luis Eslava, 91–138. Cambridge: Cambridge University Press.

Francis, David, Imraan Valodia, and Edward Webster. 2020. *Inequality Studies from the Global South*. London: Routledge.

Friedan, Betty. 1963. *The Feminine Mystique*. New York: Gollanez.

Fujikane, Candice, and Jonathan Okamura. 2000. Special Issue: 'Whose Vision? Asian Settler Colonialism in Hawai'i'. *Amerasia Journal* 26 (2): xv–xxii.

Glenn, Evelyn Nakano. 2015. Settler Colonialism as Structure: A Framework for Comparative Studies of U.S. Race and Gender Formation. *Sociology of Race and Ethnicity* 1 (1): 54–74.
Goffman, Erving. 2014 [1963]. *Stigma: Notes on the Management of Spoiled Identity*. New York: Touchstone.
Goh, Daniel P.S. 2008. From Colonial Pluralism to Postcolonial Multiculturalism: Race, State Formation and the Question of Cultural Diversity in Malaysia and Singapore. *Sociology Compass* 2 (1): 232–252.
Guy-Sheftall, Beverly. 1995. *Words of Fire: An Anthology of African-American Feminist Thought*. New York: New Press.
Hacker, Helen Mayer. 1951. Women as a Minority Group. *Social Forces* 30 (1): 60–69.
Hacker, Helen Mayer. 1975. 'Women as a Minority Group': Twenty Years Later. *Sage Contemporary Social Science* 15. Beverley Hills, CA: Sage.
Kauanui, J. Kēhaulani. 2021. False Dilemmas and Settler Colonial Studies: Response to Lorenzo Veracini: 'Is Settler Colonial Studies Even Useful? *Postcolonial Studies* 24 (2): 290–296.
Kivisto, Peter. 2012. We Really Are Multiculturalists Now. *The Sociological Quarterly* 53 (1): 1–24.
Kymlicka, Will. 1992. *Liberalism, Community, and Culture*. Oxford: Clarendon Press.
Kymlicka, Will. 1995. *Multicultural Citizenship*. New York: Oxford University Press.
Kymlicka, Will, and Keith Banting. 2006. Immigration, Multiculturalism, and the Welfare State. *Ethics & International Affairs* 20 (3): 281–304.
Kymlicka, Will, and Baogang He, eds. 2005. *Multiculturalism in Asia*, 170–195. Oxford: Oxford University Press.
Lambert, Rashaad. 2020. 'There Is Nothing Minor About Us': Why Forbes Won't Use the Term Minority to Classify Black and Brown People. *Forbes*, October 8. https://www.forbes.com/sites/rashaadlambert/2020/10/08/there-is-nothing-minor-about-us-why-forbes-wont-use-the-term-minority-to-classify-black-and-brown-people/?sh=5d37194b7e21.
Lipset, Seymour Martin. 1959. Some Social Requisites of Democracy: Economic Development and Political Legitimacy. *American Political Science Review* 53 (1): 69–105.
Maldonado, Daniel Bonilla, ed. 2013. *Constitutionalism of the Global South: The Activist Tribunals of India, South Africa, and Colombia*. Cambridge: Cambridge University Press.
Manderson, Lenore. 1997. Colonial Desires: Sexuality, Race, and Gender in British Malaya. *Journal of the History of Sexuality* 7 (3): 372–388.
May, Elaine Tyler. 1988. *Homeward Bound: American Families in the Cold War Era*. New York: Basic Books.

Miranda, Tony. n.d. *To Our Supporters*. San Francisco State Legal Defense Committee. https://diva.sfsu.edu/collections/strike/bundles/187953.

Nance, Molly. 2008. Writing Their Own History. *Diverse Issues in Higher Education* 25 (19): 12–15.

Neto, Joaõ Araújo Neto and Nestor Eduardo Araruna Santiago. 2019. Gambling with Criminal Law: The Legal Paradox of "jogo do bicho" (Animal Lottery) Criminalization in Brazil. In *Criminal Legalities in the Global South: Cultural Dynamics, Political Tensions, and Institutional Practices*, ed. Pablo Ciocchini and George Radics. London: Routledge.

O'Brien, Jean. 1997. *Dispossession by Degrees: Indian Land and Identity in Natick, Massachusetts, 1650–1790 (Studies in North American Indian History)*. Cambridge: Cambridge University Press.

O'Donnell, Guillermo. 1993. On the State, Democratization and Some Conceptual Problems: A Latin American view with Glances at Some Postcommunist Countries. *World Development* 21 (8): 1355–1369.

Obregón, Liliana. 2017. Latin America During the Bandung Era: Anti-imperialist Movements vs. Anti-communist States. In *Bandung, Global History, and International Law: Critical Pasts and Pending Futures*, ed. L. Eslava, M. Fakhri, and V. Nesiah, 232–246. Cambridge: Cambridge University Press.

Pahuja, Sundhya. 2012. *Decolonising International Law: Development, Economic Growth and the Politics of Universality*. London: Cambridge University Press.

Radics, George. 2001. Globalization, Corruption and the Structural Historical Perspective. *Philippine Sociological Review* 49 (1–2): 39–58.

Radics, George. 2019. 'First World Problems' in the 'Third World': LGBT Rights in Singapore. In *Criminal Legalities in the Global South: Cultural Dynamics, Political Tensions, and Institutional Practices*, ed. Pablo Ciocchini and George Radics. London: Routledge.

Radics, George, and Pablo Ciocchini. forthcoming. Law and Order. In *Oxford Handbook on International Law and Development*, ed. Luis Eslava, Ruth Buchanan, and Sundhya Pahuja. London: Oxford.

Radics, George, and Vineeta Sinha. 2018. Regulation of Religion and Granting of Public Holidays: The Case of Tai Pucam in Singapore. *Asian Journal of Social Science* 46 (4/5): 524–548.

Rahman, Anisur. 2019. Criminalizing adultery in colonial India: constructing the wife vs. the "other" in Islamic family law. In *Criminal Legalities in the Global South: Cultural Dynamics, Political Tensions, and Institutional Practices*, ed. Pablo Ciocchini and George Radics. London: Routledge.

Rawls, John. 1999. *A Theory of Justice*. Boston: Harvard University Press.

Rostow, W.W. 1960. *The Stages of Economic Growth: A Non-Communist Manifesto*. Cambridge: Cambridge University Press.

Salper, Roberta. 2011. San Diego State 1970: The Initial Year of the Nation's First Women's Studies Program. *Feminist Studies* 37 (3): 656–682.

Sayegh, Fayez. 1965. *Zionist Colonialism in Palestine*. Beirut: Research Center of the Palestinian Liberation Organization.

Schumacher-Matos, Edward. 2011. On Race: The Relevance of Saying 'Minority'. *NPR*, August 29. https://www.npr.org/sections/publiceditor/2011/08/29/140040441/on-race-the-relevance-of-saying-minority.

Sheikh, Danish. 2019. Privacy in Public Spaces: The Transformative Potential of *Navtej Johar v. Union of India*. In *Criminal Legalities in the Global South: Cultural Dynamics, Political Tensions, and Institutional Practices*, ed. Pablo Ciocchini and George Radics. London: Routledge.

Silva, Eduardo. 2009. *Challenging Neoliberalism in Latin America*. Cambridge: Cambridge University Press.

Slater, Dan. 2010. *Ordering Power: Contentious Politics and Authoritarian Leviathans in Southeast Asia*. Cambridge: Cambridge University Press.

Stoler, Ann. 1989. On Cultural Hygiene: The Dynamics of Degeneration. *American Ethnologist* 16 (4): 634.

Taylor, Charles, and Amy Guttman. 1994. *Multiculturalism: Examining the Politics of Recognition*. Princeton, NJ: Princeton University Press.

Therborn, Göran. 1979. The Travail of Latin American Democracy. *New Left Review*, 113.

Trask, Haunani-Kay. 2000. Settlers of Color and "Immigrant" Hegemony: "Locals" in Hawai'i.' *Amerasia Journal* 26 (2): 1–26.

Tully, James. 1995. Strange Multiplicity: Constitutionalism in an Age of Diversity. *Cambridge University Press.*

Walzer, Michael. 1983. *Spheres of Justice*. New York: Basic Books.

Weiss, J. 2007. Lesbian, Gay, Bisexual, and Transgender (LGBT) Movement. In *Encyclopedia of Activism and Social Justice*, ed. G. L. Anderson and K. G. Herr, 846–848. Thousand Oaks, CA: Sage Publications.

Wolfe, Patrick. 2006. Race and the Trace of History: For Henry Reynolds. In *Studies in Settler Colonialism: Politics, Identity, and Culture*, ed. F. Bateman and L. Pilkington. New York: Palgrave Macmillan.

Young, Iris Marion. 1990. *Justice and the Politics of Difference*. Princeton, NJ: Princeton University Press.

Part I

Rebuilding after Violence

2

The Carandiru Prison Massacre and Ongoing Military Repression in Brazil

Emilio Meyer and Marta Machado

1 Introduction

During the COVID-19 pandemic, the Brazilian Federal Supreme Court issued an order halting police operations in Rio de Janeiro's *favelas*—except in special cases—while quarantine measures were in place (Brazilian Supreme Federal Court 2020). Whereas the average of police killings was 148.5 victims from January to May 2020, after the Brazilian Federal Supreme Court ruling, the rate decreased to 46.5. In October, however, the ruling was ignored, and the rate returned to 145 victims (PSB et al. 2020). These astonishing numbers illustrate the strong connection between police activities and violence in Brazil. While violent police methods have a long-standing history

E. Meyer (✉)
Federal University of Minas Gerais, Belo Horizonte, Brazil
e-mail: emiliopeluso@gmail.com

E. Meyer
Brazilian National Council for Scientific and Technological Development, Brasília, Brazil

M. Machado
FGV São Paulo, São Paulo, Brazil
e-mail: marta.machado@fgv.br

M. Machado
Centro Brasileiro de Análise e Planejamento, São Paulo, Brazil
e-mail: marta.machado@fgv.br

G. B. Radics and P. Ciocchini (eds.), *Criminal Legalities and Minorities in the Global South*, Palgrave Socio-Legal Studies, https://doi.org/10.1007/978-3-031-17918-1_2

in Brazil, it can be argued that they gained sophistication during the Brazilian civil-military dictatorship of 1964–1985. Political repression was an essential objective of the regime and police officers used abusive illegal methods with both political opponents and common criminals. Many of those illegalities were committed by death squads, but also by formal police institutions, indicating that they shared common practices (Gaspari 2004; Manso 2020). In the public security field, the transition to democracy in Brazil reveals a pattern of continuity rather than change[1] even though institutional reforms toward human rights protections have taken place over the past few decades.

This chapter argues that the Brazilian police and Armed Forces entered the post-1988 democratic period without disturbing the national security ideology that permeated its actions during the dictatorship. Although there were attempts to democratize those institutions, these efforts were essentially unsuccessful. Additionally, courts have avoided holding police officers and the military accountable, and their omissive role further legitimized criminal deeds committed by members of the security apparatus. This chapter unpacks these issues using the Carandiru massacre of 1992 as a case study.[2] The massacre bridges the analyses of two bodies of literature, one on democratic transition and the other on police brutality, revealing both the militant truculence of police forces and institutions' resistance in dealing with state accountability and reform.

In the wake of Brazil's transition to democracy, the Carandiru case reveals a continuity of a pattern of human rights violations by the police and the fragility of the rule of law in Brazil. On October 2, 1992, after a riot broke out in the State of São Paulo Carandiru House of Detention, and with almost no efforts to placate the inmates taking place, a group of approximately 350 heavily armed agents of the military police invaded cellblock number 9. When they left, 111 inmates were dead and many wounded. No members of the police were killed. Images that showed piles of dead bodies being removed and a river of blood running down the prison stairs confronted the young constitutional democratic project. Months later, two episodes showed that the Carandiru massacre was not an isolated case. On July 23, 1993, members of the military police shot at children and

[1] In Brazil, the military police are forces responsible for maintaining public order within the states and the Federal District, subordinated to the state governments. Each state has its own military police, with its own general commander. State military police forces are distinct from national Brazilian Armed Forces. Additionally, civil police forces of the states, also subordinated to each state governor, handle crimes investigation, such as detective work and forensics.

[2] The description and the discussion of the case here rely heavily on Machado and Machado (2015).

adolescents who were sleeping on the stairs of the Candelária Church. One month later, over thirty plainclothes and hooded policemen executed 21 people in Vigário Geral, a favela in Rio de Janeiro. The list of cases committed by Brazilian public security forces over the last three decades of constitutional democracy runs long. They also illustrate what some scholars have named as "a structurally lethal pattern of activity" by the police (Oliveira 2012, 34; *see also* Lima 2019).

The absence of institutional reforms for the protection of human rights conducted by the state in Brazil translates into one of the highest death tolls caused by police members in the world. There are several long-standing systemic conditions that allow for this: the profiling of black and impoverished people as criminals due to racism; poor training and psychologically damaging work conditions for police officers; ineffective investigating and prosecution of crimes committed by police officers, especially those regarding drug trafficking; and legislative and judicial "law and order" policies. Improvements were not on the horizon with the rise of a far-right government of Jair Bolsonaro. Elected in 2018, his term began with attempts to extend citizens access to guns and a proposal to amplify police officers' legal permissions to kill. Furthermore, Bolsonaro's political statements and general discourse emboldened police officers to continue and amplify their aggressive hostilities. As a result, under his leadership, the State of Rio de Janeiro reached its highest death toll committed by policemen in twenty years.

We use the Carandiru case as a starting point to discuss the resilience of militarization of public security and the national security ideology. The importance of the case is twofold. First, it epitomizes the *modus operandi* of the Military Police and establishes a pattern of institutions absorbing and accommodating state violence within the constitutional order. It is not a coincidence that after almost 30 years of an ongoing criminal procedure in the Carandiru case that nobody has been held responsible for the excessive violence, or the resulting 111 deaths of unarmed prisoners, that took place that fateful day. Second, the case is a watershed event in the debate on institutional changes to address police violence. It propelled human rights activism and created political opportunities to discuss reforms aimed at increasing police officers' accountability, even if many of these pressures have been slow to invoke change.

This chapter aims to analyze the connections between the organization of police apparatus during the 1964–1985 dictatorship and the absence of effective reforms in the democratic period that followed. The hypothesis is that, far from being exceptional cases, torture, racial profiling, extrajudicial killings, and other illegal practices and tactics occur within the context of institutional extreme police violence uncontrolled by a justice system that allows for the impunity of police officers. Specifically, the militarization of the police of São Paulo with no reforms after 1988 preserved a logic of "national security" that harmed innocent people and targeted exclusively the black and poor. In a perverse twist of fate, the democratic period exacerbated the harm due to the role of the civil courts in guaranteeing impunity.

We begin with a discussion on the national security doctrine forged in the dictatorship—a doctrine that represented a long-standing warrior-like masculinist and truculent ethos of the police force. The doctrine also serves as a starting point to discuss the most relevant attempts to reform the police, as well as an example of the impunity guaranteed by the justice system. The chapter then turns to describe some features of the Brazilian transition to democracy, focusing on the lack of meaningful reforms in the public security field. In the next section, the chapter explores the Carandiru case and how it serves as a paradigmatic case in the lack of accountability and failure of reforms. The chapter will then proceed to discuss how attempts of the State of Rio de Janeiro to introduce improvements through "community policing" were hampered by militant legacies in the judicial system. Finally, the chapter concludes with a discussion on the current Brazilian political moment in which one can see a deeper process of militarization of the Brazilian State.

Ultimately, this chapter highlights how the military dictatorship serves as a crucial gateway to the continuity of the military rule logic in public security. In this sense, our analysis converges with Wacquant's reflection of Brazil as a case in which the militarization of urban marginality joined punitive containment in the management of dispossessed populations (Wacquant 2008). The Carandiru case is undoubtedly a case in which both logics intersect, mobilizing two structural problems in Brazilian Public Security, namely mass incarceration and police brutality.

2 Military Rule in Brazil: The National Security Doctrine and The Police

On March 31, 1964, a coup seized presidential power in Brazil, leading to a military dictatorship with civilian support that lasted for 21 years. One of the main characteristics of this regime was that it asserted a position in the global cold war based on a national security discourse of combating communism against internal and external enemies. Relying on Alfred Stepan's (1971) account of the changing paradigm for military action during the 1950s and the 1960s, Koonings (in Silva 2001, 131) points out that the traditional idea of fighting an external enemy and defending a geographic territory was supplanted by the rhetoric of a struggle against an internal enemy that could threaten the sociopolitical and moral integrity of the nation. One of the most influential scholars in developing a doctrine of national security in Brazil was Mário Pessoa (1971). He departed from the conception of a nation based on what the Superior War College[3] (*Escola Superior de Guerra*) defined as a socio-historical structure formed by a humanity's parcel that is connected by customs, habits, and also, common struggles. Instead, according to Pessoa, during the 1960s and 1970s, external security was reframed as less of a threat to the nation as compared to internal security.

This focus on internal threats became the crux of the national security doctrine and permeated Brazilian institutions throughout the 1964–1985 dictatorship. It appeared in a wide-range of acts and decrees—the last of which, Law 7.170 of 1983, is still in force.[4] The national security concept was meant to be an all-encompassing idea. As Guerra (2016, 14) highlights, the result is the incorporation of public security matters into a national security discourse. Governors only took office in 1965 after accepting the suggestions of the regime concerning who to appoint to key public security positions. Challenging the autonomy of the Brazilian federal states, in the states with a division between Military Police and Civilian Police, the commander of the Military Police became an Army's officer. Public Security Secretaries had their names approved by the Minister of Army (Guerra 2016, 17). Such institutional designs reinforced the link between the police and military logic.

Guerra (2016, 18) argues that Decree Law 667 of 1969 provided the military police the power to serve in the field as a visible force. In other words, civilian police men lost the exclusive ability to police the streets since the logic of national security allowed the military to define crime as an internal threat and be employed to fight common crimes on a daily basis. Additionally, military courts had jurisdiction over military policemen who committed crimes against civilians. In the state of São Paulo, the progressive

---

[3] A think-tank created by the military in 1949 to provide planned development for the country. The inspiration behind the creation of the Superior War College was the American National War College. *See* https://www.esg.br/a-esg/historico.

[4] The term "decree law" (*decreto-lei*) refers to acts edited by the president that had the force of law from the date they were published in the national gazette. Afterward, they should be transformed into acts by the legislative branch. The 1988 Constitution substituted the decree laws by the provisional measures and created a series of restrictions for its adoption. The main difference between decree laws and provisional measures is that the latter were automatically converted into acts if the National Congress remained in silence concerning their approval.

militarization of policing was observed through a quarrel between the Civilian Guard (*Guarda Civil*) and the Public Force (*Força Pública*) of the military that ended with the extinction of the former one by the federal Executive Order 1.072 of 1969. Ultimately, the state governor issued a decree that created the Military Police of the state of São Paulo.

Even before the Civilian Guard was dismantled, Guerra (2016, 38) mentions that officers of the Civil Guard were taught in courses on the national security doctrine, how to identify "revolutionary movements," and principles of internal security. Important organs were created with the inception of the Military Police of São Paulo: for instance, the Visible Patrol Tobias de Aguiar (*Ronda Ostensiva Tobias de Aguiar, ROTA*) was organized to fight terrorists and criminals and to act in major cases (Guerra 2016, 49).

3 Transition Without Reforms: The Absence of Changes in the Military Police Institution

In 1983, an executive order (MP No. 2.010/1983) changed the command of the Military Police of the states, changing its staff from officers of the Army to an officer of an independent corporation (Guerra 2016, 69). The Department of Political and Social Order of São Paulo (Departamento Estadual de Ordem Política e Social de São Paulo), a Brazilian government agency established in 1924 and used extensively as an oppressive tool during the Military Dictatorship, was also extinguished in 1983, although its archives and even its commanders were transferred to the Federal Police. Another executive order (MP No. 88.777/1983) became the national regulation for military policies and military fire brigades in the whole federation, restricting their direct operations to acts of war and public calamities—and it is still in force, even after thirty years of a new Constitution passed in 1988 (Guerra and Filho 2018, 160).[5]

Although military control over the political process of transition in Brazil was limited by civil society activities during the calling for direct elections to the presidency (the civil unrest movement of *Diretas, já!*) and the constituent assembly, themes such as public security were dominated by forces supporting the prior regime. For instance, there was much disagreement involving the then-Minister of the Army and the transitional

[5] *See* MP No. 887777, Chapter 2, Art 4(1) and (2).

committee which recommended that a civilian police force be exclusively in control of social order, with the Military Police only called in for support. Ultimately, the military, the bar association, and members of congress all came out against the committee's recommendation. Arguments to preserve the authority of the Military Police included the idea that it was a historical characteristic of the institution that had already been "incorporated into Brazilian culture," the rising levels of violent crimes, and the perception that the Military Police is more professionally superior to the civilian police (Guerra 2016, 91). The result was that instead of dismantling the military police in the states, or significantly reducing its power, the text of the 1988 Constitution created a policy of police duality or the militarization of the visible police and a non-cooperative federative partition.

Guerra and Machado Filho (2018, 156) see the 1987–1988 Constituent Assembly as a moment in which matters of public security that were previously regulated by statutory law were simply leveled up to constitutional hierarchy. The process went on with a further adaptation of the constitutional norms to new acts approved in the democratic period. In other words, there is much more of a continuity than of a rupture between the authoritarian and democratic periods. High rates of criminality and a huge economic crisis in the 1980s can explain why there was no social pressure toward changing a violent system of police repression. The inner *esprit de corps* of Brazilian policemen and its separation from the society in which he or she lived contributed to a system that was not motivated by a sense of public interest in improving policies since the police force mainly saw their role as controlling crime. The federalization of the police forces was a hallmark of the 1988 Constitution (Guerra and Machado Filho 2018, 164). While the 1988 Constitution created a federal backbone, it also generated a lack of communication between the federal and state governments, and an excessive decentralization without coordination. Throughout the 1990s and the 2000s, the absence of a clear federal coordination prevailed. Local governments also engaged in public security policies that maintained the militarized option of visible police.

4 The Carandiru Case: Failed Accountability and Reform Attempts

The moment of transition and the Carandiru massacre coincided with the strong urban growth caused by the rural exodus of part of the population, which was accompanied by the increase in crime and homicide rates in the country (Lima and Ratton 2011). The scenario of increasing social and racial inequalities, coupled with the economic crisis inherited from the regressive economic-fiscal arrangement of the dictatorship,[6] marked the transitional period also as a moment of exasperation of the distributive conflicts and the social tensions. The use of police forces and the entire authoritarian apparatus would remain in full operation, now aimed at controlling "the dangerous classes" (Simões Gomes 2018, 40). From the communists as the main internal enemies, police forces now targeted the black, poor, and young people that inhabit *favelas* and are involved with drug traffic (Manso 2020, 270). The rise in state violence rates in that period is notorious. Data from the military police of the State of São Paulo shows that the numbers rose from 300 deaths of civilians by the military police per year in 1981 to 1171 deaths in 1991 and 1264 deaths in 1992 (Machado e Azevedo Marques 1993, 90).

One of the elements also associated with the increase in violence was the transfer of power to the military courts in 1977 for the trial of crimes committed by the military officers (including the military police) against civilians. Military courts were, and are still, understood as institutions that guarantee a measure of impunity (Machado e Azevedo Marques 1993, 90). At the time of the Carandiru massacre, a bill was already in progress at the National Congress aimed at limiting military justice power only to military crimes and thus transferring crimes against civilians to the civil justice—a bill that became law while the Carandiru trials were taking place.

The brutal practices and the warlike ideology of the police, and impunity for military state violence, demonstrate a continuing link between Brazilian nascent democracy and its authoritarian past. While the Carandiru case highlights the warlike and violent police attitude toward its own citizens accommodated in the democratic order by the functioning of accountability institutions, it also helped to propel changes in the law—such as Projeto de Lei Numero 13/96, which passed on January 14, 1996, barring military courts from trying crimes committed by military police against civilians during the exercise of police functions (Zaverucha 1999, 66). Based on this new law, the Carandiru cases were transferred to the civil courts after having started in the military courts. The decades-long delay, and the refusal of

[6] Fiori shows how the developmental state of the military period was strong in the discipline of workers and urban citizens, and at the same time, it was weak in the face of the economic and political demands of capital and old oligarchies, who acquired advantages and monopolistic conditions, without ever committing to clear goals in terms of productivity and competitiveness. The result was an inflationary policy that punished the poor and the middle classes and increased inequality (Fiori 1994).

the appellate court to uphold the jury verdict, shows that the shift from the military courts to the civilian does not guarantee the end of impunity. The case thus uncovers how civilian courts are complicit in providing impunity to those who violate the human rights of citizens in the name of national security. In the next two sections, we address the role of the judiciary in the case and the cycle of attempted reforms initiated in the massacre aftermath.

5 The Role of the Judiciary in Guaranteeing Impunity

Almost twenty-eight years have gone by and not a single Brazilian authority has claimed responsibility for the Carandiru massacre. Brazilian judicial system institutions never even formally recognized the episode as a massacre. Documents produced by the Brazilian judicial system continue to refer to the events as a "riot" or an "uprising." The São Paulo Military Police still keeps in employment its staff who are the defendants being criminally tried for the death of 111 citizens and for injuries to 92 others (Adorno 2017). Some of these defendants even rose in the police hierarchy, while others were appointed to command positions in the Military Police or in the Public Security office in the State of São Paulo.

The trials for dozens of defendants are still pending as they have been subjected to years of delay. For example, the State of São Paulo Court of Appeals took ten years just to confirm the court order affirming the existence of probable cause and to notify the defendants of a jury trial. Jury sessions took place in the years of 2013 and 2014. After many days of long jury sessions, the police officers were finally convicted by the jury, but the State of São Paulo Court of Appeals nullified all the convictions in 2018, arguing the verdict was not supported by the evidence collected in the case. Recently, in 2021, the Superior Court of Justice reestablished the convictions through a monocratic decision, but they are still appealable.

At the Inter-American System of Human Rights, the Brazilian state was found responsible by the Inter-American Commission of Human Rights (Inter-American Commission of Human Rights 2000) for violating the right to life and to the physical integrity of citizens who were under state responsibility. The report published by the Commission in 2000 recommended that investigations be completed, families be compensated, and prison conditions be improved. None of these conditions were ever met. Albeit the non-compliance of the Brazilian state, the case was never sent to trial to the Inter-American Court of Human Rights and there has never been a follow-up to these recommendations.

In the 2018 State of São Paulo Court of Appeals ruling that nullified the convictions of the jury, one of the judges—Ivan Sartori—replicated the version used by the police officers to explain the episode. According to the appeals court judge, who relied largely on the police version of events, the police fired in self-defense after being attacked.

However, the inmates deny any confrontation and declare that they sat on the floor with their hands on their heads as soon as the police entered the cellblock. Some claim to have seen police officers firing directly at prisoners or firing against cells with automatic rifles. Inmates say that after the shooting stopped, they were obliged to carry the dead bodies out of the cells. Some claim to have been bitten by dogs while running the gauntlet. Forensic reports confirmed that deaths were summary executions and that most of the inmates were murdered after they had surrendered. The examination of the site concluded that there were no traces that would denote shots being fired by the inmates. All of the evidence indicated that a confrontation did not happen (Machado et al. 2015).

The State of São Paulo Court of Appeals has been very effective in thwarting accountability, mainly through bureaucratic delays and procedural strategies. Moreover, judges often based their justifications on pronouncements of the "law and order" and "national security" rhetoric. It is certainly not a coincidence that President Jair Bolsonaro campaigned for former Judge Ivan Sartori, a 2020 candidate in the mayor election of the city of Santos, State of São Paulo. On the one hand, the Carandiru massacre cases demonstrate the exceptional resilience of the criminal justice system. These cases have been pending for 29 years, while the majority of police killings' cases would have been dismissed much earlier (Sinhoretto et al. 2014; Vargas & Ribeiro 2008). Different from the majority of the cases tried by juries, the Carandiru case reached a conviction. The case's long life inside the system is probably explained by its complexity, international visibility, sustained media coverage, and national mobilization throughout these decades. On the other hand, the fact that a conviction was never sustained makes the case a good example of the role of the judicial system in guaranteeing impunity. Whenever a conviction associated with the massacre was close to being confirmed, an unexpected and heterodox turnaround happened and avoided the final decisions (Ferreira and Machado e Machado 2012; Machado et al. 2015).

The legal disputes within the case reveal the operationalization of elements that are common to all cases of police killings: victim demonization[7]; narratives of resistance and self-defense; the priority given to the version told by the policemen (Jesus 2016); cover ups of the crime scene; the planting of evidence; and poor investigations. The composition of the judiciary branch post-1988 is certainly more diverse and independent from state authorities than in the past. The public prosecutors have also gained more independence and more power as a horizontal check on the hierarchy of institution. Nevertheless, the transition process did not remove important authoritarian government era administrators and leaders from the justice system. Years after the transition, those who remained from the pre-1988 courts and are still professionally active are occupying important positions in the appeals courts (Braga and Shimizu 2015). Furthermore, mechanisms of ideological reproduction entrenched through highly subjective selection processes, career incentives, and self-discipline mechanisms continue to plague the system (Meyer 2021).

6 Reforms and Failures

The Carandiru cases happened in the wake of the Brazilian transition from a military dictatorship to a democracy. It also took place in the state of São Paulo, where the militant police structure was designed during the dictatorship from 1964 to 1985 and served as a model for several of the other Brazilian states (Guerra 2016, 7). At the state level, the Carandiru case generated two important innovations: the São Paulo State Police Ombudsman and the PROAR (Program for the Monitoring of Police Officers Involved in High-Level Risk). Created by decree in January 1995,[8] the São Paulo Police Ombudsman was a first in the entire country. It was permanently institutionalized five years later with the approval of Law 826 of 1997, after another highly visible violent episode, the Favela Naval[9] case. The São Paulo State Police Ombudsman is responsible for receiving complaints from the population against police officers (civil and military) and from police officers against abuses by other police officers. The model soon spread to other states

[7] This word is used by Oscar Vilhena to refer to the logic citizen/enemy. See Vieira (2015).

[8] Decree 39.900 of 1995.

[9] In March, 1997, images of an amateur cameraman were broadcasted nationally by Rede Globo (now TV Globo), showing a group of military police officers extorting money, humiliating, beating, and executing people in a raid that took place in Favela Naval, in Diadema, São Paulo.

in response to a wave of other violent attacks on the civilian population by the police.[10] Within ten years, police ombudsmen were present in fourteen states.[11]

PROAR was a program designed to give support and psychological assistance to police officers involved in fatal events, with the objective of reducing the excessive or illegal use of physical force in police actions. Police officers who reported to PROAR were also removed from the area where the event occurred and allocated to other areas. An initial evaluation showed that PROAR resulted in the decrease of police killing rates during the 1990s in the State of São Paulo—from 1190 civilians killed in 1992 to 243 in 1993, 333 in 1994, and 331 in 1995. The program faced great resistance inside the police corporation and was ultimately terminated in 2002 (Neme 1999).

At the federal level, the Carandiru cases gave impetus to the building of a strong mobilization involving non-governmental organizations, human rights activists, politicians, intellectuals, judges, and the federal government itself, which supported the approval of a law limiting military justice jurisdiction (Law 9.299 of 1996, nicknamed Lei Bicudo after its proponent). During the 1980s, there was an overwhelming sense that the problem was that military courts and their corporative character were the *loci* of impunity (Neme 1999). One immediate consequence of Law 9.299 of 1996 was the jurisdictional transfer of the criminal case related to the Carandiru massacre that started in the military courts to the common jurisdiction. The same congressman who proposed Law 9.299 of 1996 also proposed an amendment to the 1988 Constitution to include the federalization of human rights violations, allowing for cases concerning gross violations of human rights to be removed from state courts and transferred to federal courts for adjudication.[12] Four years later, it became a proposal submitted directly by the president.[13] The federalization of gross violations of human rights

---

[10] In the state of Rio de Janeiro, massacres took place in Candelária and Vigário Geral in 1993, Favela de Nova Brasília in 1995, and Cidade de Deus in 1997 and 1998. In the state Pará, 19 members of the Movimento dos Trabalhadores Sem Terra (Landless Worker's Movement) were killed in 1996 in Eldorado de Carajás.

[11] Bruno Konder Comparato, As Ouvidorias de Polícia no Brasil: controle e participação, 2005 (Ph.D. Thesis), https://www.teses.usp.br/teses/disponiveis/8/8131/tde-25052007-143115/publico/TESE_BRUNO_KONDER_COMPARATO.pdf (last visited Feb 10, 2020).

[12] See PEC 96/1992 (constitutional amendment proposal), https://www.camara.leg.br/proposicoesWeb/fichadetramitacao?idProposicao=14373 (last visited Feb 10, 2020).

[13] See PEC 368/1996 (constitutional amendment proposal), https://www.camara.leg.br/proposicoesWeb/fichadetramitacao?idProposicao=24992 (last visited Feb 10, 2020).

was finally introduced to the Brazilian legal system in the Reform of the Judiciary approved in 2004.[14] The procedure depends on a claim filed by the Prosecutor General of the Republic (*Procurador-Geral da República*) in the Superior Court of Justice (*Superior Tribunal de Justiça*) which, if it finds that the crime violated international pacts on human rights, dislodges the case from state to the federal courts.

Unfortunately, the transfer of the Carandiru case from military courts, and the federalization of human rights law, has led to little change—police brutality and impunity continue to persist. Civilian courts do not prove to be more efficient or less partial than the military courts in prosecuting police officers. The police ombudsmen have been important institutions, especially in terms of receiving complaints and releasing data, but they have no mandate to sanction or officially ascribe responsibility. Moreover, federalization of human rights violation cases has happened only in very few instances. From 2004 to 2015, the procedure was requested in only five cases and accepted in three (Almeida et al. 2014). Since 2015, another five procedures have been requested and are still being analyzed by the Superior Court of Justice.

7 The Irrepressible Violence of the Military

After the 1988 Constitution, the military police maintained an internal organizational structure similar to the Brazilian Armed Forces. Although the military police must submit to the authority of the civil state government, the state military police bodies are under the authority of the Army, through the General Inspectorate of Military Police (IGPM). Furthermore, the military warlike ethos is the informal culture of the civilian police force as well. An important reform initiative in the public security system that took place in the State of Rio de Janeiro tried to change this.

The establishment of Pacifying Police Units (*Unidades de Polícia Pacificadora, UPP's*), created in 2008 as a pilot project and institutionalized in 2011, announced a shift in the pattern of military style force against those living in favelas and against the warlike ideology. The project involved state control over territories previously controlled by drug gangs, the reduction of armed confrontations, and state officers' permanence in the favelas through

[14] See EC 45/2004 (Constitutional Amendment) http://www.planalto.gov.br/ccivil_03/constituicao/emendas/emc/emc45.htm (last visited Feb 10, 2020).

community-policing troops. The police reform attempt was designed to be coupled with infrastructural construction, public services, and social policies: the services that usually do not reach the favelas. According to a former General Commander of the Rio de Janeiro Military Police, the project's implementation was a "resounding and colossal failure."[15] Successive reports show the persistence of "old tensions" between police and communities: excessive stop and frisk practices, intimidation, and the continuance of abuse. Explanations for the failure include different questions related to implementation, lack of funding, fiscal and economic crises, an absence of project complementation with social policies, and the project's inability to circumvent path dependence (Cano et al. 2012). Other analyses question the capacity of the project itself to change the pattern of police violence since it was conducted by the military police (Franco 2014; Fichino 2012; Machado 2020). In different ways, all the reports point to the limits of the strategy to reform what would be one crucial problem in the Rio de Janeiro police forces: the military confrontational and racial selective ethos of the police. At least discursively, the UPP envisaged a different pattern of policing, the so-called communitarian policing, but it failed due to the reliance on militarization tactics.

The killing of Amarildo Dias de Souza inside the Police Pacifying Unit (UPP) in Favela Rocinha in June 2013 exposed the failure of the reform strategy[16] and the persistence of national security logic. Amarildo, a black bricklayer assistant, was taken by UPP officials and disappeared. It was soon discovered that he was tortured to death by UPP police agents. The episode coincided with the outbreak of the protest cycle that became known as "June Journeys"—a sustained series of public demonstrations in 2013. Coincidentally, the Amarildo episode happened a few days after scenes of sheer police violence against middle-class white activists and journalists went viral and dominated newspaper headlines. The middle-class white victims during this episode were not the usual "suspects," and this fact raised a never-before-seen level of support to address the problem of police violence.

The Amarildo case indeed broke the usual pattern: the prosecutor started a criminal case on the torture, disappearance of the dead body, and homicide against 25 police officers. Thirteen were convicted by the jury and the appeals court confirmed the conviction of eight, which is a very different record from the traditional destiny of the cases in the criminal justice

[15] This was quoted in one of the reports. *See* Musumeci (2017).

[16] The discussion on the UPP was previously developed at Machado (2020). See: Mariana Mota Prado & Michael J Trebilcock, Institutional Bypasses (1 ed. 2018).

system. Although police officers in this case were punished, this high publicity and severe punishments for police officers did not promote long-standing reforms. In the aftermath of the protests, a constitutional amendment aiming at an ample reform—including demilitarization—of the police was proposed by a senator.[17] The constitutional amendment never gained traction. In fact, Brazil took the opposite road.

According to the 1988 Constitution, the defense of internal order is the primary task of permanent civilian forces, but there is a provision (Article 142) that authorizes missions of the Armed Forces to act in operations to "Guarantee Law and Order" (*Garantia da Lei e da Ordem* or *GLO*) which occur in cases where traditional public security forces are exhausted, in serious situations of disturbance of order and upon orders of the constituted powers. GLO is characterized as a military operation determined by the president and conducted by the Armed Forces in an episodic manner, in a previously established area and for a limited time. Between 1992 and 2020, according to data from the Ministry of Defense, 142 GLOs were decreed—among others, 23 aimed at dealing with urban violence, 26 in cases of strike by the military police members, 22 to guarantee peaceful elections, and 39 at mega-events.[18] While most of the operations lasted from 1 to 3 months, GLOs in the favelas of Rio de Janeiro have had a much longer duration with the alleged objective of combating drug trafficking. There is a lot of criticism on GLOs, since they have been a stage for violent civilian deaths by military personnel (Viana 2018). Moreover, there are no established protocols that guarantee transparency and accountability (Rodrigues and Armstrong 2019). The normalization of GLOs has a strong impact in the militarization process of peripheral and poor areas.

GLOs in Rio de Janeiro served as preparation for more radical interventions authorized by Michel Temer, the President that took office after the impeachment of President Dilma Rousseff. In 2018, the federal intervention in Rio de Janeiro's public security even led to the control of civil and military police command posts by Armed Forces members. The federal intervention in 2018 was commanded by a general that would become President Bolsonaro's Chief of Staff (*Ministro-Chefe da Casa Civil*) and, afterward, Minister of Defense (*Ministro da Defesa*). It generated poor results and even the misuse of public funds: close to US$230 million were spent without

[17] Constitutional Amendment Proposal 51 of 2013.

[18] See https://www.gov.br/defesa/pt-br/arquivos/exercicios_e_operacoes/glo/1.metodologiaa_dea_estudo.pdf (last visited Nov 30, 2020).

major changes in public security.[19] From February to December 2018, the period of the intervention, 6041 people died—a reduction of only 1.7% in the numbers compared to 2017. Furthermore, 22.7% of the killings were perpetrated by policemen and military members. Ninety-nine state agents were killed. The so-called *chacinas*, or "slaughters," (when more than three people are killed) increased 63.6%, occurring on 54 occasions (Nunes 2019, 11). An investigation of the Tribunal de Contas da União, or the Brazilian federal accountability office, found that there was the misuse of public funding in more than 80% of the expenditures—it revealed that funds allocated for security were even used to purchase fancy seafood dinners of shrimp and cod for military members (Salomon 2020).

The federal intervention in Rio de Janeiro also allowed the Armed Forces to take control of judicial processes. In 2017, the Federal Senate approved a bill that takes homicides by members of the Armed Forces out of the hands of ordinary civilian justice, and sent the cases instead back to military courts.[20] The erosion of some of the hard-fought reform aimed at imposing checks on the actions of Brazilian police was only the beginning, foreshadowing a series of more open forms of legitimizing police executions that would soon gain space in Brazilian institutional settings. Furthermore, Jair Bolsonaro, elected President in 2018, has expressly defended police executions and even declared his intention to grant amnesty to convicted police officers. Among them, he specifically mentioned the policemen involved in the Carandiru case. Through his former Minister of Justice and Public Security, Sergio Moro, the administration sent to Congress a bill expanding the description of self-defense for police officers. It ended up not being approved. Surprisingly, these concrete measures would make little difference to the situation of police accountability. Ironically, Bolsonaro mentions his will of granting amnesty to the Carandiru officials, who in fact have never been convicted.

8 Conclusion

Police violence against activists and the poor was endemic during the civil-military regime; yet the Brazilian transition to democracy shows a "full continuity" (Pinheiro et al. 1991) of that pattern. In fact, rather than a shift,

[19] At a dollar rate of R$5.30. In *reais*, the global expenditure reached R$1.2 billion. Cf. https://agenciabrasil.ebc.com.br/geral/noticia/2019-05/intervencao-federal-aplicou-r-319-milhoes-em-equipamentos-para-o-rio

[20] Law 13.491 of 2017.

the transition meant a maintenance of repressive techniques into the daily practices of the police. The 1988 Constitution could not address significant or structural changes in the police or public security agencies. Instead, it transferred the subordination of the military police force—which continued to be the visible police—from the Army to the civilian state governments. Nonetheless, the police in the democratic transition era kept the features and practices found in the civil-military era, namely a police force that was highly militarized, hierarchical, and violent. Even though the 1988 Constitution brings explicit commitment to human rights and due process, police violence has remained a persistent dilemma in the constitutional democracy.

A series of high-profile cases—among them, the Carandiru case—combined with the massification of homicides committed by police officers against young black people in peripheral neighborhoods of large cities (not to mention the rural violence) frequently entered public debate during these past three decades of democracy. Mobilization for reform was articulated by a growing field of activism, combining international human rights, movement of mothers and families of victims, and the black movement. In some cases, tragedies functioned as opportunities to pass reforms but never led to meaningful changes. The consensus among progressive groups and the academic field was that the urgent reform of the police forces never reached the Brazilian society as a whole.

The Brazilian democratization process did not manage to dismantle the line of demonization that is used to separate citizens and criminals. Racist ideology continues to target blacks as criminals, legitimizing all sorts of human rights violations against them, from racial profiling, abusive stops and frisks, torture, mass imprisonment, and executions. The "law and order" discourse is now the new cloth of the national security doctrine. Although at the federal level there was a sequence of democratic governments working and promoting the language of human rights, no significant steps were taken to reform the public security sector, partly because police forces are organized at the state level. It is against this background that this chapter addresses the connections between the political process, the absence of reforms in the political arena, and the inner workings of the criminal justice system. The case study of judicial proceedings allows us to see that the challenges for reform are not confined to the police. On the contrary, police brutality is partially supported, and endorsed, by the justice system that continues to allow violent officers of the state to murder with impunity.

References

Adorno, Luís de. 2017. 74 PMs envolvidos no massacre do Carandiru, 58 foram promovidos [74 PMs Involved in the Carandiru massacre, 58 Were Promoted]. *UOL*, October 2, 2017. https://noticias.uol.com.br/cotidiano/ultimas-noticias/2017/10/02/de-74-pms-envolvidos-no-massacre-do-carandiru-58-foram-promovidos.htm.

Almeida, Guilherme et al. 2014. *Estudo sobre a federalização de graves violações aos direitos humanos [Study on the Federalization of Serious Human Rights Violations]*. Brasília, CNJ.

Braga, Ana Gabriela and Bruno Shimizu. 2015. Duas cenas de um genocídio (ou de por que continuamos incompetentes) [Two Scenes of a Genocide (or Why We Remain Incompetent)]. In *Carandiru (não) é coisa do passado: um balanço sobre os processos, as instituições e as narrativas 23 anos após o Massacre*, eds. Maíra Rocha Machado and Marta Rodriguez de Assis Machado. São Paulo: FGV: 271–294.

Brazilian Supreme Federal Tribunal. 2020. MC na ADPF 635 [MC at ADPF 635]. *Supreme Tribunal Federal*, June 5, 2020. https://www.conjur.com.br/dl/adpf-rio-fachin.pdf.

Cano, Ignacio et al. 2012. Os Donos do Morro: Uma Avaliação Exploratória do Impacto das Unidades de Polícia Pacificadora (UPPs) no Rio de Janeiro [The Owners of Morro: An Exploratory Assessment of the Impact of The Pacifying Police Units (UPPS) in Rio de Janeiro]. *Fórum Brasileiro de Segurança Pública.*

Ferreira, Luisa M. A., Marta R. de A. Machado and Maíra Rocha Machado. 2012. Massacre do Carandiru: vinte anos sem responsabilização. *Novos Estudos – CEBRAP* 94: 5–29. https://doi.org/10.1590/S0101-33002012000300001.

Fichino, Daniele. 2012. *Pasárgada Reconquistada? Estudo Sobre Processo de Implementação das Unidades de Polícia Pacificadora [Pasárgada Reconquistada? Study on The Implementation Process of The Pacifying Police Units]*. Masters' diss., FGV Direito SP.

Fiori, José Luis. 1994. O nó cego do desenvolvimentismo brasileiro [The Blind Knot of Brazilian Developmentalism]. *Novos Estudos* 40: 126–144.

Franco, Marielle. 2014. *UPP—A Redução da Favela a Três Letras: Uma Análise da Política de Segurança Pública do Estado do Rio de Janeiro [UPP—The Reduction of the Favela to Three Letters: An Analysis of the Public Security Policy of the State of Rio de Janeiro]*. Masters' diss: Universidade Federal Fluminense.

Gaspari, Elio. 2004. *Dictadura Encurralada*. São Paolo: Companhia das Letras.

Guerra, Maria Pia and Roberto Machado Filho. 2018. O Regime Constitucional da Segurança Pública: Dos Silêncios do Constituinte às Deliberações do Supremo Tribunal Federal [The Constitutional Regime of Public Security: From the Silences of the Constituent to the Deliberations of the Supreme Court]. 55. *Revista de Informação Legislativa* 219: 155–181.

Guerra, Maria Pia. 2016. Polícia e ditadura: Arquitetura institucional da segurança pública de 1964 a 1988 [Police and Dictatorship: Institutional Architecture of Public Security From 1964 to 1988]. *Brasília: Ministério da Justiça/Comissão de Anistia.*

Inter-American Commission of Human Rights. 2000. Report 34/00 of 04.13.2000, Case 11.291 (Carandiru) Organization of American States. Accessed November 30, 2020. http://www.cidh.oas.org/annualrep/99eng/Merits/Brazil11.291.htm.

Jesus, Maria Gorete Marques. 2016. *"O mundo que não está nos autos": a construção da verdade jurídica nos processos criminais de tráfico de drogas.* Dissertação (mestrado), Universidade de São Paulo. São Paulo.

Koonings, Kee. 2001. Political Orientations and Factionalism in the Brazilian Armed Forces, 1964–1985. In *The Soldier and the State in South America*, eds. P. Silva, Hampshire and New York: Palgrave Macmillan.

Lima, Renato. 2019. Segurança pública como simulacro de democracia no Brasil [Public Security as a Simulacrum of Democracy in Brazil]. *Estudos Avançados* 33 (96): 53–68.

Lima, Renato Sérgio de and José Luiz Ratton. 2011. *As ciências sociais e os pioneiros nos estudos sobre crime, violência e direitos humanos no Brasil.* São Paulo: Fórum Brasileiro de Segurança Pública, Urbânia, ANPOCS.

Machado, Maíra and Marta Machado (eds.). 2015. *Carandiru Não é Coisa do Passado [Carandiru Is Not A Thing of the Past].* São Paulo: FGV.

Machado, Marta et al. 2015. Massacre do Carandiru + 23: Inação, Descontinuidade e Resistências [Carandiru Massacre + 23: Inaction, Discontinuity and Resistance] In *Carandiru Não é Coisa do Passado* eds. M. Machado and M. Machado. São Paulo: FGV.

Machado, Marta Rodriguez de Assis. 2020. The Pacifying Police Units in Rio De Janeiro: A Bypass of What? *Revista Estudos Institucionais* 6 (2): 737–750.

Manso, Bruno. 2020. *A República das Milícias: Dos Esquadrões da Morte à Era Bolsonaro [The Republic of Militias: From the Death Squads to the Bolsonaro Era].* São Paulo: Todavia.

Meyer, Emilio. 2021. *Constitutional Erosion in Brazil: Failures and Successes of a Constitutional Project.* London: Hart Publishing.

Musumeci, Leonarda. 2017. *UPP: Última Chamada. Visões e Expectativas dos Moradores de Favelas Ocupadas pela Polícia Militar na Cidade do Rio de Janeiro [UPP: Last Call. Visions and Expectations of The Residents of Favelas Occupied by the Military Police in the City of Rio de Janeiro].* Rio de Janeiro: CESeC.

Neme, Cristina. 1999. *A Instituição Policial na Ordem Democrática: O caso da Polícia Militar do Estado de São Paulo [The Police Institution in the Democratic Order: The Case of the Military Police of the State of São Paulo].* Masters' diss.: Universidade de São Paulo.

Nunes, Pedro. 2019. 320 Dias de Intervenção em Números [320 Days of Intervention in Numbers]. In *Intervenção Federal: Um Modelo para Não Copiar*, ed. Observatório da Intervenção: 4–11. Rio de Janeiro: CESeC.

Oliveira, Emmanuel. 2012. Políticas públicas e estratégias de controle da ação letal das instituições policiais em São Paulo [Public Policies and Strategies to Control the Lethal Action of Police Institutions in São Paulo]. *Revista Brasileira de Segurança Pública* 6 (1).

Pessoa, Mário. 1971. *O Direito da Segurança Nacional [The Law of National Security]*. Rio de Janeiro: Biblioteca do Exército; Revista dos Tribunais.

Pinheiro, Paulo Sérgio, Eduardo Izumino and Maria Cristina Fernandes. 1991. Violência Fatal: Conflitos Policiais em São Paulo [Fatal Violence: Police Conflicts in São Paulo]. *Revista USP*: 81–89.

PSB et al. 2020. *Petição na ADPF 635 [Petition at ADPF 635]*. Accessed November 30, 2020. https://www.conectas.org/wp/wp-content/uploads/2020/11/paginador.pdf.

Rodrigues, Rute, and Karolina Armstrong. 2019. *A Intervenção Federal no Rio de Janeiro e as Organizações da Sociedade Civil [Federal Intervention in Rio de Janeiro and Civil Society Organizations]*. Rio de Janeiro: IPEA.

Salomon, Marta. 2020. *Os Desvios da Intervenção Militar [Deviations from Military Intervention]*. Piauí, September 28, 2020, https://piaui.folha.uol.com.br/os-desvios-da-intervencao-militar/.

Simões Gomes, Letícia. 2018. *A (in)visibilidade da questão racial na formação dos soldados da Polícia Militar*. Master's Dissertation, Faculdade de Filosofia, Letras e Ciências Humanas, University of São Paulo, São Paulo.

Sinhoretto, Jacqueline, Giane Silvestre and Maria Carolina Schlittler. 2014. *Desigualdade racial e segurança pública em São Paulo: letalidade policial e prisões em flagrante [Racial Inequality and Public Safety in São Paulo: Police Lethality and Arrests in Flagrante]*. São Carlos: UFSCAR.

Stepan, Alfred. 1971. *The Military in Politics: Changing Patterns in Brazil*. Princeton: Princeton University Press.

Vargas, Joana Domingues and Ludmila Ribeiro. 2008. Estudos de Fluxo da Justiça Criminal: Balanço e Perspectivas. *Anais do XXXII Encontro Anual da Anpocs*. Caxambu: ANPOCS.

Viana, Nathalia. 2018. Exército é acusado de matar inocentes em operações de segurança pública [Army Accused of Killing Innocent People in Public Security Operations]. *Pública Agência de Jornalismo Investigativo*, October 31, 2018. https://apublica.org/2018/10/exercito-eacusado-de-matar-inocentes-em-operacoes-de-seguranca-publica/.

Vieira, Oscar Vilhena. 2015. Inequality and the subversion of the rule of law. In *Law and Society in Latin America: A New Map*, ed. César Rodríguez-Garavito. New York: Routledge: 23–42.

Wacquant, Loïc. 2008. The Militarization of Urban Marginality: Lessons from the Brazilian Metropolis. *International Political Sociology*, 2 (1): 56–74.

Zaverucha, Jorge. 1999. Military Justice in the State of Pernambuco after the Brazilian Military Regime: An Authoritarian Legacy. *Latin American Research Review* 34 (2): 43–73.

3

Politics Before Law: The Penal Code of 2017 and Its Limited Protections for Ethnic Minorities in Afghanistan

M. Bashir Mobasher and Nasiruddin Nezaami

1 Introduction

In August 2017, a scandal in the Administrative Office of the President (AOP) involving a systematic campaign to remove employees of certain ethnic backgrounds from the administration dominated the headlines in mainstream and social media. The scandal was leaked when an official from the administration mistakenly posted the ethnocentric agenda on an open Telegram platform visible to all AOP employees. Soon the content of the scheme went viral, deepening public concern over the government's agenda (Noor TV Network 2014). This controversy added to growing public suspicion that President Ghani and his closest allies were attempting to institutionalize ethnic domination as several former officials including his former vice-president repeatedly accused Ghani of pursuing a Pashtun-centric governance (Afghanistan Times 2016). In response to increasing public criticism and pressure, President Ghani promised that his government would soon draft an anti-discrimination bill (BBC News 2017). Neither was that scandalous conspiracy properly investigated and sanctioned, nor was any anti-discrimination bill introduced or implemented. On the contrary,

M. B. Mobasher (✉) · N. Nezaami
American University of Afghanistan, Kabul, Afghanistan
e-mail: mobasher@american.edu

N. Nezaami
e-mail: nnasir@stanford.edu

G. B. Radics and P. Ciocchini (eds.), *Criminal Legalities and Minorities in the Global South*, Palgrave Socio-Legal Studies, https://doi.org/10.1007/978-3-031-17918-1_3

leaked records of Ghani's closest advisors revealed that some well-coordinated efforts were already in motion to purge government agencies of diverse groups even more vigorously (Kabul Art 2021). At a time when the government needed the unity of all groups and peoples against the Taliban most, it stirred up division and distrust ultimately leading to its own demise (Mobasher 2021; Hasnain 2021).

Against this backdrop, in 2017 a new Penal Code was enacted which criminalized only six discrimination-based offenses. These offenses included genocide, crime against humanity, destruction of religious sites, and the assault of religious minorities. Hate speech was limited, and new crimes associated with it were created such as inciting civil war (Art. 254), encouraging discrimination and division (Art. 256), insulting religions (Arts. 323 and 325), and "discriminatory activities on social media" (Art. 870). A few Articles regarding defamation and harassment that could encompass forms of hate speech in certain circumstances were also included (Arts. 678 and 681). The Penal Code prohibited "discrimination in administrative units," but it did not list the protected grounds (Art. 409). As a result, larger groups were more likely to utilize this Article than smaller groups who did not find themselves mentioned in explicit terms in the Code. Overall, the list of these offenses fell short of offering sufficient protection for minorities and reducing ethnic tensions as President Ghani and his administration promised in 2017.

These issues were exacerbated by enforcement agencies' and the courts' unwillingness to implement the Code properly. The Penal Code was not promoted properly, and most citizens were unaware of the few statutory protections they had against hatred-based offenses. The few times that the cases of hate crimes and hate speech were investigated and tried in the courts were for either or both of the following reasons: (a) the offense attracted massive media attention and public protests compelling enforcement agencies to investigate the crimes; or (b) the offense targeted powerful elites who then used government agencies to retaliate. In the former case, the offenders were likely to be released immediately after public outcry subsided without any trial or due process taking place. In fact, at times, offenders were rewarded handsomely when such offenses served the interests of government elites.

In this chapter, we first explore the Penal Code and its provisions. Comparing the Penal Code of 2017 with the previous Penal Code of 1976, we reveal whether and how far the new Code made progress on the particular issue of discriminatory offenses. In the second section, we examine four prominent cases of discrimination in detail. These cases reveal that: (a) the enforcement agencies were likely to start an investigation and arrest only after an offense drew media attention and ethnic tensions; (b) the offenders were likely to be released without due process soon after the media coverage of the issue and street protests ended; and therefore, (d) the offenses continued to target and harm minorities. The prevalent rule of politics, as opposed to the rule of law, was especially visible as law enforcement agencies and courts would often favor political solutions overdue process and legal remedies. Informal negotiations, public apologies, political interventions, and unwarranted mitigations were basically the norms that cut due process short during the 20 years of the Islamic Republic's regime.

2 Afghanistan's Multiethnic Society

Many consider Afghanistan to be a country of minorities since, according to most estimations, no ethnic group comprises over 50% of the population (Mazhar et al. 2012). The Afghan Constitution acknowledges 14 ethnic groups in Afghanistan, namely "Pashtun, Tajik, Hazara, Uzbek, Turkman, Baluch, Pachaie, Nuristani, Aymaq, Arab, Qirghiz, Qizilbash, Gujur, Brahwui and other tribes" (Schetter 2003). The first four ethnicities combined are estimated to comprise 90% of the population (Schetter 2003). The findings of studies regarding the exact population of each ethnicity have been controversial because no official census of the Afghan population has ever been conducted. Between 2001 and 2016, the CIA Factbook estimated Pashtuns at 38–44% of the population, Tajiks between 25 and 27%, Hazaras between 9 and 10%, and Uzbeks between 6 and 9% (The World Factbook 2021). Since 2016, the CIA Factbook stopped releasing estimations on the ethnic distribution in Afghanistan perhaps because of the unreliability of these estimations.

Legal developments in Afghanistan have rarely offered protection to ethno-religious groups and their members against hate crimes. Even though the 1976 Penal Code was the first comprehensively written Penal Code in the country, it lacked sufficient protections for vulnerable groups against hate crimes. Of the many crimes ensued by hatred and prejudice, the old Code criminalized what it termed "Offenses Against Religions." This section of the code, found in Article 347, criminalized any deliberate action that could "cause delay or disturbance to the rituals of [one of the] religion[s]," or actions that caused destruction to "places of worship or respected signs." Incitement and provocations of ethnic tensions were criminalized in the Internal and External Security Act 11 years later (1985). However, none of these laws were able to be fully enforced due to decades of war in Afghanistan.

The promulgation of the 1976 Penal Code was soon followed by the Soviet invasion of Afghanistan in 1979 and the beginning of a decade-long struggle for the freedom of the country. With the collapse of Soviet-backed government in Kabul, the decade-long struggle was followed by another decade of civil war, a period in which non-Muslim minorities experienced the worst atrocities in the history of Afghanistan. Ethnic violence and mass-murders were the political currency of the Mujahidin era (1992–1996) and the Taliban regime (1996–2001). The old 1976 Penal Code became relevant only in 2001 when the post-Taliban transitional government decided to reinstate pre-war constitution and laws. However, the war did not stop in 2001 as the Taliban regrouped to challenge the government and international forces in Afghanistan. Neither did different ethnic communities get a chance to heal. In fact, President Ghani's administration further instigated ethnic divide to the point of diffusing all socio-political fabrics that could protect his own government against the Taliban (Hasnain 2021; Mobasher and Qadam Shah 2022). Despite the reinstatement of the law in 2001, Hindus, Sikhs, and other religious minorities continued to suffer from persecution.

The new Penal Code of 2017 was an improvement from the previous law, but it fell short of providing sufficient protection for the minorities. The criminalization of hatred-based offenses in the Code was mostly reactionary as they were included in response to some popular incidents that instigated ethnic tensions rather than being the result of a normative, doctrinal discourse to address discriminatory offenses holistically. These incorporated offenses can be categorized as crimes committed by ordinary citizens and those committed by the state or organized (armed) groups in a more systematic way.

As for the first category, Articles 323–325 of the 2017 Penal Code offer some strong protections against religious discrimination by sanctioning three bigotry-based offenses: (a) the offense of disturbing and causing delays to religious rites; (b) the offense of destroying or damaging the licensed places of worship; and (c) the offense of damaging any religious symbols that are sacred to the followers of a faith. While the criminalization of these actions is an improvement, the sanctions remain insufficient. The law extends its protection only to "licensed places of worship." In other words, the law not only fails to protect "unregistered" places of worship but also reiterates the state's control over the development of any new places of worship by non-Muslim minorities, including Hindus, Sikhs, Jews, and Christians. In 2009, for instance, an underground Christian church was destroyed, and several followers were arrested (Ahmed 2014). Consequently, many Christians, consisting mostly of converts, fled the country fearing persecution (ibid.). Others continued to remain in hiding or suffer from persecution by locals and government officials alike (Ahmed 2014).

The Penal Code of 2017 also sanctions state-sponsored crimes and actions committed by organized groups targeting specific ethnic, religious, or other groups. Article 333 penalizes the Commission of five offenses against any "national, ethnic, racial, or religious groups." These offenses include "killing members of a group, causing serious bodily or mental harm to members of a group, deliberately inflicting harm on a group for the purpose of bringing about physical destruction, in whole or in part, imposing measures intended to prevent births within the group, and forcibly transferring children of one group to another group" (ibid.). In the same vein, Article 334 of the new Penal Code penalized crimes against humanity when committed as part of the "widespread or systematic" attack against civilian population "knowingly and deliberately." Among prohibited actions under this Article are the "persecution of any identifiable group or collectivity on political, racial, national, ethnic, cultural, religious, or gender[ed] grounds, and the crime of racial discrimination" (ibid.). While these crimes can be committed both at times of peace and armed conflict, Afghanistan has witnessed the perpetration of many such abhorrent actions during its four decades of conflict.

Before the enactment of the new Penal Code, many public figures and so-called political experts publicly incited to ethnic hatred, leading to ethnic tensions and public disorder. To address this issue, the new Penal Code of 2017 criminalized some forms of hate speech. Article 256(1) of the Penal Code punishes a person "who invites or provokes another person for discrimination or division on the basis of religion, race, tribe, language, or geographic region." This Article does not require discrimination or division to materialize as an act of incitement or provocation will suffice to punish the perpetrator. Although an improvement from the previous Penal Code, this Article limits the application of hate speech in several ways unless interpreted otherwise by the courts. Most importantly, under this law, in addition to the perpetrator and the victim, the Article necessitates a third party who must be incited or provoked to commit the offense. In other words, this law may not apply to cases where the perpetrators themselves wield hate-based insults toward the victims without encouraging others to engage in discrimination. Additionally, the categorization of this offense as "crimes against External and Internal security" suggests that the criminalization of this offense was not necessarily intended to protect vulnerable minorities. Rather, it was meant to prevent inciting discrimination against larger groups that could endanger the stability of the country at a greater scale.

Lastly, individuals and platforms including radio stations, visual media, and print media who may facilitate the same hate speech are not covered by the Code—at least not in explicit terms. Unless interpreted by the courts to the contrary, this Article allows a significant number of media platforms that are identity-based to propagate hatred and prejudices toward different groups. Some TV channels such as Shamshad, Zhwandoon, Farda, Noor, and Ayna are controlled by major ethno-political parties and known for promoting a particular ethnic agenda, which is new to the Afghan political discourse (Ahmed and Zahori 2014). At times, their controversial programs have resulted in public anger and ethnic tensions (Ahmed and Zahori 2014).

Cyberspace adds another layer to inter-ethnic relations, potentially widening the ethnic divide in Afghanistan. Although prominent in private and inner circles, discriminatory remarks in public have culturally and historically been discouraged for the most part in Afghanistan (Mobasher 2019). Even at times of war, ethnic leaders, and parties avoided playing ethnic cards publicly. In their media interviews and public speeches, leaders repeatedly projected themselves and their parties as national figures and institutions even if this were not actually the case. Due to its nature, social media has increasingly broken this long-standing cultural norm. Several features of social media including easy access for the users and the feasibility of creating multiple and fake accounts, provides a platform for hardliners and otherwise isolated sociopaths to engage in discriminatory and abusive speech and have an audience for it (Ibrahimi et al. 2015, 25). The internet and social media have increasingly been used for the purpose of propagating radical political agendas and the provocation of violence against different groups. This new challenge has considerably overwhelmed socially fragmented, and institutionally underdeveloped, societies such as Afghanistan. Therefore, it is no surprise that the new Penal Code has penalized hate speech in cyberspace.

Addressing hate speech in the cyber environment, Article 870(1) of the new Penal Code prohibits "ethnic, religious, sectarian, linguistic, or regional bigotry provocations" through "texts, audio, or video tracks" online. This Article not only prevents the propagation of tensions among different ethnic, religious and other groups but also provides an important protection for minorities against hate speech. Like most other hate crimes in the Code, Article 870 was indeed formulated in response to an increasing public concern over hate speech in social media. However, the law falls short of requiring the cyber mediums to remove and/or prevent hate speech on their platforms. It is important to observe that while the Penal Code criminalizes this action, no other regulatory framework is established to demonstrate the level and means of monitoring unbridled social media in the country.

With the dramatic change of regimes in 2021, the fate of the 2017 Penal Code remains to be seen. When the Taliban captured Herat province in the west of Afghanistan, they instructed courts to only decide cases based on a Hanafi understand of Islam, rather than on a secular basis.

3 The Four Cases of Unsanctioned Offenses

In this section, we probe into four well-known cases, revealing how the laws and the justice system have failed to protect minorities against discrimination. More specifically, these cases reveal a recurring pattern where hate crimes were investigated only after they drew media attention and resulted in ethnic tensions, and investigations only continued till tensions have simmered down. Most investigations were unlikely to end with trials or fair sentencing, and as a result hate crimes have continued to grow in numbers and challenge social cohesion in Afghanistan. The cases we examine below reflect discrimination against minorities in various aspects of their social, economic, and political lives in Afghanistan. The first case concerns hate speech and how the perpetrator was able to bypass the law only to repeat the same crime. The second case reveals why a very clear and long-standing law on free religious exercise has failed to protect Hindu and Sikh minorities against continued harassment and assault. The third case discusses workplace discrimination in one of the highest offices in the country: the Administrative Office of the President. The last case in this study involves ethnic discrimination and illegal disenfranchisement in the presidential election of 2014 and how the offense was rewarded with hefty patronage by the winning side.

3.1 Hate Speech: General Taqat's "Bastards"

In December of 2013, for the first time, the Attorney General's Office (AGO) summoned three individuals and eventually arrested one of them for the alleged crime of "inciting ethnic hatred" (Art. 256). The AGO proceeded with the arrest only after a mass protest began to arise against the Zhwandoon TV channel, in particular, a panel that it hosted on electronic national ID cards where some explicitly hateful remarks were aimed at non-Pashtuns by a panelist, Abdul Wahid Taqat. The Zhwandoon TV channel is owned by infamous Pashtun supremacist, Ismael Yun; both the TV and the owner have long been criticized for ethnocentrism (*see* Shahrani 2018, 91, 136). Taqat, who is a former Army General prior to the takeover of Afghanistan by Mujahideen in 1992,[1] regularly appeared on TV as a political and military expert. Due to his regular appearances in various media platforms, coupled with his unconventional and chauvinistic opinions, he was well-known among both Pashtuns and non-Pashtuns.

Since 2009, the inclusion of "Afghan" on national ID Cards, *e-Tazkiras,* has been a divisive issue in Afghanistan (Mobasher 2018). While Pashtun hardliners have unwaveringly urged the inclusion of "Afghan" as a national identity on *e-Tazkiras,* non-Pashtun hardliners synonymizing "Afghan" with "Pashtun" have advocated for the inclusion of ethnic affiliations instead (Bjelica and van Bijlert 2016). In an attempt to alleviate ethnic tensions, the parliament decided that *e-Tazkiras* would include neither national nor ethnic identities. Initially, President Ghani signed the law and ordered the National Statistics and Information Authority (NSIA) to produce *e-Tazkiras* in accordance with the new law. However, under pressure from Pashtun hardliners, President Ghani decided to issue a decree amending the law and including both national and ethnic affiliations,[2] a decision that was rejected twice by the Lower House of the parliament (Ahmad 2018).[3] Since then, the issue remained unresolved among ethnic groups as various panels were invited by different media networks to discuss whether the word "Afghan" could be a national identity for all groups.

In December 2013, a panel on the Zhwandoon channel was discussing the controversy over the use of the term "Afghan" on *e-Tazkiras*. In the panel, Mr. *Taqat* initiated his talk with a reference to the Anglo-Afghan wars:

[1] Members of a number of guerrilla groups operating in Afghanistan during the Afghan War (1979–1992) that opposed the invading Soviet forces and eventually toppled the Afghan communist government.

[2] The issue even divided the leadership in the government, as President Ghani inaugurated the issuance of ID card while CEO Abdullah declared his opposition to the distribution, which he considered an act without "national consensus."

[3] As a result, a joint committee was convened to decide about the amendment. The committee approved the law in the absence of its four members from the WJ, which led to criticism of its decision by the WJ members, who suggested that the Chief Executive Officer (CEO) must order the distribution of *e-Tazkiras* based on the pre-amendment law. The issue apparently divided even the leadership in the government, as President Ghani pushed for *e-Tazkiras* with group affiliations, while CEO Abdullah declared his opposition to this decision, which he considered an act without "national consensus".

> The Brits committed genocide against Pashtuns…because they understood that [Pashtuns] were [the ones] fighting for freedom of this land and …they are the ones that fought them …. Since Pashtuns are the real native and owners of this land, Afghanistan means Pashtana or Pashtunistan. We only call it Afghanistan because we want to share it with Tajiks, Hazaras, Uzbeks, Turkmens, and others. But we can call it Pashtunistan…This is our country. We (Pashtuns) are the real lords [and] seniors of this land. This land is built based on our blood. We do not ignore your (non-Pashtuns) sacrifices either. [That is why we] share Afghan [identity] with you. [but] you idiots, insubordinates, and bastards, who have come from other places, and don't want to share this pure and holy name [Afghan] with us. [We] don't share it either… Go to wherever you came from, if you are ashamed of [accepting] our name and identity [Afghan]. (Taqat 2013a)

His disparaging remarks against non-Pashtun groups were further aggravated by the confirmations, comments, and questions of other panelists and the anchor (Taqat 2013a). The panel and the hateful remarks by Taqat were widely condemned, and massive protests began to emerge against his speech and the Zhwandoon TV station. With the protests mounting, the AGO announced the beginning of an investigation. Soon, the AGO arrested Taqat and claimed that they were prepared to present the case to the court for trial because they were able to gather "substantial evidence" against Taqat for "inciting ethnic hatred" (Ahmadi 2013).[4] Six days later, however, Taqat was released after he made a public apology. In the apology that he released on Facebook, he clarified that he never meant to say that Afghan ethnic groups such as Uzbeks, Tajiks, Balochis, Hazaras, Pashayees, and others are bastards and idiots. He stated, "It is true that I talked [the same] about one person only referring to the then governor of Balkh, Atta M. Noor who was a hard-core opponent of the use of Afghan in *e-Tazkiras*" (Taqat 2013b).

Having been released with no charges or sanctions, Taqat appeared on another panel on the very same topic. Being unapologetic about his earlier discriminatory remarks for which he was arrested, Taqat posited that "[whoever] says that he is not an Afghan and is ashamed of the word Afghan…he is not from my country… he is a bastard" (Shab 2014). When other panelists reminded him of his apology for similar words that he used on the previous panel, he said that he was coerced to offer an apology and he did not really mean it (ibid.).

This case indicates several failures. The first was the failure of laws and particularly the old Penal Code to regulate and sanction hate speech. Although the AGO announced arresting Taqat for inciting ethnic hatred,

[4] In addition to Gen. Taqat, the AG also arrested the head of the Ansar periodical.

there was no such provision in the law to charge him with. It was only in 2017 that new Penal Code included an Article about the "incit[ement] to hatred or division" (Art. 257). The second was the failure of AGO to charge Taqat for the other offenses that were sanctioned by the law. At the very time that Taqat was in custody, legal scholars listed several offenses that he could be charged with. The offenses included "abusing", "disturbing public order" and endangering "public security" (Ahmadi 2013). Instead of charging Taqat with any or all of these offenses, AGO was content with his insincere apology (Shab 2014). The last failure was that of the Media Complaints Commission. Although the Commission issued a resolution suspending the broadcast of Zhwandoon programming for "inciting hatred," the Commission had to rely on government law enforcement agencies to implement its ruling. However, this never happened mainly due to the intervention of powerful allies in the government. All in all, these failures ensured one thing: Taqat and Zhwandoon could continue to make hateful remarks targeting non-Pashtun ethnic groups, and such remained to be the case.

3.2 Religious Persecution: Assaulting the Living and the Dead

Hindus and Sikhs are the only visible non-Muslim religious minorities in Afghanistan. According to Al Jazeera, in the 1970s, their population was over 200,000 (Kumar 2020, 2022). Today, there are only 140 Hindus and Sikh's left in Afghanistan (ibid.). Historically, Hindus and Sikhs have been the most economically vibrant groups (Salahuddin 2010). Due to their important role in trading and entrepreneurship, Hindu and Sikh arbitrated some commercial disputes in the late nineteenth and early twentieth centuries. They lived in harmony with their Muslim neighbors and celebrated both traditions' festivals together. Their population rapidly decreased, particularly after 1992, due to a series of civil wars and the rule of the Mujahideen (1992–1996) and later the Taliban (1996–2001), who actively engaged in politics of radicalization, systematic discrimination, persecution, and illegal seizure of lands, homes, and businesses (Singh 2016). The pervasive intolerance was summed up by Amrit Singh's reply to a reporter, "when we are alive, we are disrespected, insulted, and beaten…. And when we take our dead to the crematorium, which is our personal property, they won't let us burn the bodies, saying it stinks. Do we have any rights in this country or not?" (Mina 2013).

Since 2007 Hindu and Sikh communities have increasingly encountered opposition from locals regarding the cremation of their dead in Kabul

(Anwari 2007). Historically, these communities have had a designated crematorium of their own in the neighborhood of Qalacha in Kabul, which was located far from residential areas. However, in recent years, the lands in the neighborhood as well as the lands designated for crematoriums were illegally seized, and houses were built by warlords and opportunists. The government remained silent for the most part until the new illegal houses creeped over the crematorium walls. Since then, these religious minorities were subjected to increasing harassment and assaults during cremations in their own crematorium.

A violent confrontation occurred in 2007 when locals prevented a cremation ceremony by throwing stones at mourners and the dead body (Hemming 2007). Given the lack of protection from the government, many of those from the Hindu and Sikh communities protested the continued assault in front of the United Nation office in Kabul, after which the police began to intervene (ibid.). The police arrested five locals for assaulting the religious minorities (Anwari 2007). Attacking religious ceremonies was one of a few discrimination-based offenses that was explicitly listed as a criminal act in the Penal Code of 1976. Despite this, the police released the perpetrators without any charges filed. Instead, the police promised to escort Hindus and Sikhs to their cremation rites. The decision not to press criminal charges against offenders led to several negative ramifications for Hindu and Sikh communities. Most importantly, the assault on these communities continued without reprieve. Indeed, the perpetrators became more zealous in assaulting religious minorities as they gained support from some local authorities and powerful residents (Singh 2016). In 2012, cremation ceremonies encountered a massive assault that led to another protest, this time in front of the Afghan Presidential Palace (Zaheer 2012). Hindus and Sikhs were convinced that the police were not able or willing to protect them against continued assaults. Instead of investigating the crime and pressing charges against offenders, the government planned to designate a new residential area and crematorium to move Hindus outside the city of Kabul (Mina 2013).

The government proposed that these communities build the town themselves with partial government funding. Hindu and Sikh communities, however, refused to accept the proposal because the relegation of these religious minorities to a segregated town outside the city would render them even more vulnerable to extremist violence. Their refusal coincided with two ISIS attacks that led to the killing of over 45 members and the injuring of hundreds of others (Singh and Singh 2020). In the first incident, their only 2018 parliamentary candidate, Awtar Singh Khalsa, along with 18 others, was killed (BBC 2018a). In the second incident, ISIS targeted a gathering in the temple, Shor Bazar Gurdwara, in which over 25 members of these communities including women and children were killed. Scores of others were injured (Noorzai et al. 2020).

3.3 Workplace Discrimination: The Notorious Makh Kakh Agenda

An Afghanistan Independent Human Right Commission (AIHRC) report highlights the widespread discrimination against minority groups in the country (Shaheed 2019). One key example to such an increasing trend is the case of Sawabuddin Makh Kakh, who was a high ranking official in the Administrative Office of the President (AOP). In August 2017, Makh Kakh decided to share with his allies a well-prepared agenda to systematically remove Tajik and Hazara employees from AOP (Reuters 2017). The platform he used to share the file was Telegram; however, due to his unfamiliarity with the platform, he shared the file with all AOP staff, revealing the discriminatory nature of the scheme (*see* Bezhan 2017). Soon the content of the agenda slipped into public light through social and mainstream media, leading to further public suspicion of the government's involvement in systemic discrimination. Under public criticism and pressure, President Ghani directly instructed the Attorney General to investigate the case, until which no investigations were initiated by the agency based on the laws of the country.

Containing 12 points, the agenda that Makh Kakh shared on Telegram was highly discriminatory against minority groups, specifically the Hazaras. Among other things, the agenda provided instructions for Makh Kakh's co-conspirators in the AOP that specific employees should be substituted with Pashtuns because they were Hazaras, despite their "strong performances" (Shaheed 2017). The instructions repeatedly emphasized on promoting Pashtuns to key positions and supporting specific individuals who sympathized with their cause. Revealing a systematic marginalization of ethnic and religious minorities in the closest agency to the president, this revelation triggered a major public outcry in Afghanistan (*see* U.S. Department of State 2018, 36–37).

The prosecution charged Makh Kakh with the violation of national, religious, and racial equality of rights under the Law on Crimes Against Internal and External Security. Makh Kakh's trial was held late in May 2018 after the enactment of the new Penal Code of 2017 (BBC 2019). The court decided to apply the new Penal Code to Makh Kakh's case, as a result of the nature of the crime and even changed the sanction to a considerably milder punishment.[5] The court found Makh Kakh guilty of prejudicial activities on cyber space based on Article 870, which provides that "a person [who] provokes ethnic, religious, sectarian, linguistic, or regional bigotry within the society using the internet, a computer, or through publishing texts, audio, or video tracks in cyberspace," has committed the crime of bigotry on cyber space.

Because the justice system failed to charge him with employment discrimination, Makh Kakh was only punished with two years of probation (BBC 2019). It also remains unclear why Makh Kakh was the only one prosecuted and tried, while the agenda clearly pointed to an organized group of many co-conspirators in the agency. Had the judicial entities thoroughly and properly investigated the case, this could have addressed the ever-expanding discrimination pandemic in the government agencies.

3.4 Discrimination and Disenfranchisement in the Electoral Process: Fattening the Sheep

Since the second round of the 2014 Presidential Election, "fattening the sheep" has become one of the most popular phrases used to mock elections in Afghanistan. It also reminds us of why the public lost trust in electoral institutions and processes. Originally, this phrase was used by electoral officials in a series of phone calls instructing poll workers to stuff ballot boxes. The phrase "feed the sheep" or "fatten the sheep" was also used to denote instances when officials filled positions with individuals who would be loyal to a particular candidate.

The first round of the presidential election ended with no candidate surpassing the threshold of 50% votes nationwide. The two front-running candidates who had to prepare for a runoff were Abdullah, an ethnic Tajik, with over 45% of votes and Ghani, an ethnic Pashtun, with less than 32% of votes. The first round of elections revealed that most Uzbeks favored Ghani's nomination because their leader, Abdul Rashid Dostum, joined forces with him as his first vice-president candidate. Ghani scored 50–69%

[5] Article 17 of the new Penal Code asserts that, "[t]he perpetrator of a crime shall be punished based on a law which is in effect prior to Commission of the crime, unless a new law is passed which favors the accused before a final verdict is issued. A law is considered to be in favor of the accused in the following circumstance. (1) When it reduces the minimum punishment; (2) While it maintains the minimum punishment, it reduces the maximum punishment; and (3) When it reduces the punishment to a lower degree; [...] (6) Other circumstances in the new law which favor the accused.

of provincial votes in seven provinces that were populated predominantly by either Pashtuns or Uzbeks (Mobasher 2015, 402). Ghani also had the endorsement of Ismailis by forming an electoral alliance with their leader, S. Mansor Naderi, in exchange for a few seats in his administration. Most Hazaras, however, joined the Tajiks in endorsing Abdullah's candidacy due to Mohaqiq's alliance with him as his presidential running mate. In the first round, Abdullah obtained his highest proportion of provincial votes in Daykundi (75%) and Bamyan (68%), which are predominantly Hazara provinces (Mobasher 2015, 406). The substantial difference between the votes of the two candidates in the first round worried many Pashtun ethno-nationalists including those in the Independent Electoral Commission (IEC).

A series of leaked phone calls revealed the involvement of Ziaul Haq Amarkhel, the Secretary of IEC, and his assistant, Adam Khan Sirat, in a systemic electoral manipulation intersected with workplace discrimination (Mobasher 2015). In at least two calls, Amarkhel instructed officials to recruit people of certain ethnic groups who presumably had favorable views of Ghani's candidacy. In one call, for example, in response to a complaint by IEC official in Faryab province that "other [ethnic] people make the majority in our office," Amarkhel urges him to "change them all. Recruit Uzbeks. Recruit Pashtuns. It is a shame" (Noor TV 2014, 15:25). In another call, he tells a Ghani's campaign official that, "send me some useful people and make the best of my presence here…. I need 2 to 3 people in Badakhshan [a region in Northeastern Afghanistan]. I need an Uzbek and someone from Ismaelies there… [t]hey should know why they are hired. They are hired to fatten the sheep properly" (Noor TV 2014, 8:37).

The phone calls were released a few days after the police seized some suspicious trucks full of ballot papers belonging to Amerkhel on election day (2014, أفغان سلام هم وطن). Despite substantial evidence, the prosecution brought not charges against Amerkhel. Alleging that Amarkhel and many electoral officials were involved in "an industrial scale fraud" in favor of Ashraf Ghani, Presidential candidate Abdullah withdrew from the election and promised not to return until the credibility of the Commission was restored by removing all individuals involved in the plot (ibid.). Thousands of supporters of Abdullah poured onto the streets of Kabul and other big cities protesting the electoral misconducts by the IEC officials. Some powerful supporters of Abdullah, including the governor of the province of Balkh, Atta Mohammad Noor, threatened that they will cease all cooperation with the government should the Commission announce Ghani as the winner.

Abdullah's team demanded that the Attorney General's Office investigate the crime and issue a travel ban on Amarkhel. However, the Attorney General argued that they received no such complaints or charges "from the government" against Amarkhel and that they will prosecute Amarkhel as soon as they are instructed by the government to do so. This deferral of investigation and arrest to an official request from the government was a clear indication of the reluctance of the Attorney General to discharge its legal duty. Soon after his resignation, Amarkhel moved to Dubai leaving the election in such disarray that the United States Foreign Secretary, John Kerry, had to intervene and the two contending candidates had to form a national unity government, setting the electoral results aside.

There have been questions about the authenticity of the records, alleged tampering with the tapes, and the potential applicable laws to bring charges against Amarkhel. However, these questions remained unanswered and the case unresolved primarily because the Attorney General's Office never picked up the case to investigate. Instead of launching an investigation, the Attorney General encouraged presidential contenders to negotiate and resolve their electoral disputes among themselves. This approach reveals the prosecutor's office reliance on political solutions instead of a legal remedy for electoral misconduct involving systemic discrimination.

Even more problematic was the appointment of Amarkhel by President Ghani to prominent government positions afterward. After the Electoral Complaint Commission dismissed the nomination of Amarkhel in the parliamentary election of 2018 because of his previous electoral misconducts, President Ghani appointed him as his "Senior Advisor for Public and Political Affairs" (BBC 2018b). Despite substantial criticism over his appointment as the senior advisor to the president, within a few months, President Ghani rewarded Amarkhel with yet another promotion: Ghani appointed him as the Minister for Parliamentary Affairs (Sputnik 2018). Not long afterward, the president appointed him as the governor of Nangarhar province (*see* BBC 2020)—the third largest province in Afghanistan with the economically and historically significant city of Jalalabad as its capital.

This case follows the same pattern as earlier cases where an offense involving discrimination remains unprosecuted. However, it further indicates that an offender may be rewarded if the offense benefits those in power. This perhaps explains why the presidential election of 2019 was no different from the election of 2014 in terms of fraud, ethnic tensions, and inconclusive electoral results.

4 Conclusion

All cases in this study were dealt with by either informal negotiation, political mitigations, or ad hoc Commissions. The results of such solutions have been (a) mildly sanctioned or mostly unsanctioned offenders, (b) the continuation of discrimination and hate offenses, and (c) the unending suffering of the victims, especially from minority groups. One primary reason for the government engaging in political solutions and not legal ones in dealing with discrimination has been that the government was never invested in eradicating discrimination. Systematic discrimination in fact rose exponentially under President Ghani.

Ultimately, one reason for the failure of the republic and its collapse has been the further institutionalization of discrimination that led to ethnic divides rendering the state vulnerable to the Taliban's invasion. Every few days a new discrimination scandal or a discriminatory policy would test state-society relations, triggering public anger. The scandal of a systematic campaign in the Administrative Office of the President (AOP) to remove employees from certain ethnic groups as discussed in the Makh Kakh case can be seen as part of an emerging pattern. Several records of Ghani's closest circles including Hamdullah Mohib, his National Security Council Advisor, were leaked, showing that an ethnocentric agenda was being implemented even more vigorously to purge the state agencies from the presence of diverse groups. Several current and former officials of Ghani's administration including his first vice-president, Dostum, repeatedly accused the administration of ethnic discrimination.

Although Ghani presided over two national unity governments and had the set up needed to unite all political forces, Ghani reneged on his promises to be a fair power-sharing partner. From the very beginning, he made it a top priority to sideline his partners in government by firing their members in the cabinet or limiting their power by creating parallel institutions—high councils—inside the president's office under his direct control. He did the same with local governments, removing some prominent governors who could otherwise keep their provinces secured from the Taliban and replacing them with weak figures who had no intention and capacity of resisting the Taliban. While the Taliban assassinated some strong local power holders such as Abdul Razaq, the Kandahar Chief of Police, and many others, President Ghani sidelined Governor Atta, Governor Shirzoi, Marshal Dostum and the rest, leaving the country vulnerable to the Taliban's invasion.

Many still wonder how such a backward, unpopular, mostly uneducated, small, and proxy movement dismantled a government with mostly educated leaders, heavy weaponry, and a well-trained army. The answer lies in the unity of the former and the divisiveness of the latter due to scandalous and systematic discrimination against various groups. With the Taliban coming to power, the issues surrounding ethnic and gender-based discrimination prove to have severely deteriorated. The Taliban member of the de facto cabinet comprises of an absolute majority of Pashtuns. Not only are the members of the cabinet exclusively Pashtun, they also come from a specific tribes—moving backward from ethnocentrism to tribalism. From the very early stages of the group usurping power in the country, there are ample reports of enforced disappearances, forced migration, and ethnic discrimination around the country. Similarly, the Taliban has yet to open schools and higher education for girls. Public services for females are also closed and women are no longer allowed to work. While the group has publicly been claiming that they are working on the reopening of the education for females and resumption of services and jobs for women, this remains to be seen.

References

ضیا الحق امرخیل گرگ ریس جمهور با پشتاره دستگیر شد. (2014, June 14). أفغان سلام هم وطن. [President Zia-ul-Haq Amarkhail Was Arrested on Bail] YouTube, June 18, 2022, from https://web.archive.org/web/20210212204318/www.youtube.com/watch?v=iMEMnKZKtUE&feature=youtu.be.

Afghanistan Times. 2016. Dostum Blames Ghani, Abdullah for Fueling Discrimination. October 25, 2016. http://www.afghanistantimes.af/dostum-blames-ghani-adbullah-for-fueling-discrimination/.

Ahmed, Azam. 2014. A Christian Convert, on the Run in Afghanistan. *The New York Times*, June 21, 2014. https://www.nytimes.com/2014/06/22/world/asia/afghanistan-a-christian-convert-on-the-run.html.

Ahmad, Tariq. 2018. Afghanistan: Distribution of Controversial Electronic Identity Cards Launched. *Global Legal Monitor, Library of Congress*.

Ahmed and Zahori. 2014. Afghan Ethnic Tensions Rise in Media and Politics. *The New York Times*, February 18, 2014. https://www.nytimes.com/2014/02/19/world/asia/afghan-ethnic-tensions-rise-in-media-and-politics.html.

Ahmadi, Mohammad. 2013. جنرال طاقت توقیف شد، قصورش چیست؟ [General Endured Arrested, What Is Malpractice?]. *Darivoa*. https://www.darivoa.com/a/gerenral-taqat-arrested/1809302.html.

Anwari, Ramin. 2007. جدال میان سیکها و مسلمانان کابل [The Conflict Between Sikhs and Muslims in Kabul]. *BBC*, September 17. https://www.bbc.com/persian/afghanistan/story/2007/09/070917_k-ram-sikh-muslim-kabul.shtml.

BBC. 2017. غنی: قانون رفع تبعیض تدوین شود [Ghani: Legislation to Eliminate Discrimination to Be Drafted]. December 3. https://www.bbc.com/persian/afghanistan-42213666.

BBC. 2018a. کشته شدن 'تنها نامزد' سیک انتخابات افغانستان در حمله جلال‌آباد ['Only' Candidate Killed in Afghan Election 'Only' Sikh Attack in Jalalabad Attack]. *BBC News*, July 1, 2018a. https://www.bbc.com/persian/afghanistan-44677213.

BBC. 2018b. ضیاالحق امرخیل، مشاور ارشد رئیس جمهوری افغانستان شد [Zia-ul-Haq Amarkhail Became the Senior Advisor to the President of Afghanistan]. *BBC*, September 26. https://www.bbc.com/persian/afghanistan-45659249.

BBC. 2019. مخکش برای 'نقض تساوی قومی و مذهبی' به دو سال حبس تعلیقی محکوم شد [Makhkash Imprisoned for Two Years for Violating Ethnic and Religious Equality]. *BBC*, January 21. https://www.bbc.com/persian/afghanistan-46936804.

BBC. 2020. والی ننگرهار خبر ایجاد اداره امر به معروف و نهی از منکر در این ولایت را تکذیب کرد [Nangarhar Governor Denies News of Establishment of Office for the Purpose of Forbidding Evil in the Province]. October 12. https://www.bbc.com/persian/afghanistan-54501762.

Bezhan, Frud. 2017. Leaked Memo Fuels New Allegations of Ethnic Bias in Afghan Government. *Radio Free Europe*, November 20. https://www.rferl.org/a/afghanistan-ethnic-tensions-ghani-government-abdullah/28865180.html.

Bjelica, Jelena and van Bijlert. 2016. The Troubled History of the E-tazkera (Part 1): Political Upheaval, Afghanistan Analysts Network. *Afghanistan Analysts Network*.

Hasnain, Jaffar (@jaffarhasnain). 2021. Is Ashraf Ghani Responsible for the Collapse of the Government in Afghanistan? *Twitter*, August 16, 2021. https://twitter.com/jaffarhasnain/status/1427183821431115776?s=25&fbclid=I-wAR0pjgJgHZ0iSCscwASVHFARaAb1B3VjcvZJ7i8h3B_EcGIZhQFntYjs844.

Hemming, Jon. 2007. Sikhs in Afghan Funeral Demonstration. *Reuters*, September 17. https://www.reuters.com/article/uk-afghan-sikhs/sikhs-in-afghan-funeral-demonstration-idUKISL3784120070917.

Ibrahimi, Niamatullah, Musab Omer, Mohammad Irfani, and Afghanistan Kabul. 2015. Social Media and Articulation of Radical Narratives in Afghanistan. *A Research and Policy Paper*: 25.

Kabul Art. 2021. حمدالله محب: چیزهاییکه به دوستم دادیم باید پس بگیریم [Hamdullah Mohib: The Things We Gave My Friend Should Be Taken Back]. August 13, 2021. Audio, 0:44. https://www.youtube.com/watch?v=uHErmJWmjGo.

Kumar, Ruchi. 2020. Herat's Restored Synagogues Reveal Afghanistan's Jewish Past. *Aljazeera*, February 7, 2020. https://www.aljazeera.com/news/2020/2/7/herats-restored-synagogues-reveal-afghanistans-jewish-past.

Kumar, Ruchi. 2022. Deadly Attack on Sikh Temple in Kabul Leaves Community in Fear. *Aljazeera*, June 18, 2022. https://www.aljazeera.com/news/2022/6/18/deadly-attack-on-sikh-temple-in-kabul-leaves-community-in-fear.

Mazhar et al. 2012. Ethnic Factor in Afghanistan. *Journal of Political Studies* 19(2).

Mina, Habib. 2013. Hindus and Sikhs Struggle in Afghanistan. *World Wide Religious News*. https://wwrn.org/articles/40238/.

Mobasher, Mohammad Bashir. 2015. Understanding Ethnic-Electoral Dynamics: How Ethnic Politics Affect Electoral Laws and Election Outcomes in Afghanistan. *Gonzaga Law Review* 51 (2015): 355.

Mobasher, Mohammad Bashir. 2018. Identity Cards and Identity Conflicts: A Cross-National Analysis of National ID Cards and the Lesson for Afghanistan. *Indian Law Review*.

Mobasher, Mohammad Bashir. 2019. Party Laws and Party Nationalization: a Critique of Afghan Political Party Laws. *University of Bologna Law Review*, 4 (2).

Mobasher, Mohammad Bashir. 2021, September 13. What Does the Future Hold for the New Taliban Government? *MRI: InterRegional for Strategic Analysis*. https://www.interregional.com/en/non-inclusive-governance/.

Mobasher, Mohammad Bashir and Qadam Shah, Mohammad. 2022. Deproblematizing the Federal–Unitary Dichotomy: Insights from a Public Opinion Survey about Approaches to Designing a Political System in Afghanistan. *Publius: The Journal of Federalism*, 52 (2): 225–253.

Noor TV Network. 2014. وی‌ژه برنامه - افشای سندها در مورد نقش ضیاالحق امرخیل در تقلب های گسترده به نفع اشرف غنی [Special Program - Disclosure of Documents on Zia-ul-Haq Amerkhil's Role in Widespread Fraud in Favor of Ashraf Ghani]. June 23, 2014. https://youtu.be/Uux5dVmgh0s.

Noorzai, Roshan, Mohammad Niala, and Habibzada Mohammad. 2020. Sikhs and Hindus of Afghanistan in Limbo After March Deadly Attack. *Extremism Watch*, May 3, 2020. https://www.voanews.com/extremism-watch/sikhs-and-hindus-afghanistan-limbo-after-march-deadly-attack.

Reuters Staff. 2017. Leaked Memo Fuels Accusations of Ethnic Bias in Afghan Government. *Reuters*, September 21. https://www.reuters.com/article/us-afghanistan-politics/leaked-memo-fuels-accusations-of-ethnic-bias-in-afghan-government-idUSKCN1BW15U.

Salahuddin, Sayed. 2010. Afghan Hindus and Sikhs Grapple with Uncertain Future. *Reuters*, July 1. https://www.reuters.com/article/us-afghanistan-minorities/afghan-hindus-and-sikhs-grapple-with-uncertain-future-idUSTRE6610BM20100702.

Schetter, Conrad. 2003. Ethnicity and the Political Reconstruction in Afghanistan. *LSE Research Online*.

Shab, Fanuse. 2014. دیگ تعصب جنرال طاقت بجوش آمد و یکبار دیگر حرامی خطاب کرد [General's Bigotry Boiled Over and Once Again Called Haram]. December 15, 2014. Interview, 11:51. https://www.youtube.com/watch?v=uhZq0lR-DEE.

Shaheed, Anisa, 2017. ریاست جمهوری: طرح قومگرایانه دیدگاه شخصی مخکش است [Presidential Palace: Ethnic Policy Is a Makhkash's Personal Opinion]. *Tolo News*, September 19. https://tolonews.com/link

Shaheed, Anisa. 2019. Study Finds Racial Discrimination as Key Factor Behind Violence. *Tolo News*, March 25. https://tolonews.com/afghanistan/study-finds-racial-discrimination-key-factor-behind-violence.

Shahrani, M. Nazif. 2018. *Modern Afghanistan: The Impact of 40 Years of War.* Indiana University Press.

Singh, Balpreet. 2016. Plight of Afghan Skihs and Hindus in Afghanistan. *World Skih Organization of Canada* submitted to House of Common's (Canada) Standing Committee on Citizenship and Immigration. No. 23, Sess. 1, 42nd Parliament. July 2016. https://www.ourcommons.ca/Content/Committee/421/CIMM/Brief/BR8401077/br-external/WorldSikhOrganizationofCanada-e.pdf.

Singh, Naindeep and Puneet Singh. 2020. Plight of Afghan Skihs and Hindus in Afghanistan. Jakara Movement. https://d3n8a8pro7vhmx.cloudfront.net/jakara/mailings/2144/attachments/original/afghansikhs.pdf?1587524919.

Sputnik. 2014. واکنش ها به گزینش ضیاءالحق امرخیل به عنوان مشاور ارشد رئیسجمهور [Reactions to the Selection of Zia-ul-Haq Amarkhail as Senior Advisor to the President]. September 27. https://af.sputniknews.com/20180927/2705863.html

Taqat, Abdul Wahid. 2013a. !جنرال طاقت په دی وی‌ډیو بندی شو، تاسی قضاوت وکړی [General Taqat Was Arrested in This Video, You Judged!]. December 15, 2013a. Interview, 6:29. https://www.youtube.com/watch?v=nb6584MGJMk.

Taqat, Abdul Wahid. 2013b. https://www.facebook.com/haris.jamalzada/videos/479255905528661/ (video no longer available).

The World Factbook. 2021. Afghanistan. November 17, 2021. https://www.cia.gov/the-world-factbook/countries/afghanistan/.

U.S. Department of State. 2018. *Country Report on Human Rights Practices for 2017 [Afghanistan].* Bureau of Democracy, Human Rights, and Labor. https://2017-2021.state.gov/wp-content/uploads/2019/01/Afghanistan.pdf.

Zaheer, Abasin. 2012. Afghan Sikhs Protest Over Cremation. *Pajhwok Afghan News*, November 16. https://pajhwok.com/2012/11/16/afghan-sikhs-protest-over-cremation/.

4

Between Denial and Memory: A Socio-Legal Reading of Securitization Narratives in Transitional Colombia

Gustavo Rojas-Páez

1 Introduction

> As long as I speak out, my son will be alive, and he will be in the memory of the entire world. I gave birth to my son for life, but he gave life to me for the struggle.
>
> Luz Marina Bernal

The quote from human rights activist Luz Marina Bernal above illustrates the struggle to remember the victims of the extrajudicial killings of civilians conducted by the Colombian army that were sanctioned and rewarded by the state, a phenomenon referred to as "false positives." Luz Marina is a founding member of the Soacha Mothers (MAFAPO), an organization that plays a fundamental role in the denunciation of false positives in Colombia.

Luz Marina's son, Fair Leonardo Porras Bernal, was killed by the Colombian army and painted as a guerrilla leader in 2008. Although Leonardo was severely disabled, and, therefore, could not have carried the weapons of a guerrilla fighter, it took Luz Marina five years—during which she received several death threats—to prove that her son was not a guerrilla leader as stated in a

This chapter results from a research project on crimes of the powerful and Transitional Justice conducted by the author within the framework of the doctoral programme Rethinking Globalization: Challenges and interdisciplinary solutions at the University of the Basque Country.

G. Rojas-Páez (✉)
University of the Basque Country, Leioa, Bizkaia, Spain
e-mail: grojas004@ikasle.ehu.eus

G. B. Radics and P. Ciocchini (eds.), *Criminal Legalities and Minorities in the Global South*, Palgrave Socio-Legal Studies, https://doi.org/10.1007/978-3-031-17918-1_4

report of the army. Luz Marina's moral strength led her to prove Leonardo's innocence before a tribunal that declared his assassination a crime against humanity in 2013 (The Tribunal of the District of Cundinamarca 2013).

"False positives" are one of the most egregious forms of crimes of the powerful (Pearce 1976)[1] in the recent history of Colombia. These crimes consist of the extrajudicial execution of civilians, mostly male and marginalized, who were painted as guerrilla fighters and presented as legally killed combatants of illegal armed groups by the Colombian military, which were often aided by paramilitaries or organized crime groups (Gordon 2017). False positives were institutionally facilitated by a policy of incentives established by the Colombian government, which offered "a series of rewards such as money, medals and additional holiday leave to military units that achieved high body counts" (Palau 2020). It is estimated that between 2002 and 2010, approximately 10,000 civilians were victims of false positives (Rojas-Bolaños and Benavides 2017).

Holding the state accountable for crimes such as false positives poses a challenge to our understanding of criminal law within prolonged periods of violence and the ideology of "security" that supports it. In contexts of prolonged violence, lethal practices against civilians such as extrajudicial executions and enforced disappearances (hereupon ED) have been justified through securitization policies inspired by the "criminal law of the enemy". For instance, in Argentina, the National Doctrine of Security, a securitization policy rooted in the Cold War discourse against communism, was used to justify the ED of thousands of people (CONADEP 1984). By the same token, in South Africa, the imprisonment and even shooting of thousands of demonstrators was an institutional practice endorsed by the legal system of apartheid from 1948 to 1994 (Viljoen 2021).

Against this background, the purpose of this chapter is to reflect on the violent nature of the criminal law in global south countries with prolonged periods of violence through the lens of the situation in Colombia, as well as its interpretation within Colombia's legal frameworks, including the country's recently established transitional justice tribunal—*La Jurisdicción Especial para la Paz* (Special Jurisdiction for Peace) or "JEP." The primary

[1] The notion of crimes of the powerful is a very important analytical tool to understanding Colombia's long-lasting violence. As the chapter will show, the violence of the conflict in Colombia is intertwined with the rationality of the modern criminal law, which is grounded on state definitions of crime and favours an exclusionary idea of nationhood, which ignores and normalizes the structural violence endured by marginalised Colombians. In a context of prolonged violence, the impunity of crimes of the powerful has dramatic consequences because it normalizes the extermination of marginalized citizens in the name of securitization.

argument of this chapter is that criminal justice during prolonged conflict is by nature authoritarian, and ignores crimes of the powerful while systematically and historically disregarding the fundamental rights of marginalized populations. Furthermore, addressing the relationship between extrajudicial killings of civilians and criminal law in Colombia allows us to revisit a classic theme in the theoretical innards of the criminal law: the political and historical role of the state as a violent actor.

Modern criminal law promises to prevent crime through punishing individuals, and, in doing so, it overtly distorts the political and moral nature of conflicts between the state and the subjectivities that oppose its narratives regarding political order (Norrie 2017). A major consequence of the latter is that structural injustice, caused by crimes of the powerful including the state's crimes, is systematically ignored by the restricted rationale of criminal justice, which emphasizes the punishment of the abstract individual who commits crimes against and defined by the state (Norrie 2017). Thus, violence is entrenched on the grounds of criminal justice, which as O'Brien argues "discriminates unfairly between crimes of the powerful and crimes of the powerless" (O'Brien 2008, 35).

The lack of accountability of false positives and the fact that the victims of such heinous crimes are subjected to outrageous delays and the silencing of demands for justice, illustrates how the formality of criminal law in contexts of prolonged violence exacerbates and normalizes injustice. Furthermore, the stigmatization and death threats that mark the everyday lives of the victims of false positives, such as in the case of Ms Bernal as described above, show the human cost of the impunity of the crimes of the powerful and its relationship with structural violence and ostracism. Experiences such as those of the victims of false positives remind us of Walter Benjamin's analysis of the violent nature of the modern law. According to Benjamin, law is grounded in violence and its function is to preserve violence (Benjamin 2007).

Since accountability for crimes of the powerful in nations experiencing prolonged violence is difficult to achieve within the realm of the criminal law that has operated throughout periods of armed conflict, this chapter concludes with a brief discussion on Transitional Justice to explore its capacity to produce a narrative that accounts for the crimes of the powerful and its beneficiaries.

The chapter consists of two sections. The first section describes the historical and theoretical aspects of exceptionality criminal policy justified throughout the Colombian conflict. The section argues that the systemic use of exceptionality law in Colombia is illustrative of the violence of the criminal law in the country's history of prolonged violence. The latter is exemplified by the use of the Statute of Security (1978–1991) against political activists and marginalized citizens, as will be explored through the emblematic case of the extrajudicial killing of Luis Fernando Lalinde, and his mother's, Ms Fabiola Lalinde, struggle for justice. As will be seen, the narratives surrounding this case resemble those related to false positives, indicating the importance of addressing the entrenched securitization policies and discourses that have informed the criminal law of the Colombian conflict.

The second section analyzes the rationale of Colombia's Democratic Security Policy (DSP) from 2002 to 2010 and addresses its human cost: false positives. The section shows how the DSP represents a particular form of criminal law termed "authoritarian liberalism" (Iturralde 2010). In the light of this form of criminal policy, security is understood as militarization of marginalized places and subjects, and as a result, lethal practices such as the false positives become normalized. With this in mind, the section maintains that exceptionality policies endorse a restricted idea of nationhood that normalizes a violent process of "otherization". The remainder of the chapter reflects upon the narratives surrounding accountability efforts of the false positives within Colombia's transitional justice tribunal and outlines the tribunal's understanding of the violent character of the criminal law embedded in the conflict.

2 The "Statute of Security": A Historical and Theoretical Analysis

False positives illustrate the lack of empathy and disregard for the lives of marginalized citizens by the Colombian state. Understanding how this lethal practice originated and became legally justified requires a broader historical analysis of securitization discourses during the Colombian conflict. As will be seen, these discourses resulted from declarations of states of exception which became permanent legislations between 1950 and 1990 (Iturralde 2010).[2]

[2] The permanent use of the exceptionality criminal policies in Colombia corresponds to the 60-year, ongoing armed conflict. A detailed account of the conflict is beyond the scope of this chapter. However, for my argument, it is important to mention that the conflict has involved various actors, including guerrilla forces, right wing paramilitaries, and the state. According to the National Center for Historical Memory, the number of fatalities of the conflict between 1958 and 2018 account for 262,197, out of which 215,005 have been civilians and 46,813 combatants. Many experts maintain that a major element of the conflict is the inequitable agrarian structure, which has facilitated processed of dispossession and favoured the interests of local and transnational businesses elites (Coleman 2007; Molano 2015).

One of the exceptionality policies that remains deeply entrenched in the memory and in the lives of the victims of state crime in Colombia is Decree No. 1923 of 1978, also known as the "Statute of Security." This decree established prison penalties for public demonstrators, granted jurisdiction to military courts and authorities to prosecute crimes and detain people, and authorized the censorship of the media when discussing "illegal strikes" (Decree 1923, 78).

Similar to the securitization discourse that justified Enforced Disappearances in the dictatorial regimes that ruled Latin America in the Cold War, the Statute of Security was influenced by the "doctrine of national security" which was pushed by the United States to "contain communism" and focused on rooting out "internal enemies" of the state. Internal enemies under this doctrine were understood not only as guerrilla forces confronting the state in a direct way, but also any person who allegedly opposed the government's political projects (Leal 2006, 27).

According to human rights lawyer Mauricio Andreu, the implementation of the Statute of Security brought about a dramatic increase in the cases of ED and arbitrary detentions in Colombia (Andreu, as cited in Umaña 2017). For instance, Andreu maintains that in the 1970s, in a city like Bogotá with a population of nearly 3 million, over 5000 people were arrested and detained in military facilities (Andreu, as cited in Umaña 2017).

The lack of accountability of lethal practices against civilians such as Enforced Disappearances is illustrative of the impunity of the crimes of the powerful in Colombia. According to a report by Colombia's National Centre for Historical Memory (CNMH), cases of Enforced Disappearance amount to 80,514 incidences, out of which 70,587 remain unresolved. These injustices that emerge through the political use of criminal law prompt us to question the democratic nature of the Colombian state and why cases of Enforced Disappearances in a "democratic country" exceed those of the authoritarian regimes of Argentina, Chile, and Uruguay.

It is in this vein that revisiting the relationship between violence and the criminal law becomes important. The Statute of Security had legal grounds. On the one hand, the exceptionality policy was legal because article 121 of the 1886 Constitution established that the President of the Republic had the authority to declare the state of exception indefinitely in order to maintain or restore public order. On the other hand, when asked about the constitutionality of this presidential power to declare the state of exception in 1970, the Supreme Court declared that the "state of exception was the most efficient instrument to address public order issues" (Corte Suprema de Justicia

[Colombia] 1970,[3] as cited in Barreto-Rozo 2011). This not only resembles Benjamin's critique of law-making violence and law-preserving violence addressed at the outset of this chapter, but it also draws attention to the systemic violence of criminal law in countries with histories of prolonged conflict.

Article 129 of the 1886 Constitution, and its interpretation by the Supreme Court mirrors Carl Schmitt's theory about the sovereignty of the nation-state (Barreto-Rozo 2011). According to Schmitt, it is only the sovereign who can declare exceptionality laws in order to protect the constitutional order. This juridical interpretation of the political power of the state has a direct effect on the criminal law which can be observed in Schmitt's theory of a priori culpability, which Angela Davis (2016) reminds us is akin to political imprisonment. In discussing political imprisonment, Davis states that during the Nazi regime "a thief was not necessarily one who has committed an overt act of theft, but rather one whose character renders him a thief" (Davis 2016, 30).

A direct consequence of a priori culpability is the criminalization of otherness and the normalizing of lethal practices against civilians committed by the state—distinct characteristics of criminal law in nations experiencing prolonged periods of violence. As Umaña shows in his study of the ED that occurred in the Palace of Justice siege in 1985,[4] the victims of this lethal practice were not only targeted for their political opposition to the state, but also due to their socioeconomic levels (Umaña 2017). Therefore, the a priori culpability approach to criminal law in a prolonged conflict like Colombia's has led to the use of lethal violence not only against political opponents, but also against the socially excluded groups of the country. The Enforced Disappearances and the "social cleansing" campaigns of the 1980s[5] in Colombia's major cities occurred with the complicity of the police and during the time of the Statute of Security (Perea 2015).

---

[3] Sala Plena. Sentencia de agosto 13 de 1970. Magistrado ponente: Luis Sarmiento Buitrago, pp. 312–315.

[4] The Palace of Justice siege was an attack on the Supreme Court of Colombia in 1985 where members of the leftist M-19 guerrilla group took over the Palace of Justice in the capital of Bogotá. The guerrillas held the Supreme Court hostage with the intent of forcing President Belisario Betancur to trial for his actions in derailing the peace process. More than 100 people were killed including half of the Supreme Court justices. *See* Higuera Silva (2010).

[5] The indiscriminate killing of *desechables*, or disposable people. *Desechables* are typically perceived as threats to society, though the group most often targeted is street children. *See* Human Rights Watch (1994) available at https://www.hrw.org/reports/1994/colombia/gener1.htm.

The relationship between criminal law and state violence has always been a complex one. Although originating from different political experiences, Benjamin (2007) and Schmitt (1983) analyzed this relationship and provided us with differing understandings of the role of the law in a prolonged period of violence. Furthermore, the two authors put forth opposing views about the law of the nation-state and the securitization discourse that informed the Nazi regime. Despite contextual differences, these authors' ideas are useful to understanding the authoritarian notion of securitization that has informed Colombia's exceptionality policies and its judicial interpretation.

With this in mind, a theoretical remark must be made. The criminal law of prolonged periods of violence is deeply linked to nation-building processes, through which the extermination and criminalization of those who represent a threat to the nationalist project becomes both politically and morally justified. This relationship between criminal law and the nation-state is fundamental to understanding the epistemic violence that characterizes the criminal laws of Global South countries, where the violence of colonialism remains largely unresolved and continues to mark the rationale of securitization policies that are informed by a priori culpability and presented as civilizing instruments that must be endured by the socially excluded. This explains why most victims of the crimes of the powerful in Colombia belong to historically marginalized groups such as Afro-Colombians, indigenous people, *campesino* (rural) communities and the impoverished urban populations. In fact, during the years of the implementation of the statute of security, the collective rights of Afro and Indigenous communities were not fully recognized, which led to the dispossession of their lands by large landowners and local and international elites. Historically, the state's response to territorial demands of these communities has been characterized by repressive measures such as arbitrary detentions and direct criminalization. This can be illustrated by the experience of the Indigenous leader Manuel Quintin Lame, who was incarcerated more than 100 times for attempting to organize the Indigenous population against the state from 1915 to his death in 1967 (BBC 2017).

The extent of the violence deployed through the exceptionality policies such as the statute of security has prompted authors such as the Jesuit Father Javier Giraldo to describe the country's democracy as genocidal (Giraldo 1996). One particular narrative that exemplifies the everyday violence of the period that marks Giraldo's account is that of Ms Fabiola Lalinde's, which I will discuss in the remainder of this section.

3 Resisting the a Priori Culpability Approach to Criminal Law

> Alias "Jacinto", as a false positive of a fictitious and absurd war against the civilian population, finally became … LUIS FERNANDO LALINDE: arrested / tortured / disappeared / executed / denied / hidden for years / de-identified / de-humanized / finally exhumed and identified as TRUTH that denies the legitimacy of a criminal State; "Negative truth" for human dignity and for the conscious humanity of the planet. (Lalinde 2011)

Ms Fabiola Lalinde's struggle for the accountability of the extrajudicial execution of her son Luis Fernando Lalinde is a story of resistance to state crime. The event occurred in 1984 in Verdun, a rural part of the department of Antioquia.[6] The case is remarkably significant for victims of ED in Colombia and elsewhere because Fabiola Lalinde—now 83—organized the evidence of the case by herself, proving that her son was executed and subsequently forcibly disappeared by the Colombian army. Fabiola struggled for 12 years to prove that this was a case of false positives. The army denied the capture of Fernando and asserted that he could have used the alias of "Jacinto," a guerrilla fighter killed in combat. Ms Lalinde faced exile and was sent to prison after denouncing the disappearance of her son. Her imprisonment was justified under the Statute of Security (Lalinde 2011, 2018).

Ms Lalinde's experience of resistance to criminalization illustrates how human rights defenders have borne the brunt of the a priori culpability approach to criminal law in Colombia's conflict. This particular feature of the authoritarian character of the criminal law in Colombia is also related to the state's tendency to discredit and stigmatize victims of human rights violations triggered by the state's securitization narratives (UN 2012). In Colombia, this tendency has been facilitated by the implementation of exceptionality criminal policy informed by the discourses on counter-insurgency war, the war on drugs and the war on terror (Ramírez 2010).

In Ms Lalinde's case, her imprisonment resulted from a criminalization strategy through which the police placed two bags that contained cocaine in her house, and subsequently accused her of drug trafficking. The purpose of charging her with drug-trafficking was to delegitimize her narrative about the execution of her son, which with the solidarity of human rights

[6] Colombia is divided into 32 political territories called departments and a capital district.

activists and lawyers, she had managed to obtain a statement from the Inter-American Commission of Human Rights (IACHR) denouncing the drug-trafficking charges. This human rights body produced a resolution that became the first sanction against the Colombian state for human rights violations (Resolution 24/87 Inter-American Commission of Human Rights).

As indicated in an extract from Ms Lalinde's recollection of events, in which she recalls an interview with her lawyer in 1988:

> [My question] is why are there drugs in my house and in Luis Fernando's closet, if he has been missing for four years? The Answer: Human Rights organizations do not defend those involved in drug trafficking because that goes against their values, and with the drugs put in Luís Fernando's closet, the IACHR [Inter-American Commission on Human Rights] Resolution [fails]; in addition, since they found it in your home and you are the owner, you can be sentenced to 20 to 25 years in prison, with which they remove your from public life due to how uncomfortable you have made the State with your permanent complaint before international organizations… and [for the State] this serves as a means to deter other families of the disappeared who are trying to follow in your footsteps. (Lalinde 2011)

Eventually, Ms Lalinde's case was dismissed. To date, none of the members of the police who filed the bogus charges against her faced prosecution. This shows how in a prolonged period of violence, the state exacerbates the political use of criminal law against those who are deemed a threat to the realization of its political project. In Colombia, through the implementation of the Statute of Security, a priori culpability became normalized and revealed the authoritarian nature of criminal law, through which the fundamental rights of activists, human rights defenders and students are violated systematically.

Following the interpretive logic described earlier regarding the Supreme Court upholding the constitutionality of the presidential power to declare the state of exception, the court also upheld the constitutionality of the Statute of Security (Corte Suprema de Justicia [Colombia] 30 October 1978[7]). Legitimizing the authoritarian power of the state is part of what Cohen calls an "official denial," or highly organized forms of justifications which are "initiated, structured and sustained by massive resources of the modern state … a denial built into the ideological basis of the state" (Cohen 2001, 10).

[7] Sala Plena. Sentencia de octubre 30 de 1978. Magistrado ponente: Luis Carlos Sáchica.

This form of denial contributes to the continuation of structural violence caused by the crimes of the powerful in a prolonged conflict. In favouring the state's narrative on securitization, the accountability of the state is hindered, whereas the targeting and criminalization of the civilian population is legitimized. In this vein, the case of the Permanent Committee for the Defence of Human Rights is worth remembering. The Committee was created as a reaction to the Statute of Security and the human rights violations that it endorsed. Many of the founding members of the committee were assassinated, including Dr Héctor Abad Gómez, the human rights leader who helped Ms Lalinde bring her case before the IACHR (Ruiz and Torres 2019).

Thus far, I have described the historical relationship between Colombia's exceptionality criminal law and the state violence that has marked the country's prolonged conflict. In doing so, I have highlighted the authoritarian nature of the criminal law and its impact on the lives of historically marginalized groups, human rights defenders and political activists. Although Lalinde's case illustrates that some accountability of state crime has been possible within the Inter-American system of Human Rights, in local courts, the possibility for accountability has been largely prevented by "official denial", in Cohen's terms. This has given way to a context of chronic impunity of state crime in which the human impact of the a priori culpability approach to criminal law that has informed the exclusionary nation-building process of Colombia continues unabated.

A priori culpability is deeply linked to the paradigm of the nation-state. In this vein, the situation of Colombia illustrates the complexity surrounding nation-building processes in the Global South. As M. Mandani (2020, 7) suggests, the idea of the nation-state is marked by a stark contradiction: "the purpose of the state is to apply the law equally, while the purpose of the nation is to protect and valorize only members of the nation." In contexts of prolonged conflict, which is the case of many countries in the Global South, this contradiction has been exacerbated by the political use of the criminal law.

The next section will discuss the Democratic Security Policy (DSP) (2002–2010), which was the exceptionality policy that operated during the time that the false positives gained public recognition. Finally, I will draw on the narratives surrounding the accountability efforts at the Special Jurisdiction for Peace (JEP) and reflect on the tribunal's capacity to put forth a different narrative about the criminal law and its relationship with the authoritarian nature of the Colombian state.

4 Securitization in a Restricted Democracy: The Violence of the DSP

The incentives programme that led to cases of false positives was legally endorsed by the DSP. Implemented between 2002 and 2010, the DSP was an exceptionality policy and consisted of a series of securitization strategies based on the "criminal law of the enemy", which justified military interventions in marginalized neighbourhoods of major cities of Colombia, where according to the narrative of the government securitization was needed due to the presence of guerrilla forces, who were treated as organized criminality engaged in drug-trafficking (Rojas-Páez 2018).

In 2002, the DSP kick-started twelve military operations in *Comuna 13,* a district of Medellin whose inhabitants have been subjected to stigmatization and social ostracism since the 1980s (CNMH 2011). After the military interventions of 2002, the *Comuna* was controlled by paramilitaries, who carried out campaigns of "social cleansing" that meant hundreds of extrajudicial killings of mostly youngsters, whose bodies were thrown into a public dump known as *Escombrera,* one of the largest urban mass graves in Latin America, where forensic excavations have been difficult to conduct to this day (Rojas-Páez 2018).

The stigmatization of these marginalized citizens and the deployment of military forces in their neighbourhoods exemplify the continuation of the a priori culpability approach that has informed the authoritarian nature of the criminal policy of the Colombian conflict. The narrative surrounding the a priori culpability that supported the DSP was that the socially excluded are prone to criminality and therefore the radical transformation of their places becomes necessary through securitization rather than social justice measures.[8] In this vein, Manuel Iturralde (2016, 141) has maintained that the DSP is representative of what he terms "authoritarian liberalism", which is "a form of government that protects the interests of the status quo, even if violence must be used by sacrificing the rights of society's poorest and most vulnerable groups (which in Colombia account for half the population)."

The DSP was also influenced by the global expansion of the neoliberal economy, and thus, was presented as a means to guarantee security to local and international investors, mainly, extractive industries (Coleman 2018).

---

[8] This transformation is also characterized by urban development projects that lead to gentrification processes that causes a displacement of the population and broadens inequality. For an analysis of this in a comparative perspective see Cortes-Nieto and Ansari (2017).

This has proven to be detrimental for the territorial rights of Indigenous communities, *campesino,* and Afro-communities, who have faced forced displacement and deterritorialization.[9] The neoliberal idea of security entrenched in the DSP is also illustrated by the creation of specific military units to protect extractive projects in rural areas.

The DSP advanced a denial narrative of the political conflict which affected the everyday lives of marginalized Colombians and their security in different ways both in urban and in rural settings. For instance, when female leaders of the *Comuna 13*, a working-class neighbourhood in Medellín, denounced the link between the military forces and the paramilitaries which was fundamental for the "securitization" of the marginalized district, they were subjected to arbitrary detentions, inter-urban displacement and assassination such as in the case of Ana Teresa Yarce (Inter-American Court of Human Rights 2016).[10] Thus, the narrative of denial of the conflict promoted by the DSP went hand on hand with the tendency of discrediting the demands of human rights activists.

The DSP also used the War on Drugs discourse politically, against historically marginalized communities. By promoting the need of securitization of areas controlled by "narcoguerrilla forces", the government of the time implemented a massive programme of aerial spraying on coca crops, which caused displacement and disease in the inhabitants of regions subjected to aerial spraying in the departments of Chocó and Putumayo (Huezo 2017; Ramírez 2017).[11] These regions are inhabited by Afro-descent and Indigenous *campesino* communities, whose constant denunciations of the harm caused by aerial fumigation with glyphosate, were not heard by the advocates of DSP (Huezo 2017).[12] This particular aspect of the DSP draws

---

[9] As a result of the violence of displacement, which has also been caused by the armed confrontation for territorial control, the Constitutional Court has declared that more than 100 indigenous communities of the country are facing cultural and physical extermination (Constitutional order 04). Forced displacement has a direct link to the impunity of land dispossession which is historical feature of Colombia's conflict. For a recent analysis on this, *see* A. Berry (2017).

[10] Ana Teresa Yarce was a community leader at *Comuna 13*. Along with other female leaders of the Comuna, she was arbitrary detained in 2002 after military operation Orion and faced charges of terrorism. In 2004, she was assassinated by paramilitaries.

[11] Aerial fumigation has been endorsed by the US prohibitive approach to drug policy. This resulted from a US military aid programme known as Plan Colombia (1999-2015), through which Colombia became the third largest recipient of military aid in the world after Israel and Egypt. For a good analysis of the human and environmental harm of aerial fumigation, *see* Huezo (2017).

[12] The damage caused by aerial fumigation with glyphosate has been documented by several organizations. The pesticide is forbidden in many countries, including the European Union, however, it has been used in Colombia to halt coca cultivation.

attention to the structural harms caused by legal practices under the aegis of securitization and the relationship between the criminal law and the chronic impunity of the crimes of the powerful in Colombia and other Global South countries. As Atiles underscores, crimes of the powerful occur only if there is a permanent structure of power that prevents accountability through the imposition of institutional and epistemic frameworks that systematically ignore the harms inflicted on historically marginalized populations (Atiles 2018). Thus, the DSP intensifies the a priori culpability approach that has historically informed Colombia's criminal policy and emphasized an exclusionary idea of nationhood and citizenship.

The exclusionary idea of citizenship historically entrenched in exceptionality criminal law reflects forms of "cultural violence" (Galtung 1990) that have been detrimental to the lives of the aforementioned historically excluded groups. As Griffin (2019) suggests, in her analysis of the false positive case of graffiti artist Diego Felipe Becerra in 2011, cultural violence is embedded in the representational practices used to justify the death of those subjected to lethal practices by the state. In my view, the criminal law in a prolonged conflict and the denial practices that it facilitates are part of these representational practices. Diego Felipe was shot dead by a police agent when running away after spray painting under a bridge in Bogotá. The unarmed 16 year old was shot twice in the back (Griffin 2020). According to the police's testimony, the killing was justified because Diego and his friend had robbed a bus and were armed. The police unit planted a gun in the crime scene and hired a witness to confirm the cover story (Griffin 2020). This denial narrative has been normalized by the securitization policies such as the DSP, which promotes the idea that young people who engage in practices such as street art are inherently dangerous and therefore should become targets of state violence.

The deployment of securitization discourses, such as the DSP, intensified the historical stigmatization of the underprivileged, as observed by the experiences of poor and urban communities, such as Comuna 13 in Medellín and Soacha in Bogotá.[13] As a result, during the time of the DSP, inhabitants of these districts were subjected to direct state sanctioned violence,

[13] The spatial configuration of marginalized districts embodies the dynamics of social exclusion that have characterized Colombia's conflict. In fact, marginalized districts have resulted from forced migration and land dispossession.

exemplified by arbitrary detentions,[14] but also to lethal practices informed by cultural violence such as the false positives.

Against the above backdrop, I address the relationship between cultural violence and the securitization discourse that informed Colombia's criminal law throughout the conflict. An analytical tool that explains this relationship is the concept of "othering" which has been recently used by different scholars (Mbembe 2019) to pin down the violence informing the political justifications of violence within the Neoliberal globalization.

5 Othering: The Outcome of Authoritarian Criminal Law?

> Just because they were poor doesn't mean that they had no right to live. (A mother of a False Positives victim, as cited in Vivanco and Schoening 2014)

The systematic use of exceptionality criminal laws in Colombia have normalized a social process of "othering", endorsed by the exclusionary nation-building idea, which justifies the ostracization and even extermination of the socially excluded. As Gordon and Evans (2020) suggest, "that a soldier might knowingly kill an innocent civilian for such a small reward as a cash bonus or an extra couple of days leave, and generally with little coercion, suggests that there was little regard for the lives of those targeted."

Othering is a process that maintains the neoliberal social order by portraying poverty as inherently threatening (Gordon and Evans 2020). Through the process of othering, the socially excluded groups are portrayed as threats, and become targets of heinous crimes such as the false positives. Alas, the lives of these populations are not fully valued within the political imagination of those who have historically framed the image of the Colombian nation-state. Therefore, rather than the result of structural inequality, poverty and social exclusion are presented as morally reprehensible and threatening, serving to blame the poor for their poverty and their subsequent punishment (Gordon and Evans 2020).

[14] Within the DSP, incarceration rates increased dramatically. Studies show that the outrageous prison overcrowding resulted from an inappropriate use of preventive detentions, which primarily affected marginalized citizens of the country (Hernández Jiménez 2017).

As a result of the process of othering, the lives of the historically excluded groups are considered dispensable and this is why they become targets of state-sanction violence endorsed by securitization discourses and the criminal law. This situation is illustrative of the authoritarian nature of the criminal law and its dramatic impact on prolonged conflicts. The authoritarian nature of the criminal law is thus exacerbated due to theoretical principles of the modern liberal law theory. The state defines crimes and this prevents the accountability of its own criminality. Given that structural injustice is entrenched in the realm of the criminal law, which ignores collective and historical harm caused by the criminality of the powerful and authoritarian rationales such as a priori culpability, it is necessary to inquire about possibilities to overcome this form of epistemic violence.

6 Conclusion: Transitional Justice and the Continuing Failure to Prosecute Crimes of the Powerful

As the case of the Statute of Security and the DSP described in this chapter shows, in contexts of prolonged violence such as Colombia, practices of denial are legally justified by securitization policies inspired by discourses of a "friend or foe" polarization and the a priori culpability approach to criminal law. How are these practices, which justified systemic violence against civilians, to be interpreted within a transitional justice setting? In other words, what is to be done with the criminal law of the conflict and its violent rationality that informed the "othering" practices of the exclusionary nation-building process?

Observing the transitional justice settings of Global South countries shows that Colombia's experience with criminal law being used as a tool of violence and disempowerment is not unique. As Robert Meister (2011) asserts, this approach in South Africa under the apartheid regime criminal law justified the torture of the masses, causing thousands of deaths, like in the case of leader and political activist Stephen Biko.[15] In the case of Brazil, Meyer and Carvalho (2020) show in their analysis of sexual crimes

[15] Biko was the founder of the Black consciousness movement during the Apartheid regime in South Africa. He was tortured and died of brain damage in police custody on 12 September 1977. According to the official narrative of the Apartheid regime, Biko had died as a consequence of a hunger strike. In 1997, the TRC stablished that Biko died as a consequence of torture conducted by the police.

during the dictatorship, that even today, "most judges have been reluctant to accept the idea that the crimes perpetrated by state agents during the dictatorship were tantamount to crimes against humanity" (Meyer and Carvalho 2020). This occurs despite the Gomes Lund case in 2010, through which the ICtHR declared that the crimes of the dictatorship are gross violations of human rights that require investigation and prosecution (Meyer and Carvalho 2020). While in South Africa, transitional justice approaches absolved many of human rights violations, in Brazil, even an ICtHR judgement can be reasoned away under the logic of "official denials."

Whether transitional justice mechanisms will continue to fail to achieve their purported goals of enduring peace, reconciliation, and non-repetition will be put to the test in Colombia. On 26 September 2016, the Colombian government signed a peace agreement with the major guerrilla group of the multi-actor conflict of the country: the FARC (Armed Revolutionary Forces of Colombia). The peace accord meant the formal termination of the armed confrontation between the FARC and the Colombian state, which lasted for more than 50 years. The peace treaty created the JEP (Special Jurisdiction for Peace), a transitional justice tribunal charged with investigating and prosecuting crimes committed during the armed conflict. In 2019, one of the military commanders responsible for the emblematic case of false positives in Soacha was granted conditional and anticipated liberty by the JEP.[16] According to the tribunal, the commander was granted the procedural benefit because he accepted that the horrific crimes had been committed "in relation to the armed conflict" (Giraldo 2019).

According to Giraldo (2019), Ms Idaly Garcerá, the mother of one of the Soacha victims, Diego Alberto Tamayo Garcerá, appealed the decision that granted conditional liberty to one of the commanders involved in the false positive case, asserting that the crime had not been part of the armed conflict. For Ms Garcerá and her legal representatives, the ruling by JEP was wrong in associating the assassination of Diego with the armed conflict. According to the appellant: Diego's death "was not an attack aimed at any armed actor, nor one that sought to control more territory or gain an advantage, but instead it was part of a directed plan to gain personal benefits …".

Diego Alberto's case shares common elements with those of Fabio Lalinde, Ana T. Yarce, and Diego Becerra outlined in this chapter. On the one hand, the armed conflict was instrumentalized to justify their

[16] Soacha is a marginalized municipality of Cundinamarca near Bogotá. Many of the victims of the False Positives were inhabitants of this municipality. Thanks to the denunciations of the mothers of these victims, the heinous crime of False Positives of gained local and international recognition in 2008.

assassination under the aegis of securitization. On the other hand, the assassinations resulted from the a priori culpability approach to criminal law, which through the systemic exceptionality criminal policy facilitated the systemic denial of the crimes of the powerful, which have affected the lives of historically marginalized groups in Colombia. In this vein, a major challenge of JEP will be to advance a victim centred approach to criminal law, which puts forth a different rationality to state crime and the social harm that has caused. This will not be only a matter of retributive justice against individual perpetrators as modern criminal law will suggest. Addressing the historical injustice ensued by the a priori culpability approach to criminal law implemented in the country's conflicted history seems necessary. Memorialization rather than denial may pave the way for moral redress and historical justice.

References

Atiles, José. 2018. Frank Pearce and the Colonial State Crimes: Contributions to a Research Agenda. In *Revisiting Crimes of the Powerful: Marxism, Crime and Deviance*, ed. S. Bittle, L. Snider, and S. Tomnbs et al., 309–321. London and New York: Routledge.

Barreto-Rozo, Antonio. 2011. *La Generación del Estado de Sitio: El juicio a la anormalidad institucional en la Asamblea Nacional Constituyente de 1991 [The Generation of the State of Siege: The Trial of Institutional Abnormality in the 1991 National Constituent Assembly.]*. Bogotá: Universidad de los Andes, Uniandes.

BBC News Mundo. 2017. Quién era Manuel Quintín Lame, el colombiano que inspiró la primera guerrilla indígena de América Latina [Who Was Manuel Quintín Lame, the Colombian Who Inspired Latin America's First Indigenous Guerrilla]. *BBC News*, October 6, 2017. https://www.bbc.com/mundo/noticias-america-latina-41507530.

Benjamin, Walter. 2007. Critique of Violence. In *Reflections: Essays, Aphorisms, Autobiographical Writings*, ed. Peter Demetz, 248. New York: Schocken Books.

Berry, Alberto. 2017. Reflections on injustice, inequality and land conflict in Colombia. *Canadian Journal of Latin American and Caribbean Studies*, 42 (3): 277–297.

Centro Nacional de Memoria Histórica [CNMH]. 2011. *La Huella invisible de la Guerra Desplazamiento Forzado en la Comuna 13* [The Invisible Footprint of the War Forced Displacement in Comuna 13]. Report. Bogotá: CNMH. http://www.centrodememoriahistorica.gov.co/descargas/informes2011/informe_comuna13_la_huella_invisible_de_la_guerra.pdf. Accessed 31 May 2021.

Cohen, Stanley. 2001. *States of Denial: Knowing About Atrocities and Suffering*. Cambridge: Polity Press.

Coleman, L. 2018. *Global Social Fascism: Violence, Law and Twenty-First Century Plunder*. Working paper, University of Sussex, Centre for Global Political Economy, Brighton, UK.

Comisión Nacional sobre la Desaparición de Personas [CONADEP]. 1984. *Nunca Más. Informe de la Comisión Nacional sobre la Desaparición de Personas* [Never Again. Report of the National Commission on the Disappearance of Persons]. Buenos Aires: EUDEBA.

Cortes-Nieto, Johanna and Moniza Rizzini Ansari. 2017. Securitising Street Populations: Investment-Led Growth in Rio de Janeiro and Bogota. *Birkbeck Law Review*, 5 (1): 29–58.

Davis, Angela. 2016. *If They Come in the Morning*. London: Verso Books.

Galtung, Johan. 1990. Cultural Violence. *Journal of Peace Research* 27 (3): 291–305.

Giraldo, Johan. 1996. *Colombia: The Genocidal Democracy*. USA: Common Courage Press.

Giraldo, Johan. 2019. Las ineptitudes de la JEP [The Ineptitude of the JEP].

Gordon, Eleanor. 2017. Crimes of the Powerful in Conflict-Affected Environments: False Positives, Transitional Justice and the Prospects for Peace in Colombia. *State Crime Journal* 6 (1): 132–155.

Gordon, E. and E. Evans. 2020. Gente de bien y falsos positivos, el costo humano de la indiferencia social estatal [Good People and False Positives, the Human Cost of State Social Indifference]. *Dialogos de saberes,* 53: 89–122.

Griffin, Alba. 2019. *Reading the Wall in Bogotá: Imaginaries of Violence in the Urban Visual Landscape*. PhD diss.: Newcastle University, CORE.

Griffin, Alba. 2020. No somos falsos somos positivos:teorías vernáculas sobre la violencia política y cotidiana en el puente del grafitero [We Are Not False We Are Positive: Vernacular Theories About Political and Daily Violence on the Bridge of the Graffiti Artist]. In *Pedagogías de la disidencia en América Latina*, ed. Oliart, Patricia. Lima: La Siniestra Ensayos.

Hernández Jiménez, Norberto. 2017. *Derecho penal de la cárcel. Una mirada al contexto colombiano [Criminal Law of Prison: A Look at the Colombian Context Based on the Punitive Turn and the Tendency to Greater Incarceration]*. Colombia: Siglo del Hombre Editories.

Higuera Silva, Angelica. 2010. *Remember, Remember the 6th and 7th of November: Colombia 1985 Siege of the Palace of Justice*. PhD diss.: Concordia University, Canada.

Huezo, Alexander. 2017. Eradication Without Prior Consultation: The Aerial Fumigation of Coca in the Black Communities of the Colombian Pacific. *Revue Canadienne Des Études Latino-Américaines et Caraïbes [Canadian Journal of Latin-American and Caribbean Studies]* 42 (3): 375–399.

Iturralde, Manuel. 2010. Democracies Without Citizenship: Crime and Punishment in Latin America. *New Criminal Law Review: An International and Interdisciplinary Journal* 13 (2): 309–332.

Iturralde, Manuel. 2016. Colombian Prisons as a Core Institution of Authoritarian Liberalism. *Crime, Law and Social Change* 65 (3): 137–162.

Lalinde, Fernando. 2011. Un caso paradigmático de los 80 de alias 'Jacinto' como 'falso positivo [A Paradigmatic Case of the 80s of Alias 'Jacinto' as 'False Positive'] a Luis Fernando como Verdad. En Centro de Investigación y Educación Popular/ Programa por la Paz (CINEP/PPP). Negativa. *Noche y Niebla*: 220–234.

Lalinde, Fernando. 2018. *Hagan hablar al archivo, no dejen que guarde silencio [Make the Archive Speak, Don't Let It Be Silent]*. National University of Colombia. https://verdadabierta.com/hagan-hablar-al-archivo-no-dejen-guarde-silencio-fabiola-lalinde/. Accessed 31 May 2021.

Leal, Francisco. 2006. La política de seguridad democrática 2002–2005 [The Political of Democratic Safety 2002–2005] *Análisis Político* (57): 3–30.

Mandani, M. 2020. *Neither Settler Nor Native: The Making and Unmaking of Permanent Minorities*. Belknap Press: An Imprint of Harvard University Press.

Meister, Robert. 2011. *After Evil: A Politics of Human Rights (Columbia Studies in Political Thought/Political History)*. Columbia University Press.

Mbembe, Achille. 2019. *Necropolitics*. Duke University Press Books.

Meyer, Emilio and Claudia Carvalho. 2020. Sexual Crimes and Transitional Justice Before Courts in Brazil: Accountability for Crimes Against Humanity. In *Criminal Legalities in the Global South*, ed. G. Radics and P. Ciocchini, 198–215. Routledge.

Norrie, Alan. 2017. *Justice and the Slaughter Bench: Essays on Law's Broken Dialectic*. Abingdon: Routledge.

O'Brien, M. 2008. Criminal Degradations of Consumer Culture. In *Global Harms: Ecological Crime and Speciesism*, ed. R. Sollund, 35–51. New York: Nova Science Publisher Incorporated.

Palau, Mariana. 2020. The 'False Positives' Scandal That Felled Colombia's Military Hero. *The Guardian*, December 7. https://www.theguardian.com/world/2020/nov/19/colombia-false-positives-killings-general-mario-montoya-trial.

Pearce, Frank. 1976. *Crimes of the Powerful: Marxism, Crime and Deviance*. Pluto Press.

Perea. 2015. Limpieza social : una violencia mal nombrada [Social Cleansing: A Misnamed Violence]. *Centro Nacional de Memoria Histórica.*

Ramírez, Maria Clemencia. 2010. Maintaining Democracy in Colombia Through Political Exclusion, States of Exception, Counterinsurgency and Dirty War. In *Violent Democracies in Latin America*, ed. E.D. Arias and D.M. Goldstein. Durham, NC: Duke University Press.

Ramírez, Maria Clemencia. 2017. Las conversaciones de paz en Colombia y el reconocimiento de los cultivadores de coca como víctimas y sujetos de derechos diferenciados [Peace Talks in Colombia and the Recognition of Coca Growers as Victims and Subjects of Differentiated Rights]. *Revue Canadienne Des Études [Canadian Journal of Latin American and Caribbean Studies]* 42 (3): 350–374.

Rojas-Bolaños, Omar Eduardo, and Fabián Leonardo Benavides. Silva. 2017. *Ejecuciones Extrajudiciales en Colombia 2002–2010: Obediencia Ciega en Campos de Batalla Ficticios* [Extrajudicial Executions in Colombia 2002–2010: Blind Obedience On Fictional Battlefields]. Bogotá: Universidad Santo Tomás.

Rojas-Páez, Gustavo. 2018. Narratives from the Margins of the State: Resisting the Politics of Exceptionality in the Comuna 13. *Oñati Socio-Legal Series* 8 (6): 901–924.

Schmitt, Cart. 1983. *Der Hüter der Verfassung [The Guardian of the Constitution]*. Tecnos.

Ruiz, L., and E. Torres. 2019. El caso del Comité Permanente de Derechos Humanos nos dice de las violencias en Medellin [The Case of the Standing Committee on Human Rights Tells Us About the Violence in Medellin]. In *Dimensiones y perspectivas acerca de la violencia en American Latina [Dimensions and perspectives on violence in Latin America]*, ed. J. Ocaña, 269–288.

Umaña, Camilo. 2017. Impunity: In the Search of a Socio-Legal Concept Elucidations from a State Crime Case Study. PhD diss., University of Ottawa & University of the Basque Country.

United Nations [UN]. 2012. Annual Report of the UNHCR. Doc. A/HRC/19/21/Add.3.

Vivanco, José Miguel and Max Schoening. 2014. Opinion | Colombia's Compromise with Murder. *The New York Times*, November 12. https://www.nytimes.com/2014/11/13/opinion/colombias-compromise-with-murder.html.

Viljoen, Frans. 2021. South Africa Needs to Address the Lingering Legacy of Its Police Using Excessive Force. *The Conversation*, March 30. https://theconversation.com/south-africa-needs-to-address-the-lingering-legacy-of-its-police-using-excessive-force-157695.

Case Laws

Corte Suprema de Justicia [Colombia]. *Rapporteur magistrate: Luis Carlos Sáchica.* Introduced in House October 30, 1978.

Inter American Commission of Human Rights. *Caso 9620 COLOMBIA, Resolution 24/87.* Introduced in House September 16, 1988. https://www.cidh.oas.org/annualrep/87.88sp/Colombia9620.htm.

Inter American Court of Human Rights. *Yarce y otras v Colombia* [Yarce and Others v Colombia]. Introduced in House November 22, 2016. http://www.corteidh.or.cr/docs/casos/articulos/seriec_325_esp.pdf.

The Tribunal of the District of Cundinamarca. *Rad. 54498–60–01–135–2008–80006–05.* Introduced in House July 30, 2013.

Decrees and Statutes

Diario Oficial. *Decreto 1923 de 1978. Por el cual se dictan normas para la protección de la vida, honra y bienes de las personas y se garantiza la seguridad de los asociados* [Decree 1923 of 1978. By Which Rules Are Issued for the Protection of the Life, Honor and Property of People and the Safety of Associates is Guaranteed]. http://www.suin-juriscol.gov.co/viewDocument.asp?ruta=Decretos/1870140.

Part II

Economic Interests of the State

5

Formless Punishment and Exclusion: Criminalizing the Migrant Through the Indian National Register of Citizens

Suraj Gogoi

1 Introduction

It is often said that South Asia is the graveyard of social theory. It is a place where most social categories face tremendous challenges from the various social, political, and religious complexities/multiplicities prevalent in the region. Graveyard, thus, is an apt metaphor to describe the diversity and complexity of the region. Similarly, the National Register of Citizens (NRC) process is a graveyard to the existing citizenship rules and frameworks in India. NRC, along with the proposed National Population Register (NPR) and Citizenship Amendment Act (CAA) 2019 changes the categories of self, subject, community, bureaucracy, and the nature of the Indian state. This chapter explores the criminalization of migration under this legal regime. It exposes the harsh use of detention against those who are defined as illegal immigrants. Furthermore, it argues that the legal procedure experienced by those accused of illegal immigration lacks transparency and denies the accused's basic rights. The NRC is an exceptional register of citizens carried out in the state of Assam in Northeast India. First prepared in 1951 under a directive of the Ministry of Home Affairs, it is currently being updated on orders of the Supreme Court (SC) of India. Sanctioned by the SC in 2014 on the basis of The Citizenship (Registration of Citizens and Issue of National Identity Cards) Rules of 2003, the process aimed to identify

S. Gogoi (✉)
School of Liberal Arts, RV University, Bengaluru, India
e-mail: surajgogoi@rvu.edu.in

G. B. Radics and P. Ciocchini (eds.), *Criminal Legalities and Minorities in the Global South*, Palgrave Socio-Legal Studies, https://doi.org/10.1007/978-3-031-17918-1_5

"illegal immigrants" from Bangladesh who entered Assam on or after midnight of 24 March 1971. The order of the SC came on 17 December 2014 in *Assam Sanmilita Mahasangha vs. Union of India* which directed to update NRC 1951 for Assam by January 2016. The NRC made documentary evidence called "legacy data" necessary to prove oneself as a citizen.[1] The final NRC, published on 31 August 2019, excluded a total of over 1.9 million persons, effectively calling into question their citizenship and leaving them in a state of limbo.

But the NRC is more than just a headcount roster. It is a political document replete with social and cultural sensibilities.[2] Assam's NRC 1951, which was basically a rough notebook carried out by ill-trained census enumerators, became the guiding document to claim the current version of the NRC process.[3] It is just one component in Assam's multi-pronged citizenship determination regime. Furthermore, the demand and justification for such an enormous citizenship exercise came first from the Assamese nationalist whose base is primarily its upper-caste middle class, popularly called as caste-Assamese middle class. The foundation of this regional nationalism in Assam [termed in existing literature as "little nationalism"] is laid out succinctly by historian Amalendu Guha (1979, 455) in the following manner: "Little nationalism emerges as the ideology of the region-based small bourgeoisie (i.e. the regional middle classes) who feared competition from middle classes of other regions as well as from the pan-Indian big bourgeoisie. Little nationalism, therefore, stood for an exclusive control of the regional markets by their respective middle classes." The NRC, therefore, is nothing but an expression of the economic and political interests of Assamese nationalists.

[1] Legacy data is a patrilineal family tree showing ones relative to be residing in Assam before the cut-off date of 24th March 1971. It comprised two lists of documents—List A and List B. List A included 1951 NRC, electoral roll(s) up to 24 March (midnight) 1971, land and tenancy records, citizenship certificate, permanent residential certificate, refugee registration certificate, any government issued license/certificate, government service/ employment certificate, bank or post office accounts, birth certificate, state educational board or university educational certificate, Court records/processes, passport and any LIC policy. List B was meant for those candidates who could not or did not have any document that was on before 1971. This list contained 8 other documents: birth certificate, land document, board/university certificate, bank/LIC/post office records, circle officer/gaon panchayat secretary certificate in case of married women, electoral roll, ration card, any other legally acceptable document.

[2] NRC is the result of a history of the anti-Bengali sensibilities. It began in the early nineteenth century and climaxed during the Assam Movement (1979–1985) that concretized hate for the so-called outsider forever in the domain of public life.

[3] 1951 NRC was carried out in Assam alongside the 1951 census. It borrowed 11 of the 14 questions that was part of the decadal census on India. The excluded questions were: if the respondent was a displaced person, bilingual, and 'indigenous person on Assam'. It was a rough notebook of names and was by no means a rigorous practice. Enumerators also were known to leave out names of people living in hostile areas.

Yet this seemingly legal-rational process sanctioned by the SC has its consequences and is a painful and violent experience for many. The treatment of the "doubtful" or identified as "illegal" persons in the legal and administrative systems of the NRC is far from being "value-neutral" and operates based on tremendous bias. This document-heavy and resource-consuming process has driven many people to suicide and depression. It has also left millions of them impoverished, traumatised, vulnerable, violated, and disenfranchised. Thus, the spirit of this chapter is to highlight: (1) the affinity between citizenship and the criminalization of suspected foreigners in the state of Assam in India, and (2) how detention in the NRC process is a *formless punishment* and not really detention.[4] The chapter will limit our focus to institutions such as the Foreigners Tribunals (FTs) and the Border Police Organisation in Assam and the various rules, orders and acts that concern the emerging citizenship regime in India. These two institutions are crucial to the NRC process and they play a role in animating the affinity between the criminal treatment of the detenu (person who is kept under detention) and the citizenship process in NRC. Lastly, the notion of formless punishment will be discussed by looking at a Guwahati High Court Judgement and how there has been a constant violation of the due process and exceptions made in the law to forward the new citizenship regime in Assam, a brainchild of the Assamese nationalist.

2 The Foreigner, the "Illegal", and the Citizen

There are many aspects of the NRC process that begs elaborate discussion and engagement. The definition of "foreigner" and "illegal migrant" used in Indian law should be clarified for our understanding of citizenship in India. The Foreigners Act (1946) deems a "foreigner" to be "a person who is not a citizen of India".[5] This same definition of "foreigner" is used by the FTs in their NRC cases. On the other hand, The Citizenship Act (1955) which

[4] I borrow the concept of *formless* from Michel Foucault "docile body" in his work *Discipline and Punish* where the body undergoing punishment is seen as a text. The punished body can be used as a text to study both NRC and Assamese nationalism.

[5] See The Foreigners Act, 1946 2(1)a. This particular definition of the foreigner was included through an amendment in 1957 which came into effect on 19 January 1957. It brought Pakistani (primarily that of East Pakistan and present-day Bangladesh) nationals under the purview of the foreigner. Prior to this amendment, Pakistani nationals were not subjected to the provisions and rules of the Foreigners Act of 1946 (cf. White Paper on Foreigners' Issue, White Paper hereof).

came into effect on the 30th of December that year defines "illegal migrant" as a "foreigner who has entered into India" without a valid passport or other travel documents.[6] This definition makes it clear that the concept of citizen is also tied up with boundary maintenance and movement across its territorial borders. This makes the citizenship process *also* an administrative affair.

FTs were empowered by the Government of India through The Foreigners (Tribunals) Order (1964) to refer to citizenship cases and questions.[7] In the same year, the Assam State Government set up four tribunals to attend to the cases of "suspected infiltrants." The members of the tribunals were entrusted with the duty to scrutinize the cases of infiltration before serving them "Quit India notices". By 1968, there were nine FTs in Assam with headquarters in Tezpur, Guwahati, Nowgaon (2), Sibsagar, Goalpara, Dhubri, Jorhat, and Barpeta (c.f. White Paper 2012).[8] These FTs function like a civil court with the power to summon (and examine) witnesses and documents (such as List A and List B documents asked in the NRC process).[9] The FTs operated till 1983 based on the 1964 order. It was ably aided by The Foreigners Act of 1946.

The year 1983 marks a significant departure in the procedure of FTs as that same year the Illegal Migrants (Determination by Tribunals) Act (IMDT Act) was passed by the Government of India in the middle of the Assam Movement. The Foreigners Act of 1946 placed the burden of proof on the applicant or the citizen. The IMDT Act of 1983 reversed this and placed the burden of proof on the State to prove someone as a foreigner if someone's citizenship is brought into question. Two years later and after the Assam Accord was signed, Article 6A was inserted into The Citizenship (Amendment) Act of 1985. Article 6A made an exception for the state of Assam, thus changing the terms of citizenship for the state. The new Article 6A in the amendment Citizenship Act of 1985 reads as follows:

(1) Persons of Indian origin who entered Assam from specified territories (Bangladesh) before 1 January 1966 were deemed Indian citizens.

[6] See The Citizenship Act, 1955 2(1)b.

[7] Foreigners (Tribunals) Order, 1964 Gen. S. R. & O. 1401 (India). FTs are created as per Clause 2 of the Order.

[8] It is noted in the White Paper that 35,080 cases were referred to those 4 tribunals till the end of August 1965.

[9] See Foreigners (Tribunals) Order, 1964, 2 (1).

(2) Persons of Indian origin who entered Assam from specified territories between 1 January 1966 and 25 March 1971 were to be removed from electoral rolls and eligible for full Indian citizenship after ten years.[10]
(3) Persons of Indian origin who entered Assam from specified territories after 25 March 1971 were to be detected and deported.

The FTs have been very active in processing cases related to alleged "foreigners" according to the provisions laid by the Foreigners Act, 1946. The anti-foreigner agitation also known as the Assam Movement certainly acted as a catalyst to finding more alleged foreigners, the demands of which came from hardliner Assamese nationalists. In 2019, an amendment was again made to the Foreigners (Tribunals) Order of 1964 which empowered State Governments and Union Territories in India to set up their own FTs.[11] The number of cases that these FTs have processed is staggering. It is recorded that to date the Supreme Court has referred over 230,000 cases to the FTs of people who are listed as "Doubtful Voters," or in-short "D-Voters".[12] A D-voter designation can be removed only after a judgement/order given by the FTs. Between 1985 to 2016, a total of 468,934 referrals were made to the Tribunals. Of those cases, 80,194 were declared to be 'foreigners' (Amnesty International India Report 2018). And as of December 2020, there are 83,000 cases of pending D-Voters. A staggering amount of 63,959 *ex parte* judgements were passed by March 2019 (Mustafa 2019). In most of these cases, only a 24-hour notice was served to attend the hearing and are declared foreigners "without any application of mind or affording the person a chance to make an effective claim for citizenship" (Mitra 2021). These very FTs are also responsible for deciding the fate of the 1.9 million people who were left out of the final NRC list.

As noted earlier, the first set of demands for counting "illegal" citizens was placed by hardliner Assamese nationalists. Antagonism between the Assamese and the Bengalis started in the early decades of the 1830s when the Bengali language was introduced as an official language in courts and

[10] This period of 10 years is also a part of the Assam Accord (point 5.6) signed between the Government of India, the Government of Assam, and the All-Assam Students' Union (AASU) signed the Assam Accord on 15 August 1985 to end the six years of Assam Movement.

[11] Foreigners (Tribunals) Amendment Order, 2019 § 3(A)(16). Also, see Angshuman Choudhury (14 June 2019) Home Minister Amit Shah Expands Foreigner Tribunals across India, *Asia Times*.

[12] D-Voters refers to those persons whose citizenship is disputed by the Election Commission (EC) of India. The EC carried out a massive revision of its electoral rolls in 1997 and found 231,657 such cases which the SC referred to the FTs.

schools in Assam.[13] Although Assamese was introduced in 1873, by then, competition, animosity, and rivalry were already deeply entrenched. The educated Bengali who filled the colonial bureaucracy in departments such as Posts, Police, Forest, and Telegraphs in the nineteenth century were seen with sufficient hate by the emerging Assamese literati and the middle class (Barpujari et al. 1980). British stereotypes of the Assamese nobility as "indolent," "incompetent," and "corrupt" served as justifications behind the British preference of the Bengalis over the local Assamese to fill the colonial bureaucracy in Assam (*ibid*). Seemingly, it was the upper class and nobility in Assam who lost jobs because of the introduction of the Bengali language in the 1830s. This became part of the economic basis of hate of the middle-class Assamese of the Bengali irrespective of their religion.

Once Bengali language problems became a social rift in 1873, Assamese fury became directed at poor peasants from erstwhile East Bengal who started to migrate in the early decades of the twentieth century. These poor peasants migrated to Assam due to a combination of factors including but not limited to the encouragement of the colonial government to settle in the fertile riverine plains of the Brahmaputra valley, a less exploitative land tenure system in Assam in comparison to East Bengal, lower population density, and flooding (Sharma 2011). The disgruntled elite-Assamese class started forming a strong "two-level national consciousness" (Guha 1980, 962) of regional and national—national consciousness of aligning with Indian National Congress and anti-colonial consciousness and at the same time, a sense of belonging to the region of Assam with the Assamese language as its defining marker of identity. Additionally, they became very anxious about the new "immigrants" who might return as Bangla speakers in the Census, thus allegedly damaging the status of Assamese as the majority language in the region and eroding the base of the ruling class in Assam, both politically and economically. The Assamese middle class could successfully forward the narrative that the "Bengalis" (or "Bangladeshis" as they are pejoratively called in Assam) are indeed the enemy of the Assamese people and must be othered in social, political, and cultural life.[14] Numerous

---

[13] It will be pertinent to note here that Bengali replaces Persian as a court language by the British as it was getting difficult and expensive to get Persian scribes.

[14] I grew up in Assam being told to be cautious and hate the "Bangladeshi". "Bangladeshi" was always seen as unwanted, immoral, polluting beings, and is treated with disgust in everyday life. Such relations and sentiments form the moral and psychological background on which NRC must be read. Also, see Suraj Gogoi (20 October 2019) Psychology behind NRC mirrors narrow, dominating side of Assamese language, and its fragile nationalism, cultural identity, *Firstpost*.

political parties were formed in the twentieth century targeting the question of migration and Assamese culture. Important civil society organizations such as Assam Literary Society (est. in 1917) and AASU made protection of Assamese language, culture, and economy from the Bangladeshi their sole motive of organizational life. They made the "Bangladeshi" an evil, "scavenger", and "encroacher" in Assam who at once should be detected, deported, stripped of basic political and economic rights, detained, and eliminated.[15] In short, the NRC is a culmination of the material interest of the Assamese middle class which has managed to use the legal infrastructure to protect its class interest and increase its hegemony in contemporary Assam. The maze of the bureaucratic and legal ensemble created by the NRC machine must not lose sight of the history of social libido in Assam which assembles a complicated history of migration, struggle for Assamese as official language, minority politics, many partitions and cartographic redrawing, political-economy, and caste-Assamese culture.

3 NRC's Evolving Web of Enforcement

The NRC office, along with its multiple Seva Kendras,[16] worked closely with three other state-run institutions—Border Police, Foreigners' Tribunals (FTs), and Detention Centers. The Assam Border Police Organisation (ABPO) is a wing of the Assam Police which is particularly entrusted with the duty to detect and deport foreigners. The Border Police was established primarily to implement the Government of India's "Prevention of Infiltration into India of Pakistani Nationals" (PIP) Scheme (White Paper 2012). In other words, it is also a border maintenance organization. The PIP scheme aimed to deport "infiltrators" back to Bangladesh (erstwhile East Pakistan). In 2018, all the 159 Watch Posts of ABPO were made active which are in 20 districts of Assam.

The NRC, Border police, and FTs are organically related. When a case must be tried in the FT, the border police have to make a reference. However, as the burden of proof is on the suspect,[17] the border police who

[15] See Samyak Ghosh and Suraj Gogoi (14 April 2019) What do walls in Guwahati tell us about its people and their history, *The Wire*.

[16] The Seva Kendras are an essential window of the NRC operation through which people connect.

[17] In 2005 in *S. Sonowal vs Union of India* IMDT Act was repealed, thereby placing the burden of proof back to the applicant or the alleged foreigner and reverting to the terms stated in The Foreigners' Act, 1946.

refer to such cases are hardly cross-examined (Sagar 2019). When the border police send a notice saying that one is a foreigner, that notice need not be based on any reason or proof. To add to that, FTs members often refuse to give the suspects a copy of the inquiry report based on which their citizenship is questioned. Such refusal shows only one aspect of illegality involved in the NRC process. Being kept in the dark, "the suspects" have no concrete basis to prepare their defense (*ibid*). Such arbitrary powers and impunity given to the Border Police are based on a colonial law, specifically, The Foreigners Act of 1946. The FT is a quasi-judicial body because of the nature of its civil proceeding. Although it is not obliged to follow the rules of civil proceedings, under Section 30 of The Code of Civil Procedure, the FT also holds the power to call witnesses, and to use coercion. Lastly, NRC authorities are administrative agents, but the manner in which they work is similar to FT members. Such procedural similarities make them almost parallel bodies (Saikia and Gogoi 2018). In 2014, the government appointed 64 new FT members, taking the total number of FTs in the state to 100. The Guwahati High Court in 2019 issued a notification of 200 more FTs in the state and appointment of 221 new members. The High Court also reduced the age requirement from 45 years to 35 and the experience in the judicial service from 10 to 7 years to become a member of the FTs (Sagar 2019).

Moreover, under the NRC, FT's were given the power to send any doubtful voter and the people who were declared as non-citizen through the NRC process to detention centres which are housed in regional jails. At present, Assam has 6 functional detention centres located within the six jails in Assam in the districts of Silchar, Goalpara, Tezpur, Kokrajhar, Dibrugarh, and Jorhat. Sen (2020) writes about the detention facilities in the following manner:

> At least ten people died in these centers in 2019 alone. There has been a total of 30 deaths since 2016 in Assam. People who have spent time in the centers agree that they are worse than hell. There is no segregation between undertrials, convicts, and detainees....Detainees face punishment meant for criminals. In crowded prisons, the rights of detainees are erased every day to the point of being non-existent. The centers are almost like spaces of legal exception and indifference.

There is no distinction made between the ones who are detained through the NRC process and the normal convicts in these jails. This is again a case of conflating the criminal and administrative.

A White Paper notes that once a person is declared a foreigner by the FTs, they are taken to custody and kept in detention centres till they are deported or pushed back to their country of origin. The difference is "in the case of push back, there is no need for acceptance of the person by the Border Guards of Bangladesh (BGB)…. deportation, on the other hand, is a proper meeting between the Border Security Force of India and BGB" notes the White Paper. In case the BGB refuses to take back the persons, they become "stateless" (White Paper 2012). The FT's have operated with tremendous biases and have been accused by many political commentators of functioning like "kangaroo courts" (Sagar 2019).

The way FTs dispose of cases and the nature of detention that follows for declared "foreigners" shows the inhumanity of the NRC process. The first problem with the FTs is that both the aspects of *fair trial* and *fair representations* are violated. The "alleged foreigner" is already disadvantaged as the burden of proof lies on them. The first aspect of fairness is related to the right to have legal representation. It has been noted that legal aid for most cases is absent or inadequate. This failure stands in direct violation of Article 21 of the Indian Constitution which states that every person shall be treated equally before the law and legal aid is considered as an indispensable part of reasonable, just, and fair procedure. It is also related to Article 14 of the constitution which extends the provision of equality of law even to "foreigners." The second aspect related to the lack of fairness argument has to do with the nature of documentary proofs which are required if a case is referred to the FTs. The standards of the Indian Evidence Act of 1872, which is to be read in conjunction with the Criminal Law Amendment Act, is applied in those cases in which the court must scrutinize documents. In proving one's citizenship, the applicant is bound by those standards of documents stated in the Evidence Act which is that the document is to be produced in original form or through certified copies (Amnesty International India Report 2018). This gets tricky when the burden of proof is shifted to the accused because a secondary copy will be admissible only if the loss of the original can be proved, which is many times hard to do.[18] This use of the Indian

[18] Even if the document is from say 1971, it is still many decades old, and no one could have ever thought that such documents in that form would become fundamental to one's citizenship. Moreover, the standards of record-keeping even in government institutions is very poor, but to demand it from people is an unfair ask itself. To add to that, people live precarious lives in precarious times (Indian Partition, Bangladesh Liberation War, Assam Movement, communal violence) and geographies (major earthquakes have taken place in Assam, two measuring over 8 in Richter Scale, it is also a state prone to multiple floods every year). All the above are general facts, the personal events are not even considered, making the nature of admissible documents an impossible, harsh, and unreal ask for a majority of people.

Evidence Act (the Code of Criminal Procedure as well used to summon witnesses by FTs) in a quasi-judicial court like the FTs shows us how in the verification of citizenship in Assam a criminal law is used in an exceptional manner. Unlike in a criminal trial where the accused is considered innocent until proven guilty, the FTs operate on a different consideration altogether. First, unlike the criminal trial, the person here is considered as a foreigner and the process and the burden of proving otherwise is solely on the applicant. In other words, at the beginning of the trial, one is de facto assumed to be illegal. "Once a citizen" writes Mitra (2021), "is declared to be a foreigner, criminality is imputed to them." Secondly, sending someone to detention is also a de factodecision how FTs have constantly acted although there is no such need to do so. It is an exception because the applicant does not enjoy the rights that a defendant has in a criminal trial in India making the process indeed exceptionally unfair.

The second important aspect to note is that the people who are detained following the judgements of the FTs are kept in detention centres. Until 2019, there was no Detention Manual for Assam or those detained in jails. In other words, there were no guidelines on how these people should be treated during their detention period. There have been instances where the detainees have been escorted and handcuffed while taken for medical treatment. There is no such rule to handcuff them to hospital beds, but many detainees were treated as such, thus violating Supreme Court guidelines (Amnesty International India Report 2018). As of July 2021, as many as 22 children were also inside the detention centres.[19] The FTs also did not make any exception for vulnerable populations such as pregnant or lactating mothers. Cases of 102-year-old persons being kept in detention were also evident. Detention of vulnerable populations bears testimony to the extremity of punishment involved in the NRC process, a punishment which is couched as detention.

Additionally, until 2019 the principle of *res judicata* did not apply for FTs.[20] In 2018, Guwahati High Court in *Anima Khatoon v. State of Assam* noted that because *res judicata* was not applicable to FTs and their opinions are not judgements, the government or the Border Police cannot be stopped from pursuing a new case against a defendant even if another FT had already ruled on the issue. It was only as late as 2019 did the Supreme

[19] Rahul Karmakar (July 20, 2021), 22 children in detention camps for foreigners, *The Hindu*.

[20] *Res judicata* is a doctrine that simply states that if a competent court has taken a decision on a matter, or has already passed judgement on it, there is no need for a fresh suit.

Court say that *res judicata* did apply to the FTs (Saha 2021). In *Abdul Kuddus v. Govt. of India*, the Supreme Court upheld the principle of *res judicata* and argued that opinion of the FTs is an order and a decision, despite the tribunals being quasi-judicial in nature. It argued that since those opinions can be challenged by writ petitions, it would be "incorrect" to say that orders by the FTs will not be considered when determining whether the principle of *res judicata* applies to a case (Gogoi and Sen 2022). As late as 5 May 2022, the Guwahati High Court in an order upheld the principle of res judicata as laid out in *Abdul Kuddus* and observed that *Anima Khatoon* is no longer a good law and sound public policy. This gives an indication as to how unfair the FT process has been throughout in the absence of this basic legal principle people were re-adjudicated as foreigners after they were declared Indian citizens, or were summoned multiple times by NRC authorities.

All in all, the FT process leaves a huge chasm of mistreatment in the exercise of citizenship registers in Assam. In a seemingly judicial and administrative affair, not only do people lack fair trial and legal representation, the processes and outcomes themselves are not clear whether it is entirely civil or if it is criminal. Although the proceedings of the FT process are not criminal trials, the high burden of proof placed on the state is shifted to the defendant who, many times, is unrepresented, and since the process is seen simply as administrative, Constitutional guarantees present in judicial proceedings are deemed inapplicable. Everyone is treated de facto as a suspect. Moreover, the "courts often rely on the conceptual slippage between the categories of foreigner and criminal to justify harsher and punitive legal frameworks to deal with foreigners" (Mitra 2021).

Year	Event
1946	Foreigner's Act 1946
1951	Assam NRC based on 1951 Census
1955	Citizenship Act 1955
1964	Foreigners Tribunal Order allowing identification and deportation of aliens
1975	Assam Agitation and anti-foreigner movement commences
1983	Illegal Migrants (Determination by Tribunal) Act is passed & Nellie Massacre takes place in February
1985	Assam Accord signed & End of Assam Agitation
1997	Election orders revision of Electoral Rolls in Assam and introduces D-Voter
2005	IMDT Act is struck down in Sonowal v. Union of India
2008	Guwahati HC sends D-Voters to Detention Centers
2013	Centre approves FTs
2014	SC orders NRC updation
2014	64 FTs were set up
2016	Assam Home Department gives nod to Detention Centers
2016	Citizenship (Amendment) Bill tabled in the Parliament

(continued)

Year	Event
2017	First NRC draft is published in Dec
2018	Second NRC draft is published in July
2019	Final NRC is published in August

Timeline of events in Assam

4 Detention Laws, Due Process, and the NRC

The aspect of detention carried out in the NRC process is crucial in making sense of the complexities involved in the new regimes of citizenship in India. The detention of "foreigners" and "illegal migrants" have been carried out prior to the implementation of the current version of the NRC process. The process became more intense after the D-Voter category was introduced. However, the repealing of the IMDT Act in 2005 made this process more difficult for the applicant as the burden of proof was shifted to the applicant.

Several laws in the colonial period had provisions of detention. Some of those laws are the Defence of the Realm Act of 1914, the Emergency Powers (Defence) Act of 1939, and the Anarchical and Revolutionary Crimes Act of 1919 or commonly known as the Rowlatt Act, and the Bengal Criminal Law Amendment Act of 1930. The first two were emergency legislations and were framed with World Wars in mind. These laws are important in understanding the Preventive Detention Act of 1950 (PDA). In the famous *A.K. Gopalan v. State of Madras* case, the validity of the PDA was upheld. The PDA remained valid till 1969 (Aftab 2021). The Maintenance of Internal Security Act of 1971 (MISA) was another detention law that followed PDA and was used most prominently during The Emergency period in India, a 21-month period from 1975 to 1979. It remained effective till 1978. The National Securities Act of 1980 (NSA) follows MISA. NSA is still applicable today. NSA was most recently applied to a case relating to Dr Kafeel Khan who was kept in detention for allegedly participating in anti-CAA protests (ibid).[21]

Preventitive Detention is part of the Union List and the Indian Parliament has the power to enact a law for reasons connected to the "defence, foreign

[21] Although, the real reason for his detention was for he highlighted the lack of oxygen that killed 100 children in 2017 in the city of Gorakhpur in Uttar Pradesh, India. He was booked under NSA for entirely different and non-existent reasons. He spent a total of nine months in jail.

affairs, or the security of India".[22] The Concurrent List in India gives power to the Parliament at a national level and the State Legislatures to enact such laws for matters relating to maintenance of public order or supply and services related to community.[23] Entry 3 of the Concurrent List, which is also part of Article 246, allows for preventative detention for reasons "connected with the security of a State, the maintenance of public order, or the maintenance of supplies and services essential to the community." Furthermore, Entry 4 of the same List also gives the State the power to move the detained persons within India, stating that "Removal from one State to another State of prisoners, accused persons and persons subjected to preventive detention for reasons specified in entry 3 of this List."

Under clause (4) of Article 22 of the Indian constitution, a person can be detained for a maximum period of three months. During the period, as was in the case of Dr Khan, any counsel can be denied. A decision to allow representation can follow if the detention is continued after the three-month period. Clause (1) of Article 22 states that a person who is arrested "shall be informed" and will not be denied "the right to consult" with a "legal practitioner of his choice." Furthermore, Clause (2) states that the detained person will be presented in the court within a 24-hour period in front of the nearest magistrate. The exception to Clause (1) and (2) is added in Clause (3) where both 1 and 2 becomes void if the person is deemed to be an "enemy alien" of the state, thus allowing for preventive detention.[24] It is unclear whether "illegal foreigners" are deemed to be "enemy aliens," or how FTs figure in the aspect of preventive detention of those deemed "foreigners" or "D-voters."

The NRC applies the premises and punishments of detention in criminal law, while claiming to be purely administrative. While those declared as foreigners are kept in detention for administrative reasons and are not undergoing any kind of punishment, if there is no clear legitimate purpose for which a person is detained, then that detention should not be permissible. People who serve a sentence of imprisonment, even if it is for life, are indeed detained for a definite period. There are provisions of mercy, parole, and other procedural provisions such as where to be kept, how the sentence is to be served, rigorous or simple imprisonment, and so on. In the case of preventive detention/administrative detention as of now in India, there are no set procedures and guidelines for keeping people under detention.

[22] See Entry 9, List I, Union List. It is part of the 7th Schedule, Article 246 of the Indian Constitution.

[23] See Entry 3, List III, Concurrent List.

[24] See Article 22, Constitution of India, 1949.

And in the case of the NRC, unlike criminal proceedings which are *open*, FT cases are *opaque* and closed. Moreover, the person declared to be a foreigner is sent to indefinite detention, with no certainty of the length of the detention. This is indeed more inhumane and beyond punishment. I argue that all these exceptions, arbitrariness, and ambiguities in the NRC process make detention in NRC a formless punishment. FTs turn alleged foreigners into criminals, without the protections of the law and with limitless punishments.

To carry out preventative detention, there has to be a legitimate purpose. People who are declared foreigners by the FTs are not carrying any sentence of imprisonment. There is no order for detention passed by any court of law. They are simply detained for administrative reasons. If the detention is itself challenged, certain criminal laws can be invoked to keep them in detention, like the Evidence Act to dismiss the documents produced by the defendant. Thus, the only purpose of this detention is to repatriate them to their country of origin. Yet the "foreigners" identified by the NRC process and kept in these detention centres in Assam are not made under provisions such as The Passport (Entry into India) Act of 1920 (both foreigners and Indians) or the Foreigners Act of 1946, and if the detention is challenged, the government justifies detentions on the basis that the foreigner might abscond, or "vanish," with sufficient Supreme Court and High Court precedents to support this justification.

People were detained for fear that they might "vanish" and mingle with the general public. The Government claims that deportation is legitimate as they are kept in detention for this purpose. They are thus to be detained for ease of finding them should they be deported. The idea of vanishing, therefore, finds repeated mention in many judgements of the Guwahati HC. The government White Paper (2012, 38) also mentioned the need and justification for detention centres as detected persons "perform the act of vanishing." The detention centres are thus an administrative and civil extension of the FTs in Assam, although as noted earlier they are in fact imprisoned with convicts of serious and sometimes violent crimes. Many do not know what crimes have led to their incarceration. Some of them have appealed against official decisions deeming them "irregular foreigners".[25] But there is no statutory limit on the period of detention. Some have been in custody for many months, and some for years without access to parole. Such is the extent of the arbitrariness of this process and the formlessness of their detention.

[25] The Amnesty Report humanizes the "illegal" and uses the term "irregular foreigner".

B.K. Sharma, in his judgement on the Ajijur Rahman case, *Ajijur Rahman v. The Union of India & Ors* on 1 July 2011, which was initially registered under IMDT Act of 2005 (IM(D)T Case NO. 469/2001), noted that "the petitioner was to surrender before the Superintendent of Police (B), Morigaon and upon such surrender, he was to be detained in a detention camp. The Deputy Commissioner was also to ensure deletion of his name from the voter list. As the experience of this Court goes, in most of the cases, after invoking the writ jurisdiction of this Court, the declared foreign nationals defy the interim direction to surrender before the jurisdictional Superintendent of Police and commit the act of *vanishing*" (*Ajijur Rahman v. The Union of India & Ors*, WP(C) No. 2358/2011, ¶ 32 [emphasis mine]). The judge here did not shy away from showing his solidarity for the Assamese nationalists and further adds in the judgement that, "detection and deportation of such foreign nationals whose presence in the State of Assam in lakhs endangering the very survival of the indigenous people of Assam is an established fact so vividly stated by none other than the Apex Court in *Sarbananda Sonowal v. Union of India*, reported in AIR 2005 SC 2920" (*Rahman*, WP(C) No. 2358/2011, ¶ 37).

B.K. Sharma also noted two fallouts in the delay caused by the cases relating to foreigners' issues in Assam. He noted that the cases took a very long time and in this period of pendency of the case there are also issues of involvement with criminal activity on the part of the alleged foreigner. However, apart from the cases of vanishing, Sharma could cite only one case in the history of the Guwahati High Court of such a registered criminal case. Despite relying on such negligible and flimsy data, he casts a problematic position on the issue of detention. Also, in his judgement he uses "foreign national", "suspected foreigner" and "illegal Bangladeshi national/migrant" interchangeably and inconsistently and without defining what they entail. The second fallout of the delay that Sharma notes is shocking, to say the least. Sharma notes, "During the pendency of the proceedings with exorbitant delay, the suspected foreign nationals can merrily procure children(s) and the said children(s), by virtue of their birth in Indian soil, may get the protection of being Indian citizens, by birth" (*Rahman*, WP(C) No. 2358/2011, ¶ 39). The Judge also recounts towards the end of the judgement the disinterest of governments in the case of foreigners. In other words, he was questioning the purpose (and also interests) of these cases related to foreigners, the FTs, and so on. This doubt on the purpose of detention is certainly not clear, neither in the earlier cases of foreigners, nor with the NRC. Sharma's admission strengthens the ambiguity of the purpose of detention. He further notes, "In most of the cases pertaining to foreign nationals pending in this Court or which have been disposed of, neither the State Govt. nor the Union Govt. show any interest. No counter affidavits are filed unless there is clear cut direction of this Court, although, as per requirement, once a notice is issued, counter affidavits are required to be filed. It gives the impression that both the Governments are not interested in such cases" (*Rahman*, WP(C) No. 2358/2011, ¶ 44).

The Govt. of India has officially never asked any other country to take these people back. Additionally, many officials and politicians have also claimed that the NRC is an "internal process". Bangladesh Foreign Secretary Shahidul Haque said the following: "We think and have been assured that it (meaning the NRC) is an internal matter of India. PM Modi has explained to PM Hasina how India intends to include everyone in the process. Our relations are the best. But we will keep our eyes open to [how the NRC] proceeds."[26] On another occasion in 2020, foreign secretary of India, Harsh Vardhan Shringla said at an event in Dhaka that "updation of the National Register of Citizens is a process that is entirely internal to India. India assures Bangladesh that the NRC will have no implications for the country and its people."[27] These two statements made by the counterparts of both India and Bangladesh make it amply clear that the NRC is indeed an internal matter. By these admissions, the purpose of deportation becomes questionable in the NRC process as it is claimed to be an "internal affair," but surely deportation as a purpose is used in the case of detention of NRC victims to legitimize that detention. In the ambiguity of this purpose, even in a legal sense, the detention is a formless punishment. One can mourn if punishment is definite, but when there is ambiguity and uncertainty to the length of it, even mourning is beyond reach for the victim and their loved ones.[28]

This absence of a bilateral understanding and the NRC being an "internal" matter exposes the psychology of detention and its materiality. Thus, "punishing the criminal is the only possible reparation" (Laruelle 2015) because here deportation remains blocked or improbable. Such formless punishments allows the Assamese nationalist to "come to terms" with the reality and limits of the misuse of law. What detention achieves is far more painful and grotesque. It is not that everyone is sent to detention, but the possibility is floated on the horizon and the treatment is made public so that

[26] *See* Staff Report (05 October 2019) NRC is an internal, legal process, *The Hindu*.

[27] Scroll Staff Report (02 March 2020) NRC will not affect Bangladesh, entirely internal process, India's foreign secretary tells Dhaka, *Scroll.in*.

[28] About mourning and punishment see Laruelle's *General Theory of Victims*.

fear and horror never leaves the mind of the victims and potential victims. This milieu of punishment generated by the NRC process heals and nourishes the desires of the Assamese nationalist. It makes them feel powerful, as if they are the ones who are punishing the "Bangladeshi".

5 Conclusion

This chapter sought to demonstrate how the NRC process allows us to examine the affinity between the citizenship process and criminal law and how criminal law and administrative grounds of detention are often criss-crossed and misused. The people who undergo detention do not have access to the safeguards inscribed into criminal law. On the contrary, the provisions of the criminal law were used to justify detention, making the detenu face dual discrimination. Clearly, the administrative reasons and criminality are indistinct. We also see an effacement of the victims of the NRC where they experience victimhood twice—once when they are doubted and accused, and secondly, when they are sent to indefinite detention.[29]

In many ways, Thomas Robert Malthus's prophecy of overpopulation finds a new life in the NRC. His view on "overpopulation" was at best an "oxymoron" to his times as Zygmunt Bauman notes (Bauman 2003). The justification provided for the NRC finds a grim resonance with Malthus's prophecy of "principle of population", where the overpopulated (in our case migrants) are devalued, reduced to insects, and to be discarded and stripped of political rights. Those justifications are written in most bureaucratic documents that have been written on Assam like the census documents, or as we see, even the legal systems lend currency and support. The NRC also secures and strengthens the interest of the caste-Assamese middle class, even its nationalism. The legal system sides with the majority and criminalizes the migrant. They are treated as subjects (even a criminal convict is given more rights in India). Paradoxically, it is better to be a citizen than a *fidel citizen*. The NRC is a case of an insidious use of criminal law where the due process and constitutional protections are gravely limited or non-existent.

The NRC process has also brought a large section of people under the radar of surveillance. It brought together the state and a complex technological regime comprising IT companies and data collection systems under the same bureaucratic umbrella with the singular aim of filtering out "illegal"

---

29 *See* Laurelle (2015). *General Theory of Victims.*

immigrants from "genuine Indians" (Das 2020). This pervasive bureaucratic ensemble around technology has increased the suffering of people. At the same time, the surveillance infrastructure mixed with nationalism adds another layer to the authoritarian populist and anti-minority Indian state.[30] The wise and painfully true words of Bruno Rizzi about bureaucracy haunt the citizens of Assam. Rizzi (1985: 89) wrote the following in *The Bureaucratization of the World*, "Sleep peacefully, gallant knight, the bureaucracy has quite other intentions!" Once the bureaucracy grips you by your hand, even Knights can't escape. The case of NRC makes this truth loud and clear.

Acknowledgements I would like to thank Oliullah Laskar, Arijit Sen, Rohini Sen, Leah Verghese, Angshuman Choudhury, Andrew Lee, and Darshana Mitra for reading, discussing, and commenting on the chapter. They have *aided, inspired, and multiplied* my concerns and commitments I share in this paper. To Parag, Bhargabi, Abhinav, Angshuman, Shantanu, and Arijit, your presence and friendship have made me supple and kept me motivated to write, including this. I am also very grateful to George Radics and Pablo Ciocchini for their valuable comments on my chapter and for giving me the space to share my work. Part of this chapter was also presented in the *Stigmatization, Identities and the Law* Conference at NUS Law in 2020 and I thank everyone who commented on that presentation and the draft.

References

Aftab, Jasir. 2021. Preventive Detention Laws in India: A Tool for Executive Tyranny? *The Leaflet*. https://www.theleaflet.in/preventive-detention-laws-in-india-a-tool-for-executive-tyranny/. Accessed 2 Apr 2021.

Amnesty International India Report. 2018. *Between Fear and Hatred: Surviving Immigration Detention in Assam*. New York, Amnesty International USA.

Barpujari, H.K., Barpujari, S.K., and Bhuyan, A.C. 1980. *Political History of Assam (1826–1919)*. Govt. of Assam, Dispur.

Bauman, Zygmunt. 2003. *Wasted Lives: Modernity and Its Outcasts*. Polity Press.

Das, Bhargabi. 2020. How Profit-Making Technologies is Shaping the Terms of Citizenship in Assam. *Eleventh Column*, April 5, 2020.

Giddens, Anthony. 1985. *The Nation-State and Violence*. University of California Press.

[30] Surveillance is indispensable to the authoritarian state ('focusing on surveillance' is an element of totalitarian tule) as Anthony Giddens (1985) had argued.

Gogoi, Suraj, and Arijit Sen. 2022. The Gauhati HC Ruling Offers a Glimmer of Hope for Those Tangled Up in Assam's Citizenship Nightmare. Scroll.in. https://scroll.in/article/1024698/the-gauhati-hc-ruling-offers-a-glimmer-of-hope-for-those-tangled-up-in-assams-citizenship-nightmare. Accessed 3 Jun 20202.

Guha, Amalendu. 1979. Great Nationalism, Little Nationalism and Problem of Integration: A Tentative View. *Economic and Political Weekly* 14 (7/8): 455–458.

Guha, Amalendu. 1980. Little Nationalism Turned Chauvinist: Assam's Anti-foreigner. Upsurge. 1979–80. *Economic and Political Weekly* 15(41/43): 1699–1720.

Home & Political Department. 2012. *White Paper on Foreigners Issue*. Govt. of Assam. Last modified 20 Oct 2012.

Laruelle, Francois. 2015. *General Theory of Victims*. Polity Press.

Mitra, Darshana. 2021. From Citizen to Criminal: Citizenship Determination Process in India and the Limits of Due Process. *The Leaflet*. https://www.theleaflet.in/from-citizen-to-criminal-citizenship-determination-in-india-and-the-limits-of-due-process/. Accessed 27 Jan 2021.

Mustafa, Faizan. 2019. Kangaroo Tribunals: Foreigners' Tribunals Almost Another Arm of BJP Government in Assam. *Indian Express*. https://indianexpress.com/article/opinion/column/supreme-court-foreigners-tribunals-assam-nrc-6058158/. Accessed 8 Oct 2019.

Rizzi, Bruno. 1985. *The Bureaucratization of the World*. Free Press.

Sagar. 2019. Case Closed. *The Caravan*. https://caravanmagazine.in/law/assam-foreigners-tribunals-function-like-kangaroo-courts-persecute-minorities. Accessed 6 Nov 2019.

Saha, Abhishek. 2021. *No Land's People: The Untold Story of Assam's NRC Crisis*. India: Harper Collins.

Saikia, Parag Jyoti, and Suraj Gogoi. 2018. How NRC Legitimised Xenophobia in Assam. *Newslaundry*. https://www.newslaundry.com/2018/08/02/how-nrc-legitimised-xenophobia-and-chauvinism-in-assam. Accessed 2 Aug 2018.

Sen, Arijit. 2020. Covid-19 Pandemic is an Opportunity for Assam to Correct a Historic Wrong. *Polis Project*. https://thepolisproject.com/covid-19-pandemic-an-opportunity-for-assam-to-correct-a-historical-wrong/#.YTSuTNMzb0s. Accessed 9 Apr 2020.

Sharma, Jayeeta. 2011. *Empire's Garden: Assam and the Making of India*. Duke University Press.

6

(Cr)Immigration and Merit-Based Migration in Singapore: The Permanent "State of Exception"

George B. Radics

1 Introduction

In this chapter, I discuss how Singapore's merit-based immigration system exacerbates the marginalization of temporary migrant workers. Given Singapore's historical reliance on foreign labor, in the post-colonial, neoliberal environment where efficiency and utility are emphasized, this merit-based system becomes further entrenched and defined, with the bottom rungs of the hierarchy being denied fundamental rights afforded other migrants and citizens. Through an examination of how the law and the criminal justice system converge, this chapter will employ the "crimmigration" framework developed to understand the plight of migrants in the United States. It will then focus on how this crimmigration framework manifests in the Global South, particularly discussing the situation for migrant workers from India and Bangladesh in the city-state of Singapore. The chapter will highlight how when merit-based migration systems are employed in the Global South, for those who rank at the bottom of the skills hierarchy, their rights in the criminal justice system are even more precarious and permanently in a "state of exception"—insecure and subject to the ebb and flow of "security threats."

Three instances in which legal protections for migrants were suspended in Singapore due to "security" issues will be examined. The first is the Little India

G. B. Radics (✉)
National University of Singapore, Singapore, Singapore
e-mail: socrgb@nus.edu.sg

G. B. Radics and P. Ciocchini (eds.), *Criminal Legalities and Minorities in the Global South*,
Palgrave Socio-Legal Studies, https://doi.org/10.1007/978-3-031-17918-1_6

Riot of 2013, in which a riot that took place in a South Asian migrant-dominated part of town led to the passing of the Public Order Additional Temporary Measures Act, mandating the increased policing of alcohol consumption, a vice presumed to be tied to the Indian population. Next, in the context of terrorism, Bangladeshi migrant workers who were caught with radical Islamic propaganda and videos triggered the use of Singapore's infamous Internal Security Act, and 27 of these workers were swiftly detained and deported. Finally, the chapter will examine how after a COVID-19 outbreak in the worker dormitories, the Employment of Foreign Manpower (Work Passes) (Amendment) Regulations of 2020 and stricter regulations that isolated and detained the construction workers emphasized the difference between the Singaporean population and migrant workers. All three cases demonstrate how in such circumstances migrant workers are the first to be stripped of their rights when an emergency occurs, underscoring how they are often treated as security threats subject to swift, punitive measures and deportation.

The chapter will begin with a brief introduction to the predominantly Global North-focused crimmigration literature. While literature on crimmigration is primarily based in the United States , North America, and Western Europe, crimmigration is less explored beyond these contexts. Furthermore, in the Global South, the criminalization of migrants often takes place in the context of a "state of emergency"—whether it be safety, national security, or health—further complicating the application of the crimmigration literature to nations outside of the Global North. The chapter will then move on to discuss the modern-day migration system in Singapore, established to balance the needs of the highly globalized economy, while at the same time placating the anxieties of the local population. To examine how migration is managed in Singapore, the chapter will then highlight how the rights of migrants laborers in Singapore are limited, focusing specifically on South Asian migrants by examining three events and legal responses: (1) the Little India Riot of 2013 and the Public Order Additional Temporary Measures Act; (2) the uncovering of Bangladeshi Extremists and the Internal Security Act; and (3) COVID-19 and the Employment of Foreign Manpower (Work Passes) (Amendment) Regulations 2020.

2 Crimmigration and the Permanent "State of Exception"

Juliet Stumpf (2013) coined the term "crimmigration" in response to sweeping changes taking place in the United States in the late 1980's that signaled a merging between criminal and immigration law. Her argument rests on how over the past century there has been an expansion in the number of crimes that lead to deportation, immigration law violations that were originally treated as civil matters are now criminal offenses, and how local and state law enforcement are increasingly used to police migrants (Stumpf 2013, 377–379). Since Stumpf's influential piece, Menjívar et al. (2018, 2) notes that growing scholarly attention has been placed on the criminalization of immigration law, and its effect on immigrants, their families, and their communities. In the United States, much of the research has revolved around exclusion and discrimination in immigration law against Arabs (Akram and Johnson 2002; Tumlin 2004), those of African descent (Hernández 2013, 2018; Rosenbaum 2018), and the Latino community (Menjívar et al. 2018; Vazquez 2015; Gomberg-Muñoz 2015). The concept of crimmigration has also been used to describe the migration experience in Australia (Stanley 2017), Canada (Silverman and Molnar 2016) and Europe (Calavita 2003; Bosworth and Guild 2008; Barker 2012).

In the Global South, the confluence of criminal and immigration law has taken on a different and arguably more violent form. Carolina Yoko Furusho (2019) in exploring crimmigration the Dominican Republic highlights how the state openly and without restraint uses US models of crimmigration to justify state-sponsored violence against Haitian migrants. In Latin America, inter-ethnic and nationality-based conflict and prejudice drives the evolution of crimmigration laws. In Costa Rica, changes to the country's immigration law in 2008 were aimed at protecting "national security" specifically targeting Nicaraguan migrants, while in Peru, Venezuelan forced migrants are often stereotyped in the mass media as thieves, murderers, and prostitutes (Fouratt 2014; Freier and Pérez 2021). In South Africa, crimmigration has led to the proliferation of fake documents, police raids targeting of foreigners, and oppressive detention (Alfaro-Velcamp and Mark Shaw 2016). Here, xenophobia takes on the form of a *new racism* which is cultural in nature, with economic differences only deepening notions of inferiority and superiority, justifying violent attacks and programs (Tafira 2011, 115). In Asia, particularly in hyper-growth zones like Singapore, the neoliberal ethic of self-responsible citizenship makes it so that those "who cannot scale the skills ladder…are increasingly marginalized as deviant or [considered] subjects who threaten the security of the globalized milieu" (Ong 2006, 502). Thus, migrant workers who enter the country at bottom of the skills ladder must navigate between "sheer life," or achieving biological survival, and "bare life," or being designated as permanently excluded from the local community and subject to expulsion at any time (Ong 2006; Kitiarsa 2014).

Another theoretical frame that is useful in understanding the effects of the merit-based migration system is Georgio Agamben's "state of exception."

Agamben (2005) argues that built into modern law is the state's ability to assert its authority in the event of emergencies, and how when this happens, individual liberties and constitutional protections are suspended. He highlights how over the past 100 years the world has witnessed a perpetual state of "legal civil war"—from Nazi decrees to the US Patriot Act—signaling the voluntary creation of a permanent state of emergency in contemporary society. Agamben's "state of emergency" builds upon his discussion of *homo sacer*, or the Roman legal category for human beings who could be killed without being charged with homicide (Agamben 1998, 2005). Combined, he maintains that the state has the power to define whose life matters, while the "state of exception" empowers the state to suspend rights at any moment. Kitiarsa (2014) highlights that in the context of migrant lives in Singapore, these concepts "provide a systematic analytical model to gauge the harsh realities that migrants face," and how "the modern state and its sovereign power work hand-in-hand with capitalist market institutions in extracting economic value out of the bodies of migrant workers" (Kitiarsa 2014, 5).

For Singapore, a nation whose legal system was constructed by the British precisely to suppress dissidence and extract wealth through imported labor, strict migration policies and punitive measures to discipline diverse populations are historically ingrained. The next section will explore the history of South-South migration in Singapore, but also how in the post-colonial legal framework, race and crime become entangled and embedded in Singaporean immigration laws.

3 Migration Policies in Singapore

Global market forces create a demand in developed and development countries for low-cost, flexible and compliant labor, a need fulfilled by migrants on short-term contracts that render them deportable based on market fluctuations (McNevin 2006, 140). The demand for "disposable" workers in Singapore rose as the country developed economically, creating more jobs for migrant workers, primarily within occupations characterized by manual labor that locals were no longer willing to do (Huang and Yeoh 1996, 480). Moreover, both India and Bangladesh, with their geopolitical location, ecological conditions, and historical circumstances, export their labor to countries like Singapore as an important source of income for its domestic market (Ye 2016, 68; Rahman 2017). This section will first contextualize Singapore's racialized migration patterns by briefly discussing Singapore's pre-colonial migration history. Then, it will discuss Singapore's post-colonial legal framework for migrants.

3.1 Colonial Migration to Singapore

For centuries prior to the arrival of the Portuguese, British, French, and Dutch to Southeast Asia, maritime trade and migration within the region had already taken place (Bhattacharya 2011, 24). However, mass migration to Singapore was largely a product of British political and economic needs driven by "competitive capital accumulation" in the region (Abraham 1983; Stenson 1980; Brown 1974, 117). By the time Sir Stamford Raffles arrived in Singapore in 1819, the Dutch were already entrenched in the region, triggering a bitter rivalry between the two colonial powers (Kennedy 1973; Tarling 1962). The British saw Malaya as a rich source of raw materials, in particular, rubber and tin (Sandhu 1969; Stenson 1980). Such industries were not amenable to the technology of the time, and required hard physical labor to exploit the wealth embedded in the land.

To the British, their experience in administering colonies in the sub-Indian continent led them to believe that low-caste South Indian peasants were most suitable for the light repetitive tasks of plantation work (Sandhu 1969, 56). South Indian Tamils were considered "malleable and easy to manage" (Lian 2006, 123). Indian laborers were not the only migrants into the region, however. Driven from their homeland due to over-population and political conflict, the Chinese had already begun to flood the region as early as the 1820s. In fact, for the first twenty-five years or more after the British intervention in the western Malay States in the 1870s, the Chinese provided most of the labor for the British (Stenson 1980, 15). The local Malay population could also have served as labor to fuel the growth of British enterprises, but attempts to force Malays to engage in hard labor could have jeopardized the fragile relations the British had with the Malay sultanates and rulers as they tried to expand their influence and control in Malay lands (*see* Hirschman 1986; Kratoska 1983).

As a free port under the British, Singapore became the distribution center of local produce from the Archipelago, Malaya, and Indochina for shipment to Europe, North America, and China (Chiu et al. 1997). Malaya's economic boom in tin mining and the development of rubber plantations contributed to Singapore's explosive growth. Between 1824 and 1872, the total value of the colony's trade increased eight times, and Singapore quickly developed into a trading center for Southeast Asia (Buchanan 1972, 28).

Along with this growth came migrants such as laborers, mainly coolies from southern China, who were shipped to Malayan mines and plantations via Singapore. The large number of coolies passing through Singapore made it so that by the 1860s, despite the existence of British colonial officers and South Asian laborers, the city had become a predominantly Chinese territory. The large Chinese population was also due to the city's role as a major destination and coordination center for Chinese migrants bound for British territories in western Nanyang (Yeoh and Lin 2013).

3.2 Modern Singapore's Merit-Based Migration System

In post-colonial Singapore, foreign labor continues to serve an important role in the development of the nation's economy. From 1965 onwards, the newly independent nation was initially concerned with simply distinguishing between "foreign workers" and the local population. As the economy began to rely more heavily on technology-intensive industries economy, as well as the need for high value-added services, in 1988 Minister for Home Affairs S. Jayakumar raised the issue of "foreign talent" as the necessary next stage of development. To support this initiative, the government established recruitment centers in Sydney, Perth, Boston, London, Los Angeles, and Vancouver to attract highly skilled workers. Furthermore, to regulate the influx of foreign workers in Singapore, by 1998, three categories of foreign workers were introduced. These three categories led to different work passes, including the P-Pass (for professionals and executives who earn at least S$3500 a month), the Q-Pass (for mid-skilled technical staff who earn at least S$2000 a month), and the R-Pass (those primarily engaged in manual labor and domestic work, who have no minimum salary) (Low 2001, 3). By 2022, several other passes were introduced; yet foreign employment still largely falls within the three categories (P, Q, and R), except with the minimum for P-Pass (now referred to as "Employment Passes" or EP for short) raised to $4500, the Q-pass (now called "S Pass") to $2500, and R-Pass (now referred to as "Work Permits") which still has no minimum (Ministry of Manpower 2022a).

While non-Singaporean/permanent residents constitute nearly 40% of the population (NPTD 2022), Work Permit holders making up nearly 70% of the foreign worker population (Ministry of Manpower 2022b). For these Work Permit holders, the system imposes specific regulations and restrictions that are not imposed on workers or employers of other work pass categories. Work Permit holders, for example, are not entitled to bring their families to Singapore, and face restrictions on marriage to Singaporeans. Employers are required to post a S$5000 security bond before a Work Permit holder is allowed to enter Singapore. While this employer liability is discharged when a migrant worker returns home, the security bond is liable to forfeiture if a migrant worker is not repatriated when required to leave or if the migrant worker remains illegally in Singapore. The possibility of losing S$5000 amplifies employers' anxieties around workers' movements and leads to practices such as the withholding of migrant workers' passports (Ng 2010). Employers must also pay a monthly levy for each Work Permit holder they employ. Currently, the foreign worker levy ranges from S$300 to S$950 a month for each construction worker, and S$300 to S$400 for each worker in the marine sector. Although prohibited by law, considerable numbers of workers claim that their employers recover these costs through deductions from their salaries and kickbacks (Bal 2015).

Due to historical circumstances and perceived similarities between Singapore and its neighbor, initially, only migrants from Malaysia, a "Traditional Source" (TS) country, were allowed to fill Singapore's low-skilled labor needs (Rahman 2017). However, the government realized it could not meet its labor needs drawing exclusively from Malaysia. Thus, measures were taken as early as 1978 to facilitate the limited importation of unskilled labor from Non-Traditional Source (NTS) countries, which are Bangladesh, India, the Philippines, Sri Lanka, Myanmar, and Thailand. In addition, Singapore hires low-skilled foreign workers from two other sources: North Asian sources (NAS), which are Hong Kong, Macau, South Korea, and Taiwan; and the People's Republic of China (PRC). Presently, the four sources—TS, NTS, NAS, and PRC—provide the low-skilled labor needed by Singapore (Rahman 2017). NTS workers are generally allowed to work only in the construction, shipbuilding, and harbor craft industries. In other words, they are not usually allowed to work in services and manufacturing sectors. Low-skilled migrants from NAS countries and PRC are allowed to work in construction and almost all other non-construction sectors. While some of these countries were considered "non-traditional," they still reflected historical patterns of migration (i.e., regionally and from North and South Asia). This pattern of recruitment remains in place today.

4 Three Case Studies: Riots, Terrorism, and Pandemics

Singapore is known for its meticulously planned, yet strict and punitive, policies. While the upside of such law and order is the perception of safety, the costs can be harsh—particularly for foreigners at the bottom of the merit-based hierarchy. This section will examine three emergencies and the laws they invoked: (1) the Little India Riot of 2013 and the Public Order Additional Temporary Measures Act; (2) the uncovering of Bangladeshi Extremists and the Internal Security Act; and (3) COVID-19 and the Employment of Foreign Manpower (Work Passes) (Amendment) Regulations 2020.

4.1 Little India Riot and the Public Order Additional Temporary Measures Act (POATM)

In response to an unfortunate accident in which a migrant worker was ejected from a private bus and subsequently run over by it in the neighborhood of Little India, a crowd of predominantly South Asian migrant workers started pelting the bus with umbrellas, shoes, bottles, metal drain covers, and garbage bins (COI Report 2013, 21). A total of 240 officers from various Singapore Police Force (SPF) units and 56 Singapore Civil Defense Force (SCDF) officers were deployed to the scene (COI Report 2013, 37). The riot spread for about 300 m along the stretch of a major thoroughfare in the area. The riot was finally put down after two hours. (COI Report 2013, 15). Immediately following the riot, the Singapore government used the Public Order Act (POA), a law enacted in 2009 to regulate assemblies and processions in public places and provide powers necessary for preserving public order and safety, to control the area. The POA, however, was not meant to deal with emergencies, and in February 2014 was amended to specifically address the needs of Little India in the wake of the riot. The POATM not only suspended many civil rights in Little India but was primarily couched in terms of addressing the problem of alcohol, thereby painting the primary ethnic occupants of Little India, viz. South Asians, as prone to alcohol-related criminality/disorder. The Bill, as a pre-emptive measure in anticipation of future disorderliness, was eventually extended island wide.

4.2 Bangladeshi Terrorists and the Internal Security Act (ISA)

Between 16 November and 1 December 2015, the Internal Security Department (ISD) arrested 27 male Bangladeshi nationals who were working in the local construction industry under the ISA (MHA 2016). Twenty-six of them were members of a closed religious study group that were alleged to have followed to extremist beliefs and teachings of radical ideologues like Anwar al-Awlaki. They were found to be supporting the armed jihad ideology of terrorist groups like Al-Qaeda and the Islamic State in Iraq and Syria. The government also investigated an additional Bangladeshi national who was not a member of the group, but was found to be in the process of becoming radicalized and supportive of extremist preachers. He was also found to have possessed jihadi-related material. According to the government, the group members took measures to avoid detection by the authorities (*ibid.*). They shared jihadi-related material discreetly among themselves, and held weekly meetings and gatherings where they discussed armed jihad and conflicts that involved Muslims. They also carefully targeted the recruitment of other Bangladeshi nationals to grow their membership. All 26 of the Bangladeshi migrant workers immediately had their passes canceled and were repatriated, while one of the migrants was imprisoned for attempting to leave the country illegally (*ibid.*). Under the ISA, they were issued detention orders, interrogated by the ISD, detained without trial, and repatriated to Bangladesh.

4.3 COVID-19 and the Employment of Foreign Manpower (Work Passes) (Amendment) Regulations 2020

In January 2020, Singapore confirmed its first case of the corona virus disease 2019 (COVID-19) (MOH 2020). By March, a ban on all short-term visitors was announced, and by April the first set of safety distance measures called a "circuit breaker" was announced to curb the spread of the virus. Such measures included the restrictions on movement and gatherings, the closure of schools and non-essential workplaces, and the mandating of masks when outdoors. Although successful in stemming the spread of the virus, due to communal living arrangements, worker dormitories quickly became the center of COVID-19 infections, registering nearly 1000 cases a day in April. Worker dormitories were quickly placed on lockdown, with residents being confined to their rooms, rigorously tested, and moved to different locations—some on barges floating off the coast of Singapore—based on their health status. National statistics then began to report cases in the country in two categories, the "community" vs. "dormitory." Despite the eventual relaxation of the circuit breaker measures in June 2020, the government passed the Employment of Foreign Manpower (Work Passes) (Amendment) Regulations of 2020 (hereinafter EFM Regulations) which enhanced the monitoring of migrant workers by mandating employers to restrict the movement of workers, establish contact tracing, and monitor employee movements, and for workers to "keep [their] living space clean" and practice good hygiene. Over a year later, the quarantine orders on dormitories had not changed.

5 Crimmigration and the "State of Exception" in the Law

Despite the different nature of events, the remainder of this chapter will show how the law was used in a harsh and swift manner to discipline and control South Asians on Work Permits. Punishment for those on Work Permits are extreme and with limited due process, while those who do not commit crimes are subject to pervasive surveillance. Lastly, the potential of deportation leads to a precarity for these workers that is ever present.

5.1 Punishment

In contrast to the United States, and the other nations from which the crimmigration literature emerges, where due process rights between citizen and migrant can vary substantially, an important difference in Singapore is its credence in prioritizing *order* over *justice*. Singapore's governance has been described as "paternalistic and authoritative" (Chan 1996) making it extremely difficult, if not impossible, to detach crime and criminal justice data from the broader social, economic, and political contexts (Beirne and Nelken 1997). Furthermore, Singapore subscribes to the "crime control" model of justice which operates on the assumption that the primary purpose of criminal process is to repress crime, therefore prioritizing the screening and profiling suspects, efficiently determining guilt, and quickly securing the appropriate punishment (Ganapathy 2008). In contrast, the due process model presumes innocence until proven guilty, guarantees a right to defend oneself in a court of law, and acknowledges the potential for flaws in the judicial process, allowing for appeals to correct such mistakes (Packer 1964).

In response to the Little India Riot, the parliament moved quickly to pass the POATM. On 18 February 2014, the Singapore House of Parliament held a hearing on the POATM Bill. The bill was meant to address the two main concerns of alcohol and security. Firstly, with regards to alcohol, Second Minister for Home Affairs, Mr S. Iswaran stated that the POATM applies only to the community of Little India. Clause 4 of the Bill stated that within this bounded area, the consumption of alcohol is not permitted, including within licensed liquor establishments (Parliament 2014, 28). The prescribed penalty for unlawful consumption of alcohol in a public place is a fine of $1000, and $5,000 for the unlawful sale or supply of alcohol. Furthermore, without a permit, the fine for bringing in prohibited items, i.e., alcohol, is $20,000 or imprisonment up to twelve months (*ibid.*). On the topic of security, the amendment allows police officers or approved auxiliary police officers, to inspect any person present, within, or seeking to enter, the special zone, and the person's personal property, for any prohibited item or any container of alcohol. The Bill also allows officers to enter any premises, search any property within the special zone, and detain any person without a warrant (Parliament 2014, 29–30). The Bill was passed that same day, immediately after it was discussed.

For the Bangladeshi nationals accused of being extremist activities, the ISA was invoked. The ISA is a statute that grants the executive power to enforce preventive detention, prevent subversion, suppress organized violence against persons and property, and do other things incidental to the internal security of Singapore. Notable scholars such as Chua Beng Huat (2002) and Jothie Rajah (2012) have argued that the law acts more as a check on free speech in addition to, or instead of, providing internal security. While very little information is available on the investigation of the 27 Bangladeshi nationals, under the ISA, the Minister of Home Affairs has the power to detain an individual deemed dangerous to security or poses a threat to public order for two years without trial, extendable every two years (ISA, 8(1)(a)). Michael Hor (2002) reminds us that while the focus of the criminal law is on completed crime where the harm has been done, the burden of preventive detention under the ISA is, as the term suggests, to prevent harm from happening, making the law potentially effective, but also prone to being invoked improperly and mistakenly.

In response to COVID-19, the government moved swiftly to modify the existing regulations to empower employers and the government to restrict the spread of the virus in worker dormitories. Yet according to some, the regulations introduced a new set of problems. Two Singapore-based worker organizations, the Humanitarian Organization for Migration Economics

(HOME) and Transient Workers Count Too (TWC2)—issued a joint statement on the regulations, stating that employer discretion to restrict freedom of movement may deter workers from seeking help for wage violations or abuse (HOME and TWC2 2020). Furthermore, they highlighted how actions such as failure to "keep [the] living space…clean and tidy… could lead to penalties as severe as revocation of their work pass." *ibid.* For many migrant workers, such as MD Sharif Uddin, describe living in the dormitories as "a very painful life…like prison" (AFP 2021). Workers describe only being able to go to work and home, being denied leave, and feeling isolated from nature and the outside world. "We are facing psychological problems," said one worker, "fundamental rights as workers and human beings [had been breached]" he adds (*ibid.*).

5.2 Surveillance

In neoliberal contexts, surveillance plays a central part of knowledge production, with both bodies and space becoming sites of information (Ericson and Haggerty 1997; Salehin and Vitis 2020). While little is known about the Singapore government's surveillance activities, it is clear that the nation prioritizes national security over individual privacy (Jiow and Morales 2015; Wong 2013). Closed-circuit television (CCTV) cameras are ever-present at major road junctions, expressways, public areas, public housing, commercial buildings, elevators, and public transport systems (Ho 2012). Currently, over 600 CCTV cameras provide coverage of the roads in Singapore, as well as in every train, train station, and train depot (Yeo 2008). There are at least five to eight CCTV cameras on every public bus (Jiow and Morales 2015). While these surveillance mechanisms are primarily meant to capture or deter terrorist or criminal activities, they have also served to influence social behaviors (Ho 2008). Surveillance is also incorporated into urban planning, where Singapore as a cosmopolitan city is organized to best appeal to people "of the right sort" (Harvey 1990, 295). The global, cosmopolitan city is also a safe city, where rule of law prevails over ruckus and criminality (Teo 2019). As part of this process of influencing social behavior and efficiently regulating unlawful behavior, Terri-Anne Teo (2019, 210) applies Bigo's (2006) concept of "Banopticon" in which "certain groups are identified as risky, and potential criminals, requiring more governance and surveillance than others."

Immediately after the Little India Riot, South Asian low-waged migrant workers who were not implicated or convicted in the bus accident were also subject to security practices of a predictive quality. Surveillance cameras were omnipresent additions, providing round-the-clock monitoring. The continued securitization of Little India in the aftermath of the incident builds upon the idea of recurrence: that it is not an isolated incident, but one that is anticipated to have repercussions and/or a repeated occurrence (Teo 2019). These heightened security measures were also meant to deter certain behaviors such as public drunkenness. Following the riot, there was also heightened securitization of Little India and dormitories, with the installation of security cameras and biometrics, as well as the monitoring of bus terminals and schedules in order to ensure constant, scientific surveillance of the population. These measures specific to Little India constitute a form of "legal geography" that profiles and regulates the behavior of South Asian migrants, while at the same time revealing the "coercive core" of the state (Belina 2007, 331).

Furthermore, in the months after the arrests of the Bangladeshi workers, the Ministry of Home Affairs enhanced its security apparatus to further crackdown on Islamic terrorists and outlined three key areas in which Singapore's counter-terrorism strategy will be enhanced. These were: (1) improving protective security measures for buildings and premises, including expanding the video camera network, (2) enhancing security response capabilities in the event of an armed attack, and (3) strengthening community response through a new national movement called "SG Secure" (Spykerman 2016). These strategies build upon existing surveillance platforms, such as the recently rolled out "PolCam 2.0." A portmanteau of "Policing Cameras," the Police will extend the coverage of Police cameras beyond public housing blocks and car parking lots to other public areas such as town centers and pedestrian walkways (MHA 2019). The program also aims at developing and refining video analytic capabilities to automate the analysis of footage from these cameras, and flag out incidents of interest. Minister of Home Affairs K. Shanmugam in justifying the changes stated "ISIS wants to establish a caliphate in this region, encompassing Singapore ... We are in the epicenter of the caliphate that ISIS wants to establish" (Ong 2016). He added, "It is no longer a question of whether an attack will take place, but really, when is an attack going to take place in Singapore and we have to be prepared for that" (*ibid.*).

Lastly, in the context of COVID-19, the EFM Regulations places the onus on the employer to monitor the movement of employees and to deny workers the right to leave the dormitory unless granted permission by the state, or if the worker is seeking medical attention [EFM Regulations of 2020, 2C(a)(b)]. Yet Alex Au, vice president of TWC2, argues that "the dorms are built in such a way that [the government] could lock the gates at any time," adding that the government may be so pleased with the design that it might be reluctant to completely return to pre-COVID-19 rules when workers were able to move around Singapore freely (McDonald 2021). In fact, many of the changes to the worker dormitories to allow for them to be self-contained, such as the installation of gyms, canteens, and TV rooms, were in direct response to the Little India Riot and the desire to reduce the need for migrant workers to leave their dormitories (MOM 2014). In addition to the extra surveillance placed in areas of high foreign worker congregation, COVID-19 has empowered employers and the state to further restrict movement, and strictly monitor behavior within the dormitories as well.

5.3 Deportations

While deportations certainly are a form of "global police" (Walters 2002, 282) over populations, they have differentiated effects across groups. For low-waged workers and other irregular migrants, deportation is also economic punishment. As mentioned earlier, precarity of migrant work is enhanced by the intersection of immigration and labor policies, where the termination of contracts by employers generally implies deportation, especially in the employer sponsorship system of immigration found in Singapore. The uneven employer-employee dynamic that creates a "precarity multiplier" that inhibits employee claims-making against employers for fear of deportation is felt even more intensely in Singapore given how research has shown that threats and practices of deportation influence the formation of tactics used to address worker grievances in the workplace (Griffith and Gleeson 2018; Bal 2015).

Within weeks of the Little India Riot, 57 workers were deported without trial. These actions were rationalized as an appropriate response to criminal behavior by non-citizens. In a ministerial statement, Deputy Prime Minister Teo Chee Hean justified state actions with rule-based arguments around national security: "Foreign workers must know that if they flout our rules they face repatriation… [w]e need to be strict about this, to maintain the safety and security of our society" (Au-yong 2014). He added that foreigners do not have an "inherent legal right to work and stay in Singapore" and are only present "with the permission of the State." A statement released by the Ministry of Law (2013) suggests that workers were removed based on an executive decision, despite investigations that found some of their participation to be "less egregious" (Hussain 2013). The decision was founded on (a) "carefully considered decisions, commensurate with the degree of culpability of each individual;" (b) "the conditions under which foreign nationals are allowed the privilege to come here to work is that they can be repatriated if, for example, the Minister assesses them to be security threats;" and (c) the understanding that foreign nationals are not given the right to due juridical process by way of their status as foreigners, which renders them subject to repatriation, and as such have "no right under our laws to challenge the repatriation order" (Ministry of Law 2013).

In the case of the Bangladeshi migrant workers, after a formal investigation, the Work Passes of the Bangladeshi nationals were immediately canceled (MHA 2016). Twenty-six of the workers were repatriated to Bangladesh where the authorities have been informed of the circumstances of their repatriation. The remaining Bangladeshi national is currently serving a jail sentence for attempting to leave Singapore via illegal and clandestine means after learning about the arrests of his fellow group members (MHA 2016). And in the case of COVID-19, migrant worker organization TWC2 has noted that the number one concern among migrant workers that reach out to their organization is problems with transfers (TWC2 2021). Given the existing legal infrastructure, employers have the right to cancel the work permit of employees at any time, leading to immediate repatriation. Furthermore, when employees are offered a job with another employer, the original employer is informed, providing the original employer the ability to cancel the employee's work permit and trigger repatriation. Workers have a very limited window of time to apply for a transfer to another company without the current employer's consent, and COVID-19 has slowed down transfer processing times, giving the current employer even more time to frustrate the transfer. TWC2 argues that many bad employers are canceling the permits of their employees because a work permit freeze has led to a shortage of labor. Current employers do not want to raise wages to compete with other offers, so they demand employees renew their contracts or cancel their permit if they choose to go elsewhere (TWC2 2021).

6 Conclusion

Although Northern crimmigration policies have been used in many Southern nations to justify harsh and punitive legal regimes, when applied in a developed, Global South nation, punitive, neoliberal migration policies such as the merit-based migration system have harsh consequences for "low-skilled" migrants. Not only are their rights subject to suspension, but whenever an emergency takes place, they are also punished severely with little due process or recourse. As seen in this chapter, over the past decade, emergencies have been endemic in Singapore—from spontaneous civil disorder to terrorism and pandemics—and when such events take place, migrant workers are subject to immediate punishment, excessive surveillance, and repatriation orders without the right to challenge them. To illustrate this situation, the chapter has examined three events and corresponding laws: (1) the Little India Riot of 2013 and the POATM; (2) the discovery of Bangladeshi terrorists and the ISA; and (3) COVID-19 and the EFM Regulations.

While the laws in Singapore may seem excessively harsh, it is important to remember that the conditions found in the city-state are the product of entrenched colonial racialized migration practices and laws that were illiberal by design, in conjunction with the post-colonial demands of an increasingly competitive, neoliberal globalized economy. The downside to Singapore's economic success using such policies is that it gives Northern nations justification to "catch up" and implement similar skills-based hierarchies. At the moment, Northern nations that employ such merit-based systems—such as Canada, Australia, or the United Kingdom, or intend to, like the United States—have strong civil rights protections in place, while nations in the South that do not have the same relationship with rights stand risk encouraging Northern nations to roll-back such protections in order to stay economically competitive. Furthermore, for nations such as Singapore that experience high diversity, such skills-based hierarchies undermine the assumption that all human lives regardless of their profession should be treated and valued equally. Merit-based migration systems, therefore, dehumanize workers by exacerbating the effects of crimmigration for low-skilled migrant workers wherever they go, while in Southern nations, a permanent "state of exception" leads to the reduction workers' rights with each emergency, further encouraging a race to the bottom for the Global North.

References

Laws

Employment of Foreign Manpower (Work Passes) (Amendment No. 5) Regulations 2020.

Internal Security Act (ISA) of Singapore (Cap. 143, 1985 Rev. Ed.).

Public Order (Additional Temporary Measures) Act of (No. 12 of 2014).

Books and Articles

Abraham, C. 1983. Racial and Ethnic Manipulations in Colonial Malaya. *Ethnic and Racial Studies* 6 (1): 18–32.

Agamben, Giorgio. 1998. *Homo Sacer: Sovereign Power and Bare Life*. Stanford, Calif: Stanford University Press.

Agamben, Giorgio. 2005. *State of Exception*. Chicago: University of Chicago Press.

Agence-France Press [AFP]. 2021. 'Like a Prison:' Singapore Migrant Workers Suffer Under Covid Curbs. 13 November 2021.

Akram, S. M., and K. R. Johnson. 2002. Race, civil rights, and immigration law after September 11, 2001: The targeting of Arabs and Muslims. *NYU Annual Survey of American Law*, 58: 295–356.

Alfaro-Velcamp, Theresa, and Mark Shaw. 2016. 'Please GO HOME and BUILD Africa': Criminalising Immigrants in South Africa. *Journal of Southern African Studies* 42 (5): 983–998.

Au-yong, R. 2014, January 21. DPM Teo Made Call to Repatriate Those Involved in Riot. *The Straits Times*. https://www.straitstimes.com/singapore/dpm-teo-made-call-to-repatriate-those-involved-in-riot. Accessed 17 Sept 2018.

Bal, C.S. 2015. Dealing with Deportability: Deportation Laws and the Political Personhood of Temporary Migrant Workers in Singapore. *Asian Journal of Law and Society* 2: 267–284.

Barker, V. 2012. Global Mobility and Penal Order: Criminalizing Migration, a View from Europe. *Sociology Compass* 6 (2): 113–121.

Brown, M. Barrat. 1974. *The Economics of Imperialism*. Harmondsworth: Penguin Education.

Beirne, P., and D. Nelken. 1997. *Issues in Comparative Criminology*. Aldershot: Dartmouth.

Belina, B. 2011. Ending Public Space as We Know It. *Social Justice* 38 (1–2): 13–27.

Bhattacharya, J. 2011. *Beyond the Myth: Indian Business Communities in Singapore*. Singapore: Institute of Southeast Asian Studies.

Bigo, D. 2006. Security, Exception, Ban and Surveillance. In *Theorizing Surveillance*, ed. D. Lyon, 46–68. Wilan: The Panopticon and Beyond.

Bosworth, M., and M. Guild. 2008. Governing Through Migration Control. *British Journal of Criminology* 48: 703–719.

Buchanan, I. 1972. *Singapore in Southeast Asia: An Economic and Political Appraisal*. London: G. Bell and Sons Ltd.

Calavita, K. 2003. A 'reserve army of delinquents' the Criminalization and Economic Punishment of Immigrants in Spain. *Punishment & Society* 5 (4): 399–413.

Chan, J. 1996. "Legislating Feminism in a Paternalistic State" paper presented at the Joint International Conference of the Law and Society Association and Research Committee on *Sociology of Law (ISA)*, Glasgow.

Chiu, S.W., K. Ho, and T. Lui. 1997. *City-States in the Global Economy: Industrial Restructuring in Hong Kong and Singapore*. Boulder, CO: Westview Press.

Chua, B.H. 2002. *Communitarian Ideology and Democracy in Singapore*. London: Routledge.

COI Report. 2013. *Report of the Committee of Inquiry into The Little India Riot on 8 December 2013*, June 27.

Ericson, R., and K. Haggerty. 1997. *Policing the Risk Society*. Toronto: University of Toronto Press.

Furusho, Carolina Yoko. 2019. Crimmigration in the dominican republic? Decolonizing the human rights of vulnerable Haitian migrants. In *Criminal Legalities in the Global South: Cultural Dynamics, Political Tensions, and Institutional Practices*, ed. Pablo Ciocchini and George Radics. Routledge: Abingdon, Oxon [UK].

Fouratt, Caitlin E. 2014. 'Those Who Come to Do Harm': The Framings of Immigration Problems in Costa Rican Immigration Law. *The International Migration Review* 48 (1): 144–80.

Freier, L.F., and L.M. Pérez. 2021. Nationality-Based Criminalisation of South-South Migration: The Experience of Venezuelan Forced Migrants in Peru. *European Journal on Criminal Policy and Research* 27: 113–133.

Ganapathy, N. 2008. Criminal Justice Policy: Social Order, Risk and the 'Governmental Project'. In *Social Policy in Post-Industrial Singapore*, ed. C.K. Tong, and K.F. Lian. Boston: Brill.

Gomberg-Muñoz, Ruth. 2015. The Punishment/El Castigo: Undocumented Latinos and US Immigration Processing. *Journal of Ethnic and Migration Studies* 41 (14): 2235–2252.

Griffith, K.L., and S.M. Gleeson. 2018. The Precarity of Temporality: How Law Inhibits Immigrant Worker Claims. *Comparative Labour Law and Policy Journal* 39 (1): 111–141.

Harvey, D. 1990. *The Condition of Postmodernity: An Enquiry into the Origins of Cultural Change*. Cambridge and Oxford: Blackwell.

Hernández, C.C.G. 2013. Creating Crimmigration. *BYU Law Review* 6 (4): 1457–1515.

Hernández, C.C.G. 2018. Deconstructing Crimmigration. *U.C.Davis Law Review* 52(1): 197.

Hirschman, C. 1986. The Making of Race in Colonial Malaya: Political Economy and Racial Ideology. *Sociological Forum* 1 (2): 330–361.

Ho, A. 2008. Face It: You're on Candid Camera, Everywhere. *The Straits Times*, Oct 2.

Ho, A. 2012. Safeguards Needed for Govt Access to Personal Data. *The Straits Times*, Sep 15.

HOME and TWC2. 2020. Response to Post-Circuitbreaker Amendments to the Employment of Foreign Manpower (Work Passes) Regulations. https://static1.squarespace.com/static/5a12725612abd96b9c737354/t/5ef95a5861489c0a0245a119/1593399904516/Response+to+Post-Circuitbreaker+Amendments.pdf.

Hor, M. 2002. Terrorism and the Criminal Law: Singapore's Solution. *Singapore Journal of Legal Studies* 1: 30–55.

Huang, S., and B.S.A. Yeoh. 1996. Ties that Bind: State Policy and Migrant Female Domestic Helpers in Singapore. *Geoforum* 27 (4): 479–493.

Hussain, A. 2013, December 18. 28 Charged as Police Complete Riot Probe. *Today*. https://www.todayonline.com/singapore/28-charged-po-lice-complete-ri-ot-probe. Accessed 17 Sept 2018.

Jiow, H.J., and S. Morales. 2015. Lateral Surveillance in Singapore. *Surveillance & Society* 13 (3): 327–337.

Kennedy, B.E. 1973. Anglo-French Rivalry in Southeast Asia 1763–93: Some Repercussions. *Journal of Southeast Asian Studies* 4 (2): 199–215.

Kitiarsa, Pattana. 2014. *The "Bare Life" of Thai Migrant Workmen in Singapore*. Chiang Mai, Thailand: Silkworm Books.

Kratoska, P.H. 1983. Ends that We Cannot Foresee: Malay Reservations in British Malaya. *Journal of Southeast Asian Studies* 14 (1): 149–168.

Lian, K.F. 2006. *Race, Ethnicity, and the State in Malaysia and Singapore*. Boston: Brill.

Low, L. 2001. *The Political Economy of Singapore's Policy on Foreign Talents and High Skills Society*, 1–21. Research Paper Series: Faculty of Business Administration, National University of Singapore. RPS 2001–036 (BP).

McDonald, Timothy. 2021. Singapore has COVID-19 Well Under Control—But Its Migrant Workers Still Face Year-Old Restrictions. *Fortune*. 7 April 2021.

McNevin, A. 2006. Political Belonging in a Neoliberal Era: The Struggle of the Sans-papiers. *Citizenship Studies* 10 (2): 135–151.

Menjívar, C., A. Gómez Cervantes, and D. Alvord. 2018. The Expansion of "crimmigration." Mass Detention, and Deportation. *Sociology Compass*: 1–15.

Ministry of Home Affairs [MHA]. 2016. Arrests of 27 Radicalised Bangladeshi Nationals under the Internal Security Act. https://www.mfa.gov.sg/Overseas-Mission/Geneva/Mission-Updates/2016/01/press_20160120.

Ministry of Home Affairs [MHA]. 2019. Innovating to Keep Singapore Safe and Secure. https://www.mha.gov.sg/about-us/innovating-to-keep-singapore-safe-and-secure.

Ministry of Health. 2020. https://www.moh.gov.sg/news-highlights/details/confirmed-imported-case-of-novel-coronavirus-infection-in-singapore-multi-ministry-taskforce-ramps-up-precautionary-measures.

Ministry of Law. 2013, December 21. *Ministry of Law's Statements on the Repatriation of Foreign Workers* https://www.mlaw.gov.sg/news/replies/statement-on-the-repatriation-of-foreign-workers.html. Accessed 1 May 2014.

Ministry of Manpower [MOM]. 2014. *Ministerial Statement on Findings of Committee of Inquiry (COI) on Little India Riot*. https://www.mom.gov.sg/newsroom/parliament-questions-and-replies/2014/ministerial-statement-on-findings-of-committee-of-inquiry-coi-on-little-india-riot.

Ministry of Manpower [MOM]. 2022a. *Work Passes*. https://www.mom.gov.sg/passes-and-permits.

Ministry of Manpower [MOM]. 2022b. *Foreign Workforce Numbers*. https://www.mom.gov.sg/documents-and-publications/foreign-workforce-numbers

National Population and Talent Division [NPTD]. 2022. *Population Trends*. https://www.population.gov.sg/our-population/population-trends/overview.

Ng, Esther. 2010. Employer's passport to trouble. *Today* (Singapore). January 25.

Ong, A. 2006. Mutations in Citizenship. *Theory, Culture & Society*. 23 (2–3): 499–505.

Ong, J. 2016. Singapore Moves to Bolster Counter-Terrorism Security Measures. *Channel News Asia*. March 18. https://web.archive.org/web/20170709201946/; http://www.channelnewsasia.com/news/singapore/singapore-moves-to-bolster-counter-terrorism-security-measures-8156576

Packer, H. 1964. Two Models of the Criminal Process. *University of Pennsylvania Law Review* 113 (1): 1–68.

Parliament (Singapore). 2014. Parliamentary Debates. *Singapore Official Report Twelfth Parliament*, Part IV, Volume 91, Feb. 18.

Rahman, M. 2017. *Bangladeshi Migration to Singapore: A Process-Oriented Approach*. Singapore: Springer.

Rajah, J. 2012. *Authoritarian Rule of Law*. NY: Cambridge University Press.

Rosenbaum, Carrie L. 2018, September 22. Crimmigration – Structural Tools of Settler Colonialism. *Ohio State Journal of Criminal Law*, 16 (1): 9–64.

Salehin, Ahmad, and Laura Vitis. 2020. Cruising, Space and Surveillance: Decolonizing Sexuality in Singapore. *Globalizations* 17 (7): 1225–1240.

Sandhu, K.S. 1969. *Indians in Malaya: Some Aspects of their Immigration and Settlement (1786–1957)*. London: Cambridge University Press.

Silverman, S., and P. Molnar. 2016. Everyday Injustices: Barriers to Access to Justice for Immigration Detainees in Canada. *Refugee Survey Quarterly* 35: 109–127.

Spykerman, K. 2016. Better Technology, enhanced Home Team Needed to Fight Terror Threat: MHA. *Channel News Asia*. April 6.

Stanley, E. 2017. Expanding Crimmigration: The Detention and Deportation of New Zealanders from Australia. *Australian and New Zealand Journal of Criminology* 51 (4): 519–536.

Stenson, M.R. 1980. *Class, Race, and Colonialism in West Malaysia: The Indian Case*. St. Lucia: University of Queensland Press.

Stumpf, J.P. 2013. The Process is the Punishment in Crimigration Law. In *The Borders of Punishment: Migration, Citizenship and Social Exclusion*, ed. K.F. Aas and M. Bosworth, 58–75. Oxford: Oxford University Press.

Tafira, Kenneth. 2011. Is Xenophobia Racism? *Anthropology Southern Africa* 34 (3–4): 114–121.

Tarling, N. 1962. *Anglo-Dutch Rivalry in the Malay world 1780–1824*. Sydney: University of Queensland Press.

Teo, T. 2019. *Civic Multiculturalism in Singapore: Revisiting Citizenship*. Rights and Recognition: Springer International Publishing.

Tumlin, Karen C. 2004. Suspect First: How Terrorism Policy is Reshaping Immigration Policy. *California Law Review* 92 (4): 1173–1239.

TWC2. 2021. Short of foreign labour, Singapore sending workers home even when they want to stay and work. 23 May 2021. https://twc2.org.sg/2021/05/23/short-of-foreign-labour-singapore-sending-workers-home-even-when-they-want-to-stay-and-work/.

Vazquez, Yolanda. 2015. Constructing Crimmigration: Latino Subordination in a Post-Racial World. *Immigration and Nationality Law Review* 36 (2015): 713–772.

Walters, W. 2002. Deportation, Expulsion, and the International Policing of Aliens. *Citizenship Studies* 6 (3): 265–292.

Wong, T. 2013. Somebody's Watching Me; Does US-Style Prism Surveillance of Citizens' Online Outpourings Happen Here? *The Straits Times*, Jul 6.

Ye, J. 2016. *Class Inequality in the Global City: Migrants, Workers and Cosmopolitanism in Singapore*. Houndsmill, Basingstoke, Hampshire; New York: Palgrave Macmillan.

Yeo, G. L. 2008. $29m for More Cameras at MRT Stations; Work Due to Start Next Month in Move to Beef Up Commuter Safety. *The Straits Times*, Aug 29.

Yeoh, B.S.A., and W. Lin. 2013. Chinese Migration to Singapore: Discourses and Discontents in a Globalizing Nation-State. *Asian and Pacific Migration Journal* 22 (1): 31–54.

7

Colonial Legal Continuities in Post-colonial Pakistan: The *Katchi Abadi* of Qayyumabad and the Construction of Law, Ownership, and Crime

Sabeen Kazmi

1 Introduction

This chapter explores the legal language of 'formality' and 'informality' associated with land against the backdrop of a colonial legal history which works to construct specific spaces as 'criminal', 'violent', and or 'dangerous'. Using Qayyumabad, a *katchi abadi* (non-permanent settlement) located in Karachi, as a case study allows an entryway into understanding how the law and the criminal justice system function in adjudicating property rights. Drawing on post-colonial theorists such as Homi Bhabha (2004), Gayathri Spivak (1999), Franz Fanon (1967), and Edward Said (1978), as well as post-colonial legal scholars such as Margaret Davies (2002), this chapter illustrates the ongoing colonial legal legacy in the Pakistani province of Sindh.[1] Analysis of law used to colonize land during the British raj continues to function as a method of land encroachment and acquisition in present day Pakistan. Post-colonialism aims to address temporal and spatial colonial continuities in former colonies upon the termination of direct colonial rule. Said (1978) draws linkages between colonial and post-colonial

[1] Pakistan is a federation of four provinces including Sindh, Punjab, Balochistan, and Khyber Pukhtun.

S. Kazmi (✉)
Centre for Criminology & Sociolegal Studies, University of Toronto, Toronto, ON, Canada
e-mail: sabeen.kazmi@mail.utoronto.ca

G. B. Radics and P. Ciocchini (eds.), *Criminal Legalities and Minorities in the Global South*, Palgrave Socio-Legal Studies, https://doi.org/10.1007/978-3-031-17918-1_7

society, identifying the pervasive implications of colonial rule through its social, political, cultural influences in post-colonial society. One debate in the post-colonial discourse is whether a temporal and spatial reality came about with the formal end of colonial law.[2] This chapter argues that the end of colonialism never occurred, and that colonial continuities are particularly pervasive within the legal structure of Pakistan. It argues that the written laws and policies of the colonial-era Land Acquisition Act of 1894 remains unchanged in modern Pakistan, with the legislative control that was established by the East India Company over parts of India simply transferred from one group of elites to the next, continuing the efficient extraction of labor and goods from the region into the present.

The British empire used property, tenancy, and land policies and legislation as a method of control over India. Much of these colonial laws and policies were adopted verbatim by the Pakistani government post partition. Some of such laws present today include the Land Acquisition Act of 1894, permitting the acquisition of land for public purposes, and the Punjab Colonization of Government Land Act of 1912. Through these laws, and many others like them, the British served as gatekeepers and presided over all decisions ranging from law to education up till independence in 1947, when the beneficiaries of these institutions, the elite local population, replaced the colonizers with bodies who represented the natives in image but not necessarily in interest. As proxies of imperial control, elite natives and the educated bourgeoisie act as interlocutors who maintain the colonial systems of oppression.[3] They further highlight the purported dichotomy between a modern, advanced, and developed citizenry, and the dangerous, underdeveloped and rabble. These dichotomies further justify the modern-state's encroachment for the purpose of development which is often wrapped in messaging of securitization (Duffield 1999). Hidden behind development and security rhetoric is the unspoken containment of the poorest and most marginalized (Duffield 2010).

The encroachment of the state by communities deemed dangerous and underdeveloped through the language of securitization is illustrated in the

---

[2] In highlighting the problems with the term 'post-colonial,' Olaniyan (1993, 746) argues that, 'Implicit in [a] justified unease in claiming 'post-colonial' is the discriminating recognition that we are living a temporality that is not so easily, so triumphantly categorized, located as it is between the end of formal empire and, as we have all agreed, the inability to be post-colonial.'

[3] *See* Barkawi and Laffey (1999) for a discussion on the establishment of a transnational constitution of force under the banner of 'peacekeeping' and 'peace-building' implanted in former colonies through placement of the US troops.

case of Qayyumabad. The colonial legal institutions backed by imperialism construct towns like Qayyumabad as 'undeveloped' and therefore 'insecure.' By legally referring to such communities as *katchi abadis*, the name itself, '*katchi abadi*' is purposeful in that it characterizes the town as *katchi* ('unripe/underdeveloped' or 'non-permanent') and *abadi* ('development') is a constant and stark branding of non-permanency and by extension as a space of 'insecurity'. Thus, the colonial legal framework produces a social archetype wherein informality is categorically stigmatized and criminalized, justifying violence against the community and encroachment upon the land by state actors.

This chapter argues that the current legal institution of Pakistan is enmeshed in colonial legal logics illustrated through its colonial property and land reform legislations and a broken and often powerless criminal justice system. It starts off with a discussion on urban issues in Pakistan, briefly discussing the case study of Qayyumabad and the research I conducted in this community. Next, it looks at land reform regimes in the Sindh province, with a specific focus on the criminal justice system, particularly for *katchi abadis*. Finally, the chapter will explore the legal construction of "non-permanence" and how crime, danger, and illegality are associated with it.

2 Urban Issues in Pakistan

Following independence, Karachi experienced overwhelming population growth comprised of Muslim refugees fleeing India (also known as Muhajirs), in addition to an influx of laborers and peasants migrating from rural parts of Pakistan and neighboring states in search of financial opportunities. Although state leaders did their part in housing and settling bureaucrats (i.e., upper and middle class Muhajirs) the sheer rate at which the population of Karachi was expanding, along with various changes in leadership, low-income Muhajirs came to be one of the most neglected minority groups in the country. Immediately following partition, state leaders attempted to provide a temporary recourse to Karachi's burgeoning population by building *katchi abadi*, loosely translated as 'non-permanent settlements', to house displaced refugees. As far as 'permanency' goes, housing units in *katchi abadis* were defined as a dwelling that had four walls and a functional roof.

Overtime, as the non-permanent settlements aged, they continued to be neglected by the state with inadequate electricity and water supply and poor infrastructure, including the lack of transportation and sewage systems.

As the refugees and migrants moving to Karachi tripled between 1941 and 1951, state leaders failed to properly plan for and meet the needs of the fast-growing population and eventually people began to illegally occupy land and new *katchi abadis* began emerging across the city. Initially, much of the land belonged to the local provincial government (Hasan 2015, 291) and tenancy laws dictated the terms of lease agreements between the state, landowners, and farmers/labourers who worked the land (Bano 2012, 99). Today, approximately 50% of land is controlled by the Defence Housing Authority (DHA) and military cantonment boards (Hasan 2015, 220). DHA is a housing development regime with international partners and is designed to benefit retired senior military officials, politicians, elites, and investors, with its management overseen by Army General Headquarters (Siddiqua 2017, 197–217). The military has been accused of appropriating land, often resulting in the displacement of its inhabitants. The acquired land is developed for commercial and private use, and sold to investors and upper middle class or elite members of society (*ibid*). Many *katchi abadis* are fraught with contention as they attract investors for development projects who are vying for governmental support in 'winning' the land: one poignant example is that of Qayyumabad.

The Pakistani government has employed different praxis in acquiring land across the country since partition of 1947. While the land reform act has been utilized by the government to acquire land in the province of Punjab, different political and legal strategies have been established to do the same in the capital city of Karachi. This in part can be traced back to the British Raj, wherein different laws were enacted based on the colonizers' needs and what was required from the land. The entrenchment of property and land rights proposed by the British had an adverse impact on the *zamindar* (landowner class) and non-agrarian creditors to whom land had been mortgaged by the Bombay presidency (Gazdar 2009). This caused a backlash against the presidency which resulted in the successful partition of Sindh from Bombay (Gazdar 2009). The separation from Bombay allowed *zamindars* to own and control land with less state intervention. However, the *zamindars* then leased out their lands to specific castes and clans residing in Sindh known as *haaris* who worked on the lands on behalf of the *zamindars*. A significant portion of this land belonged to Hindu Varya *zamindars* who migrated to India shortly after the partition. Due to this, the *haari* claimed ownership of the property abandoned by the Hindu *zamindars* (Gazdar 2009). *Haari*, or lower caste marginalized land workers did not get to enjoy their land ownership status for very long. During the time of partition, the governments of India and Pakistan legislated policies on displacement and dispossession.

These policies promised that if migrants were able to demonstrate proof of property that they had left or lost due to war, they would be compensated for it through the allotment of land (Gazdar 2009, 16). This allotment was only provided to those who had the appropriate paperwork and proof of land ownership. Many Muhajirs who left their homes and belongings in a hurry never imagined that they would not be returning to their ancestral lands.

In Sindh, Muhajirs who were able to assert their claims of land ownership in India were given land belonging to *haaris*. The new government deemed it possible to do so through settling Muslim Muhajirs in urban areas so as to achieve political stability and building a Muslim national identity premised on the Muhajirs' cultural and socio-lingual sentiments.

3 The Case of Qayyumabad

Qayyumabad is a small *katchi abadi* wedged between a DHA neighborhood and a newly constructed motorway. It is among one of the most densely populated *katchi abadis* in Karachi and is composed of 109 acres of land shared by almost 1 million people. To contextualize, about 50% of Karachi's population live on only 8.1% of the land. This draws attention to the large class disparity experienced by the low-income population. Initially, the Karachi Metropolitical Corporation[4] proposed for an area of 163.18 acres over which to build Qayyumabad and an additional 30.32 acres of land for amenities needed for a functional residential area. Qayyumabad is also meant to be protected and 'regularized' under the Sindh Katchi Abadi Act of 1987 under which Qayyumabad is a protected settlement with ownership rights for the residents as well as entitlements to municipal services. Yet, the densely populated Qayyumabad has been a site of contention exposed to the threat of encroachment by the DHA since the 1980s. According to residents of Qayyumabad, DHA has already been successful in encroaching upon approximately 53 acres of their land with 30 additional acres of land scheduled for amenities being transferred to DHA by the Sindh government improperly through "human error."[5]

[4] The Karachi Metropolitan Corporation is a public corporation and governing body that provides municipal services in the city of Karachi.

[5] The municipality of Karachi allotted the land to the DHA who had submitted documentation support their claims that the land belonged to the organization. However, a closer look at the document illustrates either an error at best or an attempted forgery at worst (Zaman and Ali 2016).

Of the hundreds of regularized and non-regularized *katchi abadis*, my research focuses on Qayyumabad for three reasons. First, despite the risk of displacing almost one million inhabitants, the community lacks legal, political, and academic interest in protecting residents and business owners from encroachment. Informal conversations with activists and academics suggest that this may be in part due to the small size of land on which Qayyumabad sits today. Second, of the hundreds of regularized *katchi abadis* that are legally protected against land encroachment, Qayyumabad is amongst the *katchi abadi* that are most at risk of being encroached by the DHA. An in-depth analysis of laws related to the regulations of *katchi abadi* demonstrates that residents of *katchi abadis* are given little legal recourse against state agents who fail to protect the interests of the community. Third, the risk of being encroached by the DHA is due to its geographical location; it is located in between a DHA development and the motorway, and thus, the land occupied by residents of Qayyumabad is located on a valuable piece of land, garnering economic interest. However, the inaccurate representation of the community as a hub of criminal activity by the media is used as a justification for encroachment.

4 Methodology and Research Significance

During a one-month research trip in December 2019, I had informal conversations with professional stakeholders who work on land rights and displacement. The purpose of the study was to establish connections with key stakeholders working on land encroachment rights with connections to Qayyumabad. I was unsuccessful in connecting with key informants who worked with Qayyumabad, due to a lack of interest in this small piece of land. While I was unsuccessful in connecting with professionals who worked directly with the community, I was able to speak to professionals who worked on similar issues faced by residents and business owners of Qayyumabad. These professionals included politicians advocating for *katchi abadi* and their rights to land, human rights lawyers, journalists, academics, NGOs directors, and activists. These informal conversations were supplemented with site visits as well as archival analysis of news coverage on Qayyumabad.

The bulk of research on land reform, urban development, and military encroachment/violence centers Punjab as the object of academic investigation (Nasreen and Hira 2009; Ali 2014). The legal and colonial historic context of Punjab has largely contributed to this academic interest, but research conducted in Punjab is not generalizable due to Sindh's distinct history. To date, much research has focused on urban land development (Qadeer 1996), development policies (Hasan 2015), *katchi abadis* (Hasan 2006; Kirmani 2017), and land encroachment by the DHA (Rajani and Islam) and similar organizations in Karachi, focusing on the older and larger informal housing communities within city limits, such as Orangi (Hasan 2006; Bano 2017) or Lyari (Kirmani 2015, 2017). More emerging scholarship on land encroachment and development has focused on violence against indigenous communities during encroachments of land at the outskirts of Karachi by big development firms such as Biharia Town (Rajani and Islam, forthcoming). Urban development policy research in Karachi usually functions under policy-based analysis, such as the works of Arif Hasan (2006, 2015), which focus on failed structural programs and housing policies proposed by the government and pose changes in policy and governmental support as a remedy to current issues. Much of the existing research on land reform predominantly focuses on urban, housing, and resettlement policies with little concern given to the current legal system, its colonial influences, and the criminalization and stigmatization of *katchi abadi* communities.

Beyond research on policy and urban development, other studies have focused on Pakistan's military and its impact on the residents of Karachi. The work of Raza et al. (2017) illustrate that an increase in military involvement and expenditure results in income inequality and its impact on urban areas. Their data suggests that an increase in military expenditure results in an increase of military presence which leads to a heightened reliability on military intervention for the purpose of governance. This is significant because, historically, the military has been used as a response to growing violence in Karachi. Oskar (2009) looks at the impact of the increase in military presence and its impact on people living in *bastis* or slums (Oskar 2009). Meanwhile, Arshad Zaman (2016) points to four global trends which have influenced the Pakistani government's reliance on the military. Zaman argues that the re-emergence of racism and white supremacy, economic emergence of Sino-Russian Eurasia Economic agreement, and the militant extremism in India have exacerbated a greater civil-military governance and were used to develop the economy and establish sovereignty on a global platform.

5 Land Reform Regimes in Sindh

The British colonial empire wielded property law as a method to colonize land and formalize control over it. The empire employed similar tactics in India during its rule, with these tactics being co-opted by the post-colonial Pakistani state, illustrating the strong colonial legal continuities pervasive today. The laws with provisions that have carried over from the colonial era to the present include the Land Acquisition Act of 1894 permitting the acquisition of land for public purposes and Punjab Colonization of Government Land Act of 1912.

The Land Acquisition Act of 1894, Part II, Sections 4–6, empowers the state to acquire any land it requires for public purposes, a term described as 'any purpose which serves an advantage to the community and uses examples such as: hospital, railways, water, power, parks/playgrounds, residential colonies or schools.' Acquisitions of land are processed by the revenue collection authorities. The law states that land acquisition may be voluntary or compulsory. An updated version of the law has since been adopted by the Pakistani government decree entitled the Capital Development Authority Ordinance of 1960. This Ordinance gives the government power to acquire any land that it declares a necessity for the use of the state. Through this Ordinance, the Pakistani government has justified acquiring the land needed for the move of the capital of Pakistan from Karachi to Islamabad in 1966.

Similarly, the Punjab Colonization of Government Lands Act in 1912 vested the British government with the power to grant land in the colony to any person it saw fit, as long as the government was able to state the conditions under which the land was granted. Meanwhile, Section 32 states that 'in the condition that the landowner fails to demonstrate their ownership over the land, the Commissioner has the power to take possession of the land.' Additionally, Section 37 protects the decisions of the Deputy Commissioner by prohibiting anyone from filing a lawsuit challenging the decisions made by the Deputy Commissioner. Finally, Section 38 established that any action undertaken by a civil servant working within this law will be seen as a provision passed under this law. Thus, any acts of encroachment over land by agents of the state are lawful, and the displaced occupants are denied legal recourse to challenge the decisions of civil servants. Interestingly, this act remained in effect until 2001 when it was terminated under the Devolution Plan.

Shortly after the 1947 partition, the Pakistani government utilized similar rationales when acquiring land from landowners through the Land Reform

Act, and later through the Katchi Abadi Acts. The Land Reform Act has since undergone four amendments. In 1959 when the Act was first enacted through Martial Law Regulation No. 64, it imposed a ceiling over the ownership of privately owned land. Landowners were allowed 500 acres of irrigated land and 1000 acres of unirrigated land. Leniency was given to those whose crops were producing less than 36,000 units in produce. Through this Act, the government seized 2.5 acres of land which was distributed to 183,271 tenants and small landowners. The second major land reform was introduced by Martial Law No. 115 in 1972. This reform changed the allowance of land ownership from 500 to 150 acres of irrigated land and from 1000 to 300 acres of non-irrigated land. The production unit index also shifted from 36,000 to 12,000. While during the first land reform the government compensated those landowners who surrendered their land, during the second land reform no such compensation was given. Following a similar pattern, the third major land reform took place in 1977 and continued to reduce the amount of irrigated and non-irrigated land ownership from 150 to 100 acres and 300 to 200 acres, respectively. Additionally, the produce index unit decreased from 12,000 to 8000.

The main purpose of land reform was to redistribute land. These land reforms were meant to serve as a method of 'equitable' redistribution of land between landowners and their tenants. While the reform may have been successful in implementing a ceiling on how much land one individual could legally hold, it did not improve the conditions of the poor peasantry. Instead, much of the land was merely redistributed amongst the children of landowners. Moreover, the third major land reform formalized more rights for landowners who surrendered their land by allowing them first priority to lease out the land from the government. While the reform was portrayed as protecting the rights of the poor peasantry through land redistribution, in reality, it resulted in the opposite. The reform was most successful in creating favorable circumstances for the state to obtain and regulate land from rich landowners.

The Sindh Katchi Abadi Act of 1987 came as a response to the housing crisis as a result of mass migration post partition. While the upper and middle class Muhajirs were given priority during the earlier resettlement stages, the lower-class Muhajirs and migrants from Afghanistan, as well as labourers and peasants from other parts of post partition Pakistan, who migrated to the Sindh metropole, were neglected. At first the government allowed migrants to occupy public spaces such as schools, parks, and non-irrigated land because there was no other space to house them. In a way, allowing the occupation of migrants to inhabit these public spaces worked to colonize land. What followed was a series of governmental policies and legislations created to legalize the occupation of migrants on government land.

The Sindh Katchi Abadi Act of 1987 legalizes and regularizes non-permanent settlements in Karachi. While this Act has been projected as legalizing illegal settlements and empowering impoverished communities, the contents of this Act illustrate similar colonial logics as the ones illustrated in the Land Acquisition Act of 1894, the Punjab Colonization of Government Lands Act of 1912, and the post-colonial Land Reform Act of 1959. For instance, the provincial government of Sindh recognizes approximately 400 of almost 600 non-permanent settlements as 'legal,' and establishes a positive duty on the provincial government to provide the non-permanent settlements with public services such as parks, hospitals, roads, streets, clean water, sewage system, and waste collection. However, most of the settlements are severely neglected by the government. In addition, under the Sindh Katchi Abadi Act of 1987, the government has the right to acquire any land on which a non-permanent settlement is built if the land is required by the government. The act also states that any government official who neglects their duty cannot be held liable unless the complaint is filed by the director general. The sentiment of this Act closely mirrors the acquisition without consequence of colonial ideology embedded with the Punjab Colonization of Government Land Act.

6 Criminal Justice System and *Katchi Abadis*

Katchi abadis are complex social spaces. On the one hand, *katchi abadis* are needed and are thus essential for the city. The *katchi abadis* house approximately 41% of Karachi's population, making up a significant percentage of working-class families who provide domestic and physical labour such as house cleaning, cooking, driving, construction, traffic police, factory work, etc. (Fernandes 1994). The need for, and the contributions of, the residents of *katchi abadis* is undeniable. Yet on the other hand, the informality of *katchi abadis*, which are in violation of zoning laws, illegally occupied, or built on government land marked for irrigation or public usage, causes disruptions to city planning and security.

It is important to note that the emergence of *katchi abadis*, their informality, and illegality traces back to the failure on the part of the state in providing affordable housing and transportation for low-income families who work in the city. In many ways, the government allows the emergence of *katchi abadis* to offset the costs of building affordable housing, all the while socially constructing these spaces as 'informal', 'non-permanent', 'transitory', and 'crime ridden' in order to justify state sanctioned violence and the encroachment of land when required for economic or political benefit of the state.

The intersections between *katchi abadis*, crime, and the criminal justice system are complex and layered. The criminal justice system of Pakistan is informed by the Code of Criminal Procedure of 1898 and the Penal Code of 1860, both of which were developed and influenced by the British Empire prior to the empire's exit (Hameed and Jamshed 2013). Research analyzing the criminal justice system of Pakistan illustrates that the laws are antiquated, corrupt, dysfunctional, and distrusted by civilians (*ibid*). Due to the shortcomings of the criminal justice system and the mounting, skepticism by the public has significantly impacted its authority, therefore, requiring immediate procedural, legislative and administrative transformation.

While criminal law establishes the rule of the land, the criminal justice system is not always successful in exercising the punitive actions against those proven guilty. Instead, the province of Sindh functions less on the basis of legal procedure and more on a hybrid system of formality and informality. This hybrid system includes the police, rangers, military, organized mafia, ethnic political parties, and extremists who all reign over matters relating to territory and crime (Khan 2016a, b). Meanwhile, the justice system is rarely at the center of arbitration concerning land disputes against the encroachment of land by state agents. In most cases, the criminal justice system is absent, silent, or relies on informal means to handle issues concerning informality and crime.

This informality is illustrated through the case of Rehmanabad, a relatively small *katchi abadi*, housing low-income families working as domestic helpers to families close by. Despite the regularization of the *katchi abadi*, the residents of Rehmanabad were forcefully removed with the promise of better housing and amenities located at the edge of the city (Fernandes 1994). The relocation of the families cost them their homes, jobs, social connections, access to water, electricity, and affordable transportation. In addition, the forceful eviction occurred in two phases, first of which through demolishment which resulted in the death of one adult and 25 women reported being gang raped (Fernandes 1994). Furthermore, of 550 families living in the *abadi*, only 400 were compensated through the allotment of land, while the rest received nothing (*ibid*). The change in political climate saw the families returning to the *abadi* in an attempt to salvage and rehabilitate what was lost. However, the *abadi* was set on fire in which 2 infants died and 12 people were injured. In this instance, the local senator, the District Commissioner of the area and the Karachi metropolitan Corporation armed with the city police were responsible for the grave injustice against the community. The councillor used his political connections, law, and the court system to justify the encroachment and pressured the community to evict.

In the case of Rehmanabad, while law was initially invoked verbally to scare the residents into moving, the criminal justice system remained largely absent up until the last minute, in which case it was utilized by the state as an instrument used to formally establish the state's authority over the *katchi abadi*. While Rehmanabad was particularly egregious, instances of encroachment of *katchi abadis* for commercial gain continue to occur throughout the city. Similarly, Qayyumabad continues to resist further encroachment of their land by the Defence Housing Authorities. Qayyumabad town was awarded 164 acres with 106 acres for residential plots and the rest for public amenities such as park, college, and graveyard. The DHA has been attempting to extend the boundaries of its Phase VII neighborhood and has successfully taken over approximately 53 acres earmarked for private plots and 30 acres earmarked for amenities. In 2005, the residents accused provincial government officials of collusion which resulted in acceding to DHA's demand to surrender land along Korangi road near the KPT flyover (Zaman and Ali 2016). In recent years, sentiments of the residents of the town were aggravated as the DHA attempted to further encroach the town's boundaries by extending its limits into Qayyumabad's graveyard (*ibid*). Despite the demand by the justice system to surrender land to the DHA, the residents continue to resist the DHA's attempt to tear down the graveyard (Zaman and Ali 2016).

7 The Legal Construction of 'Non-Permanence'

Commenting on the colonial continuities in former colonies post colonialism, Edward Said (1978) writes about the categorization of the 'orient' by the western world and its political, economic, and cultural currency in the post-colonial world. According to Said, the colonizer holds power over the Orient or the socially constructed Other through its ability to construct the Other as fundamentally different from itself. This social construction is asserted as the unobjectionable truth through culture, society, politics, and knowledge production. The construction of the Other is established through what it is not or what it is lacking in comparison to those who have the power to construct social realities. According to Said, the Western hegemony over knowledge and knowledge production as the objectionable truth aids it in this process.

Social psychologists who study intergroup relations suggest that all groups have a propensity to describe themselves in relation to others (Sherif et al. 1961, Sherif 1966). While members of the in-group view themselves as heterogeneous, out-groups are viewed as homogeneous through stereotypical external characteristics which become the source of bias (Katz 1973). While all groups may process information by categorizing in-group and out-groups, what sets apart the western world's categorization of the Orient is the colonizer's ability to construct a narrative which seeps into the social, legal, and political society and functions as the objective truth. While Said (1978) illustrates the construction of the narrative of the Other through western knowledge, social-legal scholarship has shown that a similar process of othering occurs through the use of language in law.

Through codification, setting precedence and arbitrating disputes, the law establishes itself as the narrator, narrative, and the narrated, imbuing it with the power to construct rigid categorizations of 'legal', 'illegal', 'permanent', 'non-permanent', 'formal', 'informal', 'civil', 'uncivil', 'developed' or undeveloped', and 'domestic' or 'foreign' (Wolff 2014; Razack 2007). While these categories are not static and are heavily contested in public life, the legal institution has the authority to construct and formalize dominant narratives and the categorization of the Other, thereby, influencing the social world and its subjects (Wolff 2014). In her work on the construction of the Bedouins as illegal, Shamir (2001) argues that the displacement of the Bedouins by the Israeli state is made possible by constructing a narrative of the 'legal' and the 'illegal,' and the 'spontaneous' as opposed to the 'planned'. This dichotomization between the autonomous existence of the Bedouins versus the planned, organized, and permanent construction of Jewish state creates a legal narrative that creates the story of the Other as an unobjectionable truth (2001, 138).

Similarly, in the case of Qayyumabad and the state of Pakistan, the law constructs towns like Qayyumabad (see Fig. 1) as 'spontaneous', 'unplanned,' and 'non-permanent'. Despite legally recognizing ownership rights of homeowners in these spaces, the law refers to them as *katchi abadis,* illustrating linkages embedded within the Act which works to exploit, control, and extract land as needed. The usage of the word '*katchi abadi*' is purposeful in that it evokes a distinctly clear dichotomous status of the town.

Fig. 1 Pictures of a bustling Qayyumabad

The very characterization of the town as *katchi* (unripe/underdeveloped' or 'non-permanent') and *abadi* ('development') is a constant and stark branding of non-permanency. By continuing to call these towns *katchi abadis* shows that the state views them as non-permanent, despite their physical permanency, with generations of families, a multitude of businesses, and a deeply-rooted community putting down its roots in such spaces. The legal framework produces a social archetype of 'transitory,' 'non-belonging,' and 'temporary', which manifests into the stigmatization of not only the town but also its residents and business owners as transient, temporary, and in transition.

The political catalyst which augmented the establishment of the Sindh Katchi Abadi Act of 1987 was supposed to legalize towns such as Qayyumabad. While portrayed as an Act meant to protect the legal rights of residents of *katchi abadis*, however, the neglect of the town and its needs illustrates the state's choice in allowing its degradation. In doing so, the state chooses to allow the slow demise of the town. As the town continues to denigrate, surrounding DHA communities with significant economic and political power continue to agitate the municipal governments for their removal, which further works to serve as a justification for the state in encroachment of land. Research conducted by Quraishi (2008) argues that *katchi abadis* such as Qayyumabad are understood as 'criminal', 'violent', 'dangerous', and 'diseased' by middle and upper class Karachites. Quraishi's findings suggest that these understandings are heavily based on the occupants of the *katchi abadis* as part of an 'out-group' or 'other' which highlights differences and develops suspicion and fear. This is especially true of people who have never visited *katchi abadis* or know anyone who lives there. The demarcation of *katchi abadis* as 'unripe', 'non-permanent', and 'crime ridden' seeps into the collective subconsciousness and has varying degrees of impact on the town as well as on its relations to surrounding neighborhoods.

8 'Non-Permanence', 'Crime', and Colonial Law

Another consequence of the social construction of space as 'non-permanent' or 'crime ridden' contributes to other negative stereotypes including 'lacking,"impoverished', 'illegal,' 'dangerous,' and 'diseased'. A survey of articles about Qayyumabad reveals two main themes: (1) the town's 'lack' (poor infrastructure and government negligence); (2) the other of its 'criminality'. News articles that discussed the infrastructure generally focused on the town's suffering from municipal negligence, the lack of basic amenities, such as clean water, or the flooding of streets during monsoon season. Most of the other articles provided reports of kidnapping, hyper policing, murder, theft, terrorism, gang activities, or drug use. An article written in 2016 by *The Nation*[6] stated that:

> In Pakistan, the image of *katchi abadis* is associated with criminal activities and diseases due to the poor living conditions of the dwellers in these shanty developments. Crime is an especially important factor behind the government's policy of clearing these shanty developments. Criminal activities usually associated with *katchi abadis* in Pakistan include sale of drugs, bootlegging, harbouring people with criminal records and unchecked sale of arms and ammunition.

The labeling of *katchi abadis* as fraught with criminal activities, close associations with terrorist links, and rampant disease due to the collective socio-economic status of the neighborhood stigmatizes people who live in the community by depicting all the one million people living there as sick or criminal. As these are widely held beliefs against *katchi abadis,* it serves to justify police violence experienced by residents of *katchi abadis.*

In a comparative study conducted by Quraishi (2008), the research notes that upper- and middle-class residents of Karachi are most likely to attribute

[6] *The Nation* is one of the largest Pakistan-based newspaper printed in English and is frequently cited abroad. *See* https://nation.com.pk/about-us (accessed 13 June 2021).

katchi abadis with criminality, animosity, violence, police brutality, raids, lack of security, and perceived potential victimhood (Quraishi 2008, 165). These negative stereotypes are largely held by those residents who have never visited *katchi abadis*. Meanwhile, those who have frequented such spaces said they did not fear visitation to these spaces, nor did they ever experience hostility, violence, or criminality (Quraishi 2008, 166).The solution often offered to 'solve' crime in *katchi abadis* is development schemes undertaken by large development companies such as the DHA or Bahria Town. In doing so, DHA successfully swoops in to develop projects that systematically displace people living in these communities. Therefore, the stigmatization and projection of *katchi abadis* as dangerous and crime ridden works to displace an already marginalized community. One prominent example of this is the displacement of between 33,000 and 70,000 residents of Lyari, one of the oldest *katchi abadis* in Karachi (Gazdar and Mallah 2011). Using the rise in gang activities, prostitution, and crime in the community, the military justified their encroachment and displacement of thousands of residents as a security concern.

The link between police, informal housing, and development is seen in security-development literature which has long demonstrated the close relationship between security and development. This literature identifies that international agencies depict poverty as the cause of criminality and underdevelopment, and promote development projects to increase security. Siman and Santos (2018), for instance, argues that Brazil's involvement in key operations fighting against gang violence in Haiti's most critical and violent areas through a United Nations Stabilization Mission became a roadmap for handling crime and poverty through the use of force in its own stabilization efforts at home. Da Silva (2001), studying excessive police violence in favelas, argues that the 'bodies' living in favelas are viewed as exceptions to be excluded from the promise of universal human rights because of the spaces they occupy and the racialized, impoverished, and criminalized identities attached. Moreover, this exceptionality is only further justified through their 'non-permanence', which absolves the state from sanctioned violence (2001, 442).

The construction of spaces as 'illegal' or 'criminal' and certain people as 'exceptions' or 'others' has dire consequences. For example, in 2014, the federal government of Pakistan sanctioned the extrajudicial killings of suspects of terrorism as a method of decreasing crime through the Protection of Pakistan Act. These excessive powers have been institutionalized in addition to the already vast power given to the police instituted during colonial rule, wherein the police were often called upon to curtail revolts by the peasantry.

The Criminal Procedure Code of 1898 Section 54 was specifically used to curtail revolt and collect taxes. The Code also granted the police power to arrest any suspicious persons whom the police officer may have suspected of committing a crime, accused of committing a crime, are under suspicion for being in possession of stolen property, or are under reasonable doubt of having committed a crime. The construction of *katchi abadis* as 'criminal' with links to terrorist organizations made such locations hot spots for police raids and extrajudicial killings. Between 2014 and 2016, the specialized police force killed over 1600 suspects between 2014 and 2016 (Khan 2016a, b). During this period there was little oversight over the actions of the police in their use of excessive force, the 'suspects' were never provided due process, or even the opportunity to plead their innocence. In the event that suspects were arrested, special military courts were set up under the 21st amendment of the Pakistani Constitution to swiftly adjudicate the matter.

9 Conclusion

The case of Qayyumabad functions as a lens through which to understand the ongoing use of colonial legal frameworks in the province of Sindh today. Forty-seven years after the end of the British Raj and the birth of Pakistan, the government continues to impose antiquated and corrupt laws onto its people. The study of Qayyumabad allows us an opportunity to see the operationalization of the legal institution of Pakistan and how deeply it is enmeshed in colonial legal logics illustrated through its colonial property and land reform legislations along with a broken and often powerless criminal justice system. Despite the depiction of the Sindh Katchi Abadi Act as monumental for enshrining ownership rights and protections against the displacement and or encroachment of regularized settlements, a closer look at the language of the law and its silence illustrates colonial legal logics which only appear to be giving legal rights and recognition to *katchi abadis* without any substantive legal recourse for the displaced. Moreover, through use of language that invokes 'non-permanence' or 'informality', the criminal justice system functions to exonerate itself in the event that the state or its affiliates such as DHA legally or illegally obtains land through coercion, violence, or bribery. Furthermore, the overworked, underfunded, backlogged criminal justice system is often silent, missing, or late in adjudicating decisions with limited recourse available for those who are wronged.

While this chapter establishes links between colonial and post-colonial Pakistan, further research is required to illustrate the intentionality of the state and its affiliates in land encroachment through construction of illegality. Research in the fields of legal human-geography and security-development nexus demonstrate strong links between construction of criminality as a justification for development projects to serve the bourgeois class. While these links exist in other fields, further studies using the socio-legal approach can help to uncover intentional use of messaging of 'criminality' and 'non-permanence' by the Pakistani state and its affiliates in order to justify land encroachment and police violence.

References

Laws

Capital Development Authority Ordinance of 1960.
Land Acquisition Act of 1894.
Land Reform Act of 1959, 1972, 1977.
National Legislative Bodies. *Pakistan: Code of Criminal Procedure, Act No. V.* Introduced in House July 1, 1898. https://www.refworld.org/docid/48511ea62.html.
Protection of Pakistan Act of 2014.
Punjab Colonization of Government Land of 1912.
Sindh Katchi Abadi Act of 1987.

Articles and Books

Ali, Syed Mohammad. 2014. *Development, Poverty and Power in Pakistan: The Impact of State and Donor Interventions on Farmers*. Routledge.
Bano, Masooda. 2012. *Breakdown in Pakistan: How aid is eroding institutions for collective action*. Palo Alto, CA: Stanford University Press.
Bano, Masooda. 2017. Buying Consent: The Achilles Heel of Aid induced community Participation. *Journal of South Asian Development*, 12 (3): 213–235.
Barkawi, Tarak, and Mark Laffey. 1999. The Imperial Peace: Democracy, Force and Globalization. *European Journal of International Relations* 5 (4): 403–434.
Bhabha, Homi. 2004. *The Location of Culture*. United Kingdom: Routledge.
Da Silva, Denise Ferreira. 2001. Towards a Critique of the Socio-logos of Justice: The Analytics of Raciality and the Production of Universality. *Social Identities* 7 (3): 421–454.
Davies, Margaret. 2002. *Asking the Law Question: The Dissolution of Legal Theory*. Sydney: Lawbook Company.

Duffield, Mark. 1999. Globalization and War Economies: Promoting Order of the Return of History? *The Fletcher Forum of World Affairs*, 23 (2): 21–36.

Duffield, Mark. 2010. The liberal way of development and the development-security impasse: Exploring the global life. *Security Dialogue*, 41 (1): 53–76.

Fanon, Franz. 1967. *Black Skin, White Masks*. Pluto Press.

Fernandes, Kennet. 1994. Katchi Abadis: Living on the Edge. *Environment and Urbanization*, 6 (1): 50–58.

Gazdar, Haris. 2009. The Fourth Round, And Why They Fight On: An Essay on the History of Land and Reform in Pakistan. *PANOS South Asia*: 1–43.

Gazdar, Haris and Hussain Mallah. 2011. The Making of a 'Colony' in Karachi and the Politics of Regularization. *South Asia Multidisciplinary Academic Journal*, 5 (1): 1–21.

Hameed, Hamza and Mohammad Jamshed. 2013. A Study of the Criminal Law and Prosecution System in Pakistan. *Manzil Pakistan*: 1–32.

Hasan, Arif. 2006. Orangi Pilot Project: The Expansion of Work Beyond Orangi and the Mapping of Informal Settlements and Infrastructure. *Environment and Urbanization* 18 (2): 451–480.

Hasan, Arif. 2015. Land Contestation in Karachi and the Impact on Housing and Urban Development. *Environment and Urbanization* 27 (1): 217–230.

Katz, I. 1973. Alternatives to a Personality-Deficit. In *Psychology and Race*, ed. P. Watson. Harmondsworth: Penguin.

Khan, Taimur. 2016a. 'We Search, We find, We Kill': Inside Karachi's Gangland Purge. *World Policy Journal*, 33: 93–104.

Khan, Yousafzai Babrak. 2016b. Regularizing Katchi Abaadis is Pakistan's Need of the Hour. *The Nation*. https://nation.com.pk/18-Aug-2016b/the-regularization-of-katchi-abaadis-pakistan-s-need-of-the-hour. Accessed 18 Aug 2016b.

Kirmani, Nida. 2015. Mobility and Urban Conflict: A Study of Lyari, Karachi. *Crossroads Asia Working Paper Series* 28.

Kirmani, Nida. 2017. Resistance and Its Limits. *Economic & Political Weekly* 52 (7): 41.

Nasreen, Zahra, and Anaiza Hira. 2009. *Impact Evaluation of Katchi Abadis Regularization and Development Programme (Case Study Lahore, Pakistan)*. Lahore, Pakistan.

Oskar, Verkaaik. 2009. At Home in Karachi: Quasi-Domesticity as a Way to Know the City. *Critique of Anthropology* 29 (1): 65–80.

Qadeer, Mohammad A. 1996. An Assessment of Pakistan's Urban Policies, 1947–1997. *The Pakistan Development Review* 35 (4): 443–465.

Quraishi, Muzammil. 2008. The Racial Construction of Urban Spaces in Britain and Pakistan. *Asian Journal of Criminology* 3 (2): 159–171.

Raza, Syed Ali, et al. 2017. Dynamics of Military Expenditure and Income Inequality in Pakistan. *Social Indicators Research*, 131 (3): 1035–1055.

Razack, Sherene H. 2007. Stealing the Pain of Others: Reflections on Canadian Humanitarian Responses. *The Review of Education/pedagogy/cultural Studies*, 29 (4): 375–394.

Said, Edward. 1978. *Orientalism*. Pantheon Books.
Shamir, Ronen. 2001. Suspended in Space: Bedouins Under the Law of Israel. In *The Legal Geographies Reader: Law, Power, and Space*, ed. Nicholas Blomley. Blackwell Publishers Ltd.
Sherif, Muzafer, et al. 1961. *Intergroup Conflict and Cooperation: The Robbers' Cave Experiment*. Norman: Univ. Okland Press.
Sherif, Muzafer. 1966. *In Common Predicament: Social Psychology of Intergroup Conflict and Cooperation*. Boston: Houghton Mifflin.
Siman, Maíra, and Victória Santos. 2018. Interrogating the Security-Development Nexus in Brazil's Domestic and Foreign Pacification Engagements. *Conflict, Security & Development* 18 (1): 61–83.
Siddiqua, Ayesha. 2017. *Military Inc. Inside Pakistan's Military Economy*. Penguin Books.
Spivak, Gayatri Chakravorty. 1999. *A Critique of Postcolonial Reason: Towards a History of the Vanishing Present*. Harvard University Press.
Wolff, Leon. 2014. Let's Talk About Lex: Narrative Analysis as Both Research Method and Teaching Technique in Law. *Adelaide Law Review*, 35 (1): 3–21.
Zaman, Arshad. 2016. *Sovereign Development: A Grand Strategy for Pakistan*.
Zaman, Fahim, and Naziha Syed Ali. 2016. Qayyumabad's Long Battle Against DHA. *Dawn*. https://www.dawn.com/news/1279039. Accessed 22 Aug 2016.

8

Disciplining Colonial Subjects: Neoliberal Legalities, Disasters, and the Criminalization of Protest in Puerto Rico

José Atiles

1 Introduction

On 30 April 2020, amidst the COVID-19 pandemic, Giovanni Roberto, a well-known Puerto Rican anti-hunger advocate and organizer of *comedores sociales* (community kitchens), was arrested while leading a caravan of cars making their way through the streets of Puerto Rico's capital, San Juan. The 'caravan for life' was aimed at distributing food in impoverished communities of San Juan and protesting the government's indifference to a growing hunger crisis as Puerto Rico (henceforth PR) entered its eighth week of lockdown (Florido 2020a). Roberto was charged with obstruction of justice and violating the governor's stay-at-home order.[1] Roberto's arrest was widely criticized as an unjustified act of repression and intimidation against community organizers fighting the hunger crisis plaguing PR since 2017, when hurricane María devastated the Island, and was further exacerbated by COVID-19 stay-at-home orders (Florido 2020b). Despite a judge dismissing the charges the same day, while in detention at the police station,

[1] Issued under the Executive Order OE-2020-033 of April 12, 2020. This is the four extension, since March 15, 2020, of the shelter-at-place or stay-at-home order issued by the Puerto Rican Governor Wanda Vazquez.

J. Atiles (✉)
University of Illinois at Urbana, Champaign, IL, USA
e-mail: jatiles@illinois.edu

G. B. Radics and P. Ciocchini (eds.), *Criminal Legalities and Minorities in the Global South*, Palgrave Socio-Legal Studies, https://doi.org/10.1007/978-3-031-17918-1_8

Roberto was caught on audio chanting the following short but heartbreaking lines: "what I want is food for the poor; all I ask for, is food for the poor".[2]

Unlike Roberto's arrest, the detention of hundreds of unemployed, poor, black, and immigrants for violations of stay-at-home orders had remained invisible.[3] The majority of these arrests have been under the newly passed Law 35 of 5 April 2020, which criminalizes "any breaching of an executive order". These detentions illustrated the current law enforcement and state-violence practices taking place in PR in the wake of the economic and financial crisis, and amidst the various waves of disaster affecting the archipelago since 2016.

Following LeBrón's (2019) analysis of neoliberal policing in PR, this chapter proposes the concepts of punitive governance[4] to describe the transformations that the Puerto Rican government and US colonialism in PR are experiencing in the context of the multilayered crisis. Punitive governance is rooted in two important phenomena: abandonment and neoliberal legalities. Abandonment manifests through the rapid transformation of the Puerto Rican political economy, and the way the local government sees its role in society. It entails: (1) the intensification of neoliberal policies (i.e., the reduction of administrative and regulatory structures), privatization of public services, and implementation of austerity measures; (2) the financialization[5] of the colonial economy and the exponential rise of the public debt.

Neoliberal legality manifests through the ever-increasing accumulation of power by the local executive branch and the corresponding weakening of the constitutional and civil rights where the state of emergency becomes entrenched. It also normalizes authoritarian policing, state violence, antidemocratic legislations, and impunity for white-collar criminals

---

[2] See Pulso estudiantil: https://twitter.com/pulsoest/status/1255992256651288576.

[3] As of 2 October 2020, the PR Police had issued a total of 3356 fines, while 1003 people have been arrested in connection with alleged curfew violations. See: https://www.metro.pr/pr/noticias/2020/10/02/1003-arrestos-por-violaciones-a-la-orden-ejecutiva-desde-el-inicio-del-toque-de-queda.html.

[4] Punitive governance also goes hand in hand with Gilmore's (2007) binomial description of state power in neoliberal times as organized abandonment and organized violence. Organized abandonment is the direct consequence of the neoliberal policies and austerity measures implemented to address periods of economic crisis. These transformations of the welfare state into a police state and the generalization of organized violence against poor communities is what critical scholars have named neoliberal policing or punishment (Beckett and Herbert 2008; Cypher 2007; Harcourt 2010; LeBrón 2021; Lynch 2011; Wacquant 2009; Whitman 2011).

[5] For an analysis of how the processes of financializing the economy have led to a systemic crisis, see the work of Krippner (2011) and Lapavitsas (2013).

and state-corporate crimes. Therefore, neoliberal legalities create the legal framework for wealth extraction and plunder and for repressive policing and criminal laws that enforce social control over working and poor people, socio-environmental, anti-austerity, and anti-corruption mobilizations. That is, punitive governance is implemented to discipline Puerto Rican colonial subjects.[6]

This chapter shows how the Puerto Rican government, the Department of Public Safety,[7] and US security agencies have used punitive governance to deal with three important reactions to the economic crisis in the wake of the US imposition of the Puerto Rican Oversight, Management and Economic Stability Act (PROMESA): (1) socio-environmental mobilizations; (2) anti-austerity mobilizations; and (3) anti-corruption mobilizations. To do so, the chapter proposes a twofold analysis. Firstly, it provides a brief overview of the PR's economic and financial crisis, the proposed neoliberal solutions to the crisis, and the consequences of such solutions. By engaging with the development of neoliberal legality and the uses of the state of emergency, this section shows the processes that led to organized abandonment and social death in PR.

Secondly, the chapter analyzes the process of criminalization of the socio-environmental, anti-austerity and anti-corruption mobilizations resisting organized abandonment. These forms of resistance to organized abandonment were largely initiated by grassroot initiatives, and working-class and poor communities. Two strategies will be discussed: (1) the use of criminal law to limit freedom of speech and protests; (2) repression and the systemic deployment of state violence against protestors. These state violent reactions to socio-political mobilizations are part of a long history of criminalizing and repressive practices that must be understood against the backdrop of US colonial history in PR: that is, a long-drawn effort to discipline colonial subjects.

6 My utilization of the concept of colonial subject aims to go beyond Grosfoguel's (2002) discussion of the location of PR within the modern/colonial world-system, and his engagement with coloniality of power and colonial difference. Thus, I am interested in analyzing how organized abandonment and neoliberal legalities have reshaped the ways in which the state and the criminal law deal with Puerto Ricans in the wake of the economic crisis.

7 Created Law 20 of 2017 the Department of Public Safety became the umbrella agency for all the Puerto Rican security agencies.

2 Neoliberal Legalities in PR: *Promesa* and Organized Abandonment

As colonial subjects within the body politic of the US, Puerto Ricans have seen their human and civil rights severely restricted by the US' criminal laws, economic interventions, and natural disaster management practices. These restrictions resulting from colonialism and the historical legal accommodation of PR and Puerto Ricans within the US's rule of law have produced a colonial subjectivity. Colonial subjects, thus, experience an inclusive exclusion within the US' imperial politics. This logic of inclusive exclusion placed Puerto Ricans—especially poor, working-class, and racialized Puerto Ricans—in an exceptional space, demarcated by the denial of full citizenship and protection of their basic human and civil rights; lack of acknowledgment of their autonomy and impositions of laws and economic policies without their consent; the denial of their right to self-determination, and criminalization and repression of political mobilizations (Atiles 2016, 2019). This logic of inclusive exclusion has been exacerbated by the economic crisis and the neoliberal policies imposed by the US and PR government to manage the crisis.

It is precisely in this context that the process of criminalization of socio-environmental, anti-austerity, and anti-corruption movements must be understood as a governmental instrument to control resistance against organized abandonment, and the criminogenic (mis)management of the multidimensional crisis affecting PR since 2006. In what follows, I am going to briefly describe the Puerto Rican multilayered socio-political, economic, and humanitarian crisis and the policies implemented by the US and PR governments to address it.

PR's economic crisis began in 2006 as a result of, among other things, the elimination of the tax exemption known as Section 936,[8] which sought to encourage US corporations to establish themselves in the archipelago with the promise that they would be able to repatriate profits as soon as they were realized. After ten years of economic crisis, in 2016, the local government defaulted on and stopped paying its public debt, which amounted to $72 billion, and the per capita debt burden was $15,637 (Bhatti and Sloan 2017). To make matters worse, PR is poorer than all of the states in the United States , having a median household income of $18,626. After

[8] Section 936 of the U.S. Internal Revenue Code of 1976 (26 U.S. Code, 1976).

the default in 2016, all three branches of the US government exercised their colonial power over PR. The US Congress legislated, and President Obama signed PROMESA into law. Notwithstanding, PROMESA is accompanied by the imposition of the Fiscal Oversight and Management Board (FOMB), or a seven-member board that regulates the budget and funds of PR's government, it does not recognize the effects of colonialism in the Puerto Rican multilayered crisis.

In tandem with this, the US Supreme Court ruled on two cases that redefined the colonial condition of PR: *Commonwealth of Puerto Rico v. Sánchez Valle et al.* (2016),[9] and *Commonwealth of Puerto Rico et al. v. Franklin California Tax-Free Trust et al.* (2016). Altogether, PROMESA, FOMB, and the US Supreme Court rulings have multiple implications. First, they were justified under the rationale that Puerto Ricans were fiscally irresponsible and lack the budgetary discipline necessary to rule their economy, thus requiring US intervention and fiscal control. Second, they also emphasized that it was the duty of the United States to lead PR government efforts to manage the fiscal and economic crisis and that such efforts should be defined by US law; third, US solutions to the crisis entail a radicalization of the violence of austerity and enhance organized abandonment; and, fourth, punitive governance became legitimized as a tool to police the crisis (especially *Sánchez-Valle*). All of these create the neoliberal-legal conditions for the local government to further develop its techniques of criminalization and repression against socio-political movements.

It was amidst this reaffirmation of US colonialism, that Ricardo Rosselló (New Progressive Party [NPP]) took office on 2 January 2017. Rosselló's administration passed laws to modify or eliminate existing labor rights, and enhanced austerity and neoliberal policies. Changes included the promulgation of the Labor Transformation and Flexibility Act (Law 4 of 26 January 2017), which proposed a reform of the labor law for the private sector; the Administration and Transformation of Human Resources in the Government of Puerto Rico Act (Law 8 of 4 February 2017), which introduces a labor law reform for government employees; Enterprise Puerto Rico (Law 13 of February 20, 2017), aiming to promote economic development and growth; two different laws to encourage private investors to move to PR (Law 45 of 11 July 2018 and Law 46 of 19 July 2018); and two laws to

[9] *Puerto Rico v. Sánchez Valle* addressed a double jeopardy case, in which the Court argued that PR does not have a sovereignty different from that of the federal government when it comes to the power to criminally prosecute an accused.

encourage private capital funds to move to the Island (Law 93 of 8 August 2017 and Law 94 of 8 August 2017). It is important to note that almost every law references PROMESA, the FOMB, and the economic and financial crisis as justification for their existence.

Against this backdrop, on 20 September 2017, Hurricanes Irma and María practically destroyed the archipelago. Rosselló's administration quickly moved to implement the state of emergency as a strategy to exploit the crisis generated by the hurricanes (Atiles 2019). However, this strategy, together with the negligent and criminogenic response of Trump's administration, worsened the crisis and the living conditions of Puerto Ricans and paved the way for rapacious disaster capitalism, corruption, and fraud (Klein 2018). In the aftermath of Hurricane María, Puerto Ricans experienced a radical expression of organized abandonment by both United States and local governments. The fact that approximately 4,645 people died (Kishore et al. 2018) as a consequence of the negligent and criminogenic (mis)management of the crisis proves that organized abandonment had become the recourse in dealing with every crisis.

One of the many factors that led to the Puerto Rican Summer of 2019—the socio-political mobilizations that ousted governor Rosselló—was the corrupt practices and organized abandonment that Puerto Ricans experienced since the beginning of his administration. After Rossello resigned, Wanda Vázquez, former Secretary of Justice, became Governor of PR in August 2019. As previous governors did before, Vázquez used executive orders and issued declarations of the state of emergency to deal with the economic crisis.

In January 2020, a swarm of earthquakes severely damaged the southwestern region of the island, worsening the already precarious economic situation (Onís et al. 2020). Between 7 January 2020 and 12 March 2020, Governor Vázquez issued 18 executive orders to address this crisis. Vázquez's administration declared a state of emergency (OE-2020-20, 12 March 2020) to address the COVID-19 pandemic. Following what has become a pattern to deal with any crisis or disaster, between March 12 and December 30, Governor Vázquez issued another 51 executive orders (Atiles 2021).[10] Similarly, Governor Pedro Pierluisi (PNP), who took office in January 2021, has followed this pattern of issuing executive orders to administer every aspect of the COVID-19 pandemic and other crises. For example, between January 2nd and July 1st, Governor Pierluisi issued 15 executive orders to

[10] All the executive orders are available in: www.estado.pr.gov/es/ordenes-ejecutivas/.

address the COVID-19 pandemic. As the local administration has issued emergency measures, Puerto Ricans have been facing exponential increases in unemployment rates (in a country that was already facing 14 years of economic stagnation); lack of access to testing, proper monitoring of people infected by COVID-19, and a chaotic vaccine rollout; a dramatic escalation of families facing food insecurity; and unequal federal emergency relief (Negrón 2020).

From this brief overview, I can conclude that every disaster has been (mis) managed by the local and US government with the same set of tactics: (1) abandonment of the most vulnerable populations and emphasizing individual responsibility (rather than governmental responsibility) to recuperate after disasters; (2) systemic uses of emergency legislation and of the state of emergency to address the crises; (3) disaster capitalist policies and the intensification of austerity measures; and (4) the militarization of disaster relief and law enforcement. In what follows, this chapter will be discussing organized violence and punitive governance, as the other side of the exposed neoliberal legalities and organized abandonment.

3 Punitive Governance and Resistance in the Wake of *Promesa*

In the context in which rights are restricted in order to promote neoliberal goals, the austerity measures and organized abandonment allows for the practice of punitive governance. As LeBrón argues, punitive governance "functions as a form of crisis management that masks an inability or unwillingness to radically transform social relations and institutions in order to address pressing societal problems" (LeBrón 2019, 6). As a crisis management technique, punitive governance is intertwined with the economic and financial crisis, colonial-neoliberal legalities, and abandonment. Given this relationship, punitive governance reinforces the neoliberal understanding that there is no alternative—an understanding that has been largely resisted in PR by grassroots socio-environmental, anti-austerity, and anti-corruption mobilizations.

The Puerto Rican government's implementation of punitive governance constitutes an exemplary case of organized abandonment and organized violence in a colonized global south country. The history of PR under US colonial rule, since 1898, is rooted in the systemic use of the rule of law to legitimate plunder, violence, and the criminalization and repression of anti-colonial and socio-political movements. In PR, there is a substantial body of scholarly analyses of the processes and history of state crimes and criminalization of anti-colonial movements (Atiles 2019; Bosques and Colon 2006; Paralitici 2011; Poltevin 2000); environmental movements (Atiles 2014; Braver 2012; Concepción 1995); and student movements (Atiles and Whyte 2011; Brusi 2011; Pérez-Lizasuain 2018). Furthermore, there are important analyses of the criminalization of impoverished communities of color (LeBrón 2019), police brutality, and impunity (Kilometro 2018, 2019, 2020; LeBrón 2021). Nevertheless, there is an important gap when it comes to analyzing the impact of the economic and financial crisis and the neoliberal solutions developed by the US and local governments upon the criminal justice system and law enforcement agencies. This is particularly problematic, since there is no clear analysis of how neoliberal policing and punitive governance are implemented to criminalize poor and working-class communities, and grassroot organizations that oppose neoliberal solutions to the economic crisis.

To be sure, punitive governance was not initially intended to deal with socio-political and anti-colonial movements. Instead, for these movements, the local and US governments continued applying criminalization and repression tactics born out of counter-revolutionary and colonial practices (Atiles 2019). Hence, the application of punitive governance to criminalized socio-political movements took place in the 2010s as a result of the economic crisis and the radical neoliberal transformation of US colonialism and the PR government.

This shift of repressive and criminalization techniques has to do with a transition in the Puerto Rican socio-political mobilizations resulting from the emergence of new strategies and tactics at the local and global level as well. The socio-political movements, especially since the Occupy movement in 2011, the *Indignados* civil uprisings and the Student Strike at the University of Puerto Rico (UPR) 2010–2011 and 2017, developed polymorphous political strategies that emphasized horizontality, mutual-aid and solidarity, direct and radical democracy, assembly models, and decoloniality. These strategies were widely implemented in the context of the anti-austerity student strikes at UPR in 2010–2011 and in 2017[11]; against PROMESA and the FOMB[12]; in the community-based and mutual-aid recovery efforts

[11] For a detailed analysis of the tactics and strategies implemented by the Students strikes see Pérez (2018).

[12] For an analysis of the resistance to PROMESA and to the colonial debt see Zambrana (2021). Additionally, we should consider the opposition to PROMESA led by feminist and grassroot organization such as the Feminist Collective in Construction (Zambrana 2021).

after hurricane María[13] and the swarm of earthquakes; and in the anti-corruption mobilizations of the Puerto Rican Summer of 2019.[14] In short, all these instances produced a new understanding of grassroot and socio-political mobilizations in PR, in which a plurality of subjectivities, tactics, and strategies converged to advance a specific demand. These new tactics and strategies had empowered poor and working-class communities and grassroot organizations to hold the colonial state accountable for its organized abandonment, as well as to address the devastation generated by the wave of disasters affecting PR since 2017. Therefore, it is understandable that repressive and criminalizing tactics developed to discipline and control precarious colonial subjectivities became the way in which the colonial-neoliberal state addressed these new mobilizations born out of organized abandonment.

In light of the reconfiguration of PR punitive politics, I will be looking at practices of criminalization and repression enforced against grassroot socio-environmental, anti-austerity, and anti-corruption mobilizations in the wake of PROMESA. To do so, in addition to studying the uses of state-violence against these mobilizations, I will first discuss how the New Penal Code of PR of 2012 protected the status quo by criminalizing tactics typically used in socio-political protests. Next, I will analyze the Law 20 of 2017, which in response to Hurricane María, created the Department of Public Safety to further enhance the powers of the state to criminalize social movements. These laws and their application illustrate the intertwined relationship between neoliberal legalities and punitive governance.

4 New Penal Code of PR of 2012 and the Criminalization of Grassroot Socio-Environmental and Anti-Austerity Mobilization

The recent process of criminalization of socio-political mobilizations, and the development of punitive governance, came as part of the neoliberal administration of Luis Fortuño (NPP 2009–2013) with the enactment of the New Penal Code of PR (Law 146 of July 30, 2012). The law targeted socio-environmental and student mobilizations and labor unions and

---

[13] See Bonilla and LeBron (2019) and Davila (2017).

[14] See Bonilla (2020) and Villanueva and LeBron (2020).

criminalized their traditional mobilization tactics. The Code has suffered several amendments, specially under Rosselló's administration, including Law 27 of 19 May 2017, which strengthened some of the provisions used to criminalize socio-political mobilizations and poor communities.[15]

The New Penal Code defines trespassing as "occupying private property or machinery that are part of a construction that has the proper permits" (§ 5267c). Also, it typifies as a serious crime, punishable with 3 years of imprisonment, obstructing or stopping public or private construction works (§ 5269a). Similarly, the code criminalized the interference with tourism (§ 5269b). The Code states that any person who intentionally obstructs and/or prevents access and/or enjoyment of any tourist activity will incur crime as well, albeit less serious. Although, these articles concerning "crimes against public safety" might look irrelevant at first, it is important to bear in mind that the occupation of "construction sites, touristic areas (such as beaches), and private estates (such as farms and experimentation sites owned by big corporations, e.g., Monsanto)" are the kind of political and non-violent actions taken by communities and socio-environmental mobilizations.

A telling example is the repression and criminalization of grassroot mobilizations such as "Encampment against Coal Ashes in Peñuelas". The Encampment is a community-based organization fighting to eradicate the practice of dumping toxic ashes from coal in local landfills in the southern region of PR (Onís 2018, 2021). The organization was initially formed to demand the closure of the island's only coal-fired plant owned by Applied Energy Systems (AES),[16] and to expose the health and environmental threats impacting vulnerable communities, like the southern town of Peñuelas. The organization has shown, on the one hand, the systemic socio-environmental harm produced by state encouragement and tolerance of AES toxic dumping (organized abandonment) and, on the other hand, has exemplified the uses of the New Penal Code and the criminal justice system to coerce poor communities and socio-environmental mobilizations (punitive governance). As Santiago et al. (2020) points out, hundreds of protesters have been

---

[15] Law 27 of 2017 was passed with the intention of criminalizing protests and putting limits on free expression in PR. With this law, protests in educational, health, and construction areas are criminalized, as well as the criminalization of student, worker, and socio-environmental movements.

[16] AES has been pointed as one of the corporations involved in the corruption scandal surrounding the Rosselló administration. In addition, this corporation has systematically violated local and federal environmental regulations. After multiple mobilizations and complaints, the PR legislature passed Law 40 of 2017, which gave AES additional power to continue with the toxic dumping of ashes. For more details on the case of AES (Rosa 2019).

arrested, faced police brutality and systemic surveillance for opposing the toxic dumping of ashes in the landfill.

Another important case of repression of grassroot socio-environmental movements is the arrest of environmental organizer and leader of the Casa Pueblo initiative, Arturo Massol (on July 27, 2018). Casa Pueblo is a community-based environmentalist project born in the 1980s in the mountain town of Adjuntas, in the context of the mobilizations against the US' mining industry in PR.[17] Throughout its forty years of existence, Casa Pueblo has faced systemic repression and criminalization of its organizers and followers (Atiles 2014). This situation increased in the aftermath of hurricane María when the organization started promoting solar energy as an alternative to fossil fuel energy production (Brown 2020). It was precisely in this context that Massol was arrested. Despite his case being dismissed days after, this is an additional example of how punitive governance is implemented to discipline those who oppose organized abandonment.[18]

Furthermore, the New Penal Code establishes tampering with essential services when preventing a person from requesting or receiving help for their life, health, or physical integrity as a serious crime (punishable with 15 years of imprisonment). Chapter 339, Crimes Against Public Order and Respect for Public Authority, shows the radicalization of the criminalization measures. Section § 5336a typifies obstruction of access or work in educational and health institutions or buildings where government services are offered to the public as a less serious crime. Finally, in section § 5338, the Code describes the use of disguises in the commission of crime as a serious crime. This section is particularly problematic since it typifies that any person using a mask, hairpiece, makeup, dye, or any other costume, complete or partial, that temporarily or permanently alters in any way their physical appearance in order to alter or interfere with ordinary activities in a public educational facility, in a health facility, or inside government buildings as a crime.

All of these provisions are directly targeted at criminalizing protests by labor and student mobilizations. Using masks while in demonstrations is a common practice in PR, and elsewhere, given the long history of police

[17] For more information see: https://casapueblo.org. Similarly, in Atiles (2014) I have shown how Casa Pueblo became a key organization in the struggles against environmental colonialism. Therefore, the criminalization of its leaders comes as a manifestation of the US and PR governments effort to thwart anticolonial mobilizations that challenged US colonialism in the archipelago.

[18] As a result of the devastation generated by hurricane María, PR holds the longest blackout in the history. See: https://witness.worldpressphoto.org/the-power-of-sin-luz-life-without-power-a86ab38a5e39.

surveillance[19] and repression against workers, and socio-political and anti-colonial movements. Masks have been used traditionally as a means to protect against criminalizing techniques. Similarly, another common practice among student movements is to occupy university campuses to demand for specific changes in university or government policies. That was the case of the UPR strikes of 2010–2011 and 2017 (Brusi 2011; LeBrón 2019; Pérez-Lizasuain 2018). Therefore, those specific sections are targeting the most common practices of socio-political mobilizations and curtailing freedom of speech.

These policies proved to be essential in the criminalization and repression of the opposition to neoliberal policies imposed by the FOMB. As early as the Summer of 2016, Puerto Ricans started mobilizing against PROMESA, FOMB, and organized abandonment. "PROMISES are over" or "Jornada se acabaron las PROMESAS" was one of the first anti-austerity organizations to emerge in this context (Mercado 2016). This organization held an encampment in front of the US Federal Court in PR and held countless mobilizations against the FOMB and its members. Simultaneously, the Feminist Collective in Construction has maintained a constant mobilization against PROMESA and against the burden of austerity on poor women of color. This black feminist and intersectional collective have led numerous demonstrations and have played a key role in remaining socio-political mobilizations in PR.

Likewise, Puerto Rican communities in the US and UPR students actively protested the austerity measures imposed by the FOMB. The student strike of 2017 is particularly relevant in demonstrating this process of criminalization (Robles 2017). Only three months after Rosselló took office, in April 2017, students declared a strike at UPR that lasted until June 2017. The student strike at UPR occurred in response to the reduction of UPR's budget, for the audit of the Puerto Rican Public debt, against the privatization of public services, and in defense of public education. While it is true that the strike and student protests were criminalized and delegitimized (Carrasquillo 2020), unlike the 2010–2011 strike, the state's repression and political violence were not widely used by the administration. However, the police engaged in physical and online surveillance of students, professors, and allies of the anti-austerity mobilizations.[20]

[19] Puerto Rican movements have endured a long history of surveillance known as Carpeteo. For analyses of these processes, see LeBrón (2017) and Paralitici (2011).

[20] For more details, see Diaz Torres (2020).

The local government took an additional step in the repression and imprisonment of anti-austerity activists on 1 May 2017. After a massive demonstration, some protestors carried out acts of sabotage against Banco Popular[21] in the financial district of San Juan. In most cases, those arrested were not involved in the acts against the bank, but were arrested simply because they had been identified in previous anti-austerity demonstrations. The case of Nina Droz reflects the use of the force of law to demobilize those who oppose organized abandonment and the violence of austerity. Droz was arrested on 1 May 2017 by the PR police while carrying out acts of civil disobedience to prevent the passage of the PR police's Tactical Operations Unit. Subsequently, Droz was charged in the US Federal Court in PR with interfering in interstate commerce (Title 18 of the US Code, Section 844 [i]); specifically, she was accused of trying to set the Banco Popular branch on fire. Despite the fact that the bank's facilities were not burned down, and that the damage (mainly broken glass) was promptly repaired by the bank and the government of PR, Nina Droz was sentenced to 37 months in prison and 3 years of probation.

While the criminalization and repression of anti-austerity mobilizations was taking place, Rosselló eliminated the "PR Commission for Comprehensive Audit of Public Credit",[22] previously created by Alejandro García's administration (Popular Democratic Party [PPD] 2014–2017). With the elimination of the Commission, Rosselló showed his connivance regarding financial, economic, and colonial-political interests, which led PR to its current crisis. Thus, the role of previous colonial administrations, banks, and the corrupt practices that led PR to its current crisis were actively disguised by Rosselló's administration.[23] In opposition to the elimination of the Commission, its former members and a group of citizens created the Puerto Rico Citizen Debt Audit campaign.[24] This grassroot campaign advocated for an audit of the public debt through: (1) a popular education campaign on the needs for the audit of the public debt; (2) showing that the public debt is the result of colonial state-corporate crimes; (3) challenging austerity measure implemented by the US and PR governments to deal with

[21] Bank Popular is the biggest Puerto Rican bank and it is one of the leading players in the Puerto Rican debt crisis and has been implicated in multiple cases of corruption and state facilitated crimes (Bhatti and Sloan 2017).

[22] This led to the emergence of the Campaign to Audit the Debt. See also: https://thehill.com/blogs/congress-blog/politics/336606-opinion-puerto-ricos-debt-must-be-audited-now.

[23] See Hedge Clipper (2018).

[24] See http://www.auditoriaya.org/english/.

the economic crisis; and (4) legal mobilization. Examples of legal mobilization include challenging executive actions taken by the Rosselló and Vázquez administrations, holding accountable those who participated in a series of state-corporate crimes that propitiated the fourteen-years-long economic and financial crisis, and participating in proceedings at the US District Court in San Juan after the Puerto Rican government declared bankruptcy. Hence, it can be argued that while punitive governance was applied against colonial subjects opposing neoliberal abandonment and austerity, emergency powers have been used to protect the very corporate and financial interests that led PR to its current situation.

A year after, on 1 May 2018, there was another massive anti-austerity mobilization at the financial district of San Juan, and once again, the police engaged in excessive use of brutal force (Mazzei 2018). Despite the police recording the demonstration and that there was a significant number of journalists, to this day, there are no official reports concerning the use of force during the demonstration (Kilometro 2018). The PR police has consistently engaged in the criminogenic use of brutal force, neglected its duty to provide the public with the necessary reposts, and has concealed the identity of police-aggressors, creating an environment of impunity.

5 Law 20 of 2017, Hurricane María and Anti-Corruption Mobilizations

At the same time when PR experienced the violence of austerity, on 10 April 2017, Law 20 of 2017 was passed with the intention of creating the Puerto Rico Department of Public Safety (a consolidation of all the different agencies in charge of security). Among the agencies included in this reorganization is the police department, which has been under a Federal Court mandate reform since 2012 after the ACLU sued for Civil Rights violations (Kilometro 2018). This law is important for two reasons. Firstly, it led to the creation of the PR police department, the Bureau of Special Investigations, and the Institute of Forensic Sciences. The law technically eliminates the independence of the last two to conduct investigations against the police, creating the conditions for a lack of accountability, and impunity (Kilometro 2018).

Secondly, in article 6.10, the law gives extraordinary power to the governor in case of an emergency. Aside from reaffirming the power of the governor to declare the state of emergency, the Law established in its article 6.10, section b, that the governor can (1) amend and revoke regulations, and (2) amend and rescind orders he or she deems convenient to govern during the state of emergency or disaster. The regulations or orders issued during a state of emergency or disaster will have force of law while the emergency lasts. Furthermore, section e and f confer power to the governor to acquire property without due process in times of crisis, which was exactly what transpired during the crisis generated by Hurricane María, when Rosselló's administration used and abused these executive powers, leading to several corruption scandals (Klein 2018).

The crisis invoked by the Trump and Rosselló administrations' mishandlings of Hurricane María proves the utter inefficacy of the state of emergency and punitive governance as policies to deal with crises. That is, this authoritarian and undemocratic model has proved incapable of meeting the people's real needs, and instead, created the conditions for organized abandonment. The state of emergency and the curfew decreed by Rosselló were unable to address and solve the problems that hurricane María created. Likewise, the militarization of the archipelago by members of the Army Reserve and the National Guard did not solve the problems of shortages of fuel, water, electricity, and telecommunications (Morales 2019). This shows that, contrary to the ideologies perpetuated by colonial-neoliberalism, crises are not solved by the imposition of exceptional structures and the limitation of democracy. But rather, as Garriga-Lopez (2020), and Mulligan and Garriga-Lopez (2020) have shown, grassroot, community-based organization, mutual-aid, and radical democracy were more effective in addressing people's needs after Hurricane María. The ethic of care developed in the aftermath of Hurricane María, as Mulligan and Garriga-Lopez (2020) point out, led Puerto Ricans to the radical uprising in the Summer of 2019.

Ricardo Rosselló's resignation on the evening of 24 July 2019[25] came after more than two consecutive weeks of popular uprising, in which hundreds of thousands of Puerto Ricans protested, marched, and rallied, demanding the end of his corrupt administration. This anti-corruption uprising was catalyzed by the leak of a now infamous chat[26]; multiple corruption cases; and the negligent and criminogenic management of the aftermath of Hurricanes Irma and María. During these two weeks, the PR police engaged in excessive use of force and rioting under the justification that after 11 P.M. the

---

[25] The resignation was effective on August 2. See: https://www.nytimes.com/2019/07/24/us/rossello-puerto-rico-governor-resigns.html.

[26] See: http://periodismoinvestigativo.com/2019/07/las-889-paginas-de-telegram-entre-rossello-nevares-y-sus-allegados/.

demonstrations were no longer protected by the Constitution (Brusi 2019). At least 52 people were affected by different types of interventions by law enforcement officers during the protests. As Kilometro (2019) reports, this number does not include the hundreds of people estimated to have suffered the effects of the tear gas fired throughout the streets of Old San Juan on multiple occasions. Additionally, Kilometro (2019) argues that at least 17 were arrested and 27 injured by police baton use, firing of rubber bullets, pepper spray, tear gas, beatings, property damage, and other assaults. Kilometro (2019) reports 5 complaints regarding crowd management, use of force by police, and intimidations by law enforcement officers on social media. These intimidations were made via social media, yet Kilometro Cero reported not to have all the necessary and sufficient documentation of them as yet.

Despite the intimidation and police violence in the Puerto Rican Summer of 2019, Ricardo Rossello and his closer allies were ousted and created the conditions for a new understanding of accountability in PR. These mobilizations are also important, since they constitute, in a restricted sense, an example of anti-corruption and anti-austerity mobilizations. Moreover, the Summer of 2019 also symbolized the convergence of multiples claims and demands against punitive governance and organized abandonment

Only months after the Puerto Rican Summer of 2019, and while the earthquakes were still affecting the archipelago, and Puerto Ricans were enduring the scarcity of basic materials to deal with the aftermath of the earthquakes (many living in makeshift outdoor shelters), and people from other towns scrambled to help the affected communities, a group of citizens discovered a warehouse with thousands of recovery and relief materials. This led to a renewed set of anti-corruption protests. On Thursday, 23 January 2020, thousands of protesters gathered to demand the resignation of Wanda Vázquez, for hiding essential supplies during the earthquake emergency (Kilometro 2020). Shortly before 11:00 P.M., and after allegedly requesting the crowd to disperse 14 times, the police declared the protest illegal, and as Kilometro (2020) reports, the police proceeded to launch tear gas at the protesters and fire non-lethal ammunition. Despite these mobilizations implementing the same creativity, they did not manage to mobilize thousands of Puerto Ricans as the Summer of 2019 did.

Vazquez's administration became even more negligent and criminogenic during the COVID-19 pandemic. In response to the pandemic, the administration imposed draconian emergency measures that included the approval of Law 35 of April 2020, a new law that criminalizes the spreading of "misinformation during periods of crisis", as well as any breaching of an executive order. As I mentioned above, under this law, hundreds of persons have been arrested. Nevertheless, multiple Puerto Rican grassroot and community organizations, and socio-political mobilizations have been taking place during the pandemic. From collective kitchens, feminist pantries, community-based environmental movements to collective mobilizations, Puerto Ricans have been confronting the pandemic through building solidarity, mutual-aid, and communal systems of care, and reimagining alternative futures to organized abandonment.

6 Conclusion

As this chapter has shown, at the root of punitive governance lie two important phenomena: abandonment and neoliberal legalities. Abandonment manifests through the rapid transformation of the Puerto Rican political economy, and the way the local government sees its role in society. It entails the intensification of neoliberal policies, such as the reduction of administrative and regulatory structures, privatization of public services, and the implementation of austerity measures; the financialization[27] of the colonial economy and the exponential rise of the public debt.[28] As a result, colonial subjects have experienced the denial of their human and civil rights and with it the criminalization of those who resist colonialism, neoliberal legality and social death.

Neoliberal legality manifests through the ever-increasing accumulation of power by the local executive branch and the corresponding weakening of the republican structure and of constitutional and civil rights (normalizing the state of emergency), and the normalization of authoritarian policing, state violence, antidemocratic legislations, and impunity for white-collar criminals and state-corporate crimes. Therefore, neoliberal legalities create the legal framework for "economic development", wealth extraction, and plunder, and, for repressive policing and criminal laws that enforce social control over working and poor people, socio-environmental, anti-austerity, and anti-corruption mobilizations, while normalizing and legitimizing crimes of the powerful.

[27] For an analysis of how the processes of financializing the economy have led to a systemic crisis, see the work of Krippner (2011) and Lapavitsas (2013).

[28] For an exposition of the rise of the public debt, see Merling et al. (2017).

Key to the development of punitive governance and the reshaping of internal colonial democracy is, as mentioned earlier, the systematic uses of emergency declarations (mainly executive orders) and emergency laws. Thus, the state of emergency has served as a legal framework for the systematic appropriation and redistribution of wealth from the working and poor Puerto Ricans to the US colonial and local ruling classes, as well as for the criminalization of socio-political movements. Therefore, the state of emergency is the key legal dispositive of neoliberal legalities and organized abandonment.

These transformations have made PR a central case to understand the dynamics of criminal legalities in a colonial global south country. Not only have the PR and US governments become more authoritarian in recent years, but also, as the economic crisis and the waves of disaster unfold, organized abandonment has become the norm. A telling instance of this is that struggling for food and fighting hunger has become a punishable offense. It is in this context that we have to understand punitive governance and organized abandonment: as the neoliberal project of disciplining colonial subjects.

References

Atiles, José. 2014. The Criminalization of Socio-environmental Struggles in Puerto Rico. *Oñati Socio-Legal Series* 4 (1): 85–103.

Atiles, José. 2016. Apuntes para abandonar el derecho: estado de excepción colonial en Puerto Rico [Notes to abandon the law: state of colonial exception in Puerto Rico.]. *Cabo Rojo. PR: Editorial Educación Emergente.*

Atiles, José. 2019. Jugando con el derecho: Movimientos Anticoloniales Puertorriqueños y la fuerza de Ley [Playing with the Law: Puerto Rican Anticolonial Movements and the Force of Law.]. *Cabo Rojo: Editora Educación Emergente.*

Atiles, José. 2021. The COVID-19 Pandemic in Puerto Rico: Exceptionality, Corruption and State-Corporate Crimes. *State Crime Journal* 10 (1): 104–125.

Atiles, José, and David Whyte. 2011. Counter-Insurgency Goes to University: The Militarisation of Policing in the Puerto Rico Student Strikes. *Critical Studies on Terrorism* 4 (3): 393–404.

Beckett, Katherine, and Steve Herbert. 2008. Dealing with disorder. Social control in the post-industrial city. *Theoretical Criminology* 12 (1): 5–30.

Bhatti, Saqib, and Carrie Sloan. 2017. Broken promise. PROMESA is a mode for undermining democracy and pushing austerity elsewhere in the U.S. *ReFund America Project.* http://www.refundproject.org/#puerto-rico.

Bonilla, Yarimar. 2020. Postdisaster Futures: Hopeful Pessimism, Imperial Ruination, and *La futura Cuir*. *Small Axe* 24 (2 [62]): 147–162.

Bonilla, Yarimar, and Marisol LeBrón. 2019. *Aftershocks of Disaster: Puerto Rico Before and After the Storm*. Chicago: Haymarket Books.

Bosque, Ramón, and Javier Colón. 2006. *Puerto Rico under Colonial Rule: Political Persecution and the Quest for Human Rights*. Albany: State University of New York Press.

Brown, Alleen. 2020. Energy Insurrection. *The Intercept*, February 9, 2020. https://theintercept.com/2020/02/09/puerto-rico-energy-electricity-solar-natural-gas/.

Brusi, Rima. 2011. The University of Puerto Rico: A Testing Ground for the Neoliberal State. *NACLA Report on the Americas* 44 (2): 7–10.

Brusi, Rima. 2019. Why Puerto Rico's Cops Ignore the Constitution at Night. *The Nation*, July 30, 2019. https://www.thenation.com/article/archive/puerto-rico-police-abuse/.

Carrasquillo, Gabriela. 2020. Cronología: caso contra estudiantes tras la huelga de la UPR en 2017 [Chronology: case against students after the UPR strike in 2017.]. *Pulso estudiantil*, February 5, 2020. https://pulsoestudiantil.com/cronologia-caso-contra-estudiantes-tras-la-huelga-de-la-upr-en-2017/.

Concepción, Carmen M. 1995. The Origins of Modern Environmental Activism in Puerto Rico in the 1960s. *International Journal of Urban and Regional Research* 19 (1): 112–128.

Cypher, James. 2007. From Military Keynesianism to Global Neoliberal Militarism. *Monthly Review* 59 (2): 37–55.

Díaz Torres, Rafael. 2020. Carpeteo y criminialización de la protesta, legado de Wanda Vázquez Garced [Carpeting and criminalization of protest, legacy of Wanda Vázquez Garced.]. *Centro de Periodismo Investigativo*, August 29, 2020. https://periodismoinvestigativo.com/2020/08/carpeteo-y-criminalizacion-de-la-protesta-legado-de-wanda-vazquez-garced/.

Davila, Juan. 2017. A People's Recovery: Radical Organizing in Post-María Puerto Rico. *The Indypendent*, October 18, 2017. https://indypendent.org/2017/10/a-peoples-recovery-radical-organizing-in-post-María-puerto-rico/.

Dennis, A. 2020. Wall Street vultures razed COFINA, and now they're coming for the central government. *Eye on the Ties*. https://news.littlesis.org.

Florido, Adrian. 2020a. Advocate For The Poor In Puerto Rico Is Released After Arrest During Protest. *NPR*, April 30, 2020. https://www.npr.org/2020/04/30/848684061/puerto-rico-police-arrest-advocate-for-the-poor.

Florido, Adrian. 2020b. 'Mamá, I'm Still Hungry': In Puerto Rico, Child Hunger Becomes a Flashpoint. *NPR*, May 13, 2020. https://www.npr.org/2020/05/13/854734386/mam-im-still-hungry-in-puerto-rico-child-hunger-becomes-a-flashpoint.

Garriga-Lopez, Adriana. 2020. Debt, Crisis, and Resurgence in Puerto Rico. *Small Axe* 24 (2[62]): 122–132.

Gilmore, Ruth Wilson. 2007. *Golden Gulag: Prison, Surplus, Crisis, and Opposition in Globalizing California.* Berkeley and Los Angeles: University of California Press.

Go, Julian. 2020. The Imperial Origins of American Policing: Militarization and Imperial Feedback in the Early 20th Century. *American Journal of Sociology* 125 (5): 1193–1254.

Grosfoguel, Ramón. 2002. Colonial Subjects. Puerto Rican in Global Perspective. *Oakland: University of California Press.*

Harcourt, E. 2010. Neoliberal Penality: A Brief genealogy. *Theoretical Criminology* 14 (1): 74–92.

Hedge, Clippers. 2016. Pirates of the Caribbean. http://hedgeclippers.org/wp-content/uploads/2016/12/20161025_Hedgeclippers_ReportPR_v3-3.pdf.

Hedge, Clippers. 2018. The Golden Revolving Door. *HedgePapers*, August 21, 2018. http://hedgeclippers.org/hedgepaper-no-61-the-golden-revolving-door/.

Kilometro, Cero. 2018. Skill over force. *A critical analysis of the use-of-force statistics of the Puerto Rico Police against the people.* https://drive.google.com/file/d/0B3p2WlC_-VLibEJjc2pxZjZibWZvbGtBczNzdHVRS1JvNlU0/view?resourcekey=0-3Uqbodmkk8KLFVphsOMSxA.

Kilometro, Cero. 2019. *Documentation on interventions and cases of use of force by the Puerto Rico Police Department during the #RickyRenuncia protests.* https://docs.google.com/document/d/1--lPFG_XwMppj71-v45EHeSe5QuIq0gRTXlWvDBGbg4/edit#heading=h.2et92p0.

Kilometro, Cero. 2020. *Documentación de intervenciones y casos de uso de fuerza de la Policía durante las protestas Wanda Renuncia* [Documentation of police interventions and use of force cases during the Wanda Renuncia protests.]. https://docs.google.com/document/d/1FoPzYOVckahXGUl9MBba2QOzGcT3wblCouX-NXxdGXXg/edit#heading=h.rgldnspa1ad3.

Kishore, Nishant et al. 2018. Mortality in Puerto Rico after Hurricane María. *The New England Journal of Medicine.*

Klein, Naomi. 2018. The Battle for Paradise. Puerto Rico takes on the Disaster Capitalists. *Chicago: Haymarket Books.*

Krippner, Greta. 2011. *Capitalizing on Crisis: The Political Origins of the Rise of Finance.* Cambridge and London: Harvard University Press.

Lapavitsas, Costas. 2013. *Profiting Without Producing: How Finance Exploits Us All.* London and New York: Verso.

LeBrón, Marisol. 2017. Carpeteo Redux: Surveillance and Subversion against the Puerto Rican Student Movement. *Radical History Review.*

LeBrón, Marisol. 2019. Policing Life and Death. Race, Violence, and Resistance in Puerto Rico. *Oakland: University of California Press.*

LeBrón, Marisol. 2021. Against Muerto Rico: Lessons from the Verano Boricua. *Cabo Rojo: Editora Educación Emergente.*

Lynch, Mona. 2011. Theorizing Punishment: Reflections on Wacquant's Punishing the Poor. *Critical Sociology* 37 (2): 237–244.

Mazzei, P. 2018. Protest in Puerto Rico Over Austerity Measures Ends in Tear Gas. *New York Times*, May 1, 2018. https://www.nytimes.com/2018/05/01/us/puerto-rico-protests.html.

Mercado, Mario. 2016. Puerto Ricans' Response to the Economic Crisis Rooted in Misinformation and Frustration. *Counterpunch*, August 9, 2016. https://www.counterpunch.org/2016/08/09/puerto-ricans-response-to-the-economic-crisis-rooted-in-misinformation-and-frustration/.

Merling, L. et al. 2017. *Life After Debt in Puerto Rico: How Many More Lost Decades?* Washington DC: Center for Economic and Policy Research.

Morales, ed. 2019. *Fantasy Island. Colonialism, Exploitation and the Betrayal of Puerto Rico*. New York: Bold Type Books.

Mulligan, Jessica, and Adriana Garriga-Lopez. 2020. Forging Compromiso after the Storm: Activism as ethic of care among health care workers in Puerto Rico. *Critical Public Health*.

Negrón, Frances. 2020. Staying Alive in Puerto Rico. *Latino Rebels*, May 26, 2020. https://www.latinorebels.com/2020/05/26/stayingaliveinpuertorico/.

Onís, Catalina. 2018. Energy Colonialism Powers the Ongoing Unnatural Disaster in Puerto Rico. *Frontiers in Communication* 3 (2).

Onís, Catalina. 2021. *Energy Islands. Metaphors of Power, Extractivism, and Justice in Puerto Rico*. Oakland: University of California Press.

Onís, Catalina, Hilda Lloréns and Ruth Santiago. 2020. Puerto Rico's Seismic Shocks. *NACLA*, January 15, 2020. https://nacla.org/news/2020/01/14/puerto-rico-earthquakes-renewable-energy.

Paralitici, Ché. 2011. *La represión contra el independentismo puertorriqueño 1960–2010* [The repression against Puerto Rican independence 1960–2010.]. Río Piedras: Ediciones Gaviota.

Pérez-Lizasuain, César. 2018. *Rebelión, no-derecho y poder estudiantil: la huelga de 2010 en la Universidad de Puerto Rico* [Rebellion, non-right and student power: the 2010 strike at the University of Puerto Rico.]. Cabo Rojo: Editora Educación Emergente.

Poltevin, Rene Francisco. 2000. Political Surveillance, State Repression, and Class Resistance: The Puerto Rican Experience. *Social Justice* 27 (3): 89–100.

Robles, F. 2017. Puerto Rico's University Is Paralyzed by Protests and Facing Huge Cuts. *New York Times*, May 25, 2017. https://www.nytimes.com/2017/05/25/us/puerto-ricos-university-is-paralyzed-by-protests-and-facing-huge-cuts.html?mwrsm=Facebook&_r=0.

Rosa, Paola. 2019. Up from the ashes: Could a solar-powered uprising reshape Puerto Rico? *Grist*, September 25, 2019. https://grist.org/article/puerto-rico-applied-energy-systems-casa-pueblo/.

Santiago, R., C. Onís and H. Lloréns. 2020. Powering Life in Puerto Rico: The struggle to transform Puerto Rico's flawed energy grid with locally controlled alternatives is a matter of life and death. *NACLA Report on the Americas*, 52 (2), 178–185. https://doi.org/10.1080/10714839.2020.1768741.

Villanueva, Joaquin, and Marisol LeBrón. 2020. The Decolonial Geographies of Puerto Rico's 2019 Summer Protest. *Society and Space*. https://www.societyandspace.org/forums/the-decolonial-geographies-of-puerto-ricos-2019-summer-protests-a-forum.

Wacquant, Loïc. 2009. *Punishing the Poor: The Neoliberal Government of Social Insecurity*. Durham: Duke University Press.

Whitman, James. 2011. Of Neo-Liberalism and Comparative Punishment. *Critical Sociology* 37 (2): 217–224.

Zambrana, Rocio. 2021. *Colonial Debts. The Case of Puerto Rico*. Duke University Press.

Part III

Entrenched Cultural Values

9

"Truth" and "Consent" in Sexual Violence Reporting in Criminal Justice and Legal Contexts in Singapore

Joseph Greener and Stacy Ooi

1 Introduction

There is widespread evidence from around the world that rape and sexual assault criminal proceedings continually perpetuate the belief that victims lie about their experiences of sexual crimes (Jordan 2004; Kelly 2010; Wheatcroft and Walklate 2014). In truth, available evidence suggests that false allegations of rape are realistically between two and eight per cent, like that of any other false allegation of a criminal offence (Kelly et al. 2005; Rumney 2006). On top of this, convictions rates for rape and sexual assault are known to be extremely low and most sexual victimisation is never reported to any formal state agency. The propensity for reporters of sexual violence to be discredited or considered as providing false allegations of crimes is purportedly evident in all aspects of the criminal justice system, from the initial reporting of crimes to police departments all the way to subsequent investigation processes and questioning in court. Jordan (2004) suggested that police officers are inclined to doubt victims due to a set of heavily patriarchal and misogynist assumptions about women. According to Jordan, police investigation involves a host of stereotypical assertions

J. Greener (✉)
University of Liverpool, Liverpool, UK
e-mail: jgreener@liverpool.ac.uk

S. Ooi
Independent Researcher, Singapore, Singapore

G. B. Radics and P. Ciocchini (eds.), *Criminal Legalities and Minorities in the Global South*, Palgrave Socio-Legal Studies, https://doi.org/10.1007/978-3-031-17918-1_9

regarding victims and crimes that work to discredit accounts. These include: (1) alcohol consumption leads victims to consent but subsequently regret sexual encounters; (2) the victim is not to be believed due to past sexual encounters with perpetrator, (3) psychiatric disturbance, (4) intellectual impairment; or, (5) concealment of certain aspects of the account are proof of a false allegation. Jordan's account highlights the cultures and belief systems of criminal justice professionals who are charged with holding and perpetuating misogynist ideas, seeing women as contradictorily irrational and/or vindictive. However, research by Saunders (2012) into prosecutors and police officers in the UK brought some of the underlying processes of poor rape prosecution statistics into some question. In her study, she suggested differences in conceptions between "false allegation" and "false account": the former being a report of rape or sexual assault which did not occur, and the latter being account where significant details within the report are erroneous. Saunders (2012) effectively showed that simplistically equating the poor experiences of rape survivors within the criminal justice system to misogynist views held by criminal justice professionals did not account, systemically, for why women's experiences are so negative even when individual professionals have good will and awareness of the oppressive tendencies of the system they work within. In other words, we cannot simply explain the poor experiences of survivors with reference to patriarchal or conservative values of individual criminal justice professionals.

Contributing to these debates, this article explores the processes and practices relating to rape and sexual assault in Singapore—a nation that carries on the legacy of British colonial institutions, laws and values, but also has its own unique culture and character. In a developmentalist state that suffers from low fertility, women play an important role in the state-constructed conception of the "traditional" family as the main unit for reproduction and economic growth (Wong and Yeoh 2003). This control of women's bodies, alongside the political discourse of "Asian values," has contributed to a misogynistic and paternalistic set of institutions that create a hostile environment for those reporting rape. The following analysis is based on 11 in-depth qualitative interviews comprising of three defence lawyers, three NGO workers employed in supporting victims of rape/sexual assault, two survivors who had significant contact with the criminal justice system after rape, one medical social worker, one judge and one police officer. Although small, the sample provides an overview of the various procedures and practices relating to the treatment of victims and the requirements of investigating sexual assault and successfully bringing cases to court. Interviews took place in late 2017, lasting from around 20 minutes to an hour.

Smart (1992) argues that the law and jurisprudence are best understood as gendered and gendering and not as a pure expression of patriarchy or wholly committed to the domination of women. The application and practice of law are a "technology of gender" (Smart 1992, 40), often deeply oppressive and structuring of femininity and masculinity, but not immoveable and certainly enmeshed with various contradictions. As this article will argue, the legal context around rape and sexual assault in Singapore is equally complex (Teo 2009, 2010, 2011). The position of women has transformed as the country's regime of reproduction shifted and feminist struggle gained traction. From across our sample, we found that professionals held complex beliefs. At times, these perpetuated the rape myths (such as those discussed by Jordan 2004) but at times these beliefs were discussed because professionals were aware of the threshold of evidence needed for successful convictions in court. We discuss the problems of defending rape victims through legal processes according to two themes based on our data. Firstly, we discuss the idea of false accounts which is the data revolving around the perceived difficulties professionals feel in ensuring that survivors can provide credible and consistent accounts of the event. Secondly, the interviews uncovered problems determining consent and whether complainants can present as having clearly or provably *not* consented. The constant undermining or muddying of whether consent took place or did not reflects the wider social status of women. Together, the themes identified in the data suggested that within the criminal justice system the threshold for having claims "taken seriously" through official channels was so high that there is a systemic tolerance of sexual violence. The limited access to pursuing justice system needs to be understood in the wider context of the socio-economic location of women in Singaporean society and their role in the regime of reproduction which places "traditional" family values central to nation-building.

2 Singapore's Gender Regime: Exalting "Asian Values" and Responding to the Struggles of Women

State institutions have frequently played a contradictory role in both structuring women's oppression whilst also operating as a site of possible liberation. Women are relied on to provide essential but devalued reproductive labour. Childbearing, socialisation, maintenance of cultural practices, the nurturing of social capacities and the securing of mental and physical well-being are essential for preserving the health and capacity of labour power. Through embedding a gendered separation between the domestic sphere and the public sphere, women in most societies have been made economically dependent on the wages earned by men, rendering women subservient to men and coercing them into providing reproductive labour without receiving wages (Vogel 2013). State policies, therefore, have an interest in facilitating men's privatisation of women's bodies as a means of appropriating their reproductive capacities and labour. However, as Fraser (2016) argues, women have similarly become an increasingly important source of labour power within production as the "two-earner" family has become the predominant kinship structure in developed parts of the world. Indeed, a neat, gendered split between reproductive and productive activities has never been a reality in any historical period. Nonetheless, ideologies and practices which see men as workers and women as carers are an important naturalising and institutionalised form of oppression: reproductive labour, historically understood as women's labour, is often expected to be done by women for "free" in the home, and when it is done in the labour market it pays less.

The propensities for degrading certain gender roles to solve the contradictions of reproduction and accumulation need to be situated within a politicised conception of the state. Bob Jessop describes the state as having gender "selectivities" (2004): political parties, law, institutions, knowledge systems, discourses and welfare policies, to name a few, which make-up the core ensemble of the state are inflected with propensities to perpetuate gendered roles, stereotypes, relations and hierarchies. These conditions tend towards a reproduction of men's domination over women, maintaining higher socio-economic status for men and maleness. Yet the state is also a central site of contestation; an ever-unfolding consolidation of past and current conflicts with women's political movements clearly successful in winning improved social statuses in certain places at certain times.

Teo (2009, 2010, 2011) has described some of the complexities in Singapore's gender regime and the political and normative context of gendered nation-building. Throughout the post-independence period, the ruling People's Action Party (PAP) post-colonial government has engaged in various policy strategies which impose and sustain women's reproductive roles. Discursively, Singapore's formal nationalist discourse has consistently articulated solidarity as based on a shared set of "Asian values" which are seen to be a constellation of moral commitments to the primacy of the family, "filial piety" and heteronormativity. Whilst the construction of "Asian values" has been widely criticised as an attempt to legitimise conservative authoritarianism by appealing to tradition, Teo (2009) argues it remains a strong force in how people understand their own lives as well as giving moral weight to state policies. The housing system, along with other social policies, is at the core of a central state imperative to exalt the family as the central modality of daily life, the "proper" way to live and the central formation for securing wellbeing (Teo 2010). Most of the population dwells in state-built and mortgaged or rented Housing Development Board (HDB) properties. HDB tightly controls access to buying or renting these properties in a clear attempt to promote the nuclear family, giving priority to married couples, with singles not permitted to apply until they are 35 years old. There are now also a number of measures in place to encourage procreation within the "pro-Natalist" family (Wong and Yeoh 2003, 2). These include cash payments for having children, priority for housing, tax rebates, priority to desired schools for larger families and saving incentives. Similarly, the government's refusal to repeal Section 377a or to permit homosexual couples' access to the social policy benefits available to heterosexual couples is a further example of commitment to the "traditional" gender regime (Radics 2015). Oswin (2014) describes Singapore as having an entrenched exclusionary sexual citizenship regime, in which the range of acceptable sexualities is severely restricted.

Teo's study interviewing Singaporeans about family life and the role of women revealed that many of the respondents felt that issues of reproduction and gender equality were also issues to do with "economy, development, and national survival" (2009, 552). People in her study felt that without the continued commitment to family values, the nation would be in threat of disunity or economic collapse. In other words, perceived moral and ethical ways of living should be maintained through the state's gender regime to ensure Singapore's survival. The state has been highly active and effective in shaping the reproductive role of women and, most notably in the last few decades, has sought to encourage more female citizens to bear children. However, it has fundamentally tried to maintain the women's roles in the labour market at the same time. Today, policies still tend to favour middle class women through tax rebates and savings schemes: they give relatively meagre maternity leave and the current pressures of work and care have been managed through large scale domestic worker immigration.

Nonetheless, women's struggles have had significant impact in shifting state policies with violence against women achieving greater recognition as an issue in society. In 1996, an amendment to the Women's Charter expanded the function of government agencies in "family violence" and the setting up of Family Courts. This was a partial state admission of the problems of domestic violence, but it also clearly revolved around keeping families together, rather than providing the opportunity for divorce, and maintained the family as the primary orientation of Singapore life. Neither the Women's Charter nor the structure of social policy can be considered as empowering women to leave abusive and violent relationships. For example, the primary protection for women offered through the 1996 amendment to the Women's Charter and continuing until today is the Personal Protection Order (PPO). PPOs seek to set up an alternative system of dealing with family violence that partially criminalises offenders and is geared towards ending violence within the nuclear family. The intent is protection but largely without splitting up the family. Mandatory counselling was a primary intervention for perpetrators and victims in the original policy with the hope that therapy would prevent the breakup of family units. This remains in the form of the Counselling Order. The goal of maintaining conventional familial relations is also reflected in Ganapathy's (2008) study on policing domestic violence in Singapore. He uncovered a form of state tolerance of family violence underpinned by specific regulations and legal forces shaping policing. Police in his study were constrained by the necessary legal requirements to establish serious physical harm if criminal proceedings were to be enforced. More to the point, the primary mode of intervention that police officers could offer was referral to family counselling with the system generally discouraging criminalisation and preventing disintegration of the family unit.

In its current form, the PPO seeks to enforce a set of requirements on the abuser, such as through the Domestic Exclusion Order, which may only exclude a perpetrator from a section of the home. Overall, PPOs are the primary modality of protecting women against family violence, offering negative rather than positive freedoms: they seek to control the actions of the person who committed violence to "securitise" everyday family life. Given the ongoing rigidity of the HDB system in terms of providing housing to divorcees and single parents, victims are not empowered to shape their own violence-free futures in more far-reaching ways.

The experiences of women in Singapore are complex. Women's organisations, most notably AWARE, have built sufficient power to effect certain changes in government policy. Developmentalist policies, in tandem with various geopolitical forces, have established Singapore as a global city facilitating an expanding middle class and an increasingly consumer-based economy, contextualising the rising material power of certain groups of women. As Teo (2009) shows, however, the state, and many women themselves, continue to hold traditional perspectives regarding the appropriate role of women. Within law and government policy, some cautious concessions in terms of strengthening legal social protections have occurred, such as the bolstering of measures to prevent and criminalise some forms of violence against women. Most recently, as part of a review of the Penal Code, marital rape is now illegal and a new police department, the Sexual Crime and Family Violence Command, has been instigated. However, this is arguably not tantamount to challenging the prevailing socio-structural dominance of a patriarchal system, which ultimately continues to mobilise narrow conservative understandings of gender roles and sexualities. Recent changes seek to offer further assistance to victims and slightly more avenues for criminalising perpetrators but they do not significantly increase the opportunities for women of all classes to access the welfare support needed to re-shape their own lives.

3 Meeting the Threshold for "Truth"

Across the interviews, respondents highlighted concerns with the credibility of rape allegations. However, this was not necessarily a direct assertion that all accounts of rape were false. Whilst certain respondents clearly held the belief that victims of sexual crimes were highly likely to be lying, others felt that the real problems surrounding rape-reports was their verifiability, put differently, whether it was likely that an individual's account could be defended in court. Here, we highlight several factors which are seen to be important for determining whether accounts are viewed as credible and potentially verifiable in court. The themes identified in the data include *motivations for false allegation*, *alcohol intoxication* and *degrees of evidence for establishing "real" victimhood.*

Present amongst respondents was the belief that rape complainants had specific incentives to provide deliberately untrue accounts of sexual assault. There are two primary (mis)beliefs offered by the respondents regarding the motivations to "lie." Firstly, the idea that women frequently feel shame and regret regarding consensual sex and, secondly, the fact that survivors report rape because they have committed infidelity or adultery and wish to conceal unfaithfulness to their partners. As one defence lawyer respondent explained, he felt women frequently regretted consensual sex. For instance, in one case he felt the complainant had felt "dismissed" after the point of sexual interaction which led her to pursue a rape case against the accused: "we [the defence] said that the sex was consensual—she might regret it after, but it was not rape." As stated elsewhere in the interview, he felt he had "met vindictive women." As he described, "these girls, their inhibitions drop, they do something that they might not have done if they were in full control of themselves, and then later they regret it, should that be rape?" The police officer we interviewed clearly held the belief that the role of investigation was to uncover whether an individual was reporting a case of non-consensual sexual activity or was filing charges because she was experiencing guilt and regret: "[T]he lady can always change her mind after the act. Like example, let's say if the lady is drunk… [she] can always consent but afterward claims that she didn't consent." Another respondent also gave an example from one case where the defence team had accused the claimant of false accusation by suggesting it was an attempt to conceal infidelity,

> *…the girl had a boyfriend, she lied to him about being in X's house...she didn't tell him the truth about things, la. So that was part of our defence as well…that maybe she said all this because she was actually just trying to protect her face. Because she went to X's house secretly behind the boyfriend's back, and she had sex with him, but after that, how's she supposed to explain it to him* [her partner]*?*

Or as another respondent said '[S]ometimes girls get caught [cheating] by their boyfriends then [they] cry rape, "maybe my boyfriend will forgive me"'.

Our data showed that not only did certain respondents believe that women had motivations for making deceptive allegations, but also that these were valid strategies used by defence teams in courts of law. Gunby et al. (2012) have shown in their study of lay perceptions regarding rape that this reflects certain common-sensical views that women frequently make misleading rape allegations after regretting sexual contact, especially if they have been unfaithful. As Quinlan found in her study of police officer perceptions of rape victims, "women with apparent motives for lying" (2016, 308) were commonly seen as suspect. Our police officer respondent highlighted that the goal of interviewing a victim should be to "break" them:

> Q: *What evidence would usually show that it's not the truth?*
> A: *The interview. The initial interview. They may show signs that they're lying - but it's not up to me to judge. I can't break them. I'm not the one with [the] skilful interview skills.*

Alcohol intoxication was a common issue shaping investigation and differing processes relating to rape cases. If a case got as far as the court system, the claim that an individual was drunk to the point of unconsciousness or "blacking out", was seen to show that the person could *not* consent ("if someone is completely unconscious, obviously they cannot consent"). At the same time, alcohol consumption was seen, at times, to complicate people's memory and possibly lead them to believe they had not consented when they had.

Meeting the threshold for "truth," whether garnering support from a professional or influencing a jury judgement, can more holistically be visualised as a struggle for authenticity. Estrich makes a distinction between "real rape" and "simple rape" (1987). "Real rape" refers to situations that conform to stereotypical ideas about sexual violence—it is committed by a stranger, it involves the use of force and a weapon, and it results in physical injury, amongst other factors. At times, it is expected that a significant power differential between the perpetrator and the accused comes into play, in terms of age, size, status and so on. "Simple rape" refers to situations containing factors that might lead to the victim being taken less seriously: it is perpetrated by someone the victim knows, there are no obvious physical injuries, and weapons and significant use of force were not discernibly involved. It takes place between people imagined to be equals (e.g. intimate partners), and there is no obvious power differential between perpetrator and victim (Wheatcroft and Walklate 2014, 242). Across our interviews it was commonly shown that any form of evidence seen to corroborate "real" victimhood improved the chances of conviction.

One of our defence lawyer respondents described the difficulties in establishing "truth" in a particular case by noting that none of the evidence indicated a "usual" case of rape:

> *She admitted to not screaming. She said there was a struggle, [but this was] not corroborated by [our client's] evidence. Now…this is not a usual case of rape. It is not a case of stalking and so on. Or she behaved in such a way that led the accused to believe that she was consenting.*

Research by Bucher and Manasse (2011) explores the forms and prevalence of different responses of women who experienced attempted or realised "acquaintance rape." Using reports of rape from a US police station, they found that as many as 42% of women reported neither verbal nor physical means to communicate their non-consent. So-called freezing up during a sexual attack is known to be an extremely common response. Yet evidence of self-defence is seen as the main basis for "proving" rape, even though research shows that many rape victims do not engage in acts of self-defence.

This section has demonstrated that professionals are often seeking to ascertain the credibility of an account with any form of evidence or an account that stands up to rigorous scrutiny, which is seen to establish the basis that "real" rape occurred. What is significant here is that certain respondents held onto the idea that many women do frequently lie about rape. This leads to a blurring between what is accepted as a convincing account of sexual violence, that is an account likely to be successful in court, and then one which happened, regardless of whether there is "good" evidence or not. This leads to a situation where insufficient evidence is indicative that the complainant is "lying," even when she is not.

As we will see in the subsequent section, investigations of sexual violence often revolve around determining whether consent or non-consent can be established through evidence.

4 Proving Non-Consent

Throughout the criminal justice procedure, *identifying and establishing (and questioning and interrogating) credibility based on a convincing account of non-consent guides many investigative and legal contexts.* Across the interviews, both the survivor and the NGO workers emphasised the brutality of police investigations in the wake of sexual violence. There seems to be significant evidence that the initial investigation and questioning in police stations are shaped by the idea that victims' accounts need rigorous interrogation to ensure their credibility. Our interviews show that survivors will face an uphill battle in gaining access to justice, given the entrenched beliefs amongst some legal professionals regarding the supposed malice and duplicity of women alleging rape. Our interviews with NGO workers and one sexual assault survivor corroborate this view. The rape survivor we interviewed reported that the police officer on duty did everything he could to dissuade her from proceeding with charges.

> *This guy tried to throw everything at me. He* [the investigating police officer] *asked me "what were you wearing?", "why were you at the party?", "were you drunk?"*

When his attempts to dissuade her were unsuccessful, the officer offered to call the perpetrator and give him a verbal warning, instead of going to the trouble of making a full report. It was only when she contacted a senior police officer, with the help of an acquaintance that the officer reluctantly agreed to help her report the case. Overall, the survivor felt that her case had not been taken seriously: "The impression I got was that it was 6 pm, and I think he just wanted to go home."

One of the NGO employee respondents highlighted the significant additional difficulties facing victims of sexual assault as opposed to victims of other forms of crime:

> *Nobody questions anybody if their wallet is being stolen. You just try to figure out who the thief was, or where could it be, or whether there's evidence to prove that somebody actually stole it. But nobody questions that you're lying or you're telling the truth. [...] In that case, when it comes to rape, how hard is it to believe that somebody's been raped? How come you don't want to believe the subjective reality of that?*

As such, many victims feel pressured into dropping the case before even getting a chance to go to court. As one of our social work respondents said:

> *Police treat the victim as if they are the perpetrator. Often my victims end up feeling raped again by the police. The police will ask "Are you sure? Are you sure you didn't want sex?" Is there another way to ask questions without making my victim feel so bad? It takes a lot of courage to go down to the police. Who wants to talk to a stranger about your sexual episode?*

The moment of investigation significantly revolves around establishing whether consensual or non-consensual sexual activity took place. An NGO respondent provided an extremely harrowing example of a client who was pressured into dropping charges by an investigating officer:

> *It is the intention of the police to rattle your cage. The police are going to be very hard on you. How many can take that? I had a client with blood-soaked jeans. She carried these everywhere. Still the police asked, "Is it consensual?" She showed the jeans to the police officer, and he shoved the jeans away and asked her, "No, I don't want to see that. I'm asking you - consent or no consent?" Eventually she broke down. She gave up. It's too much shame - you drag them through the mud like that. They grinded her in the interview and kept asking if she consented, until at last she said, "I guess so." And it stuck.*

The major line of reasoning deployed in police investigations is to engage in significant questioning around consent. Most sexual encounters do not involve explicit consent and many cases of non-consensual sex do not involve verbal non-consent (Bucher and Manasse 2011). Forms of non-violent coercion may also be more prevalent than many realise, which includes, for example, threats and blackmail. When police officers or other professionals heavily emphasise on establishing consent/non-consent during investigations, victims can easily be led to feel that they are responsible by not non-consenting vigorously enough or feeling that perhaps they did consent. This kind of discussion around consent also takes place in the court setting. As one of the defence lawyer respondents recounted, the reasons behind why a victim did not shout during the attack became an issue in the courtroom:

> *I don't think I can even say whether I knew* [the victim] *was reluctant or scared. You see a bit of both, la. But at the same time it doesn't explain things like why she never shout. Cos the Judge did ask us very specifically during cross-ex, you know, "Why didn't you shout for help?"...She said "Oh I push and push and I tried very hard", y'know. Then... the judge asked her "So did you shout for help?" and she said "No". The judge asked "Why?" and her answer was that "I thought that if I screamed for help then it was no use." That's what she said.*

This is also reflected in the fact that there was significant evidence that rape cases were much simpler and likely to lead to a conviction when the respondents were seen to be unable to consent. Examples of this included situations where the victim was seriously intellectually disabled, legally underage, or in instances of incest. As one of the NGO employees noted, in such cases the police are far more likely to believe the victim and far quicker to take action:

> *In my other case where the father raped his own daughter, the police were great. They were so kind to her. The court also was so nice to her; they gave her an emergency protection order on the same day they arranged for video live-link at the Family Violence Specialist Centre. So, they were really nice. Because it was clearly non-consensual. There was no way that they could question or blame the victim, in this sense. When there's children or underaged* [victims], *those are viewed more sympathetically and taken also way more seriously.*

Indeed, one of the legal professionals we interviewed noted that cases where non-consent was easier to establish were more likely to result in conviction in court:

> *I think the question of consent is always...very fact-intensive. The task of the court would be made that much easier if there are objective facts to assist* [in arriving at a decision]. *For example, objective facts such as if the person is already quite intoxicated, or has low IQ, for that matter. But in respect of a normal woman, who is of adult age, and nothing to indicate that she has been drunk or anything of that kind, I suppose it becomes a question of her word against his. And the court will presumably look at all the facts leading up to that point. You will examine how they met, where did they go, what did they do, things like that. All the way we will examine. To see which version of the facts is likely to be true.*

This legal professional is arguing that when the case involves intellectually impaired or heavily intoxicated victims, a case of rape should be easier to establish because the individual is assumed to be unable to consent by law (see Section 90 of the Penal Code). This indicates the significance that the principle of consent has in all levels of rape and sexual assault criminal justice proceedings in Singapore. In early stages of investigation, consent becomes one of the major key points which police questioning is centred around. Evidence from respondents suggests that if survivors cannot clearly convince police of non-consensual sex in the face of brutal interrogation, then the case is unlikely to go further. Despite indication that sexual violence victims were being systematically denigrated, treated with disbelief and stereotyped as untrustworthy, defence lawyer respondents nonetheless felt that the justice system was skewed towards victims:

> *Oh it is. Definitely is. I fully and completely agree with them. I mean it's a general... just how judges treat victims also. They're always treated - I mean their [the victim's] word is always given more weight than the accused person. People are always more quick to believe the girl than the guy.*

This view does not take into consideration the high attrition rate of sexual assault cases during the police reporting process. Defence lawyers deal with cases that have already passed the initial stage of police investigations, and that have therefore passed a certain threshold requirement for evidence. Yet, high conviction rates in court do not reflect the problems with being believed at the point of reporting. Worldwide, research points to a high attrition rate of sexual assault cases at the level of the police (Jordan 2004). Cases may be dropped due to lack of evidence, or victims may withdraw charges because they are daunted by patriarchal victim-blaming attitudes amongst legal professionals (Jordan 2004; Wheatcroft and Walklate 2014).

Establishing that consent took place itself becomes something of a proxy for "proving" whether rape took place or not. In instances, where non-consent can be clearly established through evidence of physical resistance against the attacker, or the person involved is considered statutorily unable to have capacity to consent, then cases more easily find traction in criminal justice contexts, at least according to our participants. Of course, it may be the case that children's or disabled people's accounts are also subjected to considerable scrutiny for different reasons, but this was not highlighted by our respondents.

The manifestations of consent in legal settings asserts assumptions and notions regarding femininity. The idea that women might have consented without knowing or that they did not consent with the necessary intentionality constructs women's sexual desire as inherently weak or fractured. Women do not know what they really want, do not have intense sexual desire and/or are easily persuaded by men. At the same time, and utterly contradictorily, women are seen to be vindictive schemers who lie in attempts to either cover up their regret over sexual encounters or to conceal infidelity.

Arguably, these different assumptions and practices are tantamount to female victims of sexual assault as not frequently being seen as reaching the threshold of "law's person," to quote Naffine (2003). Their status as rational, moral and believable agents is compromised by constant scepticism throughout criminal and legal proceedings. The focus in many investigative procedures on whether consent occurred or did not occur emerges from the status of women's sexualities and "property in the person." As Pateman (1988) argues, gender relations are built on a certain myth-like narrative about the relationship between men and women: women have somehow consented to their subjugated position (a "sexual contract") and once they have done so, men have a right to women's bodies for sexual satisfaction and reproductive labour. In fact, what modern notions of contract offer is a simultaneous conceiving of freedom in the face of widespread oppression and domination. The obsession with determining consent masks the wider violence by men facing women, shifting it into an interpersonal issue of agreement between two parties. In essence, the principle of consent can never reflect complex realities of desire and relationships and the liberation of women's sexuality is unlikely to be found through enforcing liberal conceptions of consent. Whilst our data shows similar experiences of women in Singapore to those of many other countries, the next section seeks to connect the socio-legal processes to wider rationalities regarding the socio-economic positionality of women in the country. We argue that a connection between a degree of tolerance of sexual violence rests on prevailing contradictions around the role of women in Singaporean society, especially as imagined by the state.

5 The Logics of State-Tolerated Violence

As stated earlier and indicated in our findings, the law is a frequently gendering force or "technology" (Smart 1993, 40). What we have suggested in relation to rape and sexual assault is that false allegations persist as a dominant myth strongly shaping criminal justice practices in Singapore, thus influencing what comes to be considered as "real" rape in various formal settings. Consent/non-consent binaries are a persistent feature of proceedings as cases of rape proceed through various stages of the criminal justice system. In essence, the socio-legal system in Singapore, along with most if not all other countries, excludes the vast amount of rape cases from serious investigation or criminal proceedings. Arguably, much of the current policy and legally orientated research on violence against women does not recognise the possibility that crimes against women have deeply systemic underpinnings. The tropes about women's morality and behaviour that dominate many legal proceedings around rape and sexual violence may be more structurally founded than much of the current research claims. In the Singapore case, state-led oppression against "alternative" sexualities, for instance, has been described as a cultural legacy of colonialism (Salehin and Vitis 2019), an unfortunate consequence of history. This misses the ongoing systemic importance of maintaining the gendered regime and why dominant forces may seek to maintain certain conservative perspectives and policies for reasons that lie outside of "popular opinion" or "modernising" forces.

Radical feminist Silvia Federici's (2004) analysis of the role of violence against women in the historical development of capitalism manages to highlight the rationalities undergirding the tolerance of violence against women. Federici sees women's status as being symbolically and culturally eroded throughout the transition from Feudalism to market-based societies. She suggested that capitalism sought to enforce a new social location for women primarily as "mothers" performing domestic labour without a wage. This denigrated position for women was justified through a set of cultural norms and morals guiding "appropriate" conduct for women. Those women who retained control over their sexual and reproductive lives such as those who refused to assume the monogamous-wife role, were sexually promiscuous or assumed control over when and when not to have children, especially without the consent of men, became quintessentially immoral figures. The formation and institutionalisation of the socio-sexual regulation of women, however, was historically a deeply violent affair most evident through witch-hunts but arguably lingering to this day through policies and socio-economic systems which sanction domestic and sexual violence.

In Singapore, violence against women could frequently prove to be an uncomfortable truth negating the assumed sanctity and security of family life. As Teo (2009, 2010, 2011) has argued, a particular role for women remains central to nationalist ideological formations seeing Singapore as an "Asian values" society built on "familial piety." This ideology constructs a system of reproduction where the family is seen as the primary unit for reproduction. Nonetheless, women now occupy an improved position having negotiated state recognition and intervention on the issue of violence.

The flexing of certain state powers for intervening in domestic and sexual violence have developed over the last decades. However, these interventions continue to emphasise women's "protection" through legal and criminal justice intervention. This does not represent a more far-reaching women's empowerment which would involve deconstructing conventional understandings of family and offering material roots to economic and social independence through welfare state policies. Ultimately, by failing to take accounts of sexual violence seriously, the state tolerates its presence. In the criminal justice system, sexual violence is often discredited and victims are placed under intense and unreasonable scrutiny.

6 Conclusion

The data presented here shows that criminal justice and investigative arenas in Singapore follow international trends in their treatment of victims of sexual assault. Gendered stereotypes are institutionally embedded in legal practices and conduct. Importantly, this transcends misogynist thinking or belief systems and is inscribed in the thresholds for evidence, the critical importance of providing credible accounts and the constant interrogation of consent. Indeed, these problematic processes tended to be most extreme, admittedly from limited evidence earlier on in investigation processes. We favour a view that rape represents a form of systemically tolerated violence against women, supporting the wider gender regime, and that putting an end to sexual violence requires a systematic rehaul of the way society views women and consent. Finally, we argue that the absence of evidence to corroborate a rape claim is not proof that the incident did not occur or that the complainant is lying. To immediately jump to the latter conclusion falls prey to misogynist modes of viewing women as vindictive liars and unstable subjects. One way to begin dismantling state-sanctioned gender violence is by treating the stories of women with respect and sensitivity and committing to the "real" material empowerment of women through welfare investment and reform, opening the door to more far-reaching forms of freedom.

References

Bucher, J. and M. Manasse. 2011. When Screams Are Not Released: A Study of Communication and Consent in Acquaintance Rape Situations. *Women & Criminal Justice*, 21 (2): 123–140.

Estrich, Susan. 1987. *Real Rape*. Harvard: Harvard University Press.
Federici, Silvia. 2004. Caliban and the Witch: Women, the Body and Primitive Accumulation. *Autonomedia.*
Fraser, N. 2016. Contradiction of Capital and Care. *New Left Review* 100.
Ganapathy, Narayanan. 2008. Policing Marital Violence in Singapore. *Leiden: Brill.*
Gunby, Clare, Anna Carline, and Caryl Beynon. 2012. Regretting it After? Focus Group Perspectives on Alcohol Consumption, Nonconsensual Sex and False Allegations of Rape. *Social and Legal Studies* 22 (1): 87–106.
Jessop, Bob. 2004. The Gender Selectivities of the State: A Critical Realist Analysis. *Journal of Critical Realism* 3 (2): 207–237.
Jordan, Jan. 2004. Beyond belief? Police, rape and women's credibility. *Criminal Justice* 4 (1): 29–59.
Kelly, Liz. 2010. The (In)credible Words of Women: False Allegations in European Rape Research. *Violence against Women* 16 (12): 1345–1355.
Kelly, Liz, Jo Lovett, and Linda Regan. 2005. A Gap or a Chasm? Attrition in Reported Rape Cases. *London, England: Home Office.*
Naffine. 2003. Who are Law's Persons? From Cheshire Cats to Responsible Subjects. *Modern Law Review*, 66 (3): 317–490.
Oswin, Natalie. 2014. Queer time in global city Singapore: Neoliberal futures and the 'freedom to love.' *Sexualities* 17 (4): 412–433.
Pateman, C. 1988. *The Sexual Contract*. Stanford: Stanford University Press.
Quinlan, Andrea. 2016. Suspect Survivors: Police Investigation Practices in Sexual Assault Cases in Ontario, Canada. *Women & Criminal Justice* 26 (4): 301–318.
Radics, George. 2015. Section 377A in Singapore and the (De)Criminalization of Homosexuality. *Reconstruction* 15 (2): 1–29.
Rumney, Philip. 2006. False allegations of rape. *Cambridge Law Journal* 65 (1): 128–158.
Salehin, Ahmad, and Laura Vitis. 2019. Cruising, space and surveillance: Decolonizing sexuality in Singapore. *Globalizations* 17 (7): 1225–1240.
Saunders, C.L. 2012. The Truth, The Half-Truth, and Nothing Like the Truth: Reconceptualizing False Allegations of Rape. *The British Journal of Criminology*, 52 (6): 1152–1171.
Smart, C. 1992. The Woman of Legal Discourse. *Social & Legal Studies*, 1: 29–44.
Smart, C. 1993. Proscription, Prescription and the Desire for Certainty?: Feminist Theory in the Field of Law. *Studies in Law, Politics, and Society*, 13: 37–54.
Teo, Youyenn. 2009. Gender Disarmed: How Gendered Policies Produce Gender-Neutral Politics in Singapore. *Signs: Journal of Women in Culture and Society* 34 (3): 533–558.
Teo, Youyenn. 2010. Shaping the Singapore family, producing the state and society. *Economy and Society* 39 (3): 337–359.
Teo, Youyenn. 2011. *Neoliberal morality in Singapore: How family policies make state and society*. New York, NY: Routledge.

Vogel, Lise. 2013. Marxism and the Oppression of Women. *Leiden and Boston: Brill.*

Wheatcroft, Jacqueline M., and Sandra Walklate. 2014. Thinking differently about 'False Allegations' in Cases of Rape: The Search for Truth. *International Journal of Criminology and Sociology* 3: 239–248.

Wong, Theresa, and Brenda S.A. Yeoh. 2003. Fertility and the Family: An Overview of Pro-natalist Population Policies in Singapore. *Asian MetaCentre for Population and Sustainable Development Analysis.*

10

Between Toys and Behind Bars: Mothers in Jail in the State of Ceará, Brazil

Lara Nascimento Meneses, João Araújo Monteiro Neto and Nestor Eduardo Araruna Santiago

1 Introduction

This chapter investigates the implementation of the Early Childhood Statute (ECS—Brazilian Federal Law no. 13,257/2016) in the State of Ceará Justice System, particularly focusing on how the right of imprisoned women to raise their children is enforced in local penitentiaries and detention centres. In recent years, there has been gradual and significant growth in the number of individuals incarcerated due to provisional orders or serving sentences. Brazil reached the fourth position in the world ranking of countries with the highest incarcerated population (CNJ 2014) with more than 700,000 individuals in prison today (Statista 2021). This scenario is even more problematic as the data published by the National Survey of the Penitentiary System (INFOPEN 2018) reveals a higher rate of increase of female incarceration levels as compared with the rate of male incarceration. According to the survey, the number of women prisoners totals about 42,000, which represents an increase of 656% in relation to the incarceration rates of the early 2000s (INFOPEN 2018). One important characteristic of this new reality is that a percentage of these incarcerated women have children, leading to the enactment of provisions on the ECS and the development of policies to ensure compliance with constitutional guarantees that mothers can breastfeed their

L. N. Meneses · J. A. M. Neto · N. E. A. Santiago (✉)
University of Fortaleza (UNIFOR), Fortaleza, Brazil
e-mail: nestorsantiago@unifor.br

C. B. Radics and P. Ciocchini (eds.), *Criminal Legalities and Minorities in the Global South*, Palgrave Socio-Legal Studies, https://doi.org/10.1007/978-3-031-17918-1_10

children even if in prison, and augment the rights of women to raise and protect their children despite being incarcerated.[1]

Nevertheless, we must ask why so many women are going to jail, and how this would impact societal and family dynamics. In Brazil, almost 30,000,000 families are headed by women, and many of them are single mothers, divorced or widowed (15% of all Brazilian families) (Cavenaghi and Alves 2018). If they go to prison, incarcerated mothers leave a huge impact on support of one's livelihood; children will be alone or will be sent to state institutions to be taken care of, or even live on the streets, subject to all kinds of violence. On the other hand, incarcerated women don't want to expose their children to Brazil's prison environment (de Araújo et al. 2020).

The chapter, therefore, unpacks this overlooked legal reality analysing the enforcement and application of the ECS for imprisoned women through a review of legal cases brought on the Ceará State Court of Justice (TJCE—Tribunal de Justiça do Estado do Ceará) between 2016 and 2018. This analysis combines the protective rationale embedded in the ECS and the legal mechanisms and policies designed to protect imprisoned women's fundamental rights. Additionally, to investigate in depth what elements and configurations underpin the operation of the ECS in the implementation of the rights of imprisoned women with children, this chapter also employs a case study approach in order to understand the legal narrative supporting the enactment policies proposed by the ECS or lack thereof. Therefore, we also rely on data to critically analyse if and how the provisions of the ECS are being effectively implemented and addressed in the decisions of the Ceará State Court of Justice.

We begin by interrogating the constitutionalization of the rights of children and the youth, especially after the 1988 Brazilian Constitution embraced the so-called Doctrine of Integral Protection, abandoning the authoritarian-like legal order based on a paternalistic premise that these populations should be treated as objects of state intervention. In the second section, we highlight important quantitative information concerning women incarceration in order to demonstrate how things have, in fact, not changed at all and that women and children remain treated as objects of state intervention. The third section is dedicated to an application of the case study approach to depict female incarceration in the State of Ceará. Finally, the

[1] The Brazilian Constitution guarantees the right of the imprisoned women to breastfeed their children in prison during their time serving a sentence: Article 5, section L—"the prisoners will be guaranteed conditions, so that they can remain with their children during the breastfeeding period".

chapter concludes that the law itself is not enough to enforce the rights of imprisoned women whose rights are caught at the intersection of the courts, the law and the Brazilian imprisonment culture.

2 The Rights of Children and the Youth and the "Doctrine of Integral Protection"

In the past three decades, there has been a noticeable transformation of the Brazilian legal ecosystem. Since the enactment of the "Citizen Constitution" in 1988, the legal ecosystem has adopted a more human rights centric approach. One of the reasons behind this change was the constitutional movement to strengthen the rights of children and adolescents under a new rationale based on the Doctrine of Integral Protection. The old legal order and the Code of Minors (1979) were overturned by the new constitutional perspective enshrined in the Child and Adolescent Statute in 1990 (CAS). This new legal approach based on the Constitution currently adopted in favour of children and adolescents is the result of a complex process of transitions away from previous understandings of the role of children in Brazilian society (Custódio 2018). Previous approaches that tended to marginalize and stigmatize children and youth (Lima and Veronese 2012), began to contradict a new set of social values enshrined in a constitutional order that promoted the doctrinal construction of guarantees, principles and rules that held that the rights of children and adolescents serve as an absolute priority for State policies, deserving integral and special protection in the law. To understand how far the ECS has come in recognizing the rights of mothers and children, it is important to understand the theoretical rationale behind how children were seen in the past. In fact, it is possible to highlight three theoretical rationales used to frame the laws that applied to childhood and youth rights in the Brazilian legal order, which promoted different set of values and political-social views concerning the level of protection and can be seen: (i) in the Criminal Law of Minors; (ii) the Irregular Situation Doctrine; (iii) and the Doctrine of Integral Protection. While it is possible to identify these three different legal approaches, it is important to note that only recently has there been a focused legal approach to promote and protect children and adolescent rights: the ECA (1990) and the EPI (2016) are a translation of this new way of thinking.

The first Brazilian Constitution (1824) enacted during the monarchy (1822–1889) only mentioned the notion of minors and was much more concerned with regulating the specific situation of the Brazilian emperor who had not yet reached the majority at that time. During the final stages of the monarchy, the first Brazilian legal provisions concerning children's rights and obligations of the parent to care for them appeared. They were intended to regulate the situation of minors who violated the law, and as such, mechanisms were inscribed into the Imperial Penal Code to deal with these situations. One of the main characteristics of this period was punishment for minor offenders and the harshness and cruelty of such penalties. The Minor's Criminal Law approach was to alleviate the punishment during sentencing for populations under the age of eighteen (Bianchini 2005). During that period, children and adolescents were not considered to be of legal relevance. Only after the 1934 Constitution and its successors did sparse Brazilian constitutional provisions about childhood and youth begin to emerge (Assis et al. 2016). Socially, the absence of an effective recognition of infants as subjects in a peculiar condition of development and, therefore, deserving full protection, persisted for a long time in the country (Lima and Veronese 2012). At that time, children had no rights and the head of the family—the father—was legally authorized to decide what was best for the children (Mendes 2006).

The second legal rationale developed in Brazilian legal order to regulate children and adolescents was the Doctrine of the Irregular Situation, which dealt with minor offenders, poor and abandoned children. It was initially deployed in the first Code of Minors enacted in 1927 and, after several years of amendments, was finally consolidated in the 1979 Code of Minors. It compiled various normative provisions concerning childhood and relegated children and adolescents to a category of minors—individuals not the subject of rights but merely objects of State protection. The 1927 Code of Minors, also known as the "Mello Matos Code", embodied an assistance and protectionist normative character, intervening directly in the conditions experienced by disadvantaged children (Silva 2011). It was based on a presumed relationship between poverty and delinquency, and the law mainly focused on issues of abandonment and juvenile delinquency. Moreover, the 1979 Code of Minors revoked the previous codification and ratified the Doctrine of the Irregular Situation in Brazil, enshrining it as the legal paradigm applied to children and youths (Leite 2005). According to the 1979 Code, children and adolescents classified in an "irregular" situation were subject to a set of restrictive measures particularly aimed at addressing abandoned minors and children who violated the law (delinquents). In this regard, no distinction was made between both categories, as they were subject to the same legal treatment. Under this legal approach three categories of children could be identified: (1) minor offenders, (2) those abandoned by their respective family members and (3) individuals facing extreme poverty. These three groups were considered at risk and deserving State intervention which mainly resulted in the children and adolescents being sent to caring facilities to work under discipline and punishment. This legal model stigmatized childhood through the practice of institutionalizing children, removing them from their respective homes, and submitting them to the tutelage of the State in order to re-educate them to social interaction.

Subsequently, with the emergence of a new social order fuelled by a democratic movement and a new constitutional framework set in 1988, the traditional law and order approach applied to minors' rights were slowly transformed. These conditions ushered in a transition from the Doctrine of the Irregular Situation to the Doctrine of Integral Protection, a transition that was only enhanced by the rise of international mechanisms that promoted the reformulation of how states view and promote children and adolescents' roles in society. The United Nations 1989 Convention on the Rights of the Child, the Child and Constitution Campaign of the National Commission of the Child and the Constitution,[2] and the advent of the 1988 Federal Constitution were integral in shifting the way state and the law view and regulate children (Sposato 2009). These three different legal mechanisms were also central to enshrining the "integral protection" approach in Brazilian legal order. As the perception of children's rights began to change, legislation was passed to more effectively protect the needs of children and provide space for the development of a more encompassing set of laws and policies that promote the children and adolescent rights framework, indicating that the State, family and society are responsible for guaranteeing these rights and needs (Fachinetto 2008). This process moved slowly at first, but developed significantly after 1988. The enactment of the 1990 CAS reinforced this constitutional approach and completely transformed the paradigm previously in force: *children and youths were no longer legally recognized as problems, but as deserving protection.*

This normative transformation was the result of a significant social shift in perceptions concerning the role and the rights of children and youths in Brazilian society. Various social movements emerged in defence of the

[2]Composed of seven ministries: Education, Health, Social Welfare, Labour, Justice, Culture and Planning; plus the Brazilian Bar Association, the Brazilian Paediatrics Society, World Organization for Pre-School Education, National Council of Women's Rights, National Journalists' Federation, National Front for the Defence of Children's Rights, the National Movement for Street Boys and Girls and UNICEF.

reformulation of the legal framework regulating the rights of children and adolescents contributed significantly to break the influence of the legal rationale previously adopted. Such demands resulted in the insertion of specific provisions in the Constitution and the enactment of other protective legal mechanisms (Amin et al. 2018). Vieira (2013) establishes that the new guarantor apparatus recognizes the vulnerable circumstances of children and adolescents, listing them as an absolute priority to state policies, at the same time promoting the need to legally ensure their superior interest in the face of litigation with other actors or subjects.

Despite the advances already mentioned, the countless attempts to provide adequate specialized assistance for children and youth have not been able to cover all possible situations or, still, to fully meet the needs of such individuals, thus lacking effective implementation. One of these not fully implemented dimensions is the overlooked treatment that children of imprisoned women have been exposed to, despite the legal framework enacted to promote their rights. In order to have a better view and contextualize our approach, in the next section we highlight some important data about women incarceration, showing that the situation should be much better, considering all the legal protection given to infants and adolescents.

3 Women Deprived of Liberty and Their Children: Between Toys and Behind Bars

The gradual and significant expansion of Brazil's incarcerated population raised several questions, particularly, in relation to the female incarceration rate sharp increase in recent years. Although the male prison population is considerably higher, there has been a significant increase in the number of women imprisoned over the years. A more detailed analysis of data released by the National Penitentiary Information Survey (INFOPEN 2018) points out that between 2000 and 2016, there was an increase of 656% in the number of women imprisoned, and almost three times more than the male increase rate in the same period (293%). This increase was one of the main factors leading to the increase of research efforts aiming to decipher this phenomenon and the development of policies addressing the notorious precariousness of the prison environment and particularly the accommodation of women serving criminal sentences. Although research efforts tend to overlook the particular condition of imprisoned women with children, Braga and Alves (2015) noticed a problematic scenario due to the lack of resources and policies addressing imprisoned women's needs being impacted by bias, contributing to the neglect of their rights, particularly the ones experiencing motherhood.

There is a considerably large number of women offenders who have children and who are subjected to the disastrous conditions in the country's prison system. Moreover, there is a lack of sufficient information on the gender statistics in some states, making it even more difficult to accurately measure the number of children of women deprived of liberty. From a sample of 6,869 women (7% of the female imprisoned population in Brazil), it was found that 74% of them have children (INFOPEN 2018). Furthermore, this percentage includes countless imprisoned pregnant women and breastfeeding women subjected to a predominantly male environment which compromises not only their physical integrity, but also the adequate development of their newborn babies. Tavares and Santoro (2018) state that the crisis experienced by the Brazilian prison system in general, highlighting its structural and sanitary deficiencies, as well as the "curbing" rationale driving the lack of enforcement of inmates' fundamental rights and guarantees. When the particular condition of imprisoned women is observed, the scenario is much more precarious.

The imprisonment of mothers can have several consequences for the development of infants. It can significantly impact the formation of their personality, as well as in the perception of innumerable skills acquired during the period of early childhood. The early break in the bond established between the mother and the baby, for example, can be one of the determining factors for the emergence of behaviours that are harmful to the child's proper socialization, and in developing trusting relationships (de Araújo et al. 2020; Stella 2009). In this particular context, the Brazilian legal and constitutional system enacted several legal mechanisms to provide due protection for imprisoned women with young children and to promote adequate maternal and childcare during their time in prison, such as those established in the Federal Constitution, the Criminal Execution Law and in the CAS. These provisions deal with the need for female penal establishments to have nurseries, exclusive sections for pregnant women as well as day-care centres, all in order to provide the proper protection of infants, newborns and their mothers (Articles 83 and 89 of the Criminal Execution Law). These legal frameworks also aim to promote specialized assistance for imprisoned pregnant or breastfeeding women, coupled with gender specificities, as well as the creation of public policies that improve the treatment of women deprived of their liberty. In addition, the Bangkok Rules (United Nations 2010) establishes a set of rules for detainees particularly aiming to ensure better conditions within prison facilities. The observance of gender-specific needs and the constant incentive to apply non-custodial measures are examples of the prescribed regulations aimed at incarcerated women.

However, the normative dimension of these legal mechanisms is completely dissociated from its operational dimension, as imprisoned women and their children are in a condition of triple jeopardy (gender discrimination, imprisonment and poverty), which contributes significantly to the lack of political interest in promoting policies to enact legal provisions. One good example of this overlooked reality is the number of women provisionally imprisoned. In the State of Ceará, in June 2016, there were about 1236 women imprisoned, and 832 of them (67%) had not yet been sentenced, making Ceará the fourth highest percentage of imprisoned women without conviction in Brazil (DPN 2018: 19–21). Exploring this reality, the National Council of the Prosecutor's Office (CNMP n.d.) indicated that in 2018 the Brazilian Northeast was listed as the second region with the highest female occupation in penal establishments and concentrated the highest percentage of imprisoned pregnant women in the country, with almost double its rate. At that time, there were 5808 imprisoned women, and 105 of them were pregnant (1.80%). These numbers show that poverty plays an important role in women imprisonment, considering that this region is the 2nd poorest region in Brazil.

Ceará	Total number of imprisoned women	Number of pregnant women in jail
2015	3.082	27
2016	1.290	14
2017	1.490	24
2018	1.606	29

Source Author's elaboration, based on data collected from CNMP, *online*

Although most of the pregnant women or those who have children in the early childhood period are already housed in penal establishments that have maternal and child units, there is still a certain percentage that do not enjoy such a benefit (CNMP n.d.). This precarious situation highlights how a significant number of imprisoned women and their children are exposed to a legal reality very different from the one portrayed in the legal documents, courts and public administration. Even though already conceived as subjects of rights and, therefore, deserving special tutelage and care, women and children are overlooked and normally put aside from rights already enshrined in the law, but overlooked by courts and public authorities, as the next section will discuss.

4 The Application of the ECS at the Ceará Court of Appeals

Although it is possible to see a gradual increase of the level of legal protection of the youth and the promotion of specific rights and guarantees, over the years the lack of political interest and the absence of policies implementing these legally constructed rights represent the paradox of how the law protecting minorities operates in Brazil. Formally, the legal system promotes and enshrines these values and rights, but concretely, the implementation follows a superficial approach "for Englishmen to see".[3] This is the context of the enactment of the ECS, a Federal Law aiming to extend the normative apparatus ensuring that children and adolescents have healthy and integral development. In addition to conceptualizing early childhood as the time period encompassing the first full six years of a child's life, the ECS established guidelines for the creation of specific policies promoting the Doctrine of Integral Protection (Oliveira 2017, 31). Furthermore, it brought numerous protectionist measures in favour of preserving the integrity of the early childhood period, establishing several legislative changes in the Brazilian legal system, particularly in the ECA CSA, in the Criminal Procedure Code, and in the Consolidation of Labour Laws.

Regarding the criminal law dimension, article 318 of the Criminal Procedure Code allows the judge in charge of a criminal case involving a pregnant offender with young children to substitute provisional detention measures with home arrest. This provision applies to pregnant women at any stage of pregnancy and women with children under 12 years old or, in the case of men, as long as the infant is under their exclusive responsibility (Art. 318, sec. IV and V).[4] Thus, with the intention of addressing the reality that still persists inside female prison units, the simple fact of being pregnant, regardless of the proof that the pregnancy is at risk or that it is at an advanced stage, as well as before the existence of offspring at an age that requires essential care, legally should allow a woman to stay home and

[3] This popular Brazilian expression means to "pretend to do something or do it wrong".

[4] On 20 October 2020, the Supreme Court also granted collective Habeas Corpus no. 165,704/DF, which was filed by the Federal Public Defender's Office, establishing, the substitution of pre-trial detention for home of all parents who have children under 12 years old or disabled under their exclusive responsibility, as well as those responsible for children under 6 years of age or disabled, as long as they are indispensable to their care (art. 318, III), except in cases where the crime is committed with violence or serious threat or against own children or dependents. Unlike what happens with the mothers, it must be proven, in the specific case, that the parent or guardian is the only one responsible for the care provided for the infant.

care for her child. This particular measure benefits the child's best interest, in view of the situation of vulnerability experienced by the children of individuals deprived of their liberty that mostly have an early stage of life compromised by the absence of a family environment as well for their health development (Silva 2018).

Because article 318 states that "the judge *may* substitute preventive detention for house arrest",[5] the judge is not obliged to substitute imprisonment with house arrest (Corlassoli and Marçal 2018). Therefore, it is up to the judge to observe the peculiarities of the specific case and, if necessary, determine the withdrawal of the provisional arrest in order to ensure adequate child development. As stated by Spindola (2016), the absence of a legal imposition able to ensure the referred benefit gave rise to several judicial decisions preventing the practical application of the measure due to the lack of ruling guidelines and the higher level of discretion granted to the judge. Therefore, many contradictory decisions exist—some protecting the best interest of the child and adolescent, others sacrificing it in order to guarantee public order and the safety of the community.

In order to critically analyse the level of implementation of the policies grounded on the ECS and its regulatory ecosystem, it is necessary to investigate the numbers of women granted home arrest under article 318 of the Criminal Procedure Code, how the house arrest was enacted, and generally what was the end result of this policy. The next section will discuss the results of a survey conducted in the State of Ceará, Brazil.[6]

5 Impacts of the ECS on the Management of Imprisoned Women in the State of Ceará

The changes brought about by the ECS, particularly the provisions related to the rights of children of imprisoned women in the Criminal Procedure Code, led to a conflict between Doctrine of Integral Protection and mechanisms promoting the state's obligation to ensure public order. In order to analyse the applicability of the ECS in these cases, the authors took

[5] Emphasis added.

[6] This chapter aimed to focus on mothers due to the greater severity of the situation, taking into account imprisoned pregnant and lactating women and the resulting impacts on unborn children and newborns.

advantage of the Access to Information Law (Federal Law no. 12,527/11) and asked information to the Brazilian Ministry of Justice and Public Security, the Brazilian Ministry of Health, the Secretary of Justice of Ceará and the State of Ceará Court of Justice. We received responses—in full or partially—from January to June 2019, which gave us a better picture of how the ECS was implemented.

Concerning the budget, the Ministry of Justice and Public Security stated that the investment to maintain the routine services of female, male or mixed prison units is a state attribution. The State of Ceará Secretary of Justice and Citizenship[7] determined that there is no difference in relation to budget, maintenance expenses and specific investments for women deprived of their liberty. From this, we can infer that there is no national policy concerning expenses in favour of imprisoned women, which can bring about differences among the twenty-six Brazilian States.

From March 2016 to March 2018, The State of Ceará Secretary of Justice and Citizenship informed that, according to data provided by the Female Penal Institute, 40 children were born inside the premises, with only 2 of them being from women serving their sentences. Nevertheless, it did not inform if these women were sent home due to collective Habeas Corpus or any other judicial ruling.

The Ministry of Health did not respond to our requests, replying that under Article 13 of the Access to Information Law, it could not provide the data and could only allow researchers access to the database located at the Ministry facilities in Brasilia. Finally, with regard to the Ceará State Court of Justice, it provided quantitative data on all the decisions handed down in the State involving requests for substitution of pre-trial detention for house arrests during the period between March 2016 and December of 2018.

	Substitution of pre-trial detention for house arrests			
	2016*	2017	2018	Total
Quantity	264	352	919	1535

*March to December of 2018

	Denial of substitution of preventive prison in household			
	2016*	2017	2018	Total
Quantity	143	125	224	492

*March to December of 2018 *Source Ceará State Court of Appeals*

[7] The State of Ceará Secretary of Justice and Citizenship (SEJUS), which was extinguished and replaced by SAP (Secretary of Penitentiary Administration).

Although the State Court did not clarify why it limited the data it provided to a particular time period, the analysis of the data was revealing. It can be inferred that the number of favourable decisions made in the period mentioned demonstrates a reliance on the provisions of the ECS in the State Court, although most house arrest substitutions were made in 2018, particularly by electronic monitoring. This can be explained by the landmark judgement of the Supreme Federal Court held on the collective Habeas Corpus no. 143,641/SP (February 20, 2018) and the enactment of the Federal Law no. 13,769/18 (house arrest form imprisoned women with young children). In this case, the Supreme Court recognized the poor implementation of the ECS and determined the immediate granting of the right to house arrest of such women as a general rule, significantly contributing to the increase of cases and favourable decisions from that year on. As a result of both the Habeas Corpus and Federal Law no. 13,769/18, 2895 women were sent to their homes, according to the Ministry of Justice and Public Security.

6 The ECS and the Supreme Court: Habeas Corpus No. 143,641/SP (February 20, 2018)

Despite the enactment of the ECS and the Federal Law no. 13,769/2018, the implementation of the rights and guarantees embodied in these legal mechanisms was ineffectual. The lack of interest in promoting the necessary policies to properly implement the new legal provisions created a liminal environment where, despite being fully in force, the rules are not properly enforced, creating an ambiguous discretionary environment that promotes discrimination, corruption, uncertainty and the wreaking of law. This peculiar characteristic of Brazilian socio-legal reality, explored by Santiago and Monteiro Neto (2019) regarding the ambiguous regulatory framework found in the criminal justice system particularly in the case of gambling, required the development of advocacy strategies necessary to promote the proper enforcement of rights for imprisoned women and their children. The legal challenge made in the case by Habeas Corpus no. 143,641/SP forced the Supreme Court to review the implementation of the ECS leading to a judgement that mandated the proper application of its provisions.

The majority of women deprived of their liberty account for non-violent crimes linked to transport and small drug trade (68% of arrests). Analysing the profile, Boiteux (2016) notes that most of them are young (50%), black (68%) with little education, and the only ones responsible for the affective and financial support of their children; unemployed or engaged in precarious activities (KILDUFF 2020).

The Supreme Court ruled the immediate and mandatory conversion of preventive detention to home arrest for all pregnant imprisoned women or those who have children up to 12 years old. Only a few exceptions were made: in cases of violent criminal conduct or in cases when detention is deemed necessary by the judge. The Supreme Court decision is a good way to avoid a culture of incarceration, especially for women who suffer the most violent and long-lasting consequences of prison. As stated by Ramos (2018), despite the significant achievements resulting from the decision, especially in the fight against the culture of incarceration, there are still some questions that were not properly answered by the Supreme Court, particularly in the exceptional situations authorizing the maintenance of preventive detention at the cost of a high level of discretion to the judging body.

Furthermore, Federal Law 13,769/18 was intended to enshrine the position held by the Supreme Court through more suitable legal mechanisms. The law replaced the verb "may", which existed in the Art. 318 of the Criminal Procedure Code, finally mandating the normative command of "must", leading to an automatic presumption of conversion of pre-trial detention to home arrest. Observing the effectiveness of these changes the National Council of Justice (CNJ) already created an oversight mechanism to monitor the situation of pregnant and breastfeeding imprisoned women. The most recent data encompasses quantitative information from December 2017 to July 2019.

The data for the State of Ceará is restricted up till November 2018, making it difficult to analyse precisely the current implementation of the ECS in contrast to earlier years. On the other hand, the data presented (December 2017 to November 2018), a time period before the Supreme Federal Court ruling, reveals that the number of imprisoned women that due to pregnancy or childcare attributions should be on provisional release from prison was relatively low and stable, indicating a lower level of enforcement of their rights, as we can observe in the graphic below:

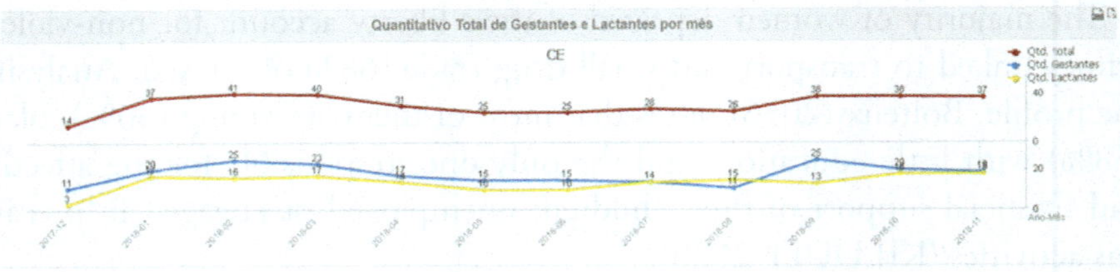

(*Source Conselho Nacional de Justiça* 2018)

Therefore, the lack of enforcement of the existing legal framework highlights how the laws aimed at promoting imprisoned women rights, reinforced by the invisibility of the issue on the political agenda and a lack of resources, create a vicious cycle, placing imprisoned women and their children in a situation where the rights promised are precarious. In other words, rather than having a law that protects women and children, social realities complicate an already messy situation in which the ECS only alleviates the effects of an already growing incarceration phenomenon and a deeply flawed criminal justice system in Brazil.

7 Conclusion

Although female incarceration has been discussed before, it is possible to conclude that the situation of imprisoned women and their children presents an interesting and overlooked phenomenon that can contribute significantly to unpack operational failures of law as an instrument to protect minorities. There are no in-depth scientific studies on the subject in Brazil and public agencies do not have accurate information about the legal status of these individuals. This reinforces their legal invisibility and contributes to increase the level of state led discrimination and harm.

From an analysis of the data provided, it can be inferred that the expressive amount of favourable decisions demonstrates a tendency to apply the ECS when possible. Regarding the specific reality of the mothers, DEPEN carried out an initial survey of the number of concessions made in 24 states of Brazil shortly after the decision by the Supreme Court in order to verify compliance with the collective HC. Until June 2018, in the State of Ceará only 104 obtained house arrest, which demonstrated that not applications of the ECS are successful (Vital 2018). On the other hand, in April 2018, the Public Defender Office of the State of Ceará (2018) reported that, according to data made available by SEJUS, in March 2018 there was a small reduction (2%) of incarcerated women for the first time in the period of 6 months, which is closely tied to the decision granted by the Supreme Court.

Nevertheless, with the increases in house arrest in 2018, it appears that although the ECS has led to significant advances in guaranteeing the best interest of children and adolescents, consisting of the initial milestone from the recent achievements in favour of children, the greatest increase occurred after the judgement of the collective Habeas Corpus by the Supreme Court, which protected the rights of all imprisoned mothers and, consequently, of their respective offspring. However, it is worth mentioning that the numerous attempts already made by legislators to ensure proper legal protection for Brazilian childhood and youth remain unable to address the culture of incarceration still prevalent in society, a fact that, combined with the absence of specific public policies, compromises the desired results, favouring the permanence of the precarious reality.

This chapter aimed to analyse the legal harms embodied in the inefficiency of legal mechanisms regulating the rights of imprisoned women who are pregnant or have children under 12 years old, and the degrading compromise of the dignity of the human person who experiences such a reality. It highlighted the exercise of motherhood within this context in order to ascertain the growing percentage of the female imprisoned, the conditions of the maternal and child units, and the struggle to enforce rights already established in the legal system. Finally, this chapter reveals a lower level of enforcement of the provisions established on the ECS in the State of Ceará. Despite the lack of information, what raises concerns about the level of interest of public bodies in shedding light in to the problem investigated, it is possible to extract certain logical conclusions from a detailed analysis of the number of cases lodged in the State of Ceará Court of Appeal, raising the need to enforce imprisoned women rights.

References

Amin, Andréa Rodrigues, et al. 2018. *Curso de Direito da Criança e do Adolescente: Aspectos teóricos e práticos* [Child and Adolescent Law Course: Theo retical and practical aspects]. In Kátia Regina, Ferreira Lobo, and Andrade Maciel (eds.). São Paulo: Saraiva Educação. ISBN: 9788547230890.

Ana Elisa et al. 2016. As crianças sua presença/ausência na legislação brasileira e a construção do direito à integridade física, à educação e à convivência familiar [Children have their presence/absence in Brazilian legislation and the construction of the right to physical integrity, education and family life]. In *Estudos sobre a violência contra a criança e o adolescente,* ed. Antonio Cecilio Moreira Pires et al. 125–167. São Paulo: Libro.

Andréa Rodrigues et al. 2018. Curso de Direito da Criança e do Adolescente: Aspectos teóricos e práticos [Child and Adolescent Law Course: Theoretical and practical aspects]. In Kátia Regina, Ferreira Lobo, and Andrade Maciel (eds.). *São Paulo: Saraiva Educação.*

Assis, Ana Elisa et al. 2016. As crianças sua presença/ausência na legislação brasileira e a construção do direito à integridade física, à educação e à convivência familiar [Children have their presence/absence in Brazilian legislation and the construction of the right to physical integrity, education and family life]. In Antonio Cecilio Moreira Pires et al. (eds.), *Estudos sobre a violência contra a criança e o adolescente,* pp. 125–167. São Paulo: Libro.

Bianchini, Edemir Nelson. 2005. *Doutrinas do Direito da Criança e do Adolescente [Doctrines of Child and Adolescent Law.].* Lajeado/RS: Centro Universitário Univates.

Boiteux, L. 2016. *Encarceramento feminino e seletividade penal* [Female incarceration and criminal selectivity.]. Rede de Justiça Criminal: Discriminação de gênero no sistema penal. Accessed April 5, 2021. https://redejusticacriminal.org/pt/portfolio/encarceramento-feminino-e-seletividade-penal/.

Braga, Ana Gabriela Mendes and Paula Pereira Gonçalves Alves. 2015. *Prisão e políticas públicas: Uma análise do encarceramento feminino no estado do Ceará* [Prison and public policies: An analysis of female incarceration in the state of Ceará.]. *Revista Pensar. Fortaleza* 20 (2): 302–326.

Cavenaghi, Suzana, and José Eustáquio Diniz. Alves. 2018. *Mulheres chefes de família no Brasil: Avanços e desafios [Women heads of families in Brazil: Advances and challenges.].* Rio de Janeiro: ENS-CPES.

Código de Processo Penal. 1941. *Decreto-Lei n. 3.689, de 3 de outubro de 1941* [Decree-Law No. 3689 of October 3, 1941.]. Accessed September 15, 2019. http://www.planalto.gov.br/ccivil_03/decreto-lei/del3689.htm.

Conselho Nacional de Justiça (Brasil). 2014. Novo diagnóstico de pessoas presas no Brasil [New diagnosis of people arrested in Brazil.]. *Departamento de monitoramento e fiscalização do sistema carcerário e do sistema de execução de medidas socioeducativas—DMF.*

Conselho Nacional de Justiça (Brasil). 2016. Regras de Bangkok [Bangkok rules.]. *Regra das Nações Unidas para o tratamento de mulheres presas e medidas não privativas de liberdade para mulheres infratoras.*

Conselho Nacional de Justiça (Brasil). 2018. *Cadastro Nacional de grávidas e lactantes* [National Registry of pregnant and nursing mothers.].

Constituição (Brasil). 1824. *Constituição Política do Império do Brasil* [Political Constitution of the Empire of Brazil.].

CNMP – Conselho Nacional do Ministério Público. n.d. *Sistema Prisional em Números* [Prison System in Numbers]. Accessed September 14, 2019. https://www.cnmp.mp.br/portal/relatoriosbi/sistema-prisional-em-numeros?fbclid=IwAR3rUyWbm7dtWROq0l4g0MQDVtXYpNhA83jm-0-VUrGqmaWQGaRNjSpD_J4.

Constituição (Brasil). 1988. *Constituição da República Federativa do Brasil* [Constitution of the Federative Republic of Brazil.]. Brasília, DF, Senado.

Corlassoli, Thaís Mara Bottega and Julia Dambrós Marçal. 2018. Prisioneiras: Violações cometidas aos direitos das mães e gestantes nas penitenciárias brasileiras e a decisão do HC 143.641 pelo STF [Prisoners: Violations committed to the rights of mothers and pregnant women in Brazilian penitentiaties and the decision of HC 143,641 by the Supreme Court.]. *Revista Jurídica FADEP Digital* 2 (4): 299–322.

Custódio, André Viana. 2018. Teoria da Proteção Integral: pressuposto para a compreensão do Direito da Criança e do Adolescente [Theory of Integral Protection: presupposition for the understanding of the Right of children and adolescents.]. *Universidade de Santa Cruz do Sul* (29): 22–42.

de Araújo, Priscila França et al. 2020. Behind bars: the burden of being a woman in Brazilian prisons. *BMC International Health and Human Rights* 20 (1): 1–9.

Defensoria Pública Do Estado Do Ceará. 2018. *Defensoria contabiliza 104 mulheres beneficiadas com prisão domiciliar após HC Coletivo* [Defender's account counts 104 women benefited from house arrest after COLLECTIVE HC.].

Departamento Penitenciário Nacional (Brasil). 2017. *Levantamento Nacional de Informações Penitenciárias* [National Survey of Penitentiary Information.]. Brasília, DF.

Departamento Penitenciário Nacional (Brasil). 2018. *Levantamento Nacional de Informações Penitenciárias: INFOPEN Mulheres* [National Penitentiary Information Survey: INFOPEN Women.]. Brasília, DF.

DPN – Departamento Penitenciário Nacional. 2018. *Levantamento Nacional de Informações Penitenciárias: INFOPEN Mulheres*. Brasília.

Estatuto da Criança e do Adolescente (ECA). 1990. *Lei nº 8.069, de 13 de julho de 1990* [Law No. 8069 of July 13, 1990.].

Estatuto da Primeira Infância (EPI). 2016. *Lei nº 13.257, de 08 de março de 2016* [Law No. 13,257 of March 8, 2016.].

Fachinetto, Neidemar José. 2008. *A garantia do direito à convivência familiar e sua relação com as políticas públicas: uma análise interdisciplinar* [The guarantee of the right to family life and its relationship with public policies: an interdisciplinary analysis.]. Master's diss., Santa Cruz do Sul.

Kilduff, Fernanda. 2020. Seletividade punitiva, racismo e superencarceramento no Brasil [Punitive selectivity, racism and superincarceration in Brazil.]. *Vértices (campos Dos Goitacazes)* 22: 787–804.

Lei de Execução Penal (Brasil). 1984. *Lei n. 7.210, de 11 de julho de 1984* [Law No. 7210 of July 11, 1984.].

Lei de Execução Penal (Brasil). 2018. *Lei n. 13.769, de 19 de dezembro de 2018* [Law No. 13,769 of December 19, 2018.].

Leite, Carla Carvalho. 2005. *Da doutrina da situação irregular à doutrina da proteção integral: aspectos históricos e mudanças paradigmáticas* [From the doctrine of irregular situation to the doctrine of integral protection: historical aspects and paradigmatic changes.]. Juizado da Infância e da Juventude. Tribunal de Justiça do Estado do Rio Grande do Sul, Corregedoria-Geral da Justiça.

Lima, Fernanda da Silva and Josiane Rose Petry Veronese. 2012. *Os direitos da criança e do adolescente: a necessária efetivação dos direitos fundamentais* [The rights of children and adolescents: the necessary realization of fundamental rights.]. Coleção Pensando o Direito no Século.

Mendes, Moacyr Pereira. 2006. *A doutrina da proteção integral da criança e do adolescente frente à Lei 8069/90* [The doctrine of the integral protection of children and adolescents in the face of Law 8069/90.]. Master's diss., São Paulo.

Oliveira, Rafaela Costa e Silva. 2017. *Prisão domiciliar como medida garantidora dos direitos das crianças que estão no cárcere com suas mães* [House arrest as a measure that ensures the rights of children who are in prison with their mothers.]. Trabalho de Conclusão de Curso, Brasília.

Ramos, Anna Carolina Meira. 2018. *Maternidade e prisão domiciliar na jurisprudência do Tribunal de Justiça do Rio Grande do Sul* [Maternity and house arrest in the case law of the Court of Justice of Rio Grande do Sul.]. XXVII Encontro Nacional do Conpedi, Porto Alegre.

Santiago, Nestor Eduardo Araruna and Joao Araujo Monteiro Neto. 2019. Gambling with criminal law: The legal paradox of "jogo do bicho" (animal lottery) criminalization in Brazil. In Pablo Ciocchini and George Radics (eds.), *Criminal Legalities in the Global South*. Routledge.

Silva, Bruna Larissa Pontes da. 2018. *A proteção à primeira infância dos filhos de mulheres presas e os possíveis reflexos do julgamento do Habeas Corpus coletivo n. 143.641—STF* [The protection of early childhood of the children of imprisoned women and the possible reflections of the judgment of the collective Habeas Corpus n. 143.641—STF.]. Brasília, Trabalho de Conclusão de Curso.

Silva, Gustavo de Melo. 2011. Adolescente em conflito com a lei no Brasil: da situação irregular à proteção integral [Adolescents in conflict with the law in Brazil: from irregular to comprehensive protection.]. *Revista Brasileira de História & Ciências Sociais* 3 (5).

Spindola, Luciana Soares. 2016. *A mulher encarcerada no sistema penal brasileiro: a busca de soluções para as especificidades do gênero feminino no tocante à maternidade* [The woman imprisoned in the Brazilian penal system: the search for solutions to the specificities of the female gender with regard to motherhood.]. Artigo (Especialização), Instituto Brasiliense de Direito Público.

Sposato, Karyna Batista. 2009. A constitucionalização do direito da criança no Brasil como barreira à redução da idade penal: Visões de um neoconstitucionalismo aplicado [The constitutionalization of the right of children in Brazil as a barrier to the reduction of the criminal age: Visions of an applied neoconstitutionalism.]. *Revista Brasileira De Ciências Criminais* 80: 80–118.

Statista. 2021. *Countries with the largest number of prisoners as of July 2021*. Available at: https://www.statista.com/statistics/262961/countries-with-the-most-prisoners/.

Stella, Cláudia. 2009. O impacto do encarceramento materno no desenvolvimento psicossocial dos filhos [The impact of maternal incarceration on the psychosocial development of children.]. *Educere et. Educare, Revista de Educação* 4 (8): 99–111.

Supremo Tribunal Federal (Brasil). 2018. *Habeas Corpus coletivo n. 143.641* [Habeas Corpus collective n. 143.641.]. São Paulo, Relator: Ministro Ricardo Lewandowski.

Tavares, Natália Lucero Farias and Antônio Eduardo Ramires Santoro. 2018. *Transcendências da pena: análise do encarceramento de gestantes e mães com filhos em fase de aleitamento* [Transcendences of the penalty: analysis of the incarceration of pregnant women and mothers with children in the breastfeeding phase.]. XXVII Encontro Nacional do Conpedi, Salvador, Bahi.

Vieira, Cláudia Maria Carvalho do Amaral. 2013. *Crianças encarceradas—a proteção integral da criança na execução penal feminina da pena privativa de liberdade* [Incarcerated children—the full protection of the child in the female criminal execution of the custodial sentence.]. Universidade Federal de Santa Catarina, Curso de Pós-Graduação em Direito, Programa de Doutorado, Florianópolis.

Vital, Danilo Governo. 2018. *pede que HC a mães presas seja executado 'de forma compulsória'* [asks HC to imprisoned mothers to be executed 'compulsorily'.]. Revista Consultor Jurídico.

11

The "War on Drugs" in Philippine Criminal Courts: Legal Professionals' Moral Discourse and Plea Bargaining in Drug-Related Cases

Pablo Ciocchini and Jayson Lamchek

1 Introduction

When Rodrigo Duterte assumed office in 2016, he unleashed one of the most infamous campaigns to allegedly tackle the illegal drug market in the Philippines. Thousands of people were executed by death squads because of this aggressive campaign. The widespread extra-judicial killings (EJKs) have attracted the attention of critics of the government, as well as local and foreign scholars. However, EJKs were not the only terrible consequence of Duterte's campaign. The government claims that 223,780 people were arrested in drug-related cases between 2016 and 2019 (OHCHR 2020). The impact of these arrests and the resulting detentions has been neglected by much of the literature, as has the role of legal professionals in managing them. Some observers have even downplayed the relevance of detentions in the campaign, arguing that imprisonment rates did not rise during Duterte's campaign (Johnson and Fernquest 2018, 375).

Illegal detentions were certainly less atrocious violations of human rights than EJKs, but they often result from illegal arrests or actions by police, including by planting evidence (Associated Press 2017). Legal professionals,

---

P. Ciocchini (✉)
University of Liverpool, Liverpool, UK
e-mail: p.ciocchini@liverpool.ac.uk

J. Lamchek
University of New South Wales, Sydney, Australia

G. B. Radics and P. Ciocchini (eds.), *Criminal Legalities and Minorities in the Global South*, Palgrave Socio-Legal Studies, https://doi.org/10.1007/978-3-031-17918-1_11

particularly public prosecutors and judges, decide upon the continuation of these detention and the fates of detainees. But faced with the massive number of detentions and being aware of the illegality of many of them, legal professionals chose to encourage defendants to plead guilty. By doing this, they contributed to the legitimation of the police behaviour in the context of the "war on drugs". Furthermore, there is consensus among critics that Duterte's "war on drugs" has targeted the poor (e.g. The Drug Archive 2018; Amnesty International 2017). In fact, the Filipino society at large shares this view (Reuters 2017). Nevertheless, Duterte has maintained a high approval rating and his deadly campaign has been strongly supported by the population. Scholars explained that this is the result of Duterte's success in addressing both Filipino society's anxiety against drugs and the middle and upper classes' fear of crime (e.g. Curato 2017; Kenny 2019). However, this theory does not satisfactorily explain how it was possible to authorize such levels of violence against the poor (Lara Jr. and de la Rosa 2020; Thompson 2020). Why do most of the population appear to approve of violence against the poor as a solution to the problem of drugs and crime (Lamchek 2017; Social Weather Station 2018)? Why is there continued support for the "war on drugs" despite its failure to curb the drug problem (Allard and Lema 2020; Cepeda 2020)?

To begin to understand this paradox and chart alternatives, this chapter acknowledges that the conditions for this campaign were set by decades of neoliberalism (Harvey 2007) which has led not only to rampant poverty and inequality but also to the poor being seen as primarily responsible for the breakdown of social order. In this chapter, we argue that neoliberalism created the economic deprivation and the moral framework for the "war on drugs" which informed the work of legal professionals in mediating and effectively justifying the violence in the "war on drugs". Duterte's discourse that drug addicts and peddlers are sub-human and beyond the pale of the law is central to the justification of violence. But we should not lose sight of similar moral discourses against the poor that circulate throughout society of which Duterte's discourse is but an extreme version. Based on interviews with legal professionals working in the criminal courts of the City of Manila about the impact of a new judicial rule on plea bargaining in drug cases. It argues that legal professionals support plea bargaining partly due to a firmly, though apparently unconscious, class bias held against defendants, which is expressed as moral judgements against the poor.

In the following sections, we point out the absence of serious discussion on the "war on drugs" as class conflict and how the chapter advances such a discussion. We then describe the interview methodology used in this study before presenting the findings in subsequent sections. We then elucidate how legal professionals' condescending attitudes towards poor litigants in drugs-related cases are illustrated through quotations from interviews with respondents. We conclude by reflecting on what our findings imply about the "war on drugs" as class conflict and the role of legal professionals in that conflict.

2 The "War on Drugs" as a Neoliberal War Against the Poor

While the Philippines' "war on drugs" has obvious class dimensions, most studies of Duterte's signature policy have avoided directly elucidating it as class conflict. Most scholars have focused on political communicative factors, such as Duterte's populist style (e.g. Curato 2016, 2017; Kenny and Holmes 2020) to explain the rise of the "war on drugs" as a form of "penal populism". Attempts towards a more materialist or political economic explanation of the Philippine "war on drugs" are rare. Highlighting the bluntness of the chief instrument of the "war on drugs", Sheila Coronel's focuses on police corruption and the payoffs for police who commit killings (Coronel 2017) hints at institutional-historical and economic dimensions to drug-related EJKs. Lara and dela Rosa (2020) propose an "economic sociology" approach to the Philippines' "war on drugs" that looks at payoffs for communities in terms of the differing economic interests and effects on everyday political struggles of different sections of drug-affected communities.

In contrast, this chapter highlights the role of neoliberalism in authorizing the violence against the poor. Wendy Brown's understanding of neoliberalism as a project of "markets-and-morals" (Brown 2019, 15) can help us to understand Duterte's terror and the weaponization of morality against the poor. Neoliberal reason has simultaneously promoted the submission of politics to economic goals (and consequently favoured authoritarian regimes) (Brown 2019, 28) and the replacement of social justice mechanisms with the responsibilization of individuals for their own social improvement (Brown 2019, 37–39). Furthermore, such responsibilization has been based on traditional reactionary values. This leads to the weaponization of morality against the poor as the breakdown of social order is blamed on the poor's defective morality or failure to make the right choices to improve themselves. In the case of the Philippines, the neoliberal weaponization of morality against the poor is expressed in the embrace of the unrestricted use of state-led violence against drug peddlers and addicts as a method of imposing order in a highly unequal social context.

Since the mid-1980s and despite the different administrations, neoliberal policies have controlled the Philippines' economic programmes (Tadem 2018). While these policies have achieved significant economic growth, they have notably worsened the country's economic inequality and left a third of the population in poverty (Batalla 2018). However, in the last two decades a new middle-class was formed in large urban centres under these policies (Rivera 2018). Neoliberal policies did not only transform the Philippine economy, but they also introduced a narrative that blamed local cronyism for its failures (Bello 2009). Under this narrative, the poorest sectors, heavily dependent on patronage networks dominated by local elites with access to state resources, became seen as responsible for the country's underdevelopment. Neoliberal "moral politics", i.e. politics underpinned by moral judgements about the poor and the middle-class have ascended in the decline or absence of class-conscious interest politics in the country (Kusaka 2017). Reproducing a neoliberal morality, the middle-income group perceives the poor as "undisciplined" or lacking in the moral qualities requisite to good citizenship, hence, the need to discipline them and shape them into law-abiding citizens. This is visible in the use of the pejorative term *masa*, that denotes flawed moral values, to refer to the poorest sectors of the population (Garrido 2019). This confrontation has been intensified by the unequal development of urban centres, in which middle-class enclaves coexist alongside urban slums. It is in this context that we read the "war on drugs" as a neoliberally driven war against the poor.

By highlighting legal professionals' moralizing discourse, this chapter illuminates how moral politics, which has been elucidated in the political sphere, and also operates in the criminal justice system. Often touted as possibly offering human rights-respecting alternatives to the "war on drugs", legal professionals within the criminal justice system work within material and ideological constraints imposed by neoliberalism. This chapter illustrates the limits of criminal justice-based solutions through the example of plea bargaining in drug cases.

3 Methodology

This chapter is based on 50 interviews conducted with public prosecutors (27), judges (9), clerks of courts (2), and public attorneys (12) working in Regional Trial Courts (RTCs) and Metropolitan Trial Courts (MeTCs) in the City of Manila between May and November of 2018 (Table 1). While RTCs handle criminal cases with punishment over six years of

Table 1 Interviews

Interview #	Role	Gender	Date
1	Public Prosecutor	Female	21–05–18
2	Public Prosecutor	Female	21–05–18
3	Public Prosecutor	Male	21–05–18
4	Public Prosecutor	Male	21–05–18
5	Public Prosecutor	Female	21–05–18
6	Public Prosecutor	Female	21–05–18
7	Public Prosecutor	Male	21–05–18
8	Public Prosecutor	Male	21–05–18
9	Public Prosecutor	Female	22–05–18
10	Public Prosecutor	Male	22–05–18
11	Public Prosecutor	Male	22–05–18
12	Public Prosecutor	Female	22–05–18
13	Public Prosecutor	Female	22–05–18
14	Public Prosecutor	Female	22–05–18
15	Public Prosecutor	Female	22–05–18
16	Public Prosecutor	Female	22–05–18
17	Public Prosecutor	Male	22–05–18
18	Public Prosecutor	Male	23–05–18
19	Public Prosecutor	Female	23–05–18
20	Public Prosecutor	Female	23–05–18
21	Public Prosecutor	Female	23–05–18
22	Public Prosecutor	Male	23–05–18
23	Public Prosecutor	Male	23–05–18
24	Public Prosecutor	Female	23–05–18
25	Public Prosecutor	Male	23–05–18
26	Public Prosecutor	Female	23–05–18
27	Public Prosecutor	Female	23–05–18
28	Assistant Clerk of Court	Female	05–06–18
29	Branch Clerk of Court	Female	05–06–18
30	Judge	Male	05–06–18
31	Judge	Male	05–06–18
32	Judge	Female	05–06–18
33	Judge	Male	05–06–18
34	Judge	Male	06–06–18
35	Judge	Female	06–06–18
36	Judge	Female	06–06–18
37	Judge	Female	06–06–18
38	Public Attorney	Male	06–06–18
39	Public Attorney	Male	06–06–18
40	Judge	Male	06–06–18
41	Public Attorney	Male	22–11–18
42	Public Attorney	Female	22–11–18
43	Public Attorney	Female	22–11–18
44	Public Attorney	Male	22–11–18
45	Public Attorney	Male	22–11–18
46	Public Attorney	Male	22–11–18
47	Public Attorney	Female	22–11–18
48	Public Attorney	Male	22–11–18
49	Public Attorney	Male	22–11–18
50	Public Attorney	Male	22–11–18

imprisonment, MeTCs handle minor crimes. Half of the interviewees were female. Most of the interviews took place in the library of the building in which the courts are located, Manila City Hall, and the rest in the interviewee's office. The interviews were audio-recorded and lasted between 15 min to 1 h.

The interviews were semi-structured. They focused on the different judicial reforms recently implemented to reduce the courts' backlog, problems faced during the criminal procedure, and their working relationship with other agencies of the criminal justice system. There was a special focus on the handling of drug-related cases prosecuted during the conduct of the government's "war on drugs". We were particularly interested in understanding how legal professionals approached their work considering the problematic behaviour of the Filipino police, the notorious EJKs, and the overrepresentation of the lower classes among both victims and defendants.

4 Legal Professionals' Working Practices

Because of the "war on drugs" campaign, drug-related offences have become by far the most common cases in criminal courts (DOJ, n.d.). Most of these cases involve small-time pushers and users. Indeed, the Vice President of the Philippines underscored that, as a result, the Philippine Drug Enforcement Agency was only able to seize one per cent (1%) of the total supply of illegal drugs in the country despite undertaking a "war on drugs" for many years (Cepeda and Cepeda 2020). A former police chief admitted that the anti-drugs strategy mostly targeted low-level operatives, stating "[f]or almost three years, we were arresting the street pusher or the courier. After we have arrested the drug courier, we stopped" (Allard and Lema 2020). Furthermore, the Philippine police force has openly admitted and they targeted small-time drug pushers, supposedly because their budget constraints made going after big-time syndicate bosses less workable (Recuenco 2020). In 2018, 28% of all cases brought by the prosecution to court were drug offences (DOJ, n.d.).

Drug cases were originally handled by special RTCs in Manila; however, the massive influx of cases due to the "war on drugs", prompted the Supreme Courts to distribute drug cases among regular courts. This resulted in every RTC being flooded with drug cases. Drug-related cases have impacted even MeTCs, which have no jurisdiction on these matters (Section 90 Republic Act 9165). As public attorneys explained to us, at the peak of Duterte's campaign, cases related to violations of local ordinances (e.g. drinking alcohol and urinating in public, or illegal gambling in the street) were used by police to build drug cases. Police used violations of local ordinances to justify strip searches that result in drug charges. A public attorney described this: "They cannot arrest a drug offender on the act of selling or on the act of using it, so they have to find a way to arrest these drug offenders, and their way is to create a story like they were urinating, or they were not wearing a helmet [while riding a motorbike] ..." (Interview #42). To deal with this police strategy, public attorneys from MeTCs prioritize defending clients against these minor cases, despite their relatively lenient potential punishment, because if they win, the legal grounds for seizure of evidence on which the drug case is based falls. These cases in turn add to the MeTCs' workload. As one public attorney put it,

> We know that violations of ordinances pending before the Metropolitan Trial Courts are initial violations in order to charge that person with ... violation of RA 9165 [Comprehensive Dangerous Drugs Act]. So, we have an unwritten procedure wherein we need to defend the accused no matter what the cost until we have heard any result as to the charge filed against him in the Regional Trial Court. (Interview #50)

Blinkie (2019) has persuasively argued that these ordinances disproportionately impact the poor. She argues that though these laws were in place before Duterte came to power, it was under his presidency that they were intensely enforced (ibid, 14). Thus, the targeting of the poor is a common pattern visible among cases directly or indirectly related to illegal drugs. It is in this context, that we explore the moral discourse that justify legal professionals' role in legitimizing state violence against the poor.

The class bias of the criminal justice system is not only reflected in the selectivity of the cases that are prosecuted but also in its institutional organization and budget allocation. Public prosecutors as well as public attorneys are overwhelmed with their workload, but the latter more so than the former. The pressure of relieving their workload as fast as possible shapes their legal strategies. As a respondent explained: "...with respect to us as public prosecutors, and the public attorneys, a rule here is the less paperwork the better because of the bulk of the work. We don't have the time to really prepare lengthy pleadings ... so if allowed, we would make our manifestations shorter already..." (Interview #16). Facing the shortage of personnel young lawyers joining the Public Attorney's Office are asked to immediately represent defendants in courts, despite their lack of experience. Although, this was viewed as a career opportunity to a public attorney interviewed (Interview #49), it also means that defendants are placed in a disadvantageous position in the criminal process.

Public prosecutors are required to conduct an inquiry, called preliminary investigation, in criminal cases where the penalty is more than four years, two months, and one day (Rule 112, Revised Rules of Criminal Procedure). These are not thorough investigations. They are limited to inspect police reports and, in some cases, to call the victim or witnesses to expand their testimony before them. In most cases, the evidence is based on the victim's and some direct witness testimony, with the latter usually from police officers. As a public attorney explains, "usually there are no other witnesses who, there are no other persons [who had] witnessed the arrest that was made by the police officers" (Interview #44). Therefore, case investigation is almost exclusively done by police and prosecutors tend to take that investigation at face value. This is very problematic because the prosecutors interviewed were well aware of the serious shortcomings of police work. This also results in favouring simple cases based on the testimony of the victim and some direct witnesses (usually the intervening police officers) as the main evidence, that are accordingly disposed of quickly.

Drug-related cases are supposed to be the exception to this rule because the law on illegal drugs requires strict procedures to be carried out when arresting the suspect and handling the evidence seized at the moment of arrest (Section 21 Republic Act 9165). Hence, public prosecutors are supposed to scrutinize the legal strength of the case presented by police. However, under the current context of the "war on drugs", public prosecutors' exercise of control over the legal strength of the police's case is constrained by the fear of appearing to favour drug suspects. As a public attorney explained, "judges and … prosecutors are afraid of, like, dismissing a case outright, or acquitting the accused after just a little time … because they are being watched by the Government" (Interview #43). This fear is not merely of being seen as inefficient or inept, but of being accused of being "a protector of drugs" (Interview #17) and, consequently "…placed in the list of narco court prosecutors or narco judges…" (Interview #19). This fear is not unfounded as Duterte has repeatedly publicly accused judges to be paid by drug lords (Corrales 2016). Years of public accusations between politicians and senior governmental officials built a profound distrust over state actors' behaviour (Ciocchini 2019). This mistrust provides fertile ground for Duterte to threaten legal professionals, particularly judges and prosecutors, whose actions seem to oppose his "war on drugs".

Public attorneys also face a serious challenge under the current context of the "war on drugs". According to a public prosecutor: "… you can hardly find any witness who will testify for the accused unless it's a family member or some really concerned citizen that really would like the truth to be known, that the accused has done nothing wrong..." (Interview #15). Consequently, "the defence basically relies on the testimonial evidence of the accused (...) usually the defence is just [to] deny [the accusation]" (Interview #18). Alternatively, public attorneys may choose to target the legality of the police procedures. The law prescribes strict procedures in drug-related cases to handle the evidence and the arrested suspects to prevent planted evidence and other potential malpractices by law enforcement officers (Republic Act 9165, Sections 21, 27 and 29). Thus, public attorneys' strategies are centred around potential breaches of those requirements to the chain of custody by police officers. A prosecutor admitted with certain frustration:

> the defense is merely tasked to see the break of the event whilst they establish that there was a break in that procedure, that's already a fine point [for] the acquittal, so that is very easy. (Interview #18)

The seriously flawed work of the police makes this strategy very significant. Illegal police practices are also key in winning cases that are constructed around the violation of a minor offence, such as local ordinances, and that police used to justify body searches and seizures for potential drug-related cases. Thus, as a public attorney explained, they coordinate their work with other public attorneys working in lower courts: "we usually monitor the case before the MeTC ... if, for example, the lower court found that he is not guilty of the crime charge[d], or there is no sufficient basis for him to be held [for] trial in that case, we usually use that as a defence in our drug[s] cases" (Interview #44). They work to find the breaches of the legal procedures in the police intervention:

> The police officers do not know the very provisions of that ordinance itself (...) so, [the arrest] is really defective. Second, most of these police officers [tell] the same kind of story from one case [to another], I see almost copy/paste. So, if I am the judge and I handle this type of cases almost every day of my life I can immediately spot or see the problem and that kind of complaint or statement made by the police officers ... because what they say in court is different from what they stated in the affidavit. (Interview #49)

In conclusion, public attorneys' strategies are usually based on identifying legal flaws in police procedures. The fact that they are successful with these strategies show the lack of credibility of police before the courts. However, it also shows that despite that lack of credibility, the police's version of the events is preferred over the defendant's. This is an indication that defendants are assumed to be morally flawed, and therefore deserving punishment, regardless of the facts of the case, as will be discussed in further detail in the next section.

5 Legal Professionals' Moral Discourse

Morality is clearly seen by legal professionals as a marker of class. Legal professionals distinguish themselves from poor litigants through their differing morals, particularly relating to their sense of law and justice. In their accounts, poor complainants and defendants value justice less and are largely driven by their material needs. For example, a respondent said, poor litigants prioritize their material needs over the need for legal justice:

> [I]n poor Filipino families, their argument of justice would be: what will happen to my family now that my husband was murdered, my husband was killed and he was the one who earned money for this family and so on and so forth (...) So their idea of justice would be a financial compensation for the loss. So, it is, I would say that it is still justice (...) It's still justice but it's just not the kind of justice where someone goes to jail, or someone goes free... (Interview #3)

Similarly, another prosecutor explained her difficulties dealing with poor complainants due to their supposed economic mentality and prejudice against legal professionals. She claimed that victims and defendants mistrust prosecutors because they are not paying for their services and could be bribed by others. She affirmed that victims resent not being able to afford a private lawyer and being forced to resort to the services of the public attorney. In this way, legal professionals interpret the mentality of defendants and complaints from the lower classes as economically driven. This attitude was also expressed by some public attorneys interviewed.

> [T]he litigants sometimes tend to complain, why is the fiscal focusing on this case and not in my case .... [I am] not being treated equal .... Most of our clients in court are indigents and that their mentality is that when you tend to lose the case they will think that you did not really focus, you did not give more attention to the their case [and] they will say that you are being paid, somebody bribed you for that, or that you are focusing on other cases.... (Interview #2)

However, such mistrust is also fuelled by some prosecutors' disdain for poor defendants. For example, a prosecutor refers to victims who live in slums as "those people" and describes the efforts to locate them, as a "luxury of time" that he cannot afford:

> [I]t's really hard to find those people and I don't have the luxury of time to locate them one by one (…) The problem arises when the complainants were—you know—just ordinary persons, who live in the slum areas, where the process servers or even the postman would dare not go and I will be like: how am I supposed to get in touch with these people? (Interview #15)

We also found a paternalistic and condescending attitude in some legal professionals. For example, a public prosecutor, when explaining the conditions of cases handled by MeTCs, explicitly referred to the defendants' socio-economic background to explain their irrational and emotionally driven behaviour.

> With the Metropolitan Trial Courts, there [are] lots of emotions involved, they will be shouting at each other, you have to pacify them … and you have to really explain to them because it boils down [to the fact] that they are part of more marginalized part of society so you have to really be patient with them and explain to them the situation. The problem with them is that once they hear something which might not be true, they take it as the whole truth, and they would even argue with us…. (Interview #16)

Legal professionals describe drug-related cases in such a way that defendants, victims, witnesses, and others involved in drug-related case are said to be thoroughly corrupted by criminality by reason of their poverty. As a public prosecutor argues: "…[T]he City of Manila is densely populated. So, if you have more population, and the population mainly consists of those persons below the poverty line … [then] misdemeanours, crimes, are usually committed by [them]…" (Interview #18). Legal professionals often emphasize the social environment of the poor as determining their defective morality. Thus, being distanced from this kind of social environment—as the legal professionals themselves are—may improve the poor's morality. Another public prosecutor's response illustrate this approach:

> [A]side from drugs, it's the problem with the community. … it would be better if we take the child away from that neighborhood because if you return the child to his parents, within the same neighborhood, with the same vices, the same temptations, you cannot rehabilitate the child. (Interview #21)

As is evident, legal professionals exhibit a condescending attitude towards defendants and complainants that is based on the assumption that poor litigants are “economically minded” and that poverty, drug abuse and criminality are linked in a deterministic way. As we will explore in the next section, the combination of the legal professionals’ attitude together with the heavy workload and intense political pressures, lead them to see plea bargaining as a way to deal with these problems.

6 Plea Bargaining and Its Impact

6.1 An (Il)legal Solution

The state’s narrative of the “war on drugs” puts pressure on legal professionals to respond to the drug problem more efficiently for swift justice. The police’s drive to arrest an unprecedented number of drug suspects translates to the massive influx of drug cases into the justice system. Prosecutors, public attorneys, and judges manage this deluge of drug cases by embracing the device of plea bargaining, newly introduced by the Supreme Court to drug cases. Given the weakness in the police’s construction of drug cases, conviction is often in serious tension with the duty and commitment of prosecutors, public attorneys, and judges as legal professionals to decide cases on the basis of law and evidence. At the same time, acquittals appear anathema both to the government’s aggressive anti-drugs campaign and legal professionals’ own moral judgement of drug users. Plea bargaining allows legal professionals to avoid these unwanted outcomes and satisfies their belief in rehabilitation. Thus, this section develops the preceding section on prosecutors’, public attorneys’, and judges’ moral discourse against poor defendants by showing how this moral discourse affects the justice system’s response to drug cases.

6.2 Reintroducing Plea Bargaining

The massive inflow of cases as a consequence of the “war on drugs” overwhelmed judicial courts’ workload. Disposing of those cases was further complicated by the banning of plea bargaining for drug-related cases under the provisions of Section 23 of the Republic Act No. 9165, a prohibition intended to prevent potential collusion between prosecutors and drug offenders. Thus, the combination of a cascade of new cases brought by police, prosecutors, and judges unwilling to dismiss cases despite their apparent weakness to avoid being called out by the government as supporters of the drug trade, the trial is left as the only alternative. The institutional reaction to this crisis was produced by an uncoordinated, but implicitly conscious, effort by legal professionals to legalize plea bargaining for these cases.

In June 2016, six months after Duterte unleashed his "war on drugs", the Public Attorney's Office (PAO), filed a motion to enter into a plea bargaining agreement in a drug-related criminal case (Estipona V. Judge Lobrigo, G.R. No. 226679). Although the prosecution and the judge opposed the motion, they acknowledged there was merit in the request. The PAO submitted a petition before the Supreme Court of the Philippines challenging the constitutionality of the ban on plea bargaining. It was argued that the denial of plea bargaining was arbitrary and amounted to infringing the right to equal protection of the laws and to due process. The Supreme Court ruled in favour of the petition and declared unconstitutional the prohibition on plea bargaining. Following that decision, the Supreme Court adopted a framework that prescribes for each offence the acceptable lesser offence that can be agreed.

6.3 Legal Professionals' Embrace of Plea Bargaining

In the context of the Philippines, plea bargaining has become an elegant compromise in the eyes of legal professionals. Firstly, it significantly reduces their workload since they can close the case without the hassles an adversary procedure represents for them. Moreover, every actor can claim it as a victory for themselves. For public prosecutors and judges, it guarantees convictions so they can satisfy the government's expectations while avoiding dealing with the weakness of the cases arising from problematic police work. As a public prosecutor stated:

> [Plea bargaining] is [a] welcome move for us, as prosecutors, because it lessens the burden of prosecuting these cases. We do not have to present the police officers anymore; we do not have to present evidence anymore; and we are guaranteed with a conviction. It is a win for us ... because getting a conviction with drug cases is very hard ... because of the technicalities and well we all know the police officers are not as reliable as they should be ... (Interview #16)

Thus, though plea bargaining is presented as a compromise among the parties involved, it is actually imposed on vulnerable defendants. Plea bargaining is justified institutionally because it aligns with the punitivism demanded by the government and can be presented by neoliberal technocrats as an effective and efficient way of disposing of cases. Lastly, legal professionals can justify their actions by associating plea bargaining with rehabilitation and present the sentence as an intervention on behalf of the defendant.

According to public attorneys, defendants prefer to enter into negotiations, even if this results in a sentence and criminal record, because they are already "marginalized" so they only care about being released as soon as possible: "the majority of the detainees come from the marginalized sectors—based on my experience—… the record of conviction does not matter to them, they just wanted to start a new life immediately. To live free from all these legal delays…" (Interview #49). Therefore, for public attorneys, a conviction based on plea bargaining "would be considered as a favourable disposition … because we were able to secure a lesser penalty" (Interview #44). The argument among PAO lawyers is that plea bargaining benefits "both the defence and the prosecution …, in a way we are also correcting the drug behaviour of the person, so the conviction says a lot that you know you do not get to do it again" (Interview #41). So, while the penalty "is not proportionate" by pleading guilty they can even aspire to be released under probation: "every plea of guilty to a lesser offence I always file an application for probation". (Interview #41)

There are two significant aspects of this narrative. First, the weaknesses of the cases are downplayed. This is seriously problematic for defendants, given that, as legal professionals all agreed, the irregularities and inadequacies of police work would normally result in their acquittal. Further, given that irregularities of police conduct are rampant, downplaying them results in systematically failing to challenge massive detentions and police abuse as a structural problem. As a respondent explained: "So far most of [the] drugs cases are acquittals so apparently the courts do not believe the stories of the police or also that the police are not able to present their evidence properly … well there is also the[il]legality [of] the arrest" (Interview #47). There are serious flaws in the way police proceed: "the problem is really with the, sadly with the, with the compliance and the performance of the police officers in their functions because … it affects the prosecution … if they were not really compliant with the requirements of the Comprehensive Drugs Act, then during the trial, the Public Attorney's Office will grill them on cross examination…". (Interview #22)

According to legal professionals, it is not merely negligence which is the reason behind weak police work, but serious problems of police officers' integrity: "most of my drug cases are for acquittal … sometimes [the cases] are just fabricated, they are just concocted by the police officers that's why..." (Interview #36). Similarly, another legal professional stated that "...cases that came in starting 2016 up to today, 2018, I would even say more than 90% of the cases involve, what we call in essence and just general essence, planted evidence by the police" (Interview #31). With plea bargaining, legal professionals facilitate abandonment up the challenge to these irregularities in police conduct, legitimizing massive detentions and guaranteeing convictions.

Second, legal professionals unproblematically assume that all defendants are drug users, regardless of the evidence, and even when legal professionals believe the cases were fabricated by police. Thus, they require all defendants who undertake plea bargaining to undergo rehabilitation.

> I think because they know for themselves that they're actually using, it just so happens that at the time that they were arrested they were not maybe they were not actually doing this offence. But within themselves they know that they were maybe they are using it.... (Interview #20)

The condescending attitude of legal professionals towards poor litigants in drug-related cases jives well with the rehabilitation ideal. Defendants need to change their life and the sentence is an opportunity for them to do that. It is through this moral discourse that plea bargaining is justified:

> ...there is still justice [in cases disposed by plea bargaining] because they (defendants) are in prison so before I will release them, I talk to them that that you must reform, do not use drugs anymore. (Interview #34)

Thus, plea bargaining is thought to preserve "justice" both for society which demands some punishment and the defendant who is afforded the chance to rehabilitate. A lesser sentence is in a sense a more rights-respecting solution than EJKs, but it reproduces the perception of the poor as factually if not legally guilty of involvement in drugs and hence morally defective.

6.4 Continuing Detentions

The narrative deployed by legal professionals presenting plea bargaining as a legal solution favours their interest to reduce their workload while complying with the government's expectations and avoiding tensions with the police. However, the institutional material conditions hardly mean plea bargaining serves defendants' interests as well. The government has not shown real intention in promoting rehabilitation policies, as revealed by lack of dedicated centres and programmes. "...A rehabilitation centre (...) can house so many thousands of people. But they do not have the budget to maintain this (...) so those who are convicted are now supposed to undergo rehabilitation [but] have not been brought to the rehabilitation centre" (Interview #30).

Rehabilitation facilities often require fees to be paid to cover various expenses: "the rehab centre ... for a while they were requiring fees for 600 pesos for the drug test, for the uniforms..." (Interview #36). This lack of resources led to another layer of class discrimination within the already biased justice system. Rehabilitation becomes a privilege for those who can afford it: "...we're trying to come up ... with whether the accused is capable of paying the rehabilitation with the private rehabilitation centre. Maybe if they allow that maybe that will also decongest the jails" (Interview #26).

The lack of places in rehabilitation facilities mean defendants remain in jails. To deal with this problem, some legal professionals interpret the time defendants spent in prison as time spent on rehabilitation, and accordingly release the defendants. However, others leave detainees waiting in jails until rehabilitation facilities have available beds, showing the limits of their stated interest in the defendants' well-being.

> [For] those who already spent six months inside the jail without them transferring to the rehabilitation center, we file motion for the discharge of the accused .... That incarceration inside the jail can be deemed as a rehabilitation considering that there is no more access to drugs during that period. (Interview #38)

As we have shown, the whole narrative that justifies plea bargaining around the idea of offering the defendant a second opportunity assumes defendants are drug addicts that require rehabilitation. Although not openly discussed, that narrative assumes that all defendants will opt for plea bargaining instead of facing the trial. However, the context in which defendants decide is heavily restrictive, leaving very little room for real volition.

Drug-related offences are not bailable, and even if they were, most defendants could not afford to pay bail, so they are in detention during the criminal process. The conditions of such detention are extremely unappealing, i.e. the jails are critically overcrowded. Not surprisingly, defendants: "... prefer to admit to a lesser offence rather than be incarcerated" (Interview #36). As a public attorney explained, even in those cases that there are clear chances of acquittal, the problem is the time it might take to obtain it:

> I would really try to convince my client and tell them that, you see we are after justice here. If you really say you are innocent then I say we have to go fight for it. But then again, I am not the one who is in prison, every day I go home to my family, I eat good food, I sleep comfortably but they do not have that kind of privilege because they are in jail. (Interview #15)

And this situation is even worse if you are poor, because inside jails and prison, economic inequality is perversely reproduced: "… in the Philippines a day in detention is a day in oblivion …. Especially when those in detention facilities are poor, if you don't have any money you cannot buy your own food…" (Interview #18). If despite all these, defendants still resist to plead guilty, some legal professionals resort to threatening defendants to reduce their workload:

> I've heard of judges here in Manila … [who have] a very high disposition or disposal rate, but it seems from my impression that there is somehow—I hate to use the word 'force'—but they have, in so many words, let the accused know that you better take this option of plea bargaining […] whether you really did it or not and they will reduce it. (Interview #31)

To sum up, the use of plea bargaining in drug-related cases in the "war on drugs" exposes legal professionals' bias against poor defendants. The benevolent punitivism of legal professionals based on a deeply-rooted class bias has legitimized the brutal violence deployed by the state.

7 Conclusion

The poor are under a real threat of being victimized by EJKs in the Philippines' "war on drugs" as well as being detained by police without sufficient evidence. Thus, criminal courts and legal professionals are called upon by those seeking alternatives to the "war on drugs" to provide a human rights-respecting solution to this urgent problem. In this chapter, we examine one solution, namely, plea bargaining in drug-related cases which the Philippine Supreme Court introduced to cope with the deluge of drug-related cases before the criminal courts. The chapter provided a critical perspective on plea bargaining as continuing a neoliberal logic. This logic denies the need for social justice mechanisms in favour of individual responsibility and leads to the weaponization of morality against the poor (Brown 2019).

The chapter revealed that plea bargaining was underpinned by a moralistic orientation towards the poor and the privileging of moral solutions to the violence of the "war on drugs". The moral discourse engaged in by legal professionals to justify plea bargaining is based on a condescending view of poor litigants. Class bias manifests not only as some type of moral punitivism that demands drug users to be punished regardless of the evidence of the case, but also as a paternalistic punitivism that justifies such punishment as an opportunity for moral rehabilitation. We found that plea bargaining served legal professionals' multiple interests. In plea bargaining, legal professionals found a solution that balanced their individual and institutional needs to lighten their heavy workload, the governmental and societal pressure to punish those suspected of drug offences, and their personal belief in the fairness of rehabilitative measures. Furthermore, plea bargaining enabled lighter punishments and drug dependency treatments that helped legal actors to frame their behaviour as benevolent and based on a rehabilitative approach.

Through moral discourse, legal professionals participate in obscuring the "war on drugs" as a class conflict. They believe poverty causes criminality and drug addiction or participation in the illegal drug trade, but fail to engage in a deeper questioning of the material conditions that produce poverty. Poverty is taken as a given social environment—from which legal professionals are distanced by reason of their education and training—and through plea bargaining, the poor is offered, nay, forced into, moral betterment and nothing more. Thus, the analysis showed the limits of a judicial solution to human rights abuses in the "war on drugs" and revealed the continuity of the neoliberal logic and strategy of the moral politics of the "war on drugs" in and outside the criminal courts.

References

Allard, Tom and Karen Lema. 2020. Exclusive: 'Shock and awe' has failed in Philippines drug war, enforcement chief says." *Reuters*, February 7, 2020. https://www.reuters.com/article/us-philippines-drugs-performance-exclusi-idUSKBN2010IL.

Amnesty International. 2017. Philippines: Duterte's 'war on drugs' is a war on the poor. *Amnesty International*, February 4, 2017. https://www.amnesty.org/en/latest/news/2017/02/war-on-drugs-war-on-poor/.

Associated Press. 2017. Philippines police plant evidence to justify killings in drug war, says report. *The Guardian*, March 2, 2017. https://www.theguardian.com/world/2017/mar/02/philippines-police-plant-evidence-to-justify-killings-in-drug-war-says-report.

Batalla, Eric Vincent. 2018. Bypassing industrial development. In *Routledge handbook of the contemporary Philippines*, ed. Mark Thompson and Eric Vincent Batalla, 211–224. Abingdon: Routledge.

Bello, Walden. 2009. Neoliberalism as hegemonic ideology in the philippines: Rise, apogee, and crisis. *Philippine Sociological Review* 57: 9–19.

Blimkie, Alicia. 2019. *Crime and poverty: Criminalization and empowerment of the poor in the Philippines* (IHRIP Working Paper Series 7, p. 1). Singapore: IHRP.

Brown, Wendy. 2019. *In the ruins of neoliberalism: The rise of antidemocratic politics in the west*. New York: Columbia University Press.

Cepeda, Mara and Karen Cepeda. 2020. '1 over 100': Robredo Calls Duterte's drug war a 'failure'. *Rappler*. https://www.rappler.com/nation/robredo-duterte-drug-war-failure-icad-report.

Ciocchini, Pablo. 2019. The politics of judicial actors in the philippines's 'war on drugs.' In *Criminal legalities in the global south*, ed. Pablo Ciocchini and George Radics, 145–165. Abingdon: Routledge.

Coronel, Sheila. 2017. Murder as enterprise: Police profiteering in duterte's war on drugs. In *A Duterte reader: Critical essays on Rodrigo Duterte's early presidency*, ed. Nicole Curato, 167–198. Ithaca, NY: Cornell University Press.

Corrales, Nestor. 2016. *Duterte's new drug list: 40 judges, '1 page' for Chinese suspects*. Inquirer.Net, September 21. https://newsinfo.inquirer.net/817675/dutertes-new-drug-list-40-judges-1-page-for-chinese-suspects.

Curato, Nicole. 2016. Flirting with authoritarian fantasies? Rodrigo Duterte and the new terms of Philippine populism. *Journal of Contemporary Asia* 47 (1): 142–153.

Curato, Nicole. 2017. Politics of anxiety, politics of hope: Penal populism and Duterte's rise to power. *Journal of Current Southeast Asian Affairs* 35 (3): 69–89.

Department Of Justice. n.d. *DOJ open government data*. Department of Justice. https://www.doj.gov.ph/open_data.html.

Felbab-Brown, Vanda. 2017. The human rights consequences of the war on drugs in the Philippines. *Brookings*, August 8. https://www.brookings.edu/testimonies/the-human-rights-consequences-of-the-war-on-drugs-in-the-philippines/.

Garrido, Marco. 2019. *The patchwork city: Class, space, and politics in Metro Manila*. Chicago: University of Chicago Press.

Harvey, David. 2007. *A brief history of neoliberalism*. Oxford: Oxford University Press.

Johnson, David, and Jon Fernquest. 2018. Governing through killing: The war on drugs in the Philippines. *Asian Journal of Law and Society* 5: 359–390.

Kenny, Paul. 2019. Populism and the war on drugs in southeast Asia. *The Brown Journal of World Affairs* 25 (2): 121–136.

Kenny, Paul, and Ronald Holmes. 2020. A new penal populism? Rodrigo Duterte, public opinion, and the war on drugs in the Philippines. *Journal of East Asian Studies* 20 (2): 187–205.

Kusaka, Wataru. 2017. *Moral politics in the Philippines: Inequality, democracy and the urban poor*. Singapore: National University of Singapore Press.

Lamchek, Jayson. 2017. A mandate for mass killings? Public support for Duterte's war on drugs. In *A Duterte reader: Critical essays on Rodrigo Duterte's early presidency*, ed. Nicole Curato, 199–218. Manila and New York: Ateneo de Manila University Press and Cornell University Press.

Francisco, Lara and Philline C. Nikki de la Rosa. 2020. Collusion or collision? The war on drugs in the philippines. *Estudios Socio-Juridicos* 22 (2): 1–51.

OHCHR. 2020. Situation of human rights in the Philippines. *OHCHR*. https://www.ohchr.org/Documents/Countries/PH/Philippines-HRC44-AEV.pdf.

Recuenco, Aaron. 2020. Why the police are busting more big-time drug dealers. *Manila Bulletin*, June 14. https://mb.com.ph/2020/06/14/why-the-police-are-busting-more-big-time-drug-dealers/.

Reuters. 2017. Most Filipinos believe drug war kills poor people only, survey shows. *Reuters*, October 2. https://www.reuters.com/article/us-philippines-drugs-idUSKCN1C71HH.

Rivera, Temario. 2018. The middle class in society and politics. In *Routledge handbook of the contemporary Philippines*, ed. Mark Thompson and Eric Vincent Batalla, 363–375. Abingdon: Routledge.

Social Weather Station. 2018. June 27–30, 2018 social weather survey: Satisfaction with national admin's campaign against illegal drugs at net +65. *Social Weather Station*.

Tadem, Teresa Encarnacion. 2018. Technocracy and class politics in policy-making. In *Routledge handbook of the Contemporary Philippines*, ed. Mark Thompson and Eric Vincent Batalla, 262–272. Abingdon: Routledge.

The Drug Archive. 2018. The drug killings: Who, what, where, when, how? *The Drug Archive*. https://drugarchive.ph/post/26-the-drug-killings-who-what-where-when-how-master.

Thompson, Mark. 2020. Explaining Duterte's rise and rule: 'Penal populist' leadership or a structural crisis of oligarchic democracy in the Philippines" *Philippine Political Science Journal* 41: 5–31.

Part IV

Criminalization of Diversity

12

Circuits of Law: Everyday Criminalisation of Transgender Embodiment in Istanbul

Ezgi Taşcıoğlu

1 Introduction

Criminal law has long played a key role in governing non-normative genders and sexualities. From sex in public spaces to same-sex relationships in private, practices and identities that do not conform to the social order of heteronormative intelligibility have been the subject of considerable penal sanction. In this chapter, I look at the case of trans women[1] of Istanbul, Turkey where, unlike in many global North and South jurisdictions, LGBTI identities have never been formally criminalised by law but have been a frequent target of criminalisation in the daily practices of legal institutions.

My interest here lies in a particular instance of the containment strategies of trans women by law in urban Turkey that can be traced to the early 2000s: the move away from inflicting direct physical violence towards an increasing reliance on the law that effectively and efficiently turns trans

[1] I deploy the term 'trans' as an umbrella term to refer to people "who have undergone hormone treatment or surgery to reconstruct their bodies, and to those who cross gender in ways which are less permanent" (Hines 2007a, para. 1). As such the category denotes a wide range of diversity and difference of gendered embodiment and experience, including transgender, transsexual, cross-dresser, queer gender and other gender non-conforming identities (Whittle 2006, xi). 'Trans woman' addresses any person who was assigned male at birth and identifies as woman.

E. Taşcıoğlu (✉)
Keele University, London, UK
e-mail: e.e.tascioglu@keele.ac.uk

G. B. Radics and P. Ciocchini (eds.), *Criminal Legalities and Minorities in the Global South*, Falgrave Socio-Legal Studies, https://doi.org/10.1007/978-3-031-17918-1_12

women's bodies into unlawful occupiers of the urban space (Taşcıoğlu 2020). While on the surface, these deployments of the law—namely misdemeanour fines and criminal law trials—result in a diminished number of reported cases of torture and violence, I argue that they reflect less of a change of the underlying normative concerns around sex, gender and sexuality than an enhancement and expansion of the punitive capacity of the neoliberalising state under the Justice and Development Party (AKP) government.[2] I will show the ways through which trans women's bodies, marked as unlawful, are expelled to spaces outside the 'circuits of security' (Rose 2000) by the applications of misdemeanour laws and criminal laws. I argue that these employments of the law (dis)place trans women into constant circulation within and between different circuits of the law that work on and through various jurisdictions (Valverde 2014) and that makes it possible to govern in certain ways at the intersections of the formal and the informal.

The chapter takes, as a point of departure, trans gender citizenship scholarship that has successfully demonstrated trans people's unequal access to the rights of citizenship (Couch et al. 2008; Field 2007; Hines 2007b; Monro and Warren 2004; West 2013). Going beyond the static notion of citizenship as a legal status, my aim is to examine trans women's daily encounters and interactions with the law that constitute their citizenship *on the ground*. The next section sets out this theoretical framework at the intersection of transgender citizenship and socio-legal literature on everyday life. After an account on the construction of gendered and sexualised citizenship in the context of Turkey and my methodology, the empirical sections of the chapter look at the governance of trans women by law, by combining analyses of legal texts, life story interviews conducted with trans women in 2012–2013 and publications of LGBTI and sex worker organisations from Turkey.

2 Transgender Citizenship and Law in Everyday Life

The relatively recent emergence of a socio-legal interest in transgender citizenship is closely linked to the interdisciplinary work on citizenship. This main body of citizenship literature has focused on theoretical debates of

[2] Justice and Development Party is the ruling party in Turkey that has maintained its control over Turkish politics in an increasingly authoritarian manner under the leadership of Recep Tayyip Erdoğan since its coming to power in 2002 (Baykan 2018).

citizenship as a formal status (Marshall 1964; Turner 1986) and charted the historical and institutional developments of the concept (Kymlicka 1998; Soysal and Soyland 1994; Young 1998). Explorations of the social situatedness of the citizen person have been another key line of inquiry. These studies showed that citizenship practices cannot be reduced to legal/formal status and that modern rights relationships are simultaneously a question of inequality (Brubaker 1992, 1996; Joseph 1996; Somers 1993).

Feminist and queer studies of citizenship have been particularly crucial in exposing the patriarchal and cis-heteronormative assumptions that underpin dominant paradigms of citizenship and rethinking aspects of citizenship such as rights, public–private distinctions and political community (Bussmaker and Voet 1998; Evans 1993; Lister 1997; Pateman 1988; Plummer 1995; Richardson 2000). At the intersection of transgender and citizenship, a wide array of interactions between the trans citizen and state institutions have been the focus of transgender citizenship scholarship (Monro 2005; Monro and Warren 2004; West 2013) spanning the importance of the amendment of formal documentation for the enjoyment of citizenship rights (Couch et al. 2008) to uneven access of trans people to rights including rights to employment, parenting and marriage (Currah et al. 2006) and the failure of legal texts to offer trans people protection against discrimination and violence (Field 2007). These studies have significantly addressed the call for transgender studies to move away from a preoccupation with identity towards an interrogation of the institutional powers and their effects on trans people's lives (Namaste 2005).

Following this critical line of work on citizenship, this chapter goes beyond the static notion of citizenship as either a legal status or a philosophical concept and focuses on the institutional practices that distribute rights associated with formal citizenship unevenly across the population, which renders some citizens less valuable than others. Once seen this way, citizenship becomes an empirical question to be answered by an analysis of the making and unravelling of citizens' experiences. One step in answering this question is to unpack the unitary notion of the 'state' (Sharma and Gupta 2006) and to see 'citizenship' as a variable field of discourses and practices that constitute the state and citizen interaction. Law can be understood as one of such key constitutive institutional sites of encounters between citizens and the state where citizenship is (re)defined, negotiated and contested (Koğacıoğlu 2003).

The "constitutive nature of law" has been a focal point in "law in everyday life" literature that emerged as a novel way of looking at how law and legal processes construct everyday life (Ewick and Silbey 1998; Sarat 1990).

Informed by a Foucauldian understanding of power (Foucault 1978, 1979, 1991), this take on everyday experiences with the law did not make the study of formal institutions less important but advocated an investigation of law and legal institutions from the perspectives of actors through their everyday experiences with the law. However, as Mariana Valverde (2010) highlights, probably due to the lack of contact between socio-legal scholars and citizenship studies circles, little work has been done on analysing the citizenship/law nexus. This chapter attempts to combine these two lines of studies, that of citizenship and law in everyday life, through an empirical examination of the ways through which the actual workings of the law structure and shape "different varieties or forms of citizenship" (Valverde 2010, 229). My analysis will pay specific attention to the multi-scalar modes of governance and law's capacity to work at different legal orders (Valverde 2009) in devaluing certain citizens and (dis)placing them to the margins.

3 Modern Law and the Making of the Familial Citizen in Turkey

Beginning with the decline of the Ottoman Empire and followed by the founding of the Turkish Republic in 1923, modernisation has constituted an integral part of Turkey's political, economic and social history. Unlike many modernisation projects in the global South, the modernisation of Turkey—as a country which has never been colonised—did not start in a colonial or postcolonial setting. Rather it was the ruling elite of the Ottoman state and then of the early Turkish Republic regime that implemented a modernisation programme upon the people of the country.

Law occupied a specific role in the realisation of the desired transformation. The abolition of the Sultanate and the constitution of the Republic in 1923, the abrogation of the Caliphate[3] in 1924 and the outlawing of the religious orders in 1925 were closely followed by the replacement of Muslim law by Swiss, French and Italian codes in 1926. The declaration of the Republic as secular in the constitution of 1937 turned Turkey into the first Islamic country to transition to a secular state. These changes in the socio-legal terrain decisively transformed customary notions of justice and brought them in line with the requirements of a modern legal system. The formal law became the testimony of the newly established state-citizen relationship,

[3] The spiritual leadership of the Muslim world that had resided with the Ottoman Empire since 1571.

with its promise of equality to all the citizenry regardless of their gender, class and religious identity and identifications.

The wide-ranging process of transformation informed the gender hegemony in modern Turkey. The figure of the Turkish woman as emancipated and equal to the male citizenry was cast as a key marker of the level of civilisation attained by the Republic (Arat 1997; Gole 1997, 86). The granting of women's suffrage rights in 1934, the introduction of a secular dress code and the encouragement of women's increased access to the public sphere, including institutions of education and the labour force, were listed among important accomplishments of the new regime with regard to greater gender equality (Arat 1997). Yet, the limits of the state-led emancipation of women have been evident in the gendered nature of Republican citizenship and the unequal gender relations between women and men (Berktay 2001; Kandiyoti 1987; Sirman 1989). Nükhet Sirman (2007), in her influential analysis of familial citizenship in Turkey, explicates the constitutive feature of the family in the making of the public and private domain, in the cultural pronouncements of entitlements as well as the wording of policy. The inclusion of women into public space is closely tied to women's social recognition as wives and mothers in the domain of family and as desexualised, virtuous and chaste loyal servants of the nation (Berktay 2001; Kandiyoti 1988). The hegemonic and dominant roles of gender dichotomy between men and women inscribe themselves into women's interactions with law and state institutions, undermining women's individual rights at the expense of the family-related ideals and reinforcing the family as an institution (Koğacıoğlu 2005; Özar and Yakut-Cakar 2013). The rise of the Islamist AKP (Justice and Development Party) in 2002 consolidated this central role of family in shaping the texture of everyday experiences and institutional life in Turkey, with its religious-conservative gender politics which perceives women and men as *essentially* different, as captured by several public announcements made by the party's leader Recep Tayyip Erdogan and other high-profile politicians (Cindoglu and Unal 2017).

Within this context, the boundaries of sex/gender are highly surveilled and policed, and any transgression of the gender dichotomy is disciplined, punished or banished. One of the most emblematic representations of the institution of sex/gender dichotomy in institutional life in Turkey has been the pink and blue ID cards issued to women and men, respectively. In order to be legally recognised as their gender, trans people have to go through a lengthy medico-legal process to prove that they fit into the defined boundaries of certain bodily configurations and gendered performances (Zengin 2014). Everyday violence at the hands of state institutions, law enforcement officers and ordinary citizens deeply structure gender non-conforming lives, especially of trans women (Kaos 2007; Lambdaistanbul LGBTI Association 2010; Ördek 2014, 2016; Taşcıoğlu 2015, 2020). My aim in this chapter is to focus on the predicament of trans embodiment in Istanbul, and on the shift away from physical violence towards an increasing reliance on 'law' in efforts to police, remove and banish trans women's bodies from public spaces. I argue that trans women's social existence is expelled out of the familial by law and executive actions, and once expelled, they become parts of a marginalized population, targets of governmentality.

In tracing the legal texts and their applications that distribute less value to trans embodiment and push them to the margins of social and institutional life in Istanbul, this chapter further situates its analysis within AKP's neoliberal policies since it came into power. Under the rule of Recep Tayyip Erdogan, since 2002, Turkey underwent a rapid and significant socio-economic and legal transformation. Unlike its predecessor Islamist parties, AKP has embraced economic liberalisation (Tugal 2009) as well as prioritised the accession to the European Union. The legal reforms that were introduced to bring the country in line with the Copenhagen criteria entailed amendments done to the Criminal Law, including changes to pre-trial detention provisions as well as the reforms to the Turkish National Police in order to address human rights abuses, particularly torture under illegal detention following unrecorded arrests and/or in police facilities. This chapter will look at these transformations from the perspective of trans women in Istanbul, Turkey and demonstrate their effects on trans women's encounters with the law.

4 Methodology

This chapter is based on life story interviews I conducted with 12 trans women in 2012 and 2013, close readings of LGBTI and sex worker organisations' publications, and analyses of relevant legal texts. Life story interviewing—a qualitative, in-depth method of data collection—reveals people's articulation of their lived experiences at the intersection of the social and the personal (Riessman 1993; Plummer 1995; Franzosi 1998; Engel and Munger 2003). This method situates participants' voices at the very heart of the research and gives them significant control over the direction and content of their narratives. Instead of imposing a question-and-response structure (Chase 2003), the interviews were loosely structured to allow participants to convey how the law affects their lives and livelihood.

I recruited research participants via my previous acquaintances among trans women formed since 2006 through my engagement with LGBTI organisations in Istanbul. Two trans women I first reached out to put me in contact with other potential participants, who then offered more names. At all initial meetings, I introduced myself and explained in detail the project's aims, methods and implications. This approach allowed me to build trust gradually by affording potential participants sufficient time to consider their participation and opportunities to ask questions. After agreeing to participate in this study, at the start of each interview the participants were reminded of the project details and their rights to confidentiality, to refuse to participate and to revoke consent. Their informed consent was obtained on these terms.

The participants ranged in age from 27 to 76. Their education levels varied significantly, from those who did not complete their primary education to university degree holders. Different educational achievements, however, did not seem to play a key role in determining their life trajectories. Eight participants were sex workers and two were *kolihouse*[4] managers who previously worked as sex workers. The other two participants had quit sex work several years ago; one was a street lottery ticket seller and the other was an NGO staff member. Working in the sex industry is common for trans women in urban Turkey (Lambdaistanbul LGBTI Association 2010), and the interlacing of their gender identity with sex work profoundly shapes their life conditions.

All interviews, except for one, were carried out in the homes of participants: some of whom used these locations for their work. The one interview outside of the home was conducted in a teahouse. Eight of the 12 interviews took place over more than one session, oftentimes due to the sex worker participants' working patterns. Sometimes interviews did not start immediately if a participant had a client when I arrived, or interviews had to be cut short because of a phone call from or arrival of a client. The longest interview spanned five meetings and lasted more than nine hours. All interviews were conducted in Turkish, and transcribed and translated into English by me. All participants are identified here with pseudonyms. Although Turkish is a gender-neutral language, I use the English pronouns 'she' and 'her' when referring to my research participants and not the gender-neutral pronouns. Both choices reflect the participants' self-identification and use of gender categories in making sense of and describing themselves and their embodied experiences.

[4] *Kolihouse* (house of intercourse) in trans women's slang refers to a flat (usually run by an elderly trans woman) that offers trans sex workers hourly rent rooms.

5 Misdemeanour Laws and Fines: Everyday Policing in Istanbul

Although the Turkish state never openly criminalised trans women or sex workers, sex work regulations in Turkish laws have historically worked in conjunction with the on-the-ground operations of police forces to exclude trans women from regulated spaces of sex work and from urban spaces, rendering them open targets of violence at the hands the state and legal actors as well as ordinary citizens (Taşcıoğlu 2020). The systematic exclusion of trans women usually took place outside the confines of formal law in police stations, police cars, streets or on the outskirts of the urban areas, where trans women were tortured, raped, murdered, with little recourse to legal protection against discrimination or persecution. In the 2000s, however, a change manifested for trans women in the ways through which Istanbul police forces treat and punish them: "Now we don't experience the same things," Melisa said, "but this time the fines make us suffer to the bone."

The fines Melisa refers to are issued under the Misdemeanours Law (Law no. 5326) that was introduced into the Turkish legal framework in 2005 as part of the European Union accession process. With the introduction of the Misdemeanours Law, some minor offences that were previously covered by the Criminal Code lost their 'criminal' attribute and were transformed into 'misdemeanours' that are considered to be likely to cause harassment, distress and nuisance in public life. The Misdemeanours Law authorises local authorities and police forces to deal with these newly established misdemeanours, including gambling, drunkenness, excessive noise, occupying the street, failing to disclose one's identity to a public official or polluting the environment, among others.

The introduction of the Misdemeanours Law signalled the shift Melisa identified in her interview, marked by a move away from violently targeting trans women's bodies towards managing their public existence via on-the-spot fines issued by the police. Other research participants reported similar experiences: Trans women's appearance in public spaces at any time of day or night, or walking on the sidewalk or standing in a street corner, even if not for sex work purposes, is labelled by the police as a misdemeanour under the Misdemeanours Law. Didem, telling me about her experiences as a trans sex worker in Istanbul since 1990's, states:

> Now they came up with this idea of fining! Whenever they see you on the street, it doesn't matter if you are out there for sex work or shopping or hanging around. They fine you with the accusation of occupying the street, [or] preventing the police from fulfilling its duty.

The emergence of trans embodiment as a routinised target of the misdemeanour fines calls to mind O'Malley's (2009) influential analysis of the use of monetary sanctions by Western European countries. For O'Malley, increasing reliance on fines for legal governance is closely related to the rise of consumer society and the spread of monetised risk management as an alternative to incarceration. Rather than eliminating, punishing or disciplining the wrongful behaviour, fines in O'Malley's account represent an aim of controlling the flow and distribution of the offending behaviour without moralising the wrong-doer (O'Malley and Valverde 2014, 329; see also Bentham 1962). In the case of the trans women of Turkey, I suggest that the application of the misdemeanour fines indicates both economising and moralising missions of penal policies and practices: The monetary penalty imposed on trans embodiment, while making possible a certain way of urban governance by regulating trans women's circulation in the city, operates with a normalising, moralising aim of sustaining the normative structures of sex/gender.

The stated aims of the Misdemeanours Law go some way towards shedding light on the juxtaposition of these two sides of fines. In the words of the General Directorate of European Union, the introduction of the Misdemeanours Law aimed at "*speeding up* the provision of justice; ensuring its *quick, efficient* and *economic* implementation; *reducing* the workload of the judiciary; and preventing *waste of time and labour* of officials" (The General Directorate of European Union 2008, 12, italics mine). The focus on speed, efficiency and cost–benefit analysis of the legal reform is significant here, in that it points to the economising orientation of the legal reform and the newly established legal sphere of misdemeanours law. The aims of the Misdemeanours Law as stated in the law itself, on the other hand, point to its moral character: 'to protect public order, general morality, general health, the environment and the economic order.' The vagueness of the language, coupled with its economising logic, endow the authorities with a licence to devise and apply strategies to fulfil the broad aims of the Misdemeanours Law in an effective manner. The effectiveness of misdemeanour fines indeed lies in the ease of their on-spot application, purging the streets from trans women at lower economic and political cost. Fines are easy to issue, require less resource and time and confer the state with a higher level of legitimacy in the national and international community, compared to other forms of punishment such as torture or abduction.

Misdemeanour fines, as a monetary transaction, clearly create a financial incentive for the police to issue and collect fines. The revenue from fines contribute to the budget of the local authority the police work under, and moreover, there exist individualised incentives to encourage police officers to issue fines and collect revenue for their public employer: the bonus system. The points-based system for police officer assessment allocates certain 'bonus points' to different categories of crimes and misdemeanours depending on arrests made for 'serious' crimes and misdemeanour fines collected (ILGA 2014; Gönen 2016; Ördek 2014). Consistent with the economic orientation of the Misdemeanour Law, the bonus system, in this way, constitutes an internal system process that subjects police officers' conduct to measurement, quantification and evaluation (Feeley and Simon 1992).

Under these conditions, it is not difficult to imagine that trans women emerge as an easy, everyday target for police officers. Trans women's accounts show the reach of the Misdemeanours Law into their everyday lives and its disruptive effects on their living and working conditions. Many research participants paid thousands of Turkish liras in fines; many also spoke of hardships that they must endure to pay these fines. There were occasions when they were fined several times in a day. Cansu, for instance, told of a winter night when she "was fined four times, and lost exactly 368 liras in fines." Yet the fines she was issued did not stop her from doing sex work but forced her to move between various sex work spots regularly during the same night. She had to be on the street for 7–8 h to earn her living, and additionally, to compensate her earnings lost to the fines. Misdemeanour fines condemn them to a vicious circle of being fined and doing sex work, even if at the risk of subsequent fines.

Kemal Ördek, in their report for *Red Umbrella Association* (2014), calls these administrative fines a tool for taxation on trans women's informal sex work practices. Other scholars have also focused on the function of fines as a form of taxation (Harris 2016; Harris et al. 2010; Kohler-Hausmann 2014; Natapoff 2015). Considering that fines target trans women as trans women, not necessarily as sex workers, one can argue that misdemeanour fines represent a two-fold, interrelated debt relationship between the Turkish state and trans women: first, in their economic dispossession by the seizure of their income in the form of fines, and second, in their construction as debtors of the state who are obliged to repay for their transgression of the boundaries of familial citizenship. The new exchange animated by economic exploitation, cost efficiency and generation of revenue through the collection of fines simultaneously produces debt for trans women and reconfigures and polices particular gender arrangements.

6 Criminal Trials: At the Intersection of the Formal and Informal

Changing legal landscapes and policing strategies means that ongoing conflict between the police and trans women on the streets has been increasingly taken to the courthouse. This entails encounters for trans women with a new scale of law and the introduction of new spatio-temporalities into their lives. The second circuit of law that this chapter focuses on is criminal trials. I particularly look at how the formal and the informal become enmeshed in trans women's encounters with the judiciary in ways that strips them of their capacity to argue their case and seek justice against accusations of the police.

Almost all the trans women I interviewed for this research had gone through a number of criminal cases of similar kinds, some still pending at the time of our interviews. Most of their appearances in court were driven by similar interactions with the police, and in most of these cases they were prosecuted based exclusively on police allegations. Parallel to the use of the Misdemeanours Law by the police, some of these allegations were related to their sex work practices; some were just aimed at criminalising trans women's presence in public spaces. Derya counted: "I have 2–3 cases that go on at the moment. But if I count the earlier ones, they would make around 15–20. All of them are about the police." In one of these trials, Derya was accused of indecent behaviour, based on the claim of a police officer that she was seen naked on the street. She was found guilty and sentenced to six months in prison by the local court of Şişli. In the other case, she was being tried for insulting a police officer and hindering him from fulfilling his duty.

The operation of the law at the courthouse that emerges from trans women's narratives is one intertwined with spaces and relationships that lie outside a strict formal and impersonal juridical operation. Law was, on the one hand, regarded as an instrument of the state, and on the other, as a space where actors contest with each other to get the upper hand through mobilising formal and informal means and legal or extra-legal forms of capital. Either way, in these criminal trials, the judiciary appeared to be more concerned with the conveniences of the police rather than with trying to uncover what really happened, often undermining or sometimes even violating legal rules and procedures.

In her indecency case, Derya recognised "homophobia" in her first face-to-face encounter with the judge in the courtroom. She recalls, "I saw the eye of the judge. I said 'Allah!' to myself, 'this is a very bad man. Completely. A homophobic man. It is so clear that he is looking to me with disgust."

Her feeling was proven true throughout the rest of the trial. She had to deal with the judge's reliance on a false witness and fabricated evidence when her accuser police officer brought a witness: "The [police officer] hires and brings a false witness there and gets me condemned." Derya noticed that the judge guided this witness with direct questions, which for her was an obvious breach in procedure: "[The judge] tells [the witness] what to say. 'She was naked, wasn't she?' The judge says this, and the man replies 'Yeah'." Derya offered further evidence to prove that the allegation of the police officer was not correct, including the recordings of surveillance cameras at the scene, but the judge refused her request and closed the case: "No," she recalled him saying, "I found you guilty. I sentence you to six months." Although for Derya it was evident that the combination of facts and rules should have led to her acquittal, the legal authorities involved in her case—police officers, prosecutors and judge—refused to be guided by legal rules and evidence, and a decision was made with no consideration of possibly exonerating evidence. Derya ironically paralleled the way the judge made his decision to "divine inspiration":

> What is the evidence? Show me the evidence! Although there is no evidence, you are still guilty. I asked for evidence, one piece of evidence. You postponed the trial for three months to collect evidence and what evidence did you come up with? Nothing. There is no evidence. 'The conviction has come.' 'The conviction has come that the crime is committed.' 'The conviction has come to the judge.' 'I arrived at the conviction.' Oh yes, he got divine inspiration! He made his decision that I committed this crime, meaning that I walked naked on the streets.

Coming from above like divine inspiration, in these instances trans women felt directly targeted by the state due to their gender identity. The attitudes and decisions of judges were usually deemed as a mere reflection of the state's stance towards trans women.

The second way trans women found themselves disadvantaged in the courtroom relates to the consequence of their social status and their disconnection from networks that might provide them an advantage. The law that appears here is a malleable one that can be influenced from the bottom-up through an interaction of legal practices with local norms and informal practices. The ability to exploit one's local networks of power and to employ informal connections in order to advance one's interests in the courtroom becomes visible. "The courts side with the powerful ones. If you have a man, your case is done," Deniz said. Referring to having informal connections that one can put to work in the courtroom, "having a man" becomes a manifestation of power concentrated in the informal, interrupting the requirements brought about by the formal law.

The exclusion of trans women from familial citizenship seems to be crucial in shaping their interactions with the law in the courtroom. While accusations levelled against them to revolve around their public appearance that transgresses normative categories of gender, their inability to perform socio-legally expected familial bonds increased their sense of marginality. Canan thought that having the support of her family in the courtroom would have given the court "a better image," one that could have had an impact on the way the judge thought of her and her case; it would have shown that she was not disowned by her family. For Tuğçe, the lack of support from her family was the key reason behind her imprisonment sentence: "This is really a fact. If you are unowned, if you don't have anyone, anyone behind you, if you don't have anyone, if you have no family, no family support, if you don't have anyone behind you to support you, you get really smashed."

In contrast to the immediacy of the on-the-spot misdemeanour fine, trans women spend a great amount of time in courthouses for their trials. Their experiences of the criminal justice system are strictly conditioned by the institutional temporalities—postponement, waits and delays. Derya, comparing her earlier experiences at the hands of police violence at police stations, to her treatment at courthouses said:

> Before they used to take and release you after ID check. They used to beat you and hit you with a baton two-three or five-six times and release you. Now they take you to court and make you crawl from pillar to post. You go to trial ten times. One single trial! What is the difference? There is no difference. It got even worse. Much worse!

By imposing on trans women these episodes of waiting and moving back and forth between the courthouse and everyday spaces, the institutional time frame works as a further means through which the law enhances its power and recreates trans women as an object of its power (Auyero and Swistun 2009).

This new mode of management of trans women by the law influences how trans women use urban spaces and organise their lives and behaviour. Handan Anne closed her *kolihouse* as a result of her sentence: "I had to close the *kolihouse*. I cannot risk being tried again. One friend is in prison now because of reoffending, for 11 months." Derya felt under pressure to watch and control herself in her interactions with the police when on streets, concerned that any act or any utterance of hers could be used against her in trials:

> Because there is this police chief, Aziz Yalcinkaya. He does this to all transvestites. He provokes on purpose, so that you say something to him against which he can press charges. Now I don't say anything. What can I do? Even if he hits, I don't speak out. Because I will have a trial with him now.

The consequences of these policing performances are persistent, and multiply their governmental effects because even when they are not actualised they exist as potential threats for trans women. Both Melisa and Cansu shared with me their feelings of insecurity and fear when they are out on the streets, and Derya told me that whenever she sees a police officer, she cannot help but feel that he will harass her. "Most of my friends are depressed. We are imprisoned in our houses. Is walking on the street, shopping a misdemeanour?" Melisa asked. The policing and criminalisation of trans women work not only through enactment but also through latency—by creating a chronic condition of anticipation of legal intervention. It permeates into trans women's lives as a constant potentiality and places them under a constant threat of criminalisation even in the most mundane daily matters and exchanges.

7 Conclusion

This chapter analysed life story narratives of trans women in Istanbul, providing rich accounts concerning their encounters with the law as they live their lives at the intersection of various forms of legal power. In writing this chapter, I sought to avoid the omissions that arise from doctrinal studies that limit the scope of their inquiries to the letter of the law, but also those of socio-legal approaches that rely on legal formalism or concentrate on questions of policy. This stream, which dominates the study of law and society in Turkey and abroad, takes legal thinking's normative frameworks at their face value and abstains from interrogating law in any way beyond these self-referential normative frameworks. Such an approach consequently remains limited to pointing out deficiencies or gaps between legal texts and practice and does not leave analytical room to examine and understand the effects of legal power in the lives of social actors.

The chapter also departed from mainstream research of citizenship which sees citizenship as a formal status and does not go further into the questions of the differentiated and stratified experiences of citizenship. Instead, it scrutinised law as one of many possible terrains where encounters between citizens and state take place and where the state gets solidified in citizen's lives through low level everyday interactions. Rather than the top-down declarations of citizenship in law in the books as belonging to a community of right holders, it argued that citizenship takes shape mainly in everyday encounters and confrontations. This indicates the need to understand citizenship as an ongoing process, rather than one depending solely on a pre-existing set of rules.

The narratives of trans women I interviewed conveyed the pervasive and insidious entanglement of their everyday lives by the police and criminal law trials. They described how the applications of misdemeanours law and criminal law limit their access to public spaces in an effective manner. The Misdemeanours Law, in everyday practice of policing in Istanbul, emerged as an effective, time saving and revenue generating mechanism that impoverishes and at the same time removes trans women from the public gaze. Trans women's management via criminal law trials, on the other hand, subjects them to another mode of operation of the law at the courthouses that intertwines formal and informal operation. Between the immediacy and frequency of the Misdemeanours Law and the slow temporality of criminal law trials, trans women's bodies are marked permanently as unlawful on the ground. These developments in the legal management of trans women point to the rise of governmental logic where the public officials claim to control circulation in the name of security order and morality. Foucault notes the emergence of this new formulation of power:

> No longer that of fixing and demarcating the territory, but of allowing circulations to take place, of controlling them, sifting the good and the bad, ensuring that things are always in movement, constantly moving around, continually going from one point to another, but in such a way that the inherent dangers of this circulation are cancelled out. (Foucault 2007, 65)

I argued that the (dis)placement of trans women into constant circulation is coupled with the extensive web of practices that circulate trans women's bodies without familialising them: when related to the family they are always the constitutive outside. As such it becomes normal to reduce them to their bodies (Agamben 1998, 2005), and their very bodily existence and performances turn trans women into targets of police/legal power that checks, controls and channels their everyday presence, bodies and behaviours.

Until very recently, Turkey was praised for its exemplary democracy as a model for the Middle East in European and North American contexts, from the media to academia. Turkey's EU candidacy, long at the centre of foreign policy agenda, also triggered legal reforms to comply with EU conditionalities that reinforce that view. My analysis of trans women's experiences during this period, however, add to the line of studies that show how legal reforms do not always bring about the expected transformation but can be accompanied by novel strategies for creating and maintaining social order (Koğacıoğlu 2003; Çalı 2010; Bahçecik 2015; Babül 2017). Sharpe (2002, 191) argues that "the study of transgender/law relations within critical legal scholarship [...] offers to inform thinking about law more generally and its changing regulatory strategies around bodies." Considering the rapidly changing broad socio-political context of Turkey since the completion of this research, the criminalisation of trans embodiment also sheds light on the importance of attending less on grand moments or processes of the law and more on the everyday and the ordinary where the law takes a life, unfolding in the social and the political.

References

Agamben, Giorgio. 1998. *Homo Sacer: Sovereign Power and Bare Life*. Stanford, CA: Stanford University Press.

Agamben, Giorgio. 2005. *State of exception*. Chicago: Chicago University Press.

Arat, Yeşim. 1994. Women's Movement of the 1980s in Turkey: Radical Outcome of Liberal Kemalism? In *Reconstructing Gender in the Middle East: Tradition, Identity and Power*, ed. M. Göçek and S. Balaghi, 100–113. New York: Columbia University Press.

Arat, Yeşim. 1997. The Project of Modernity and Women in Turkey. In *Rethinking Modernity and National Identity in Turkey*, ed. S. Bozdağan and R. Kasaba, 95–112. Seattle: Washington University Press.

Auyero, Javier, and Débora Alejandra. Swistun. 2009. *Flammable: Environmental Suffering in an Argentine Shantytown*. Oxford and New York: Oxford University Press.

Babül, Elif. 2017. *Bureaucratic Intimacies Translating Human Rights in Turkey*. CA Stanford: Stanford University Press.

Bahçecik, Şerif Onur. 2015. The Power Effects of Human Rights Reforms in Turkey: Enhanced Surveillance and Depoliticization. *Third World Quarterly* 36 (6): 1222–1236.

Baykan, Toygar Sinan. 2018. *The Justice and Development Party in Turkey Populism, Personalism, Organization*. Cambridge: Cambridge University Press.

Bentham, Jeremy. 1962. *The Works of Jeremy Bentham: The Constitutional Code*. New York: Russell and Russell.

Berghan, S. 2007. *Lubunya*. Istanbul: Metis Yayincilik.

Berktay, Fatmagül. 2001. Osmanlı'dan Cumhuriyet'e Feminizm. In *Tanzimat ve Meşrutiyetin Birikimi: Modern Türkiye'de Siyasi Düşünce Cilt 1*, ed. M. Alkan, 348–360. İletişim Yayınları: Istanbul.

Brubaker, Rogers. 1992. *Citizenship and Nationhood in France and Germany*. Cambridge: Harvard University Press.

Brubaker, Rogers. 1996. *Nationalism Reframed: Nationhood and the National Question in the New Europe*. New York: Cambridge University Press.

Bussmaker, Jet, and Rian Voet. 1998. Citizenship and Gender: Theoretical Approaches and Historical Legacies. *Critical Social Policy* 18 (3): 277–307.

Calı, B. 2010. The logics of supranational human rights litigation, official acknowledgment, and human rights reform: the southeast Turkey cases before the European Court of Human Rights, 1996–2006. *Law & Social Inquiry*, 35 (2): 311–337.

Chase, Susan E. 2003. The Way We Were, Are, and Might Be: Torch Singing as Auto Ethanography. In *Turning Points in Qualitative Research: Tying Knots in a Handkerchief*, ed. Y.S. Lincoln and N.K. Denzin, 276–296. Oxford: Altamira Press.

Cindoglu, Dilek, and Didem Unal. 2017. Gender and Sexuality in the Authoritarian Discursive Strategies of new Turkey. *European Journal of Women's Studies* 24 (1): 39–54.

Couch, et al. 2008. Transgender People and the Amendment of Formal Documentation: Matters of Recognition and Citizenship. *Health Sociology Review* 17 (3): 280–289.

Currah, Paisley, Richard M. Juang, and Shannon Minter. 2006. *Transgender Rights*. Minneapolis: The University of Minnesota Press.

Edelman, Elijah Adiv. 2014. 'Walking While Transgender': Necropolitical Regulations of Trans Feminine Bodies of Colour in the Nation's Capital. In *Queer Necropolitics*, ed. J. Haritaworn, A. Kuntsman, and S. Posocco, 172–190. Abingdon: Routledge.

Engel, David, and Frank W. Munger. 2003. *Rights of Inclusion: Law and Identity in the Life Stories of Americans With Disabilities*. Chicago: University of Chicago Press.

Evans, David. 1993. *Sexual Citizenship: The Material Construction of Sexualities*. London: Routledge.

Ewick, Patricia, and Susan S. Silbey. 1998. *Commonplace of Law: Stories From Everyday Life*. Chicago: University of Chicago Press.

Feeley, Malcolm M., and Jonathon Simon. 1992. The New Penology: Notes on the Emerging Strategy of Corrections and its Implications. *Criminology* 30 (4): 449–474.

Field, Ann-Marie. 2007. Counter-Hegemonic Citizenship: LGBT Communities and the Politics of Hate Crimes in Canada. *Citizenship Studies* 11 (3): 247–262.

Foucault, Michel. 1978. *History of Sexuality, Vol. I: An Introduction. New York: Pantheon Books.*

Foucault, Michel. 1979. *Discipline and Punish: The Birth of the Prison.* New York: Vintage Books.

Foucault, Michel. 1991. Governmentality. In *The Foucault Effect: Studies on Governmentality*, ed. G. Burchell, C. Gordon, and P. Miller, 87–104. Chicago: University of Chicago Press.

Foucault, Michel. 2007. *Security, Territory and Population: Lectures at the Collège de France 1977–1978*. New York: Palgrave Macmi.

Franzosi, Roberto. 1998. Narrative Analysis: Or Why (and how) Sociologists Should be Interested in Narrative. *Annual Review of Sociology* 24 (1): 517–555.

General Directorate of European Union. 2008. Avrupa Birliği'ne Aday Ülke Olarak Türkiye'de AB Uyum Yasalarının İç Hukuka Etki ve Katkısı. Available at: http://www.abgm.adalet.gov.tr/yayinlar/belgeler/ekutuphane/ABUyumYasalarininIcHukukaEtkisiVeKatkisi.pdf (accessed January 2018).

Göle, Nilüfer. 1997. Secularism and Islamism in Turkey: The Making of Elites and Counter-Elites. *Middle East Journal*, 51 (1): 46–58.

Gönen, Zeynep. 2016. *The Politics of Crime in Turkey: Neoliberalism, Police and the Urban Poor*. London: I. B. Tauris.

Harris, Alexes. 2016. *A Pound of Flesh: Monetary Sanctions as Punishment for the Poor*. New York: Russell Sage Foundation.

Harris, Alexes, Heather Evans, and Katherine Beckett. 2010. Drawing Blood from Stones: Legal Debt and Social Inequality in the Contemporary United States. *American Journal of Sociology* 115 (6): 1753–1799.

Hines, Sally. 2007a. (Trans)Forming Gender: Social Change and Transgender Citizenship. *Sociological Research Online* 12, no. 1 (2007a): 181–194.

Hines, Sally. 2007b. *Transforming Gender: Transgender Practices of Identity, Intimacy and Care*. Bristol: The Policy Press.

ILGA. 2014. *Human Rights Violations of LGBT Individuals in Turkey*. Ankara: Ayrinti Basimevi.

Joseph, Suad. 1996. Gender and Citizenship in Middle Eastern States. *Middle East Report* 26 (1): 4–10.

Kandiyoti, Deniz A. 1987. Emancipated But Unliberated? Reflections on the Turkish Case. *Feminist Studies* 13 (2): 317–338.

Kandiyoti, Deniz A. 1988. Slave Girls, Temptresses and Comrades: Images of Women in the Turkish Novel. *Feminist Issues* 8 (1): 35–50.

Kaos G. L. 2007. LGBT Bireylerin İnsan Hakları Raporu.

Koğacıoğlu, Dicle. 2003. *Law in Context: Citizenship and Reproduction of Inequality in an Istanbul Courthouse*. PhD diss.: Stony Brook University.

Koğacıoğlu, Dicle. 2005. Citizenship in Context: Rethinking Women's Relationships to the Law in Turkey. In *Citizenship and the Nation State in Greece and Turkey*, ed. F. Birtek and T. Dragonas, 144–160. London: Routledge.

Kohler-Hausmann, I. 2014. Managing Justice and Mass Misdemeanors. *Stanford Law Review* 66 (2): 611–693.

Kmlicka, W. 1998. "Multicultural Citizenship" in Gershon, S. (eds.), *Citizenship Debates*, Minneapolis, University of Minnesota Pressy.

Lambdaistanbul LGBTI Association. 2010. "İt iti ısırmaz." *İstanbul: Lambdaistanbul.*

Lister, Ruth. 1997. *Citizenship: Feminist Perspectives*. Basingstoke and London: Macmillan.

Marshall, Thomas Humphrey. 1964. *Class; citizenship, and social development*. Garden City: Double Day.

Monro, Surya. 2005. *Gender Politics: Citizenship, Activism and Sexual Diversity*. London: Pluto Press.

Monro, Surya, and Lorna Warren. 2004. Transgendering Citizenship. *Sexualities* 7 (3): 343–362.

Namaste, Viviane. 2005. *Sex Change, Social Change: Reflections on Identity, Institutions and Imperialism*. Toronto: Women's Press.

Natapoff, Alexandra. 2015. Misdemeanor Decriminalization. *Vanderbilt Law Review* 68 (4): 1055–1116.

Pat, O'Malley. 2009. Theorizing Fines. *Punishment and Society* 11 (1): 67–83.

O'Malley, Pat and Mariana Valverde. 2014. Foucault, Criminal Law, and the Governmentalization of the State Foundational Texts, In *Modern Criminal Law*, ed. in M. D. Dubber, 317–334.Oxford: Oxford University Press.

Ördek, Kemal. 2014. *"Kayıtsız" Alanda "Kayıtlı" "Soygun": Trans Seks İşçilerine Yönelik Bir "Vergilendirme"*. Aracı Olarak İdari Para Cezaları. Ankara: Kırmızı Şemsiye Derneği.

Ördek, Kemal. 2016. *Türkiye'de Trans Olmak: Dışlanma, Ayrımcılık ve Şiddet*. Ankara: Kırmızı Şemsiye Derneği.

Özar, Şemsa and Burcu Yakut-Cakar. 2013, November–December. Unfolding the invisibility of women without men in the case of Turkey. *Women's Studies International Forum*, 41 (1): 24–34.

Pateman, Carole. 1988. *The Sexual Contract*. Cambridge: Polity Press.

Plummer, Ken. 1995. *Telling Sexual Stories: Power, Change and Social Worlds*. London: Routledge.

Richardson, Diane. 2000. Constructing Sexual Citizenship: Theorizing Sexual Rights. *Critical Social Policy* 20 (1): 105–135.

Riessman, Catherine Koher. 1993. *Narrative Analysis*. London: Sage Publications.

Rose, Nikolas. 2000. Government and Control. *British Journal of Criminology* 40 (2): 321–339.

Sarat, Austin. 1990. The Law Is All Over: Power, Resistance, and the Legal Consciousness of the Welfare Poor. *Yale Journal of Law and the Humanities* 2 (2): 343–379.

Selek, Pinar. 2006. *Maskeler, Süvariler, Gacılar*. Istanbul: Istiklal Kitabevi.

Sharma, Aradhana and Gupta, A. 2006. *Introduction. Rethinking Theories of the State in an Age of Globalisation*. In *The Anthropology of the State: A reader*, ed. A. Sharma and A. Gupta. Oxford: Blackwell Publishing.

Sharpe, Andrew. 2002. *Transgender Jurisprudence: Dysphoric Bodies of Law*. New York and Abingdon: Routledge.

Sirman, Nükhet. 1989. Feminism in Turkey: A Short History. *New Perspectives on Turkey* 3: 1–34.

Sirman, Nükhet. 2007. Constituting the Modern Family as the Social in the Transition from Empire to Nation-State. In *Ways to Modernity in Turkey and Greece*, ed. Ç. Keyder and A. Frangoudaki, 176–190. London: I. B. Tauris.

Somers, Margaret R. 1993. Citizenship and the Place of the Public Sphere: Law, Community, and Political Culture in the Transition to Democracy. *American Sociological Review* 58: 587–620.

Soysal, Yasemin Nuhoglu, and A.J. Soyland. 1994. *Limits of Citizenship: Migrants and Postnational Membership in Europe*. Chicago and London: The University of Chicago Press.

Taşcıoğlu, Esen Ezgi. 2011. What Do Transgender Women's Experiences Tell Us About Law? Towards an Understanding of Law as Legal Complex. *Oñati Socio-Legal Series* 1 (1): 1–25.

Taşcıoğlu, Esen Ezgi. 2015. Violence, Survival and Knowledge in Trans Women's Lives in Turkey. *Oñati Socio-Legal Series* 6: 1452–1470.

Taşcıoğlu, Esen Ezgi. 2020. States of Exception: Legal Governance of Trans Women in Urban Turkey. *Social & Legal Studies*. https://doi.org/10.1177/0964663920924780.

Tugal, C. 2009. *Passive Revolution: Absorbing the Islamic Challenge to Capitalism*. Stanford: Stanford University Press.

Turner, Bryan S. 1986. Personhood and Citizenship. *Theory, Culture and Society* 3 (1): 1–16.

Valverde, Mariana. 2009. Jurisdiction and Scale: Legal "Technicalities" as Resources for Theory. *Social Legal Studies* 18 (2): 139–157.

Valverde, Mariana. 2010. Practices of Citizenship and Scales of Governance. *New Criminal Law Review* 13 (2): 216–240.

Valverde, Mariana. 2014. Studying the Governance of Crime and Security: Space, Time and Jurisdiction. *Criminology & Criminal Justice* 14 (4): 379–391.

West, Isaac. 2013. *Transforming Citizenships: Transgender Articulations of the Law*. New York: NYU Press.

Whittle, S. 2006. Foreword. In *The Transgender Studies Reader*, ed. S. Stryker and S. Whittle. New York and Abingdon: Routledge.

Young, I. M. 1998. Polity and Group Difference: A Critique of the Ideal of Universal Citizenship. In *The Citizenship Debates*, ed. S. Gershon. Minneapolis: University of Minnesota Press.

Zengin, Aslı. 2014. Sex for Law, Sex for Psychiatry: Pre-Sex Reassignment Surgical Psychotherapy in Turkey. *Anthropologica* 56 (1): 55–68.

Laws Cited

Kabahatler Kanunu [Misdemeanours Law] No. 5326. Introduced in House March 30, 2005.

Türk Ceza Kanunu [Turkish Criminal Law] No. 5237. Introduced in House September 26, 2004.

13

Reaffirming Womanhood: Young Transwomen and Online Sex Work in the Philippines

Veronica L. Gregorio

1 Introduction

It's not just About the Money.

I encountered this quote several times in my conversations with young transwomen who engage in online sex work. Sex work, while illegal in the Philippines, provides these transwomen with the opportunity to make a living and forge meaningful connections with others in an often hostile and dangerous environment. Thus, the quote above was frequently followed by other phrases such as "it's also about being confident," "being recognized as woman and/or being desired as a woman," or "about having sexual partners."

Despite the positive outlook, *transpinays,* or Filipina transwomen, are in fact among the most susceptible to gender-based violence (GBV) and discrimination in the country. Cases of harassment and hate crimes continue to increase, and loopholes in legislation makes the protection of their rights extremely limited. Since 2010, the murder of at least 50 transgender or gender non-binary individuals have been recorded across the archipelago (Redfern 2021). The most notable case is that of Jennifer Laude who was murdered in 2014 by a US Marine whose sentence was cut short when President Rodrigo Duterte pardoned him in September 2020. In terms of legislation, transwomen are treated as criminals through Article 200,

V. L. Gregorio (✉)
National University of Singapore, Singapore, Singapore
e-mail: v.gregorio@u.nus.edu

G. B. Radics and P. Ciocchini (eds.), *Criminal Legalities and Minorities in the Global South*, Palgrave Socio-Legal Studies, https://doi.org/10.1007/978-3-031-17918-1_13

or the "grave scandal" provision, of the Revised Penal Code. Due to the vagueness in defining what constitutes a "grave scandal," or when an individual is deemed to be "offending against decency or good customs," they can be readily arrested or detained. For instance, in 2019, when *transpinay* Gretchen Diez confronted a female janitor who denied her entry to the women's restroom in a mall in Quezon City, Gretchen was escorted to the security room, handcuffed, and brought to a police station. Other forms of discriminatory practices are found in universities, public spaces, and workplaces. Reports include forcing transwomen students to wear male uniforms, cut their hair, and use male pronouns. In public spaces and workplaces, transwomen are being asked to leave restaurants and to quit work because of the no-crossdressing policies (for more details see David 2015; Health Policy Project 2015; Joseph-Collins 2012; Restar et al. 2019; International Gay and Lesbian Human Rights Commission 2012).

In this chapter, I explore the role of the law in enforcing the marginalization of, and the production of criminality among, Filipina transwomen. Notably, the law prevents Filipina transwomen to be recognized as females and forces them to retain their male given birth names. By doing so, it reaffirms the Filipino society's prejudice against those who do not conform to traditional gender roles. Facing such discrimination, Filipina transwomen resort to illegal sex work, in particular online sex work, as both a means for living and a safe space to be recognized as women.

In the following sections, I will outline how colonial histories and legislative bodies impact LGBTs. Next, I will elaborate how sex work is currently being studied—from victimhood to empowerment. Following this, I will present how the internet complicates sex work and cybersex debates. I will also discuss my fieldsite, methods, and life history analysis. Next, in discussing LGBT rights in the Philippines, I will reflect on the case of Jennifer Laude. Finally, the conclusion will highlight how sisterhood and family ties influence the life decisions of young transwomen.

2 Including Transwomen in the Conversation

The experience of violence and discrimination against the trans-community can be seen throughout the world. Trans-people in South and Southeast Asia, however, despite their historical and widespread existence in the region, are particularly vulnerable to institutional and social violence as a result of imported laws and values (Joseph-Collins 2012; Winter 2009). Anti-sodomy laws enacted by British colonizers in Singapore, Malaysia, Brunei, and Myanmar continue to criminalize LGBT identities and limit LGBT rights (Radics 2021). The role of hijras or transwomen in India changed from being providers of blessings for newborn babies and newlywed couples to being labelled and prosecuted as prostitutes (Chakrapani et al. 2018). In the case of the Philippines, in the pre-colonial era, respected shamans (also known as *babaylans*, *katalonans*, and *bantuts*) were often transwomen. Their status changed dramatically during Spanish colonization as clergies accused shamans of blasphemous witchcraft. In the post-colonial era, efforts to move beyond colonial-Spanish morality can be seen in the Anti-Discrimination Bill or SOGIE (Sexual orientation and gender identity expression) Equality Bill first filed in 2000. It remains the longest running unpassed bill in Philippine Senate history after two decades of debates. Lawmakers often use religious reasoning to continue delaying the passage of the bill. Furthermore, lawmakers go as far as to question the boundaries of the plus sign (+) in LGBTQIA+ to imply that it extends to necrophilia and paedophilia (Layug-Rosero 2019).

In the specific context of *transpinays*, Philippine law explicitly denies recognition of gender reassignment surgeries. In *Rommel Jacinto Dantes Silverio v. Republic of the Philippines* (G.R. NO 174689: October 22, 2007), Rommel Jacinto Dantes Silverio filed a petition to change her name and sex to Mely in legal documents after she completed her sex reassignment surgery. The Supreme Court denied her request on the basis of Republic Act 9048 (RA 9048) or the “Clerical Error Law of 2001” Section 5 which states,

> no petition for correction of erroneous entry concerning the date of birth or the sex of a person be entertained except if the petition is accompanied by earliest school record or earliest civil documents such as, but not limited to, medical records, baptismal certificate and other documents issued by religious authorities; nor shall any entry involving change of gender corrected except if the petition is accompanied by certification issued by an accredited government physician attesting to the fact that the petitioner has not undergone sex change or sex transplant.

Mely, who identifies as a woman, and who has undergone medical procedures to be recognized as a woman, will have to retain the name Rommel in her legal documents in the Philippines. Unfortunately, her case will continue to be applied to every other Filipino trans-person who will attempt to file a petition for a name change.

These historical, social, and legal realities shape the lived experiences of being LGBT in the Philippines, particularly in the diverse southern island of Mindanao. Despite its massive size and population, with power being centralized in Manila and the northern island of Luzon and with many parts of Mindanao experiencing decades of Muslim Christian conflict, research on LGBT identities in Mindanao is scant. However, pioneering works such as Johnson's (1995, 1997) ethnographic studies in a Muslim town in Jolo Sulu analysed 50 *bantut* (gay) life histories. Similar to my own work, Johnson (1998) also discusses the ways in which *transpinays* in the 1990s "worked for love," exchanging sexual favours for money and ultimately in search for lasting relationships. This chapter explores similar themes, but analyses them in the shadow of discriminatory laws and in the context of an even more integrated world with the advent of the internet.

In this chapter, I explore how Filipina transwomen navigate everyday life in hostile social environments in which the law severely restricts their opportunities. My analysis focuses on how such violence affects their transition from youth to adulthood. I am particularly interested in the horizontal dimension of this transition (Wyn and White 1997), which refers to common experiences based on age, compulsory education, global or regional historical events, and the joining of the labour force. The young *transpinays* in this study are positioned at a period where they grew up with access to information about the violence that LGBTs are experiencing but also were kept informed about the rights and options that LGBTs from outside the Philippines enjoy. At the same time, the young *transpinays* are also digital natives who developed great comfort in using the internet for socialization and other activities such as sex work.

3 Sex Work in the Philippines

Prostitution or sex work is illegal in the Philippines. Article 202 of the Revised Penal Code (enacted in 1930 and amended by RA 10,158 in 2012) states that women found guilty of prostitution will be arrested, fined, or both.[1] Despite the existence of this law, the sex industry in the Philippines

[1] "Any person found guilty of any of the offenses covered by this article shall be punished by *arresto menor* or a fine not exceeding 200 pesos, and in case of recidivism, by *arresto mayor* in its medium period to prison correctional in its minimum period or a fine ranging from 200 to 2000 pesos, or both, in the discretion of the court." Atty. Ruby Roselle Tugade, Fellow at the Center for International Law in Manila, highlights that the law raises an interesting legal issue—if transwomen are not legally recognized as women in the Philippines (and the State cannot do so according to the *Silverio* ruling), they technically can't be held liable under Art. 202, which only penalizes "women."

continues to thrive due to legislative loopholes. For instance, in Angeles City Pampanga, known as one of the country's red-light district, sex workers from bars skirt around the law by registering as "entertainers" (there is no jurisdiction for "freelancers" who work outside establishments) (Redfern 2019). Despite the criminalization of sex work, a network of organizations like PREDA Foundation, Voice of the Free (previously known as Visayan Forum), and Talikala Foundation have emerged to advocate for the welfare and rights of women and children who were trafficked into sex trade.

Discussions regarding prostitution in the country are heavily influenced by class-based narratives on "oppression" and "female subordination." However, sex work is different from sex trafficking. The latter includes deceiving individuals, promising them a different job and then forcing them into prostitution while the former conveys consent and clear transactions between the buyer and seller. Despite the obvious distinction, sex workers are generally considered or seen by the public as individuals who were forced and therefore need to be saved. Parmanand (2019) challenges this perspective on sex workers as victims and reveals how laws, civil society organizations, and external donors create an anti-sex work environment. In her work, Parmanand interviewed leaders and members of the Philippine Sex Workers Collective (PSWC), which was established in 2013. PSWC is an offshoot of the first sex worker led organization in the Philippines, also known as Women Hookers Organizing for their Rights and Empowerment (WHORE), established in 1989.

In Southeast Asia, Law (2000) locates sex workers from Thailand, Philippines, and Indonesia in the global discourse regarding HIV/AIDS. She demonstrates how "the introduction of peer education (by NGOs) in Southeast Asia have successfully challenged the stereotype of the prostitute as (always) a victim" (126). Even if prostitution is illegal in all the three countries mentioned, authorities choose to overlook the phenomenon and establishments get away by providing different labels to the workers. Given the increase of HIV/AIDS rates in the region by the 1990s, NGOs developed projects to engage with the sex workers—to encourage them to participate in education campaigns and to access blood tests from government health clinics.

Transwomen sex workers in the Philippines are understudied. In most cases, reports on transwomen sex workers are only found in new reports about police raids and in extreme cases on violence inflicted upon them when they are said to have "lied" to their customers about being a woman. This paper aims to study trans sex work through three intersecting dimensions. First, it moves sex work discussions from the streets and bars to the digital or online realm. Second, it makes visible the experiences of young transwomen. Lastly, as opposed to discussing sex worker agency or empowerment, this chapter instead uses the notion of youth-to-adult transitions from the fields of the sociology of youth and family.

4 The Internet: Making Everyone Accessible to the World

In 2000, only 1.98% of the Philippine population had access to the internet. However, the latest data shows that such access has increased to 43% (World Bank 2019). The accessibility of the internet gave way to faster and better communication, but it also opened the country up to the cybersex industry. Child pornography and online abuse became so rampant that Republic Act 10,175, or the Cybercrime Prevention Act, was passed in 2012. The law defines cybersex as "wilful engagement, maintenance, control or operation, directly or indirectly, of any lascivious exhibition of sexual organs or sexual activity, with the aid of a computer, for favour or consideration."[2]

Despite efforts to restrict cybersex through the passing of RA 10,175, the Philippines has "become the global epicentre of the live-stream sexual abuse trade" (Brown 2016). NGO reports and scholarly works on online sex work or digital prostitution is not new. However, in the Philippine context, it continues to focus on women as sex workers and children as vulnerable victims. I posit that the internet has made everyone accessible to the world—this includes transwomen who are marginalized in the Philippine sex work environment. As I will demonstrate in the following sections, the internet has opened up the world of transwomen in terms of being accepted as women by foreign clients (mostly Europeans, American, and Australians) and in creating a profile of their own that allows them to identify themselves as women.

In engaging the cybersex debate, I relate with the work of Mathews (2017) on adult/Asian cam models (ACMs) in the Philippines. Similar to the works of Parmanand (2019) and Law (2000), Mathews explores the agency of female ACMs. He argues that "cam modelling provides women an opportunity to earn income in a way that is both economically and socially

[2] From https://www.officialgazette.gov.ph/2015/08/12/implementing-rules-and-regulations-of-republic-act-no-10175/.

convenient to them" (180). Moreover, I use the work of historian Jonathan Coopersmith (2006) to underscore the need to theorize cybersex as a service or e-commerce. He calls for the integration of cybersex in broader academic studies in the field of economics (on consumption and labour relations) and even geography in terms of the diffusion of cybersex at varying rates across the globe.

5 Research Background

The Philippines consists of three major islands: Luzon, Visayas, and Mindanao. Mindanao is the second largest island in the country in the southern part facing Celebes Sea and Indonesia. A majority of the interviews for this research took place in the Davao Region of Mindanao. According to the official website of the main city of the region—Davao City—it serves as "the gateway for the entire Mindanao island [and is] the centre of development in Mindanao." Davao City has a land area of 2444 sq km and a population of 1,673,832 which is spread out in 182 barangays. Around 80% of the population are Roman Catholic, 18% are Protestant, while the rest belong to non-Christian faiths. Davao City is home to 11 ethno-linguistic tribes including Maranao, Tausug, Maguindanaon, Iranun, Sama, Ata, Kagan, Tagabawa, Ovu-manuvo, Matigsalog, and Klata-guiangan. In terms of mother tongue, most Davaoeños use Cebuano followed by Tagalog. A local dialect is used by few while in educational institutions and business communities, English is the official medium.

The data for this work is based on my PhD research. For this research, I conducted ethnographic research since 2018 and online interviews in early 2020 and mid-2021 as part of what I call "ongoing and mediated fieldwork"—a research process wherein I was continuously in touch with the community members, albeit virtually. This also includes being able to participate in community events and be invited to family gatherings despite the geographical distance (Gregorio 2020). Some examples include joining wedding ceremonies via Instagram live and catching up with other community members individually through Facebook messenger. I use life history as a key method in order to account and uncover the experiences and emotions of the young transwomen. The face-to-face interviews are in-depth, and it uses semi- or non-standardized questionnaires. Conversations were done in Tagalog and English. The mediated aspects of my fieldwork were conducted over Facebook video calls and Instagram direct messages as return visits became impossible due to the COVID-19 pandemic.

Conducting research about transwomen and online sex work is challenging. My positionality as a PhD researcher invited several questions from the participants. One remark that I will always remember is, "*Ate*,[3] does that mean you will be a doctor and you can help us access pills and hormones?" to which I responded by explaining that I am in a different field from medical doctors. They eventually understood when I clarified that I hope to be a professor in the future. Additionally, being an elder female in my late 20s (but not old enough to be their mom or aunt) helped in relating to them as a sister or *Ate*. Since their neighbours and cousins knew of me even prior to meeting them, this established a trust that allowed me to ask deep and personal questions in my interviews. Also, being open to the participants about my personal life goals helped in fostering a safe environment wherein they could also share their own aspirations about the future.

6 Growing up Trans in Mindanao

I met Kathryn, Nadine, and five other young transwomen when I was attending a week-long community event. When I met them, their ages were between 20 and 24. I focus on Kathryn and Nadine as I have spent more time with them, and they agreed to be interviewed even after the event. We also maintained consistent communication even after my fieldwork and even planned to meet again either in Manila or Davao City.

Kathryn is from an agricultural family. Her parents and extended relatives have known about her sexuality since childhood. As she shared, "When they saw me dancing in birthday parties as a kid, they already knew!" The relatives are open about her cross dressing which began in her teenage years. Her elder cousins would sometimes pass on to her their pre-loved dresses, skirts, and sandals. After studying high school, she decided to go to Davao City and be an online sex worker. I asked if this was related to the economic needs of her family and two other younger siblings. She then explained that her parents actually do not ask for any money and they even wanted her to pursue university, but she rejected the idea. Her priority was to save money and have a sex change operation in Thailand. She mentioned that she knows people who were able to do it even without university degrees, and so she was eager to do it too.

[3] Elder sister.

Nadine on the other hand is from an indigenous group in Mindanao. Her parents found out about her sexuality during high school. When she was younger, she would leave the house to meet friends and they would change their clothes to dresses and heels before hanging out in malls or the park. At first, her father was extremely upset because she is the eldest son, but he eventually accepted the situation with the help of Nadine's mom. Nadine started taking hormone pills in high school, but the supply depended on her friends who could buy it illegally in hospitals. When Nadine reached college, she met other transgender women who introduced her to online sex work.

Kathryn and Nadine met in the apartment where other transwomen online sex workers were living. They ran in different social circles but a common friend asked them if they wanted to explore online sex work. As we continued our conversation, Kathryn mentioned Ate Angelica (also a transwoman, in her late 20s). Angelica owns the apartment where Kathryn and Nadine stayed. She guided them about transitioning and gave them contacts and information on where to get hormone pills and injections. Angelica went to Thailand few years ago for her sex reassignment surgery and just last year (2019) for her forehead reduction surgery and teeth whitening treatment.

As Kathryn was talking about Angelica, Nadine jumped in and explained that Angelica used to also engage in cybersex until an Australian guy, a former customer, proposed that she be his girlfriend. They have been together for about three years. The same guy sent money for Angelica's multiple operations and if everything goes according to plan, Angelica will fly to Australia to marry him and settle down. For Nadine, their Ate Angelica is the life #goals and a source of inspiration for younger transwomen.

In a separate conversation, I asked both Kathryn and Nadine about their families. I asked them how they explained their stay in Davao City to their parents. I was also curious about whether their parents knew about their online activities. The two explained that they do not hide their activities from their families. As a matter of fact, because they wanted to help out other younger gay relatives and neighbours, as their Ate Angelica did for them, they are open to discussing their online sex work with whoever who asks. In this sense, the parents and siblings are aware of their activities even if they do not talk about the details.

Over time, I managed to meet some of Nadine's neighbours and cousins. They described Nadine's job as "panandalian kasi nag-iipon" (momentary while she saves money for her operation) and followed by a comment that "online lang naman kaya wala talagang nangyayari" (it is just online so nothing is really happening). With these life histories and narratives, I divide my analysis into two parts: (1) the patterns related to independence and sisterhood and (2) the formation and strategies of achieving specific goals as a young transwoman. These two parts will be discussed in the next two sections.

7 On Independence and Sisterhood

From the multi-pronged aspects of residential arrangements, economic needs, and management of romantic relationships (Lanz & Tagliabue 2007; Punch 2002; Sironi & Furstenberg 2012), the idea of longing for independence can be found among the youth globally. For the young transwomen who participated in this study, the freedom to live out the gender they identify with signifies independence. While there were challenges in expressing this desire to their families, the continuous efforts to live independently and support mostly from their mothers, helped in fostering acceptance in the home. A symbolic acceptance in the home is the changing of honorifics from "kuya" (elder brother) to "ate" (elder sister) by the younger siblings and cousins. As extended kin and neighbours hear this, they too start to teach small kids to call the young transwomen as ate or tita (aunt). Here, I find that the independence to live as a transwoman is collectively provided by families and neighbours.

In another aspect, connectedness through sisterhood, while often used to refer to relations between ciswomen (Chadwick & DeBlaere 2019; Gregorio 2018; Siegel 2007), is seen as Nadine and Kathryn interact with Angelica and her cohort. As a group sharing similar identities and forming their goals, sisterhood can be referred to in two relational ways. First as "friends" and second as "siblings." Friendship develops as they are introduced to each other while siblingship occurs as the generational hierarchies between the "ate" and the "bunso" (youngest sibling) are identified. These relationships intersect because both the acts of guiding and scolding are present in the interactions inside and outside their work stations. In one instance, Kathryn told me that she got scolded by Angelica because she did not tell them where she went for two days and they became worried for her safety.

When the young transwomen return home to visit, they sometimes ask their friends from the apartment to join and introduce them to their families. Parents also call them "anak" (child) and siblings also call them "Ate." I believe that this action of introducing fellow young transwomen to their families signals that the family does not have to worry about them doing online sex work because they are not alone, and they have friends who they can rely on if there are problems.

8 #Goals: Sex Operation and Settling Down

In theorizing cybersex as a service, I found that the long-term plan of these *transpinays* was to save enough money for various operations related to sex change and beautification. While beautification here refers to a dominantly Western standard of beauty (whiter skin, straight teeth, larger breasts and thighs), the point is that they plan it carefully and seriously.

The next major #Goals is to settle down. In Johnson (1997, 195), he found that his gay participants interpret live-in or cohabitation with a man as the "apex of possible gay men relationships… affirming of a man's true affection and of a gay's feminine identity." Similarly, I found that young transwomen attempt to forge romantic relations with their foreign clients online as they do not see potential partners in their own localities. Johnson (1997, 207) also highlighted how local relationships were seen as denying or subverting gays' transgender identities, while relationships abroad (such as in Sabah and Saudi Arabia) affirmed them. This is important to note because it shows how online sex work serves as a venue for the participants to meet men who they know will be open to having a relationship with transwomen and more importantly, are willing to take them overseas for marriage and lifelong partnership. This also stems from the fact that same-sex marriage and LGBT marriage is still not allowed in the Philippines. In 2017, the congress filed the House Bill 6595 or Civil Partnership Act to grant same-sex couples the same benefits and protection as spouses in marriage. However, the bill has not yet been voted on.

The key difference with my participants compared to Johnson's (1997) is that their goals for romantic relationships are complemented by their goals of sexual reassignment surgeries in Thailand. Moreover, the plans become more concrete as these women watch their Ates go through the process. From the passport application, selection of a clinic in Bangkok, to the actual operation and adjustments, access to information from these Ates is complemented by information online. Furthermore, despite the massive challenges associated with the surgery and with travel, Bangkok to them is seen as a "land of lady boys," a place where their dreams can become more of a reality.

9 Journey for Philippine LGBT Rights

Perhaps the biggest win for advocates of LGBT rights in the Philippines is the formation of *Ladlad* (Tagalog for unfolded) in 2003, which is the sole LGBTQ political party in Asia and the world (Radics 2019a). An even more recent win is Geraldine Roman's—the first nation's transgender politician—election to the House of Representatives in 2016. In terms of mass movements and organizations, large LGBT organizations have emerged, such as *Bahaghari* (Tagalog for rainbow) and Babaylan (based at the University of the Philippines).[4] While it is a major step for LGBT people to participate in the political arena, violence and stigma against transwomen is still prevalent.

In 2014, Jennifer Laude was killed by United States Marine Joseph Scott Pemberton in a motel room. According to reports, the two met in a bar while Pemberton was on a break after participating in military exercises in Olongapo City. Pemberton's lawyer asserted that "he acted to defend his honour when he discovered that Ms. Laude had a penis but that other factors led to the altercation, including his fear of being scammed" (Whaley 2015). The acceptance of "panic defence" in courts puts LGBT community members' lives in jeopardy as it serves as a justification for homicide and provides perpetrators a defence to escape punishment (Williams 2020). Furthermore, when Laude's German fiancée of four years, Marc Sueselbeck, scaled the fence of the military camp where Pemberton was then being detained, Sueselbeck's actions caused confusion among Filipinos. Pemberton's killing of Laude was understood as a crime but Sueselbeck's proclamation of love for Laude was deemed incomprehensible.

This case shows how violence against transwomen is prevalent in the sex work industry and how the stigma of transwomen being undeserving of true love is still present in Philippine society. In many ways, the young transwomen I interviewed arrange their plans carefully not just because of the desire to live as a woman and have a long-term life partner, but also because of fear of facing violence and possible death. Online sex work can be seen as a way for *transpinays* to protect themselves from violence, as the men on the other side of the camera cannot hurt them and can turn the camera off if they do not want the service of a transwoman. Chatting online is also their way of slowly revealing their identity and personal details with potential partners. According to Kathryn, conversations online give both sides time to get to know each other and for the man to decide if he is interested in pursuing a romantic relationship with a transwoman.

In September 2020, President Duterte issued a pardon to Pemberton. Activists and LGBT groups condemned the decision. Highlighting the intersection of gender, neocolonialism, and rights, the LGBT group Bahaghari

[4] For a more comprehensive perspective on the history of LGBT movements in the country, see (Evangelista 2017, 2018; Ramos 2014).

stated that, "For as long as the United States maintains hegemony over our military, economy, and politics, there will be no #JusticeForJennifer and for the Filipino LGBTQ+" (BBC News 2020).

10 Conclusion

To conclude, I return to the fields of sociology of youth and sociology of family. As the data demonstrates, generational relations are important in the youth-to-adult transition stage of young transwomen. The sisterhood from one cohort of elder transsisters to the younger ones, or from Angelica's cohort to Nadine/Kathryn's cohort, is vital in the learning process in two aspects. First is in terms of financial control and gender transitioning, and second is in terms of formation of life goals. Both Nadine and Kathryn shared that Angelica's cohort taught them how to negotiate for higher payment and for extra gifts from their regular clients. The social circle of the younger cohort also becomes wider as they meet more people through Angelica and they manage to establish their own networks. As discussed, these networks of transwomen allow younger cohorts to have more access to information about gender transitioning.

Additionally, the role of the family is very much visible in the youth-to-adult transition phase that these *transpinays* experienced. As the families do not stop these young transwomen from engaging in cybersex to save money, it also implies that they do not find issues with their transdaughters undergoing the said operation. This is because besides the fact that young transwomen are proving to their parents that they are self-sufficient, parents accept that after the operation, their *bakla* or *bayot* son will be coming back home as a daughter. Although reinforcing a problematic gender binary, the transition helps families recognize and make sense of the identity formations of their transchildren.

Going back to Laude's family, Talusan (2015) reported that Jennifer started to support her family, using income made from webcamming, gifts from foreign boyfriends, and local sex work in 2007 (when she was still 20 years old). Julita Laude, Jennifer's mother, similar to the parents of the young transwomen from Davao, did not know exactly what Jennifer was doing but knew that Jennifer was spending a lot of time on the internet at night. Julita was also fully aware that Jennifer identified as a woman and that she underwent breast implant surgery. As transwomen undergo operations and return home as daughters, parents, and siblings become more open to the idea that she will be marrying and settling down with her own family in the future. Thus, in Angelica's case, one can see her coming home as a woman and with a foreign partner. Sadly, for Jennifer, she was never able to achieve this as her life was cut short.

The despite the difficulties in passing legislation to protect LGBT people in the Philippines and elsewhere throughout the region, looking at its neighbours in Southeast Asia, I posit that there is still hope for the Catholic nation.[5] For instance, in Singapore, the LGBT movement called Pink Dot SG continues to grow and gain support despite government intervention to ban foreigners from participating in its annual gathering (Radics 2020, 2019b). In Malaysia, the work of Goh (2020) on transmen and their construction of their subjectivities vis-à-vis political and faith discourses also show the increasing visibility of the LGBT community. Similarly in Indonesia, Tumpag (2016) shows how transwomen communities proactively create their social space through establishing their own businesses and continuing to practice Islam as women. As we continue to expand our understanding of LGBT positionalities in the twenty-first century vis-à-vis sex work and new technologies, we have to recognize their views that it's not just about the money but rather about their own bodily autonomy and long-term life goals.

Acknowledgements This work was first presented at the Philippine Queer Studies Conference in October 2020 (via zoom). The author would like to thank the conference organizers and audience for providing comments and questions that refined the arguments of the paper. The author is also indebted to the NUS Sociology graduate students writing group participants who helped in the development of the manuscript. Lastly, the author is thankful to the editors, George Radics and Pablo Ciocchini for providing an early career scholar a space in this volume.

[5] Tugade reminded me that the Supreme Court in denying to strike out provisions in the family code that only recognizes marriage between a man and a woman, the court stated that "this Court sympathizes with the petitioner with his obvious longing to find a partner. We understand the desire of same-sex couples to seek, not moral judgment based on discrimination from any of our laws, but rather, a balanced recognition of their true, authentic, and responsive choices. Yet, the time for a definitive judicial fiat may not yet be here" (Jesus Nicardo M. Falcis, III Vs. Civil Registrar General, G.R. No. 217910. September 3, 2019. p. 107). Also, in 2019, the Safe Spaces Act was passed which prohibits gender-based harassment in the streets and public spaces. The law specifically protects against "misogynistic, transphobic, homophobic and sexist slurs" (Republic Act 11313: Safe Spaces Act, Sec. 4; *See also,* A. Madcasim abd C. Dayday [2019] *Defending "Safe Spaces": Hate Speech and the Constitutional Mandate to Uphold the Dignity of Communities. Philippine Law Journal,* Vol. 92, Iss. 4 (2019).

References

BBC News. 2020. Jennifer Laude Case: Duterte Pardons US Marine Over Transgender Killing. *BBC News*, September 8, 2020. https://www.bbc.com/news/world-asia-54063247.

Brown, Andy. 2016. Safe from Harm: Tackling Webcam Child Sexual Abuse in the Philippines. *UNICEF*, June 3, 2016. https://www.unicef.org/stories/safe-from-harm-tackling-webcam-child-sexual-abuse-philippines.

Chadwick, Caleb, and Cirleen DeBlaere. 2019. The Power of Sisterhood: The Moderating Role of Womanism in the Discrimination-Distress Link Among Women of Color in the United States. *Sex Roles* 81 (5–6): 326–337.

Chakrapani, Venkatesan, Peter A. Newman and Ernest Noronha. 2018. Hijras/Transwomen and Sex Work in India: From Marginalization to Social Protection. In *Transgender Sex Work and Society*, ed. L. Nuttbrock, 214–235. Harrington Park Press

Coopersmith, Jonathan. 2006. Does Your Mother Know What You *really* Do? The Changing Nature and Image of Computer-Based Pornography. *History and Technology* 22 (1): 1–25.

David, Emmanuel. 2015. Purple-Collar Labor: Transgender Workers and Queer Value at Global Call Centers in the Philippines. *Gender & Society* 29 (2): 169–194.

Evangelista, John Andrew G. 2017. Mula sa Kinaroroonang Ideolohiya: Kontrobersya Tungkol sa 'Unang' Pride March sa Pilipinas [From ideology: Controversy About 'First' Pride March in the Philippines.]" *Saliksik* 6 (2): 256–296.

Evangelista, John Andrew G. 2018. Beyond Partying: Characterizing the LGBTQ Movement in the Philippines. *Philippine Social Sciences Review* 70 (2): 45–74.

Goh, Joseph N. 2020. *Becoming a Malaysian Trans Man: Gender, Society, Body and Faith*. New York: Springer Singapore.

Gregorio, Veronica. 2018. The Only Exception: Teenage Pregnancy in the Philippines. *Review of Women's Studies* 28: 1–28.

Gregorio, Veronica. 2020. Farm and Familialism in Southeast Asia: Gender and Generational Relations in Malaysian and Philippine Villages. PhD Diss., National University of Singapore.

Health Policy Project, Asia Pacific Transgender Network, United Nations Development Programme. 2015. *Blueprint for the Provision of Comprehensive Care for Trans People and Trans Communities*. Washington, DC: Futures Group, Health Policy Project.

International Gay and Lesbian Human Rights Commission. 2012. Human Rights Violations on the Basis of Sexual Orientation, Gender Identity, and Homosexuality in the Philippines. *106th Session of the Human Rights Committee for the Fourth Periodic Review of the Philippines*. Geneva: UN Human Rights Committee

Johnson, Mark. 1995. Transgender Men and Homosexuality in the Southern Philippines: Ethnicity, Politicalviolence and the Protocols of Engendered Sexualities Amongst the Muslim Tausug and Sama". *South East Asia Research* 3 (1): 46–66.

Johnson, Mark. 1997. *Beauty and Power: Transgendering and Cultural Transformation in the Southern Philippines*. New York: Berg.

Johnson, Mark. 1998. Global Desirings and Translocal Loves: Transgendering and Same Sex Sexuality in the Southern Philippines. *American Ethnologist* 25 (4): 695–711.

Joseph-Collins, Nadine. 2012. Globalization and Discriminatory Practices Against Trans-Women in the Philippines. *International Forum* 15 (2): 85–101.

Lanz, Margherita, and Semira Tagliabue. 2007. Do I Really Need Someone in Order to Become an Adult? Romantic Relationships During Emerging Adulthood in Italy. *Journal of Adolescent Research* 22 (5): 531–549.

Law, Lisa. 2000. *Sex Work in Southeast Asia: The Place of Desire in a Time of AIDS*. London: Routledge.

Layug-Rosero, Regina. 2019. What You Should Know About the SOGIE Equality Bill. *Cosmopolitan*, September 19. https://www.cosmo.ph/lifestyle/sogie-bill-philippines-a613-20190919-lfrm.

Mathews, Paul William. 2017. Cam Models, Sex Work, and Job Immobility in the Philippines. *Feminist Economics* 23 (3): 160–183.

Parmanand, Sharmila. 2019. The Philippine Sex Workers Collective: Struggling to be Heard, Not Saved. *Anti-Trafficking Review* 12: 57–73.

Punch, Samantha. 2002. Youth Transitions and Interdependent Adult–Child Relations in Rural Bolivia. *Journal of Rural Studies* 18 (2): 123–133.

Radics, George. 2020. 'First World Problems' in the 'Third World'? LGBT Rights in Singapore. In *Cultural Dynamics, Political Tensions, and Institutional Practices*, ed. P. Ciocchini and G. Radics. London: Routledge.

Radics, George. 2019a. Human Rights in Asia. In *Global Encyclopedia of Lesbian, Gay, Bisexual, Transgender, and Queer (LGBTQ) History, ed.* H. Chiang et al., 1st ed. 784–789. Charles Scribner's Sons.

Radics, George. 2019b. "#Ready4Repeal? Viewing s 377A of the Singaporean Penal Code Through the Lens of Legal Actors and Artists. *Australian Journal of Asian Law* 20 (1): 1–14.

Radics, George. 2021. Challenging Antisodomy Laws in Singapore and the Former British Colonies of ASEAN. *Journal of Human Rights* 20 (2): 211–227.

Ramos, K. 2014. *History of the Filipino Lesbian Movement (1992–2013)*. Philippines: University of the Philippines.

Redfern, Corrine. 2019. In Philippine Red-Light District, an Uphill Struggle to Battle Trafficking and Abuses. *The Washington Post*, November 18, 2019. https://www.washingtonpost.com/world/asia-pacific/in-philippine-red-light-district-an-uphill-struggle-to-battle-trafficking-and-abuses/2019/11/17/43a6470a-bad3-11e9-b3b4-2bb69e8c4e39_story.html.

Redfern, Corrine. 2021. I'm Scared Every Damn Day: In the Philippines, Violence Shadows Trans Lives. *The Fuller Project*, January 7, 2021. https://fullerproject.org/story/im-scared-every-damn-day-in-the-philippines-violence-shadows-trans-lives/.

Restar, Arjee J., E. Karina Santamaria, Alexander Adia, Jennifer Nazareno, Randolph Chan, Mark Lurie, Theo Sandfort, Laufred Hernandez, Susan Cu-Uvin, and Don Operario. 2019. Gender Affirmative HIV Care Framework: Decisions on Feminizing Hormone Therapy (FHT) and Antiretroviral Therapy (ART) Among Transgender Women. *PLoS ONE* 14 (10): e0224133.

Siegel, Deborah. 2007. *Sisterhood, Interrupted: From Radical Women to Girls [Sic] Gone Wild*. London: Palgrave Macmillan.

Sironi, Maria, and Frank F. Furstenberg. 2012. Trends in the Economic Independence of Young Adults in the United States: 1973–2007. *Population and Development Review* 38 (4): 609–630.

Talusan, Meredith. 2015. How the Killing of a Trans Filipina Woman Ignited an International Incident. *Vice*, February 27. https://www.vice.com/en/article/xdm7b4/the-trial-of-a-us-marine-accused-of-killing-a-trans-filipina-woman-starts-today-will-he-go-free.

Tumpag, Laurence Anthonie. 2016. *Beyond Adat: Transwomen Boldly and Innovatively Navigating Their Communities in Central Java, Indonesia*. Illinois: Northern Illinois University.

Whaley, F. 2015. U.S. Marine Testifies in Killing of Transgender Woman in Philippines. *New York Times*. https://www.nytimes.com/2015/08/25/world/asia/us-marine-joseph-scott-pemberton-testifies-in-transgender-killing-in-philippines.html.

Williams, Jennifer. 2020. Ban 'Panic Defence', Save LGBTQ Lives. *Aljazeera*, October 22. https://www.aljazeera.com/opinions/2020/10/22/ban-panic-defence-save-lgbtq-lives.

Winter, Sam. 2009. Lost in Transition: Transpeople, Transprejudice and Pathology in Asia. *The International Journal of Human Rights* 13 (2–3): 365–390.

World Bank. 2019. *Individuals Using the Internet (% of Population)—Philippines*. World Bank. https://data.worldbank.org/indicator/IT.NET.USER.ZS?end=2019&locations=PH&start=1994&view=chart

Wyn, Johanna and Rob White. 1997. Chapter 5: Youth Transitions. In *Rethinking Youth*, 94–119. London: SAGE Publications.

14

A Queer *Chinkhoswe*: Re-imagining the Customary in Malawi

Nigel Timothy Mpemba Patel

1 Introduction

In December 2009, the headline on the front-page of The Nation newspaper in Blantyre, Malawi, read "Gays Engage!" (Somanje 2009). Reporting on the *chinkhoswe,* a traditional Malawian matrimonial agreement ceremony,[1] held between Tiwonge Chimbalanga Kachepa (hereafter Tiwonge) and Steven Monjeza Soko (hereafter Steven), the story propelled queerness into the contemporary Malawian political arena. Subsequently, in the criminal case *of R v Steven Monjeza Soko and Tiwonge Chimbalanga Kachepa* (hereafter *R v Soko and Kachepa*) the couple were charged and convicted under provisions of the Penal Code: Steven for "buggery or having carnal knowledge of the second accused," and Tiwonge for "buggery or … permitting the first accused person to have carnal knowledge of him against the order of nature" (*R v Soko and Kachepa*, 2). In the alternative, they were both charged and convicted for "the offence of indecent practices between males" (ibid.).

[1] The Chichewa term *chinkhoswe* is often translated as an engagement ceremony as it sometimes is in the *R v Soko and Kachepa* judgment. However, the term 'engagement' often implies a later marriage ceremony. This is not always the case in the Malawian context and shows the difficulty with translation. The ceremony is in fact one form of a valid marriage that can be enter into. Thus, the translation I prefer is matrimonial agreement ceremony.

N. T. M. Patel (✉)
United Kingdom Supreme Court, Solicitor, UK
e-mail: nigeltpatel@gmail.com

G. B. Radics and P. Ciocchini (eds.), *Criminal Legalities and Minorities in the Global South*, Palgrave Socio-Legal Studies, https://doi.org/10.1007/978-3-031-17918-1_14

The maximum sentence of "14 years imprisonment with hard labour" was delivered for the main conviction of "buggery and permitting buggery" (ibid., 21). Re-reading the newspaper article now, I recall being troubled by how the press framed the story as a gay marriage between two men. I later came to understand why this was when I learnt that Tiwonge, who was assigned male at birth, identified and was largely socially accepted as a woman. Nonetheless, the events were a lesson in prejudice to queer[2] Malawi that our sexual and gender identities were condemned and acting upon them would criminalize us.

Reflecting on this moment a decade later, I realize that the *chinkhoswe*, beyond simply platforming queer life in Malawi, also positioned queerness in a direct relationship with local customs. Hence, this chapter will unpack the relationship between queerness within customs through the significant Malawian tradition of *chinkhoswe*. An analysis of the literature contextualises Steven and Tiwonge's *chinkhoswe*, giving rise to and framing the question: Where does the queer African appear, if at all, in the customary? (Hoad 2016, 1). This provides the basis of a critique of the *R v Soko and Kachepa* judgment. That is, it fails to take living customary law seriously and entrenches the narrative that queerness is 'un-African'. The chapter then considers an interview with Tiwonge which locates her as a queer African figure within custom, culture and traditional practice. In doing so, I hope to show the complexities and possibilities of overcoming criminal law through queering the customary.

The regulation and criminalization of queer Africans has occurred through law and politics in an international, national and customary context. These regimes address queerness in differing ways which create discourses that speak on, for and against queerness (Hoad 2016, 1). Steven and Tiwonge's *chinkhoswe* is a moment that highlights the tension between these differing regimes. This first section will firstly explore the historical place of queerness in Malawi, and then draw from the literature on Steven and Tiwonge's *chinkhoswe* in relation to anti-queer national legislation and international human rights law. The chapter then will engage in a discussion on the politics concerning queerness in Malawi through the customary practice of *chinkhoswe* by first examining the criminal law arguments deployed in *R v Soko and Kachepa*, and then the same event as experienced by Steven

[2] An umbrella term, not a closed list and not to be confused with a one-size-fits all idea. Often understood to mean those marginalized based on sex, sexuality and gender. Indicative of the diversity within sex, gender and sexuality and so operating to promote association between those who transgress cisnormativity and heteronormativity.

and Tiwonge (Kabwila 2013, 376). The chapter will demonstrate how the responses to Steven and Tiwonge's *chinkhoswe* are the product of the fraught history of queer genders and sexualities in Malawi. Accordingly, I suggest the *chinkhoswe* and surrounding events—dominantly represented as a moment of urgent crisis or the product of psychologized African homophobia—cannot be robustly understood without recognition of the historical impact of colonisation on gender and sexuality, and the criminalization of LGBT identities, in Malawi and the wider Africa.

2 A Queer Legal History of Malawi

The Republic of Malawi can be found in south-eastern Africa, comprising several Bantu ethnic groups, Asians and Europeans. As a British protectorate from 1891 to 1964, many of its laws, including the criminalization of same-sex activity (particularly between males), and more widely queerness in Malawi, was in its origin a result of British imposition. The first codification of colonial sodomy laws occurred during the British rule of India in 1825 (Kirby 2011). The Indian Penal Code (1860) which later spread to other British colonies criminalized a variety of sexual acts such as thigh sex, oral sex, anal sex or any form of intimacy that was not related to procreation. The ideology behind the punishment and stigmatization of queerness was based on Victorian interpretations of Christian morality, which condemned transgressive genders and sexualities (Browne 2017; Johnston 1987, 408). The colonial preoccupation with same-sex sex between males had a basis in anxieties that these acts undermined significant material interests of the colonies (Jeater 1993, 194–195). That is, the healthy male body, a central source for labour extraction for the colonial project, was threatened by the 'sodomite' (Biruk 2014; Epprecht 2013).

Queerness in Malawi did not however begin at colonisation, pre-colonial Malawi had a long history of queerness (Msibi 2011). The forceful colonial shaping of sexualities and genders should not result in the romanticisation of queerness in pre-Colonial Africa. Heteronormativity was still pervasive. Transgressive sexualities and genders were topics that were largely erased from the Malawian discourse. Colonialism supported and magnified this. The introduction of Victorian Christian morality further altered the gender and sexual practice of pre-colonial African societies. The laws in place during the colonial period, including the penal laws criminalizing male same-sex sex, remained in place after Malawi gained its independence in 1964 (Mwakasungula 2013). Along with these laws, the negative perceptions towards queerness also persisted and continue to colour the dominant socio-political landscape (Mawerenga 2018; Msosa 2018; The Other Foundation 2019).

In post-colonial Malawi, queerness becomes more complicated. The case of *R v Soko and Kachepa* occurred in a historical context where queerness was largely erased. Thus, the public ceremony that the couple held incited and exposed the interaction between national, international, customary law and politics. National laws, rooted in colonialism, were used to prosecute the couple, and this section considers these laws and the national and governmental rhetoric surrounding them. In the international sphere, relevant human rights law on the issue and the international politics of donor funding are currently a key force shaping the ways queerness is perceived in Malawi. Much of the academic literature on Steven and Tiwonge's case is seen through an international lens. There are sufficiently fewer culturally focused sources on the queer *chinkhoswe*, and those that exist are often from traditional authorities and are largely dismissive of the act. There are however other sources that have begun to explore the relationship between the way queer people currently interact with African culture (Hoad 2016; Biruk 2014). These sources help to begin to locate the queer African in the customary.

At the national level, Malawi adopted a final Constitution with a Bill of Rights in 1995. Section 20(1) provides that:

> Discrimination of persons in any form is prohibited and all persons are, under any law, guaranteed equal and effective protection against discrimination on grounds of race, colour, sex, language, religion, political or other opinion, nationality, ethnic or social origin, disability, property, birth or other status. (Constitution of the Republic of Malawi 1995)

While gender or sexuality are not included, this is not a closed list. It is possible that their inclusion could be argued for under "other status". Despite this, Malawi's laws continue to persecute queerness. A violation of equal protection, section 153 of the Malawi Penal Code, which Tiwonge and Steven were convicted under, deals with "unnatural offences". It states that:

> Any person who—
> (a) has carnal knowledge of any person against the order of nature;
> (b) has carnal knowledge of an animal; or
> (c) permits a male person to have carnal knowledge of him or her against the order of nature,

shall be guilty of a felony and shall be liable to imprisonment for fourteen years, with or without corporal punishment. (Malawi Penal Code 1999, §153)

Furthermore, Section 156 deals with "indecent practices between males". It states that:

> Any male person who, whether in public or private, commits any act of gross indecency with another male person, or procures another male person to commit any act of gross indecency with him, or attempts to procure the commission of any such act by any male person with himself or with another male person, whether in public or private, shall be guilty of a felony and shall be liable to imprisonment for five years, with or without corporal punishment. (Malawi Penal Code 1999, §156)

Following the conviction of the couple under these laws, a series of comments from government officials condemned Tiwonge and Steven. The Deputy Minister of Information and Civic Education is noted as having said "that as far as the Malawi government was concerned there were only two homosexuals in Malawi namely Steven Monjeza and Tiwonge Chimbalanga" (Kumintengo 2012, 23). Disregarding the existence of queer Malawians, the words contribute to the historical project of queer erasure. It was also stated that "if there were any other homosexuals in country they were to come out in the open and face arrests" (ibid.). Following this, the Malawian Police Force embarked on a directive to arrest and prosecute queer people (Smith 2010).

The tactic of positioning queerness as foreign to Malawian culture was also being reproduced at the highest level of government. The president at the time, Bingu Wa Mutharika, stated that Tiwonge and Steven had "committed a crime against our culture, our religion and our laws" (Browne 2017, 10). Furthermore he "is on record to have vowed that under his leadership he would never legalise homosexuality" (Kumintengo 2012, 23). In line with his statements, the national movement was in fact regressive. Parliament further criminalized queerness in November 2010 by passing the Penal Code Amendment Bill which was then ratified by the president in January 2011 (McKay and Angotti 2016, 399). The amendment in the provision section 137(a) deals with "indecent practices between females". It states that:

> Any female person who, whether in public or private, commits any act of gross indecency with another female person, or procures another female person to commit any act of gross indecency with her, or attempts to procure the commission of any such act by any female person with herself or with another female person, whether in public or private, shall be guilty of an offence and shall be liable to imprisonment for five years. [Malawi Penal Code 1999, §137(a)]

The Malawian High Court announced a review on the constitutionality of the anti-queer laws in 2013, but there has been no decision on the issue since the initial announcement. In 2014, a moratorium on the anti-queer laws was announced by the government (US Department of State 2016). However, this moratorium was challenged by religious leaders and subsequently annulled by the Mzuzu High Court (UK Home Office 2017). Arrests of queer Malawians still continue to take place (Kalimira 2018). Additionally, the Marriage Divorce and Family Act (hereafter the MDFA Act) came into force in 2015. This Act recognizes the validity and equal status of civil marriages to customary marriages, religious marriages and marriages by repute or cohabitation. However, the capacity to enter a marriage is limited to "persons of the opposite sex" (MDFA 2015, §14). In a similarly reductionist move, sex is defined as being "in relation to the gender of a person, means the sex of that person at birth" (MDFA 2015, §2). This gender essentialist and homophobic law functions to keep marriage out of the reach of queer Malawians (Demone 2016, 384).

While changes to national law may highlight an increasingly anti-queer position, the place and perceptions of queerness in Malawi is also shaped by international action, through law and politics. Malawi is party to many international treaties that contain human rights provisions for protections of queer people.[3] However, these only go so far. Kabwila (2013, 376) states that the international human rights discourse is "imperial, parasitic and [one of] vulture character." While this is a severe critique, this position does raise a problem in the human rights narrative which "depicts an epochal contest pitting savages, on the one hand, against victims and saviours, on the other" (Mutua 2001, 201). In international law, discussions of human rights this can result in an essentialized reduction of Malawian culture as an anti-queer monolith. This feeds into the national narrative by masking queer voices that emanate from within the Malawian cultural discourse.

[3] These include the African Charter, United Nations Convention Against Torture, Convention on the Elimination of Discrimination Against Women, CRC, International Covenant on Civil and Political Rights (ICCPR), ICCPR Optional Protocol and International Covenant on Economic, Social and Cultural Rights.

Additionally, the linkage between human rights and international donor aid has contributed to framing the queer movement for freedom as a foreign agenda (Biruk 2014). This "can jeopardize increased awareness, education and information on LGBTI issues through constructive civil debate" (Browne 2017, 26). Aptly diagnosing the problem, Sharra (2012) writes that Western donors' "loud pronouncements have wrecked the chances of local ownership in the debate and created the appearance of a foreign agenda that is using the economic vulnerability of African governments and their over-dependence on aid to engage in what is being seen as cultural imperialism." In Malawi, these neo-colonial undercurrents contribute to the resentment towards queerness. This further casts the human rights discourse as an external intrusion and has a negative impact on the possibility for indigenous ownership of the queer movement.

Yet, signalling the importance of international action on the lives of queer Malawians, Tiwonge and Steven were pardoned by President Mutharika following an instructive visit by the UN Secretary General Ban Ki Moon (Biruk 2014, 449). The Malawian public's responses largely involved debates on whether the President was "correct 'to bow down to the West'" manipulating queerness into a proxy for issues of national sovereignty (ibid.).

3 Customary Laws and Chinkhoswe

The customary law in Malawi, whilst not homogenous, is largely matrilineal, as this system is applied in more geographical areas than the patrilineal system. Two central differences between the systems are that in a matrilineal system "when a man marries, he goes to live in the woman's village" and the children born to married women are affiliated to her and her village (Roberts 1964, 77; See also Mwabene 2005). However, in a patrilineal system the woman moves to the man's village and the children are affiliated to him. Neither of these is a strict practice; in each system parties can agree on variations or to depart from the custom depending on circumstances. The matrilineal system is the one under which Steven and Tiwonge had their *chinkhoswe* so I will only be considering this system. While matrilineal practices differ slightly across tribes, there are "common features in terms of conducting their marriages" (Mwabene 2005, 7).

It is also important to note the difference between official *customary law* and *living customary law*. Official customary law is customary law that has been codified (Grant 2006, 16). It is "the customary law captured in statute and precedent, and was directly influenced by … English legal principles."

(Himonga and Nhlapo 2014, 16). This form has largely been cast under colonial and patriarchal dominance (ibid.). Incorporated into statute and the system of precedent, the hybrid customary principles created under these oppressive systems are cemented in the official customary law. Conversely, the living customary law is flexible (Himonga and Bosch 2000). It is constituted by people's practices, "namely what they do and believe they ought to do as opposed to just what the state and courts believe they ought to do" (ibid., 319).

Under living customary law, there are generally five main requirements for a valid Malawian matrilineal customary marriage. The first requirement is capacity (Mwabene 2005, 10). This is largely centred on reaching adulthood, which is not attained at an exact age but rather after the completion of initiation. Secondly, the consent of the *ankhoswe* (marriage guardian)[4] "is essential for the validity of a person's marriage" (Mwabene 2005, 11).[5] This has been emphasised by the courts in *Manchichi v. Manuel* (Case No. 1 of 1979 N.T.A.C. [Malawi]) where the court found, "[w]e know that marriage is a social agreement between two persons, but in order that such marriage may acquire legal recognition under traditional customary law, the agreement must be sanctioned by the establishment of *chinkhoswe*." Thirdly, initiation—or having engaged in ceremonies that mark adulthood, such as circumcision for males, or virginity rituals for girls—is often a constitutive element of marriage capacity. However, at present, "this requirement is being disregarded" (Mwabene 2005, 13). The fourth requirement is "the acquisition of the right to cohabit" which arises from the consent of marriage guardians (ibid.). The fifth requirement is a marriage payment in the form of a chicken (ibid.). In addition to these requirements, there are common formalities that are often observed, whilst not essential, such as "the assent of parents and elders" (ibid.). Overall, the literature on customary marriages is largely in terms of cisgender heterosexual couples, but there is nothing to suggest that a marriage outside of this would not be valid.

Evident in the consideration of these requirements is the adaptability of living customary law. Embracing this dynamic nature, Steven and Tiwonge conducted a *chinkhoswe*. The living customary law provided them with the space to inhabit the customary. Despite this, the perception that queerness is foreign and corrupts the Malawian cultural fabric persists within the minds

---

[4] Known as *ankhoswe* in Chichewa also translates to marriage advocate for the *chinkhoswe*. Generally, the title given to the senior brother or maternal uncle of each spouse. See also BP Wanda (1988, 126–128).

[5] See also *Mbewe v Nyirenda* Civil Appeal No. 49 of 2003 HC (Mzuzu Registry) (Unreported) where Court noted marriage guardian was necessary requirement for valid customary marriage.

of many Malawians (Mwakasungula 2013, 359). Following the arrest of Tiwonge and Steven, like the government and religious leaders, traditional leaders also condemned queerness as un-Malawian (Malamba 2012, 39). In a study done by Malamba (2012), a focus group was held with four traditional leaders. Similarly to the state president, they all "agreed that same-sex relationships are alien to Malawian culture," speaking about queerness as a Western phenomenon (ibid.).[6] One traditional leader commenting "[t]his is not how we were taught by our parents to live. This is not part of our culture. These are things coming from the white people" (ibid.). Underlying this response is the idea that queerness in the post-colony should be rejected in the customary because queerness is racialized as exclusively within the paradigm of whiteness. Furthermore, entangled with the cultural rejection of queerness is religion. The colonial context produced a hybrid Christian customary. Thus, the position of institutions like the Malawi Council of Churches (MCC) who argue that queerness contradicts "Malawi's rich traditions, culture, and its spirituality as a God-fearing nation" fuels the abstraction of queerness from culture (Bvumbe 2011).

The rejection of queerness in Malawi on the basis of culture pervades all levels of Malawian society. Notably, those who use religion to argue that queerness is un-African from a cultural standpoint have been critiqued as being duplicitous. Mutua (2011, 460) points out that the imposition of religion, particularly Christianity, as a colonial tool to dominate Africans is often overlooked. Malawian culture is then paradoxically conceptualized as rejecting queerness on the basis of it being foreign, while Christianity is authentically embraced into its culture. Despite the fact that the notion of queerness as un-African is historically inaccurate, the inconsistency here shows that the rejection of queerness on a cultural basis is not logically based on it being alien. Furthermore, the hybridly Christian customary is a further indicator of the flexibility and adaptability of custom, culture and tradition. Mutua's critique also picks up on the traditional leaders "rush to talk about culture like it is a pure concept" (Kabwila 2013, 387). Traditional leaders, acting in a despotic fashion, essentialize Malawian cultural discourses. This contributes to state and religious sponsorship of queerphobia. This, in turn, feeds into the international narrative that depicts African culture monolithically. Thus, the grand effect is that queer cultural subjectivity is masked on an international, national and customary level.

[6] However, see also Msosa (2019). This study deals in part with traditional approaches to queer terminology. Msosa highlights that people expressed more tolerant views to queerness when indigenous language was used to discuss it.

4 The "Crime Against Malawian Culture": A Queer *Chinkhoswe*

Based on the legal and customary structure discussed earlier, the court in *R v Soko and Kachepa* judgment ruled that Steven and Tiwonge's *chinkhoswe* was a "crime against Malawian culture." While many scholars have focused on their analysis of the court's decision by interrogating its conflict with the Malawian Constitution and international law (Phooko 2011), my critique draws from Crystal Biruk (2014) and Neville Hoad's (2016) evaluations of the judgment, locating queerness within the customary. As will be discussed, the court in *R v Soko and Kachepa* positions itself as the sole authority on Malawian culture, and in the process fails to take customary law seriously. At the core of this is a tension between an official customary law approach to the law and a living customary approach to the law. The former manifests as a rigidly hierarchical approach to customary law which functions to preserves cisnormativity and heteronormativity, while the latter, the flexible approach, provides endless possibilities for queering.

Faced with the existence of queerness within custom, in the form of a perceived gay *chinkhoswe*, the court places itself as the guardian of Malawian culture. The court concludes, based solely on the prosecution's argument, that a matrimonial agreement "in a Malawian setting indeed takes place between a man and a woman" (*R v. Soko and Kachepa* 2010, 15). The judgment makes it clear that they view the traditional matrimonial agreement between Steven and Tiwonge as abhorrent (Kumintengo 2012). The irony in this case is that the two accused were largely recognized in the community as man and woman. Furthermore, the perception that the accused were both men conducting a gay marriage also emphasises how living, community recognized, customs provide a space for a queer challenge to formal Malawian criminal laws that have been politicized.

The court states that the queer *chinkhoswe* "transgresses the Malawian recognized standards of propriety since it does not recognize the living of a man with another as husband and wife" (*R v. Soko and Kachepa* 2010, 16). The court's interpretation of customary law here bypasses any consideration of the community who participated in the *chinkhoswe*. This is indicative of an attempt to appropriate the power to speak authoritatively on Malawian customary law. Rather than moving towards the plurality of authority that is associated to living customary law, the court's approach reinforces an interpretation of customary law that keeps it outside the reach of queer Malawians and the wider population. Not dissimilar to the traditional authorities, the court attempts to become a cultural despot.

This is further evident in the sentence that the court handed down. The judgement states that Malawian society is not "ready at this point in time to see sons getting married to other sons … or smile at her daughters marrying each other" (*R v. Soko and Kachepa* 2010, 23). The *chinkhoswe* is "not seen as simply a breach of the Penal Code, but termed … a 'crime against Malawi's culture'" (Price 2011, 553). Assuming the self-constructed role of cultural custodians, the court entrenches the idea that queerness is foreign to Malawian culture. The judgement in fact likens the couple's actions to the crime of hijacking. This culminates in what the judge refers to as a "scaring sentence" of the maximum fourteen years imprisonment with hard labour (*R v. Soko and Kachepa* 2010, 24). Queerness is made foreign to Malawian culture as it is cast as a corrupting influence on morality.

Despite dismissing the *chinkhoswe* as invalid, the judgement does however contain slight ambivalence to the possibility that the *chinkhoswe* was legitimately held under customary law. The court refers to the *chinkhoswe* ceremony as an "engagement or purported engagement" (*R v. Soko and Kachepa* 2010, 19). Furthermore, the defence, arguing for a mitigation of sentence, states that "sending them [the couple] to prison is like sending married people to prison" (*R v. Soko and Kachepa* 2010, 23). The court finds this argument "grossly wrong" for equating the queer *chinkhoswe*, monikered referred to as "a bizarre marriage", to the "normal practice of any other lawful marriage in Malawi" (ibid.). Despite this, these moments of ambivalence are signifiers of queer custom. They call us to ask what might have happened had the state not intervened (Hoad 2016, 10). The custom in this situation had provided for this "bizarre" re-imagining of cultural practice: a re-imagining which rendered culture incomprehensible to the courts who could not see the customs beyond the historical shackles of cisnormativity and heterosexuality.

Furthermore, in positioning itself as a cultural authority, the court does not take living custom seriously. The court never looked at whether the *chinkhoswe* could have been valid. The judgment fossilises the interpretation that customary law's exclusion of queerness is in line with the Penal Code's criminalisation of same-sex relations. Customary law is instrumentalized insofar as the *chinkhoswe* becomes solely a tool to determine whether the couple had anal sex. In a clear parallel to the colonial administration, there is a preoccupation with same-sex relations between perceived men, reducing the proliferations of queer cultural experiences down to the simple act of anal sex. Yet the court's approach—privileging official customary law—is troubled by Tiwonge's queering of gender (*R v. Soko and Kachepa* 2010, 9). This is particularly due to Tiwonge's cultural existence as a woman within living custom where gender is not determined by the physical body. In using a medical examination of Tiwonge to determine her gender, the court places on a pedestal the sex-gender binary that queer Malawi subverts.

> Underlying the [witness] testimonies are hints that Tiwonge was a proper woman in many ways—attending church regularly and seeking to follow traditional womanly protocols for a proper engagement and marriage to Steven. Retrospectively, then, we might read the series of acts recalled during the trial—a pastor's agreement to take on a role as a traditional marriage counsellor (*ankhoswe*) to the couple when asked by Steven, the engagement photographer's willingness to serve as a marriage advocate for Tiwonge, the loaning of *zitenje* [traditional waxed cotton fabric] to Tiwonge by Flony, the admission of Tiwonge into a church congregation as a woman, and her employment in women's work at a lodge—as individual acts that accumulatively verified Tiwonge as a 'woman' in her community. Indeed, locally, Tiwonge was known by the nickname 'Auntie Tiwo'. (Biruk 2014, 458)

Inherent in the living customary law is the possibility for queer manifestation. This is not to say that living customary law is not laden with exclusionary sex, gender, and sexuality norms. Rather, living customary law allows these exclusionary norms to be contested in ways which can be productive to forming radical communal and relational conceptions of sex, gender, and sexuality that go beyond biological categories and determinism.

The mere inclusion of queerness in official customary law is not a desirable solution for queer equality. The possibility for queer people to utilize the changing living customary landscape is limited under official customary law. The attempt to codify, i.e. solidify, queerness, which by its nature is fluid, is futile. Codification will likely reinstate colonial and patriarchal principles within the relationships of queer Malawians. On the other hand, an approach to queer jurisprudence informed by the idea of living customary law allows for the creation of queer imaginaries that go beyond the present way in which we view relationships and ourselves.

5 It's Our Culture Too: Re-imagining the Customary

Despite the court asserting itself as an authority capable of "protecting" Malawian culture, this final section will explore the actual experience of Steven and Tiwonge's *chinkhoswe*, from the lenses of both personal and the customary. Amid growing interest in and attention to how African experiences can challenge some of the assumptions of dominant Anglo-European queer theory (see Watson 2010), I decided to interview Tiwonge, who was largely objectified during the *chikhoswe* affair, rather than framed as a thinker and bearer of queer theory.[7] The in-depth interview was carried out face to face in Chichewa,[8] recorded and then transcribed and translated into English. The included selections from the interview are in no way a full representation of Tiwonge and her experiences. However, her narrative is a valuable account of the experiences and thoughts of a Malawian whose labour has contributed to the queering of the customary. The analysis of the qualitative interview with Tiwonge shows the agency that queer people can exercise in their occupation of the customary.

5.1 Pre-*chinkhoswe*

While this chapter focuses on the *chinkhoswe*, this should not be taken to reduce queer Malawian cultural existence to this sole tradition. Rather, the *chinkhoswe* has become the site of the main cultural contestations concerning queerness. In my general observations, the *chinkhoswe* is a tradition through which many Malawians view their and others' relationships to Malawian culture.

Importantly, Tiwonge's existence as a simultaneously cultural and queer figure extends well before the *chinkhoswe*. Tiwonge commented that when questioned about her gender, by people who perceived her as a man, she would explain to them that:

> In my village, I lived with my uncle, chief Chimbalanga. He saw that I was a girl. When people were rude to me, he told me not change anything about myself and that I was a girl from the home of the Chimbalangas.

> I am a woman, like any other woman, like your mother, your sister. I was born a girl, but I was bewitched.

> I am a woman like the wife you go home to every night.

[7] Steven, the other party to the *chinkhoswe*, passed away in 2012. The couple were no longer in a relationship at the time of his passing.

[8] The main language used in Malawi.

Tiwonge's recollections of all her responses to moments where her gender had been put under interrogation drew on culture and relationships. Echoing the witness statements in the *R v Soko and Kachepa* judgment, Tiwonge was culturally accepted as a woman. This upholds Oyewumi's (2002, 4) analysis that "in many African cultures … relationships have little to do with the nature of human bodies." That is, beyond the western system of biological determinism, Tiwonge's gender is culturally situated and affirmed by her membership in kinship structures.

The gendered affirmation Tiwonge experienced within the customary can perhaps explain her comfort to adapt cultural practices to suit her position in context of the *chinkhoswe*. This queer occupation destabilizes the traditional imperative towards biological family and reproductive futurity as the only legitimate framework to build worlds.

Despite the judgment referring to the *chinkhoswe* as a "bizarre" practice, the fact remains that queer Malawians have been privately having *chinkhoswes* (Gevisser 2014). The only difference with Steven and Tiwonge was that they had a public ceremony.

Having framed the focus of this chapter on culture, there are two things that I want to draw from Tiwonge's experience. Firstly, culture constitutes a site for resistance. This is denoted when Tiwonge points out in her interview that she had done nothing wrong culturally by having a *chinkhoswe*. This contests the idea put across by the court in the *R v Soko and Kachepa* judgment that the Penal Codes' criminalization of same-sex sex accords with custom. Instead, Tiwonge's account shows how custom is a potential source of defiance against laws crafted in the colonial period. Secondly, the police questioning of Tiwonge on whether the *chinkhoswe* was in fact staged for financial reward illustrates the potential negative effect of international aid on Malawian queer resistance. The politicization of donor aid in a Malawian cultural context robs queers of narratives that might centre their agency, rather than framing them as 'bought' by the West.

Building on this idea of resistance, Tiwonge presented a challenge to the Malawian or queer dichotomy.

> People have said that what I did was not Malawian, many people still speak about it today. They say that I am not Malawian because of the way I acted. I am from Malawi. I was born into the family of a chief, traditional authority Chimbalanga. I was born and bred in Malawi. Yes, people say a lot of things, but I am Malawian.

Tiwonge's assertion of ethnic belonging demonstrates the connections between Malawian culture and queerness. This offers a notable shift in the knowledge, views and discourses concerning queerness which helps to make connections with pre-colonial histories of queerness in Malawi.

Culture provides a powerful resource for queer people to assert their interests. Speaking on politics and culture, Tiwonge simultaneously claims her Malawianess and queerness. Culture is conceptualized as furthering a pluralist agenda, and in doing so, enables social change. Resisting the systematic silencing and denial of queerness that was instigated during colonisation, Tiwonge's cultural labour works to "unmute, unsee, and unlearn the outright erasure of multiple forms of evidence of queerness" (Nyanzi 2015, 134).

In my final interview with Tiwonge, she highlighted the importance of solidarity, both in an inter-queer sense and across differing cultures. This resonates with my definition of queer.[9] Making connections between the cultural experiences of people with transgressive sexes, sexualities or genders across Malawi and the wider Africa can expand the struggle against persecutory laws. This solidarity requires the building of relationships with people no matter how different we seem at the surface.

6 Conclusion

As in all cultures, there is an unmistakeable history of queerness in Malawian culture. The contemporary international, national and cultural systems that speak for and against queerness often cast or recast culture in confined ways that mask the complex relationship between culture and queerness. The *chinkhoswe* in many ways defines Malawian norms of gendered and sexual behaviour. Thus, while sexuality and gender imaginaries that implicate exclusionary norms are still at play in the queer *chinkhoswe*, it creates the possibility for queer Africans to begin to re-imagine the customary outside of heterosexual and cisgender norms. This possibility provides a mode for queers Africans to desire and resist in a way that furthers a queer African futurity.

Queerness and custom are both amorphous: the fluidity of queerness is complimented by the flexibility of living custom. In many ways "Queerness is not yet here. Queerness is an ideality … a structuring and educated mode

[9] See Footnote 2.

of desiring that allows us to see and feel beyond the quagmire of the present" (Muñoz 2009, 1). In a similar fashion, the *chinkhoswe* is a tradition that constitutes a possible future. It reveals the possibilities for the diverse queer community to further entwine queerness with culture. Thus, the queering of the *chinkhoswe* allows for us to "dream and enact new and better pleasures, other ways of being in the world, and ultimately new worlds" (ibid.).

Marriage has been roundly critiqued for being a cisnormative, heteronormative and patriarchal institution (Conrad and Nair 2010). This raises the valid concern: is a queer customary marriage possible at all? Or is what we have here, in Steven and Tiwonge's *chinkhoswe,* an African form of homonormativity and transnormativity? This chapter offers one explanation: when queerness is allowed to destabilize legal discourses and entrenched criminal laws centred around official interpretations of customary law, the cisnormative, heteronormative and patriarchal institution of marriage becomes challenged. Steven and Tiwonge's *chinkhoswe* configures living customs as a site of queer struggle. Recognizing the queerness in living customary law allows us to then celebrate this queer *chinkhoswe*, without making it the archetype of queerness. Under a living customary lens the queer *chinkhoswe* is just one of many articulations of queer Malawi. In other words, it only marks a moment in the development of a radical queer politics. A politics that is not just inclusionary of queerness under culture, as a form of tolerance, but one that reconfigures the ordinary. This *chinkhoswe* teaches us to look at queer lives first and hold culture accountable to what we need, rather than looking to culture to see how much of queer life can be fit into it.

This chapter presents a reading of queerness and culture in the Malawian locale, offering a "relational, historicized, and contextualized understanding" of queerness in Malawi (Spurlin 2001, 186). This provides the basis of a critique of the *R v Soko and Kachepa* judgment which highlights the importance of living custom for developing a flexible and non-prescriptive archive and future for queer Malawian culture.

Steven and Tiwonge's *chinkhoswe,* an example of living custom, provides an entry point into thinking about queerness in decolonised terms, a thinking "that neither follow[s] the prescriptive and [often] colonising human rights discourse" and troubles "the essentialism of Malawian culture" (Kabwila 2013, 376–377). I have argued that Steven and Tiwonge's *chinkhoswe* subverts the idea that queerness is un-African. Furthermore, the interview lifts the shadow cast by political and legal regimes to show that Tiwonge is a queer figure who exercises agency within the customary. Looking closely at the queer *chinkhoswe,* a decade after it happened, it serves as a reminder that the dichotomy between Malawian culture and queerness is false; that is, one can embrace queerness and culture at the same time. This creates the possibility for queer Malawians and queer Africans to begin re-imagining the customary and our relationships to it.

Tiwonge Chimbalanga (Aunty T)
Image used with permission from Iranti-Org

References

Laws

Constitution of the Republic of Malawi, 1995.
Marriage, Divorce and Family Relations Act of 2015 (Malawi).
The Penal Code Amendment Act of 2011 (Malawi).
The Penal Code Chapter 7:01 of the Laws of Malawi [as amended to Act No. 8 of 1999].
The Indian Penal Code of 1860 (India).

International Instruments

UN Committee on Economic, Social and Cultural Rights, General comment no. 21, Right of everyone to take part in cultural life (art. 15, para. 1a of the Covenant on Economic, Social and Cultural Rights), 21 December 2009, E/C.12/GC/21.

Cases

Doreen Chikayera v Manuel Mteteka Civil Cause No. 70 of 2004, Mulunguzi Magistrate Court (Unreported).
Manchichi v. Manuel Civil Appeal Case No. 1 of 1979, N.T.A.C. (Unreported).
Mbewe v Nyirenda Civil Appeal No. 49 of 2003 HC (Mzuzu Registry) (Unreported).
R v Steven Monjeza Soko and Tiwonge Chimbalanga Kachepa 2010 MWHC 2 (Malawi Chief Resident Magistrate's Court).

Articles and Books

Biruk, Crystal. 2014. Aid for Gays': The Moral and the Material in 'African Homophobia' in Post-2009 Malawi. *The Journal of Modern African Studies* 52 (3): 447–473.
Browne, Philip. 2017. *Canaries in the Coal Mines: An Analysis of Spaces for LGBTI Activism in Malawi Country Report*. The Other Foundation.
Conrad, Ryan, and Yasmin Nair. 2010. *Against Equality: Queer Critiques of Gay Marriage*. Melbourne: Against Equality Press.

Demone, Bradley. 2016. LGBT Rights in Malawi: One Step Back, Two Steps Forward? The Case of *R v Steven Monjeza Soko and Tiwonge Chimbalanga Kachepa*. *Journal of African Law* 60 (3): 365–387.

Epprecht, Marc. 2013. *Hungochani: The History of a Dissident Sexuality in Southern Africa*. London: McGill-Queen's Press.

Gevisser, Mark. 2014. Love in Exile. *The Guardian*, November 27. https://www.theguardian.com/news/2014/nov/27/-sp-transgender-relationship-jail-exile-tiwonge-chimbalanga.

Grant, Evandé. 2006. Human Rights, Cultural Diversity and Customary Law in South Africa. *Journal of African Law* 50 (1): 2–23.

Himonga, Chuma, and Craig Bosch. 2000. The Application of African Customary Law under the Constitution of South Africa: Problems Solved or Just Beginning. *South African Law Journal* 117 (3): 306–341.

Himonga, Chuma, and Thanabantu Nhlapo. 2014. *African Customary Law in South Africa: Post Apartheid and Living Law Perspectives*. Cape Town: Oxford University Press Southern Africa.

Hoad, Neville. 2016. Queer Customs against the Law. *Research in African Literatures and Film* 47 (2): 1–19.

Jeater, Diana. 1993. *Marriage, Perversion and Power: The Construction of Moral Discourse in Southern Rhodesia, 1890–1920*. Oxford: Claredon Press.

Johnston, Sir Harry Hamilton. 1987. *British Central Africa: An Attempt to Give Some Account of a Portion of the Territories under British Influence North of the Zambesi*. London: Methuen.

Kabwila, Jessie. 2013. Seeing Beyond Colonial Binaries: Unpacking Malawi's Homosexuality Discourse. In *Queer African Reader*, ed. S. Ekine and H. Abbas, 376–392. Oxford: Pambazuka Press.

Kirby, Hon Michael. 2011. The Sodomy Offence: England's Least Lovely Criminal Law Export? *Journal of Commonwealth Criminal Law* 1: 1–33.

Kumintengo, Josephine Lucia. 2012. *The Narrow Road Towards a Possible Decriminalisation of Consensual Sodomy in Malawi*. PhD dissertation, University of Cape Town.

Malamba, Manuel. 2012. *The Controversy of Homosexuality: A Critical Look at the Issues That Make Legalizing Homosexuality in Malawi Difficult*. PhD dissertation, University of Gothenburg.

Mawerenga, Jones Hamburu. 2018. *The Homosexuality Debate in Malawi*. Mzuzu: Mzuni Press.

McKay, Tara, and Nicole Angotti. 2016. Ready Rhetorics: Political Homophobia and Activist Discourses in Malawi, Nigeria, and Uganda. *Qualitative Sociology* 39 (4): 397–420.

Msibi, Thabo. 2011. The Lies We Have Been Told: On (Homo) Sexuality in Africa. *Africa Today* 58 (1): 55–77.

Msosa, Alan. 2018. *Human Rights and Same-Sex Intimacies in Malawi*. PhD dissertation, University of Essex.

Msosa, Alan. 2019. *Under Wraps a Survey of Public Attitudes to Homosexuality and Gender Non-conformity in Malawi*. The Other Foundation.

Muñoz, José Esteban. 2009. *Cruising Utopia: The Then and There of Queer Futurity*. New York: New York University Press.

Mutua, Makau. 2001. Savages, Victims, and Saviors: The Metaphor of Human Rights. *Harvard International Law Journal* 42: 201–246.

Mutua, Makau. 2011. Sexual Orientation and Human Rights: Putting Homophobia on Trial. In *African Sexualities: A Reader*, ed. Sylvia Tamale, 452–462. Oxford: Pamabazuka Press.

Mwabene, Lea. 2005. Divorce in Matrilineal Customary Law Marriage in Malawi: A Comparative Analysis with the Patrilineal Customary Law Marriage in South Africa. PhD dissertation, University of Western Cape.

Mwakasungula, Undule. 2013. The LGBT Situation in Malawi: An Activist Perspective. In *Human Rights, Sexual Orientation and Gender Identity in the The Commonwealth: Struggles for Decriminalisation and Change*, ed. Lennox Corinne et al., 359–379. London: University of London Press.

Nyanzi, Stella. 2015. Knowledge Is Requisite Power: Making a Case for Queer African Scholarship. In *Boldly Queer: African Perspectives on Same-Sex Sexuality and Gender Diversity*, ed. Theo Sandfort et al., 125–135. Hague: HIVOS.

Oyewumi, Oyeronke. 2002. Conceptualizing Gender: The Eurocentric Foundations of Feminist Concepts and the Challenge of African Epistemologies. *Jenda: A Journal of Culture and African Women Studies* 2 (1): 1–9.

Phooko, Moses Retselisitsoe. 2011. Homosexuality and Privacy: Rep v Soko & Another under the Magnifying Glass. *Malawi Law Journal* 5 (1): 55–74.

Price, Louise. 2011. The Treatment of Homosexuality in the Malawian Justice System: *R v Steven Monjeza Soko and Tiwonge Chimbalanga Kachepa*. *African Human Rights Law Journal* 10 (2): 524–533.

Roberts, Simon. 1964. Matrilineal Family Law and Custom in Malawi: A Comparison of Two Systems. *Journal of African Law* 8 (2): 77–99.

Sharra, Steve. 2012. Debating Homosexuality and Human Rights in Malawi. https://wagingnonviolence.org/feature/debating-homosexuality-and-human-rights-in-malawi/. Accessed 10 May 2018.

Smith, David. 2010. Malawi Launches Operation against High-Profile Gay and Lesbian People. *The Guardian*, February 16. https://www.theguardian.com/world/2010/feb/16/malawi-operation-against-gays-lesbians.

Spurlin, William J. 2001. Broadening Postcolonial Studies/Decolonizing Queer Studies. In *Postcolonial, Queer: Theoretical Intersections*, ed. John C. Hawley, 185–205. Albany: State University of New York Press.

The Other Foundation. 2019. Under Wraps: A Survey of Public Attitudes to Homosexuality and Gender Non-conformity in Malawi. http://theotherfoundation.org/wp-content/uploads/2019/09/Other-Foundation-Malawi-Paper-v7.pdf. Accessed 1 Oct 2019.

United Kingdom Home Office. 2017. Country Policy and Information Note Malawi: Sexual orientation and gender identity. https://assets.publishing.service.gov.uk/government/uploads/system/uploads/attachment_data/file/678301/Malawi_-_SOGI_-_CPIN_-_v3.0__February_2017_.pdf. Accessed 10 May 2018.

United States Department of State. 2016. Country Report on Human Rights Practices—Malawi 2015 (Section 6). http://www.state.gov/j/drl/rls/hrrpt/2015/af/252701.htm. Accessed 10 May 2018.

Wanda, Boyce P. 1988. Customary Family Law in Malawi: Adherence to Tradition and Adaptability to Change. *The Journal of Legal Pluralism and Unofficial Law* 20 (27): 126–128.

Watson, Patricia. 2010. *Queer Malawi: Untold Stories*. Johannesburg: Malawi's Centre for the Development of People (CEDEP) and Gay and Lesbian Memory in Action (GALA).

Newspapers

Bvumbe, Bishop Joseph. 2011. Statement by Lutheran chairman of the Malawi Council of Churches (MCC). *The Sunday Times*, February 20.

Kalimira, Samuel. 2018. Suspected Gay Arrested in Mzuzu. *The Daily Times*, April 25.

Somanje, Caroline. 2009. Gays Engage! *The Nation*, December 27.

Index

G. B. Radics and P. Ciocchini (eds.), *Criminal Legalities and Minorities in the Global South*, Palgrave Socio-Legal Studies, https://doi.org/10.1007/978-3-031-17918-1

The manufacturer's authorised representative in the EU is Springer Nature Customer Service Centre GmbH, Europaplatz 3, 69115 Heidelberg, Germany. If you have any concerns regarding our products, please contact ProductSafety@springernature.com

Printed and bound by CPI Group (UK) Ltd, Croydon, CR0 4YY
28/09/2026
02224074-0013